A MONASTIC COMMUNITY IN LOCAL SOCIETY: THE BEAUCHIEF ABBEY CARTULARY

A MONASTIC COMMUNITY IN LOCAL SOCIETY: THE BEAUCHIEF ABBEY CARTULARY

edited by
DAVID HEY, LISA LIDDY, and DAVID LUSCOMBE

CAMDEN FIFTH SERIES
Volume 40

CAMBRIDGE
UNIVERSITY PRESS

FOR THE ROYAL HISTORICAL SOCIETY
University College London, Gower Street, London WC1 6BT
2011

Published by the Press Syndicate of the University of Cambridge
The Edinburgh Building, Cambridge CB2 8RU, United Kingdom
32 Avenue of the Americas, New York, NY 10013-2473, USA
477 Williamstown Road, Port Melbourne, VIC 3207, Australia
C/Orense, 4, Planta 13, 28020 Madrid, Spain
Lower Ground Floor, Nautica Building, The Water Club,
Beach Road, Granger Bay, 8005 Cape Town, South Africa

© Royal Historical Society 2011

First published 2011

A catalogue record for this book is available from the British Library

ISBN 9781107016460 hardback

SUBSCRIPTIONS. The serial publications of the Royal Historical Society, *Royal Historical Society Transactions* (ISSN 0080-4401) and Camden Fifth Series (ISSN 0960-1163) volumes, may be purchased together on annual subscription. The 2011 subscription price, which includes print and electronic access (but not VAT), is £121 (US $203 in the USA, Canada, and Mexico) and includes Camden Fifth Series, volumes 38, 39, and 40 (published in April, July, and December) and Transactions Sixth Series, volume 21 (published in December). Japanese prices are available from Kinokuniya Company Ltd, P.O. Box 55, Chitose, Tokyo 156, Japan. EU subscribers (outside the UK) who are not registered for VAT should add VAT at their country's rate. VAT registered subscribers should provide their VAT registration number. Prices include delivery by air.

Subscription orders, which must be accompanied by payment, may be sent to a bookseller, subscription agent, or direct to the publisher: Cambridge University Press, The Edinburgh Building, Shaftesbury Road, Cambridge CB2 8RU, UK; or in the USA, Canada, and Mexico: Cambridge University Press, Journals Fulfillment Department, 100 Brook Hill Drive, West Nyack, New York, 10994-2133, USA.

SINGLE VOLUMES AND BACK VOLUMES. A list of Royal Historical Society volumes available from Cambridge University Press may be obtained from the Humanities Marketing Department at the address above.

Printed and bound in the United Kingdom at the University Press, Cambridge

CONTENTS

LIST OF ILLUSTRATIONS — vi

FOREWORD — vii

INTRODUCTION — 1

GLOSSARY — 35

MAPS — 36

THE BEAUCHIEF ABBEY CARTULARY — 39

APPENDICES

   I. The Leake Family Cartulary — 261

   II. The Royal Confirmation of 1316 — 269

   III. Concordances — 277

BIBLIOGRAPHY — 281

INDEX OF PERSONS — 287

   Persons other than witnesses — 287

   Witnesses — 294

INDEX OF PLACES — 301

LIST OF ILLUSTRATIONS

Maps

1. Beauchief abbey: local properties
2. Beauchief abbey: properties in Derbyshire, Leicestershire, Nottinghamshire, and Yorkshire

Both maps ©Paul Coles.

Figure

Frontispiece: 'Beauchief abbey, in the present state', engraving, from S. Pegge, *An Historical Account of Beauchief Abbey* (London, 1801), plate VIII.

FOREWORD

The late Professor George Potter, former Head of the Department of Medieval and Modern History at the University of Sheffield, transcribed the Cartulary of Beauchief Abbey with a view to publication, but unfortunately his transcripts are lost. The publication project was revived by Professor David Luscombe, of the same department (by then the Department of History), with the aid of a grant from the University of Sheffield, and most of the first seventy-four folios were carefully transcribed by Dr David Postles during his time as Archivist at Sheffield Archives and before he took up a new appointment at the University of Leicester. Meanwhile, Colin Merrony, of the Department of Archaeology at the University of Sheffield, and his students had shown by excavation and fieldwork that the physical remains of the abbey and its surrounding estate were more extensive than had been believed. Tony Smith's research into the Fairbank collection at Sheffield Archives had led to similar conclusions, and Patricia Wheeler had collected most of the available documentary evidence in her 1996 dissertation for the Certificate in Archaeology of the Division of Adult Continuing Education at the University of Sheffield. A grant made by the Humanities Research Board of the British Academy to Professor David Hey of the same Department made possible the appointment of Lisa Howarth (now Lisa Liddy), who had recently completed the MA course in Medieval Studies at the University of York, to complete the transcriptions and to provide the headnotes to the charters. Later, her computer expertise was invaluable in completing the final version of the text for publication. Professor David Smith of the Borthwick Institute at the University of York (which, by happy chance, had a microfilm of the Cartulary) gave valuable assistance and encouraged the project throughout. The late Madeleine Blaess of the Department of French in the University of Sheffield kindly helped with the sections that were written in Norman French. Dr Charles Fonge, of the University of York and of the Modern Records Centre in the University of Warwick Library, very kindly provided transcriptions of relevant charters found in the Leake family Cartulary. We later received much valuable assistance with the Derbyshire charters from Philip Riden, the Derbyshire County Editor of the *Victoria County History*, and we have very gratefully followed and incorporated many of the knowledgeable suggestions he has made. Not least by any means, we also warmly thank the very helpful staff in the Sheffield Archives and Local Studies Library, in the Derbyshire Record Office at Matlock, in the British Library, and – especially – in the Library of the University of Sheffield, as well as Paul Coles in the University's Department of Geography for drawing the maps. Finally, we are very grateful to Dr Hester Higton for the thoroughness of her work as copy-editor and for the numerous helpful suggestions she has made.

David Hey, Lisa Liddy, and David Luscombe
March 2011

Frontispiece: Beauchief Abbey c. 1801

INTRODUCTION

Beauchief in Sheffield is a beautiful hillside at the foot of which, near the river Sheaf, and on the still wooded south-western fringes of the city, are the remains of the medieval abbey that housed, from the late twelfth century until the Henrician Reformation, Augustinian canons belonging to the Premonstratensian order. Augustinian canonries were generally modest places, although for reasons that have been persuasively advanced by the late Sir Richard Southern, this fact should never obscure the breadth of their significance in the wider history of medieval urban and rural localities:

> The Augustinian canons, indeed, as a whole, lacked every mark of greatness. They were neither very rich, nor very learned, nor very religious, nor very influential: but as a phenomenon they are very important. They filled a very big gap in the biological sequence of medieval religious houses. Like the ragwort which adheres so tenaciously to the stone walls of Oxford, or the sparrows of the English towns, they were not a handsome species. They needed the proximity of human habitation, and they throve on the contact which repelled more delicate organisms. They throve equally in the near-neighbourhood of a town or a castle. For the well-to-do townsfolk they could provide the amenity of burial-places, memorials and masses for the dead, and schools and confessors of superior standing for the living. For the lords of castles they could provide a staff for the chapel and clerks for the needs of administration. They were ubiquitously useful. They could live on comparatively little, yet expand into affluence without disgrace. Consequently there were many who were willing to contribute their crumbs. In return they satisfied many modest requirements. For the moderate landowner they provided a religious house where he was received as lord and patron. For the smaller benefactor they provided a place of burial and masses for his soul. They ran many small schools, many hospitals and places of retirement for the sick and aged, for pregnant women, for the blind, for lepers. In an increasingly busy and practical age they appeared to give more than the Benedictine monks.[1]

Most Augustinian canonries were independent but Premonstratensian canons belonged to an order that brought together, under a common observance, religious communities found in almost every

---

[1] R.W. Southern, *Western Society and the Church in the Middle Ages*, The Pelican History of the Church, 2 (Aylesbury, 1970), ch. 6.ii: 'The new orders', p. 248.

part of western Europe.² The order had a monastic character that made it less likely that an abbey such as Beauchief would be founded in a town or that it would not be primarily a place of strict religious observance. But, with these differences noted, the charters found in its Cartulary, which we edit for the first time, amply illustrate the many functions of an Augustinian community in England between the second half of the twelfth century and the end of the fourteenth, serving and being served by its local and neighbouring communities in the ways that Southern describes.

Foundation

Beauchief was one of only three abbeys in medieval Derbyshire, all of them houses of Augustinian regular canons, the other two being in the south of the county at Darley and Dale. Nor was the county well served by friars, the Dominican friary at Derby being the only one in the county, whereas Yorkshire's towns had nineteen, including two in Doncaster and one at Tickhill. Darley abbey was founded by Robert Ferrers, second earl of Derby, *c.*1146. Very little of the buildings survives but its charters do and they have been published.³ Like Beauchief, Dale abbey (which was sometimes referred to as Stanley Park) was a Premonstratensian house, founded about the year 1200. The site has been excavated and some architectural fragments survive, as do the abbey's charters, which have also been published.⁴ The endowments of both these small abbeys were concentrated in the southern half of Derbyshire. Beauchief abbey, on the other hand, was founded as a daughter establishment of Welbeck abbey in Nottinghamshire upon the gift of land by Robert FitzRanulf, formerly sheriff of Nottinghamshire and Derbyshire, and lord of Alfreton and Norton in Derbyshire, Edwalton in Nottinghamshire, and Wymeswold in Leicestershire. Two versions of the foundation charter have survived: the first dates from the reign of Henry II (**3**);⁵ the second, which gives a more detailed description of the boundaries of the estate, is known from a royal confirmation of the reign of Edward II (**4**). The canons of Beauchief always responded to visitations by giving their

---

²'If we take an extensive view of the communities living under the Rule of St Augustine, it must be judged the most prolific of all medieval religious Rules. The number of communities in the thirteenth century which acknowledged this Rule as their guide is beyond any certain calculation, but it would run to many thousands' (*ibid.*, p. 249).
³R.R. Darlington, *The Cartulary of Darley Abbey*, 2 vols (Kendal, 1945).
⁴A. Saltman (ed.), *The Cartulary of Dale Abbey*, Derbyshire Archaeological Society Record Series, 2 for 1966 (London, 1967).
⁵Numbers in bold type indicate charter numbers in the Cartulary.

foundation date as the feast of St Thomas the Apostle, 21 December 1183. However, Richard, Bishop of Coventry, to whom the original charter was addressed, had died by that time, and Albinus, Abbot of Darley, who witnessed both documents, had died by 1176. The likely explanation for these discrepancies is that, although land had been granted for the use of the proposed abbey by 1176, the 'official opening' was late in 1183. The abbey was dedicated to St Mary and St Thomas the Martyr, who was canonized in February 1173. The original grant must therefore have been made between 1173 and 1176.[6]

The Premonstratensian order had been founded in 1120 at Prémontré, in a secluded and marshy valley near Laon in northern France, as an order whose communal life and organization was modelled on that of the Cistercians while being supportive of preaching and parochial work outside the cloister. The White Canons, as they were popularly known, were regular canons who lived under a rule that was less strict than that of the monks, but they sang the daily offices in the abbey church, shared a common dormitory and the frugal diet of the refectory, and were obliged to follow the statutes of their order. Regular inspections by visitors, who were appointed by an annual general chapter, ensured common standards of liturgy, accommodation, dress, and conduct. The first English abbey of the new order was established at Newhouse (Lincolnshire) in 1143; Welbeck abbey was founded ten years later. More than fifty successful Premonstratensian communities were established in Britain, mostly between 1150 and 1210, but the order failed to expand subsequently.[7]

Beauchief is the Norman French name for the 'beautiful headland' that lay on the north-western edge of the parish of Norton, just inside Derbyshire. The Latin version of the name was *Bellum Caput* or *Abbatia de Bello Capite*.[8] The foundation was of modest size compared with the great Benedictine abbeys of northern England. Visitations during the fifteenth century regularly named the abbot and twelve to fourteen canons. The surnames of the abbots and canons suggest that most of them came from the neighbourhood of the abbey.[9] The number

---

[6] See H.M. Colvin, *The White Canons in England* (Oxford, 1951), pp. 103–106 for the background. It is not clear why the foundation date should be that of Thomas the Apostle and not that of Thomas Becket. See also Janet Burton, *Monastic and Religious Orders in Britain, 1000–1300* (Cambridge, 1994), pp. 56–60.

[7] R. Harte and C. Merrony, 'Two way traffic: the importance of Beauchief abbey as a case study for the Premonstratensian order in England', *Review of Archaeology in South Yorkshire, 1994–95* (Sheffield, 1995), pp. 81–88.

[8] K. Cameron, *The Place-names of Derbyshire*, II (Cambridge, 1959), p. 208.

[9] S.O. Addy, *Historical Memorials of Beauchief Abbey* (Sheffield, 1878), p. 136; see also Claire Cross and Noreen Vickers, *Monks, Friars and Nuns in Sixteenth Century Yorkshire*, Yorkshire Archaeological Society Record Series, 150 (1995), p. 3.

of lay brothers and other assistants and servants is not known, but as the abbey church was 200 feet long they probably far outnumbered the canons. When the abbey was dissolved on 4 February 1537, it was valued at only £126 3s 4d, thus bringing it well below the threshold value of £200, under which the smaller religious establishments were dissolved according to the Act of 1536.

Robert FitzRanulf's original grant of an estate in Norton extended from the river Sheaf, which formed the boundary of Derbyshire in the north-west, as far as Abbey Brook and Chancet Wood in the north and the spring and stream by the present Twentywell Lane in the south-west. (Twentywell is a corruption of St Quentin well, which was named after the abbey of St Quentin, not far from Prémontré.[10]) The estate consisted of uncleared hazel scrub beyond the clearances that had recently been made by local peasant farmers on the border of the manor. By charter **6**, the founder extended his original grant of land to the south as far as the border between the hamlet of Greenhill in Norton parish and Birchitt in the parish of Dronfield. Later grants enlarged the estate on the northern side of Abbey Brook as far as the river Sheaf, beyond Hutcliffe Wood and towards Woodseats and the abbey's new water mill on a site that became known as Norton Hammer. After the Dissolution, the compact estate of 780 acres around the abbey was known as the extra-parochial Liberty of Beauchief; much of it is shown on a map of Strelley Pegges's estate drawn by William Fairbank in 1762.[11] The parish of Norton and the adjacent chapelry of Dore and Totley in the parish of Dronfield both lay just within Derbyshire and the diocese of Coventry and Lichfield, on the border with the parish of Sheffield, the county of Yorkshire, and the Archbishopric of York. The river Sheaf and its tributary the Meersbrook both have names that were derived from this boundary.[12] Norton mill, small properties in Norton Lees and by the Meersbrook, and the advowson and tithes and so forth of Norton church were given to the canons by the first charters, as were similar rights to the churches of Alfreton (Derbyshire), Wymeswold (Leicestershire),

---

[10] Cameron, *The Place-names of Derbyshire*, II, p. 285.

[11] Sheffield Archives, Fairbank collection, BEA 1. The acreage is given in J.M. Wilson, *The Imperial Gazetteer*, I (London and Edinburgh, 1870), p. 135. The foundation charters refer to Beauchief as being in 'Doreheseles', i.e. the hazel woods of Dore, though the abbey's estate was actually across the Dore boundary (formed by the Limb brook and the river Sheaf). The adjoining Ecclesall Wood was known as Hazlehurst when Sir Robert of Ecclesall enclosed it within his park in 1319 (J. Hunter, *Hallamshire*, ed. A. Gatty (London, 1869), p. 342). Hazels therefore seem to have been characteristic of this part of the Sheaf valley.

[12] A.H. Smith, *The Place-names of the West Riding of Yorkshire*, VII (Cambridge, 1962), pp. 131–132, 137. Sheaf is an Old English word meaning 'boundary'. Meersbrook is from 'mere', also a boundary.

and Edwalton (Nottinghamshire), and part of the demesne land at Wymeswold. Later members of the FitzRanulf family granted further land at Wymeswold.[13] Robert's grant of the tithes of his parish churches was of vital importance in supporting the canons, especially in their early years.[14]

Norton, Alfreton, and Wymeswold (but not Edwalton) formed part of the Honour of Tickhill, Roger of Busli's great Norman estate centred on Tickhill castle on the Yorkshire–Nottinghamshire border. Domesday Book records that Ingram (an Old French or Old German name) held Norton and Alfreton of Roger of Busli. We do not know whether he also held Edwalton and Wymeswold because no tenants-in-chief were recorded in the Nottinghamshire and Leicestershire folios of Domesday Book (Wymeswold lies just across the Nottinghamshire boundary in Leicestershire, a few miles south of Edwalton).[15] Ingram's son, Ranulf of Alfreton, was the father of Robert FitzRanulf, the founder of Beauchief abbey.[16] Ranulf was sheriff of Nottinghamshire and Derbyshire for many years and was succeeded by his son, who held the same offices between 1165 and 1170.[17] Beauchief abbey also received grants of land from the lords of other manors within the Honour of Tickhill: Beighton, Dore, Pleasley, and Rowthorne (Derbyshire); Billingley, Goldthorpe, Kimberworth, Scholes, Swinton, and Thorpe Hesley (South Yorkshire); and Bilby, Egmanton, Marnham, and Perlethorpe (Nottinghamshire). The chief religious houses within the honour were the Benedictine priory at Blyth and the Augustinian priory at Worksop (both in Nottinghamshire).

Within a generation, the abbey attracted grants of large stretches of moorland for grazing cattle and sheep in adjoining manors a few

---

[13] A pedigree of the family is given in S. Pegge, *An Historical Account of Beauchief Abbey* (London, 1801), p. 20.

[14] The database of Pope Nicholas IV's *Taxatio*, prepared by the late J.H. Denton and others and showing the valuation of English and Welsh parish churches and prebends listed in the ecclesiastical taxation assessment of 1291–1292, gives the following assessments: Norton £8, Alfreton £10, Wymeswold £25 13s 4d (http://www.hrionline.ac.uk/taxatio). There is no entry for Edwalton. Dronfield, which was appropriated in 1399, was valued at £40.

[15] P. Morgan, *Domesday Book: Derbyshire* (Chichester, 1978), p. 16; W. Page (ed.), *Victoria County History of Nottinghamshire*, I (London, 1906), pp. 259–279; idem (ed.), *Victoria County History of Leicestershire*, I (London, 1907), p. 325. Roger of Busli had few possessions in Leicestershire but held an extensive estate in Nottinghamshire and many manors in Derbyshire and South Yorkshire. Edwalton formed part of the lands of Roger of Poitou in 1086.

[16] Pegge, *An Historical Account of Beauchief Abbey*, pp. 20–23; Robert FitzRanulf witnessed the foundation charter of Welbeck abbey and gave his church at Osberton to Worksop priory. He also had property in Derbyshire at Monyash, Rowsley, Calver, Hassop, Blackwell, and Dronfield, and in Nottinghamshire at Nuthall, Thurgaton, Watnall, Woodborough, Bramcote, Markham, Ollerton, and Bilby.

[17] Colvin, *White Canons*, pp. 103–104.

miles south-west of Chesterfield, halfway between the FitzRanulf manors of Norton and Alfreton. Serlo of Pleasley, the great-grandson of his namesake who was the Domesday Book owner of Ashover and Glapwell, granted a bovate of land with a toft and croft and common rights in the parish of Ashover; his neighbour, Robert Brito (or the Breton) of Walton, gave a wood up to the Ashover boundary; and Warner (otherwise Warin) of Beeley donated the site of Harewood, where the abbey built a grange. Warner's son Serlo soon gave the canons extra land there.

Further endowments

In the early decades of the thirteenth century more grants were made by the same families and by some new ones. The founder's son donated nine bovates and another 24 acres in Wymeswold, as well as smaller acreages at Beauchief and Troway (Derbyshire); the lords of Beeley continued their support; and Richard of Glapwell allowed the canons to rent three bovates on his manor, with pasture for a plough team and 160 sheep. The abbey's Obituary commemorated John Rocester, lord of Dore, 'who gave us all his land in Dore', but his charter is not included in the Cartulary. About the same time, at least three more granges were established: by Walter Barry, lord of Teversal (Nottinghamshire), at Stanley; by Robert of Furness at Birley, within his manor of Beighton (Derbyshire); and by Gerard of Furnival at Fulwood, within his lordship of Hallamshire (South Yorkshire). Furnival's gift was an especially significant new donation, for the previous lords of Hallamshire, the Lovetots, had granted the large tithes of their extensive lordship to the Benedictine abbey of St Wandrille, near their place of origin in Normandy, and the small tithes and other properties to the Augustinian priory that William and Emma of Lovetot had founded at Worksop (Nottinghamshire).[18] At Sheffield the Furnivals had inherited a castle and a thriving market town that the Lovetots had established at the confluence of the Sheaf and the Don; and in the 1270s Thomas of Furnival III built a formidable new stronghold there that dominated Sheffield and the lordship of Hallamshire for nearly four centuries. Another foothold in South Yorkshire was established in 1227 when Adam of Saint Mary, lord of Rawmarsh (which he subinfeuded from the Deincourts, an East Midlands baronial family who witnessed many Beauchief charters), made a modest gift at Upper Haugh. The abbey also acquired some

[18] D. Hey, *Historic Hallamshire* (Ashbourne, 2002), pp. 27–29.

urban property, notably in Chesterfield, where the present rectangular market, once surrounded by burgage plots, had been laid out at the edge of the old town in the early or mid-twelfth century. However, the bulk of its estate was in village fields or on the Derbyshire moors, within or immediately across the borders of the wapentake of Scarsdale, which covered north-east Derbyshire around the market town and minster church of Chesterfield.

The Chaworths

The FitzRanulf line ended in 1242 with the death of Thomas of Alfreton, when his two sisters became co-heiresses. The elder sister, Alice, married Sir William Chaworth, lord of Marnham (Nottinghamshire); the younger, Johanna, married Robert, the son of Richard of Lathom (Lancashire).[19] William Chaworth's son, Thomas, who came of age in 1247, is usually regarded as the co-founder of Beauchief abbey because of the substantial nature of his gifts. His surname was written in many different ways in medieval documents (but not in the Cartulary) and is thought to have been derived from Chaurces (now Sourches), near Le Mans.[20] The Chaworths, too, were prominent knights in the Honour of Tickhill. The oldest extent of the honour shows Robert Chaworth holding half a knight's fee in Marnham and a third of a knight's fee in Wadworth (South Yorkshire). Thomas Chaworth I was active in promoting his Derbyshire properties: in 1252 he and Robert of Lathom obtained a royal charter for a Monday market and a three-day July fair at Alfreton, and five years later he created deer parks around his manor houses at Alfreton and Norton.[21] Upon his death in 1315, he was succeeded by his grandson, Sir Thomas Chaworth II (d. 1347), who in turn was succeeded by his son, Sir Thomas Chaworth III (d. 1370). The Chaworths were benefactors to and patrons of Beauchief for several

---

[19] Pegge, *An Historical Account of Beauchief Abbey*, p. 20; R. McKinley, *The Surnames of Lancashire* (London, 1981), p. 55.

[20] A pedigree of the Chaworths is given in Pegge, *An Historical Account of Beauchief Abbey*, p. 110. The first four generations spelt their name Chaurces, etc. See the *Oxford Dictionary of National Biography* entry on the Chaworth [de Cadurcis] family (*per. c.*1160–*c.*1521).

[21] J. Hunter, *South Yorkshire: the history and topography of the Deanery of Doncaster*, II (London, 1831), pp. 249–250; an effigy in Wadworth church is thought to be that of a Chaworth; the branch there was succeeded by the Fitzwilliams. A branch of the Chaworths lived at Rawmarsh (South Yorks) after George, the third son of Sir Thomas Chaworth, married the heiress of the Rawmarsh estate in Henry VI's reign; the Chaworths remained there until the reign of James I (*ibid.*, II, p. 47). Another branch was seated at Harthill (South Yorks) from at least Edward IV's reign until 1674 (*ibid.*, II. pp. 140–141). For the grants of a market and parks, see *Calendar of Charter Rolls, Henry III*, I, 1226–1257, pp. 400 and 472.

generations and were buried within the abbey precincts; for example, Thomas Chaworth, who died in 1483, was described in the Beauchief Obituary as 'our advocate'.[22] Most of the charters numbered **17** to **91** relate to grants from the Chaworths.

Other benefactors

Other benefactors, some of whom were also buried in the abbey, are listed in the abbey's Obituary, though their gifts are not always recorded in the Cartulary. For example, each year on 18 June a Mass was said for 'Radulph Musard, our canon and assistant brother [. . .] for he gave us Hanley and Wadshelf, and a golden chalice with a golden cross'.[23] Some of the Furnivals, lords of Hallamshire, were buried in the choir, including Sir Gerard of Furnival I, who gave valuable pasture rights to establish the grange at Fulwood and '20s rent from his mill at Sheffield, to maintain light in our church',[24] and Sir Thomas of Furnival I, who enlarged the grange and confirmed all the donations of his ancestors in Hallamshire.[25] The good will of the Furnivals' successors, the Talbots, earls of Shrewsbury, was essential because the lords of Hallamshire were the canons' most powerful neighbour. Thus we find that in 1466 the abbot granted an annual fee of five marks to the earl for life in return for his 'very potent counsel, support, protection and aid'.[26]

The minor lords who were neighbours (and often retainers and kinsmen) of the FitzRanulfs, Chaworths, and Furnivals appear as benefactors in the Cartulary and sometimes in the Obituary. Some made grants with no strings attached; others asked for a rent, or imposed a time limit. In the latter half of the thirteenth century, Sir Ralph of Ecclesall (son of Sir Robert and one of the knights of the

---

[22] Addy, *Historical Memorials of Beauchief Abbey*, pp. 28–29; Obituary, 3 March. The Norton and Alfreton branch of the Chaworths ended with the death of Thomas Chaworth in 1483, leaving his sister Joanna, the wife of John Ormond, as his heir. Alfreton church has a wall monument to John Ormond and Joan Chaworth (who died in 1507), though the brasses are missing. The north transept of Langar church (Notts) in the Vale of Belvoir contains the sixteenth-century tombs of the Chaworths of Wiverton and later tablets to the Chaworth-Musters of Annesley.

[23] *Ibid.*, p. 40. These grants are not recorded in the Cartulary, but are listed (except for the golden cross) as nos **30** and **31** in the *Inspeximus* of 1316; see also nos **32** and **33**. At the Derbyshire eyre of 1281, the abbot of Beauchief showed a charter concerning the vill of West Handley 'which Richard Musard held in chief of king John grandfather of the king'; see A. Hopkinson (ed.), *The Rolls of the 1281 Derbyshire Eyre*, Derbyshire Record Society, 27 (2000), p. 181 and n. 2.

[24] Addy, *Historical Memorials of Beauchief Abbey*, p. 53.
[25] *Ibid.*, p. 37.
[26] Pegge, *An Historical Account of Beauchief Abbey*, pp. 226–227.

Furnivals and also lord of a sub-manor within Hallamshire that lay on the opposite bank of the river Sheaf to the abbey) made a significant commitment when he granted the canons his corn mill on the river Sheaf, at an annual rent of four marks, in order to maintain a canon to celebrate Mass in his chapel. He went on to grant other properties in Attercliffe, Sheffield, Dronfield, and Mattersey (Nottinghamshire). His example was soon followed by the Hauselins, the principal tenants of his sub-manor, and by the Costenoths of Wadsley, another sub-manor of Hallamshire. Meanwhile, the granges at Fulwood and Strawberry Lee benefited from grants of moorland pastures from the lords of Hathersage and Padley and, later, from William of Meynell Langley and William of Dronfield.

The abbey continued to attract valuable property gifts in the late thirteenth and early fourteenth centuries. The Chaworths were staunch supporters who made several new grants in the neighbourhood of the abbey and in their manor of Alfreton, some of which supported a canon to pray at a new altar within the abbey church. The services of serfs were transferred to the abbey, and revenue was boosted by grants of corn and fulling mills and coal mines. The Reresbys, lords of Ashover, and other neighbouring landowners, including Walter Chauz of Brampton, extended the canons' pasture rights across the moors near their grange at Harewood. Meanwhile, in South Yorkshire, more grants came from the Hallamshire sub-manors of Ecclesall and Wadsley and from further afield at Scholes, Thorpe Hesley, Swinton, Billingley, and Goldthorpe. This generosity declined swiftly in the 1320s, however, after the nation had suffered badly from harvest failure and livestock plagues, long before the catastrophe of the Black Death. In the second half of the fourteenth century, new donations came only in a trickle until Ralph Barker's generous gift of the rectory and advowson of Dronfield church in 1399.

Derbyshire was of little strategic or economic importance under the Normans, and so few castles and no Benedictine, Cistercian, or Cluniac monasteries were established there. The income that might have supported the foundation of abbeys and priories within the county was diverted instead to cathedrals and monasteries beyond the county's borders. In 1093, for instance, the large parishes of Ashbourne and Chesterfield, with their chapelries, were granted by the king to the new cathedral at Lincoln. Soon afterwards, distant monasteries established granges in many parts of Derbyshire in order to farm the properties that they had been granted: for example, the Cistercians of Louth Park (Lincolnshire) and the Cluniacs of Lenton Priory (Nottinghamshire) set up granges on the edges of Barlow. Even when preaching orders became popular, few religious houses were sited within the county.

It seems that Beauchief was regarded as the 'home' abbey for the wapentake of Scarsdale, which, as has been mentioned, covered north-east Derbyshire around the market town and minster church of Chesterfield. The grants of property that were received from within Derbyshire were confined there or were from immediately across its moorland border, and no other religious house was established within the wapentake. The founder's manors of Norton and Alfreton lay at the northern and southern edges of the wapentake respectively. Other grants to the abbey were of properties just across the Nottinghamshire border near Alfreton, or within Hallamshire and other parts of South Yorkshire to the north of Norton. The more important Beauchief charters were witnessed by the leading landowners in the neighbourhood, even though only a few of these lords donated land themselves. The 1312 confirmation of charters was a particularly well-orchestrated event, headed by Thomas of Furnival, lord of Hallamshire, and Edmund Deincourt, lord of several Derbyshire manors, including Morton near Alfreton and Holmesfield near Norton, and the head of the junior branch of the Deincourts of the barony of Blankney (Lincolnshire). They were followed by the leading knights of Scarsdale and Sir Robert of Ecclesall.

Personal names in the Cartulary

The founder, who called himself Robert son of Ranulph, and his descendants did not possess an hereditary surname; indeed, charter **64** (dated 1210–1225) names his granddaughter as 'Alice daughter of William son of Robert of Alfreton'. By the thirteenth century, however, the other barons and knights who appear in the charters either as grantors or witnesses had Norman or Breton surnames that were already fixed and hereditary. The Furnivals came from Fourneville, the Deincourts from Ancourt, the Chaworths from Sourches; while other landowners who made fleeting appearances in the charters included Barry, Bullon, Chauz, Jorrs, Picard, Pierrepoint, Normanville, and Wasteney. In other families, nicknames eventually became surnames: Bret or Breton, Cade, Foljambe, Herries, Mousters, and Rufus. We might suspect that some knights who adopted the names of their English properties, such as the four generations of the Ecclesalls, were also Norman in origin.

Nearly all the deeds in the Cartulary date from before the 1330s, so it is unsurprising that grantors and witnesses from lower down the social level did not possess hereditary surnames. Instead, they were recorded by such names as 'Hugh son of Adam at the spring in Greenhill', 'John the swane son of Adam of Greenhill', 'Adam son of John of the

Cliffe', 'Richard son of Adam the cook of Sheffield', or 'Simon son of Henry son of Gunnild of Sheffield'. Others were recorded by their occupation: 'Richard the ditcher', 'Ellis the carpenter', 'William the tanner', 'Peter the weaver', and so forth. Clerks and chaplains naturally served as literate witnesses, and a group of men from local farmsteads were often called upon: 'Thomas of Norton Lees', 'John and Peter of Birchitt', 'Peter of Barnes', 'Thomas of Dronfield Woodhouse, clerk', and 'John of Stubley, clerk'. Their names reveal that the pattern of settlement that is first shown on Peter Burdett's 1767 map of Derbyshire had been created by the thirteenth century.

Although the personal names recorded in the Cartulary are overwhelmingly Norman French, some Old English or Old Scandinavian personal names were still in use in the late twelfth and thirteenth centuries. The peasants who had cleared the assarts near the site chosen for the abbey included Clebern, Gamel, and Hacon, though others had names that had been introduced by the Normans: Gerard, Gervase, Hugh, Peter, and Robert. The Old English names Uchtred and Weremund were still in use soon afterwards, but 'Robert son of Godric of Darley' shows how a father with an Old English name chose a Norman one for his son. Likewise, an Ashover man with the Old Welsh name Madoch christened his son John, once the saint's name had become popular; Gunnild of Sheffield chose the Norman name Henry for her son, while Gunnild of Chesterfield chose the Breton name Alan for hers; and the Norman names of Robert, Richard, and William were chosen for the sons of Edwin of Chesterfield, for Thoke, the serf of Hugh Hauselin of Little Sheffield, and for Gamel of Ecclesall respectively. The low status of pre-Conquest personal names is revealed by their rarity among the witnesses; they occur few and far between when compared with the names that became hugely popular under the Normans. In the Beauchief Cartulary, the most popular personal names were William, Robert, and Roger, followed by John (which was rising fast in popularity throughout the land), Thomas, Hugh, Ralph, Adam, Henry, Walter, and Peter. Other Norman personal names included Ellis, Gilbert, Giles, Lambert, Odo, Philip, Reyner, Serlo, Warin, and Walter, with Alan and Brian from Brittany. The twenty-one women's names in the charters were all Norman and were spread thinly, with no favourite choices.

Parishes and other churches

Robert FitzRanulf's original grant (**3**) included the churches of Norton, Alfreton, Edwalton, and Wymeswold, and canons from Beauchief served as vicars at each of them. Thus, the vicars of Norton included Thomas of Alfreton, canon of Beauchief (1325); William Kychyne, who was at the visitation of the abbey in 1475; John Croke (1490), former sub-cellarer and sub-prior of the abbey; and John Sheffield, alias Greenwood (1510), the last abbot.[27] FitzRanulf may have been responsible for the Norman south doorway and the arches of the north side of the nave at St James's, Norton, and the carved heads that frame the great Perpendicular east window seem to represent an abbot and a canon. In 1524 the Bishop of Coventry and Lichfield, Geoffrey Blythe (who was born at Norton Lees), provided the vicar of Norton with a 'chantry house' in a croft on the west side of Norton Green, where ten dairy cows were to graze; the vicar also received a corrody or grant of ale and bread each week.[28] The medieval work of the large church of St Mary, Wymeswold dates from the early fourteenth century onwards, that at Holy Rood, Edwalton from a few decades later.[29] At St Martin's, Alfreton, the earliest architectural remains date from the thirteenth century.[30] The visitation of 25 May 1494 named one of the canons as vicar of Alfreton and another as chaplain of Alfreton chantry, which may have stood on abbey property at the Riddings.[31]

The visitations of the second half of the fifteenth century regularly name beneficed canons at Norton, Alfreton, and Wymeswold, but not at Edwalton. The *Valor Ecclesiasticus* (1535)[32] likewise makes no mention of Edwalton. The abbey's connection had been broken long before. The *Valor* does, however, record the church of St John the Baptist, Dronfield, which was not included in FitzRanulf's original grant. The witnesses in the Cartulary include Sir Henry of Brailsford,

---

[27] H. Armitage, *Chantrey Land* (London, 1910), pp. 2–3. Armitage gave no source for this information. He also wrote that Thomas of Dronfield (1380) later became abbot of Beauchief. 'Thomas de Dronfield, formerly vicar of Norton, who died A. D. 1425' (Addy, *Historical Memorials of Beauchief Abbey*, p. 41) is commemorated in the longer version of the Obituary (20 June; see pp. below) but is not listed in D.M. Smith (ed.), *The Heads of Religious Houses: England and Wales, III, 1377–1540* (Cambridge, 2008), p. 563. For 'John Grennwood (Greynwod) *ulius* Sheffield', who was confirmed as abbot of Beauchief in 1519 and died in 1536, see *ibid.*, pp. 563–564.

[28] Addy, *Historical Memorials of Beauchief Abbey*, pp. 129–132; Armitage, *Chantrey Land*, pp. 32–36; Sheffield Archives, Norton parish church deeds, 21.

[29] N. Pevsner, *The Buildings of England: Leicestershire and Rutland* (2nd edn, revised by E. Williamson and G.K. Brandwood, Harmondsworth, 1984), p. 430; idem, *The Buildings of England: Nottinghamshire* (2nd edn, revised by E. Williamson, Harmondsworth, 1979), p. 119. The chancel for which the canons were once responsible at Edwalton fell down in the seventeenth century.

[30] N. Pevsner, *The Buildings of England: Derbyshire* (2nd edn, revised by E. Williamson, Harmondsworth, 1979), p. 155.

[31] R. Johnson, *A History of Alfreton* (Ripley, n.d.), pp. 36–37.

[32] J. Caley and J. Hunter (eds), *Valor Ecclesiasticus Temp. Henr. VIII. auctoritate regia institutus*, 6 vols (London, 1810–1834); the entry for Beauchief abbey is in vol. III (1817), pp. 172–174.

former patron of Dronfield church, and his younger son, Roger of Brailsford, whom he appointed as rector; they seem to have been responsible for the building of the fine chancel there in the early fourteenth century. The abbey did not own the rectory and advowson until 1399, when Ralph Barker of Dore and Dronfield Woodhouse donated the advowson and Pope Boniface IX appropriated the rectory to the use of the abbey. On 2 December 1399 the rector resigned and the canons appointed John Wykwall as their vicar; four years later, they built him a vicarage.[33]

Granges

As we have seen, most of Beauchief's endowments were received in the first century and a half of the abbey's existence. During this period, granges were established to supervise the farming of the abbey's properties, but in the later Middle Ages the abbot and canons of Beauchief followed the common practice of leasing their lands to tenants. Pegge quotes a large number of leases from the fifteenth and sixteenth centuries. The Glapwell charters show that some lands passed to Darley abbey, but the *Valor Ecclesiasticus* indicates that the main body of endowments remained intact until the Dissolution.

The lands that were granted by benefactors may have been farmed at first by lay brothers whose outlying farmsteads, or granges, were similar to contemporary farmhouses but sometimes also distinguished by the addition of a chapel.[34] The charters provide few definite references to granges, except when grants were confirmed or new lands were donated. Seven granges can be identified but it is possible that one or two more existed. Even when the abbey leased its lands to secular farmers, the word 'grange' was retained, but the nineteenth-century fashion for calling houses 'grange', with no historical justification, causes some confusion; neither Bradway Grange Farm nor Norton Grange is named in the Cartulary, though the abbey did possess two properties at Bradway[35] at the time of the Dissolution. The predecessor of a Georgian house known as 'The Grange' at Dronfield was referred to in 1738 as 'the Grange house or parsonage'.[36]

---

[33] Pegge, *An Historical Account of Beauchief Abbey*, pp. 97–99; Addy, *Historical Memorials of Beauchief Abbey*, pp. 115–116. See charters **218–219**.
[34] For monastic granges, their buildings and staffing, see C. Platt, *The Monastic Grange in Medieval England: a reassessment* (London, 1969).
[35] Pegge, *An Historical Account of Beauchief Abbey*, pp. 67–68.
[36] Sheffield Archives, Ce R/64.

A home farm or grange was built close to the abbey on the site of the later Beauchief Hall. Pegge wrote that, after the Dissolution,

> The Strelleys never made use of the abbey as a house to live in, but dwelt at the Grange. And after Edward Pegge [his ancestor] began to erect his present mansion, the walls of the abbey and its enclosures were mostly carried away for the purpose of accomplishing that, and other buildings.[37]

Two inventories of Beauchief abbey mention the contents of this grange and list the livestock. The first, dated 21 November 1393, notes the foodstuffs 'in the manor and storehouse at Beauchief Grange' and lists 41 cows, bullocks, and heifers, 172 wethers, ewes, and lambs, 8 horses, mares, and foals, and 17 pigs and young pigs.[38] The Dissolution inventory, taken on 2 August 1536, includes 'Household stuff at the grange' and lists the livestock as 12 oxen, 13 cows, 2 bulls, 17 young beasts, 120 ewes, hogs, and other sheep, 2 horses and 1 mare, and 20 pigs, and the farm equipment as two corn wains, three dung carts, three ploughs, one sled, and some yokes.[39]

Three miles up the valley, just in sight of the abbey, a grange was built in a clearing on the edge of the moors at Strawberry Lee.[40] A farmhouse stood on this site until 1936 but now only some ruined walls remain. An extensive green grazing area is surrounded by moorland on all sides: a deep gulley provides a natural boundary with the moorland of Brown Edge to the south, Blacka Hill rises to the north, and Totley Moss stretches away to the west. By an undated charter (**159**) the canons acquired common of pasture for goats and other animals at Strawberry Lee. The first mention of a grange (**161**) dates from the middle decades of the thirteenth century,[41] when Matthew of Hathersage made a grant of common pasture on Hathersage Moor for the livestock at the canons' granges of Fulwood and Strawberry Lee. The canons received similar grazing rights for their livestock at Strawberry Lee on the adjoining Padley Moor in 1285 (**163**). The stump of the Lady Cross, mentioned in **161**, survives in its original position on the moors, over a mile away from the grange.[42] In the later middle ages the grange was leased by the canons: in 1461 to John

---

[37] Pegge, *An Historical Account of Beauchief Abbey*, p. 207.
[38] *Ibid.*, appendix 5.
[39] *Ibid.*, appendix 10; Addy, *Historical Memorials of Beauchief Abbey*, pp. 138–143. A small, late medieval barn was sited close to the abbey: see S.R. Jones, 'A king-post barn of late medieval origin at Beauchief Abbey House, Sheffield, NGR SK 333821', *Transactions of the Hunter Archaeological Society*, 23 (2005), pp. 11–18.
[40] OS ref. SK 285799.
[41] Cameron, *The Place-names of Derbyshire*, II, p. 265. A William Fairbank field-book survey of 1812 is difficult to interpret but shows that the cultivated area was smaller before the parliamentary enclosure of the surrounding moors (Sheffield Archives, FB 126, p. 70).
[42] OS ref. SK 273783.

Faunchall, for sixty years; and in 1530 to Thomas North, for seventy years.[43] Upon the Dissolution, Strawberry Lee was sold to Sir Nicholas Strelley, who also acquired the main estate at Beauchief.

The present Fulwood Grange Farm,[44] three and a half miles north of Strawberry Lee, is the successor to the grange mentioned in **161**. The Beauchief Obituary names Sir Gerard of Furnival, lord of Hallamshire, as the man who gave 'sufficient pasture in his forest of Fulwode for 30 cows, with young under three years old, and one acre of land to build our lodges upon'. Gerard had become lord of Hallamshire in the 1190s upon his marriage to the heiress Maud of Lovetot; he died on the fifth crusade in 1218 or 1219 and was buried in Normandy.[45] His descendant, Sir Thomas of Furnival, 'gave land to enlarge our grange in Fulwode'.[46] In 1514, William Holland took a forty-year lease of the grange.[47] Upon the Dissolution, Fulwood Grange was acquired by Francis, earl of Shrewsbury, and so it once more became part of the lordship of Hallamshire.

The abbey's largest grange beyond Beauchief was sited on the eastern edge of Beeley Moor, where a farmhouse still bears the name of Harewood Grange.[48] Warner or Warin of Beeley, in the late twelfth or early thirteenth century, made the original grant of Harewood, with pasture on the moors for 100 oxen and cows, 20 horses with their young, and 100 sheep (**164**). Further grants (**165–190**) by Warner's descendants and by neighbouring landowners extended the grazing area to the western side of Beeley Moor and into the parish of Ashover and the chapelry of Walton. Some of the boundary stones on these moors probably date from the times of these grants. By the fifteenth century the grange was being leased: on 29 September 1431 it was taken by William of Stone of Harewood for thirty years but, as Stone was described as already 'of Harewood', the lease was probably a renewal.[49] In 1507 Sir John Blackiswalle, the chantry priest of Dronfield, took a lease for eighty years,[50] and in 1524 Christopher Blackwall took an eighty-year lease to keep 120 wether sheep.[51] William

---

[43] Pegge, *An Historical Account of Beauchief Abbey*, p. 197.

[44] OS ref. SK 284854.

[45] Addy, *Historical Memorials of Beauchief Abbey*, p. 53. S. Lloyd, *English Society and the Crusade, 1216–1307* (Oxford: Clarendon Press, 1980), p. 102.

[46] Addy, *Historical Memorials of Beauchief Abbey*, p. 37.

[47] Pegge, *An Historical Account of Beauchief Abbey*, p. 157.

[48] OS ref. SK 312680. The name means 'boundary wood', for it stood on the parish and wapentake boundary (K. Cameron, *The Place-names of Derbyshire*, I (Cambridge, 1959), pp. 44–45).

[49] British Library, Wolley charters, i, 14 (I.H. Jeayes, *A Descriptive Catalogue of Derbyshire Charters in Public and Private Libraries and Muniment Rooms* (London and Derby, 1906), no. 258).

[50] British Library, Wolley charters, i, 15 (Jeayes, *Derbyshire Charters*, no. 265).

[51] Pegge, *An Historical Account of Beauchief Abbey*, p. 137.

Blackwall held the lease at the Dissolution, when the estate was sold to Sir Francis Leake of Sutton.[52]

Less is known about other granges. Robert de Furness, lord of Beighton, was commemorated in the Obituary because 'he gave us our grange of Birlay with the adjacent lands', together with a meadow in Beighton and common of pasture for 200 sheep in Westwood.[53] The place-name means 'byre clearing'[54] and the site may be identified with Birley Farm, two and half miles south of Beighton and a mile southwest of Killamarsh.[55] Pegge mentions an eighty-year lease dated 1468 to John Austin of 'the grange at Barley [*sic*] beneigh [i.e. within] the lordship of Beighton'.[56] The grange may have included the lands at Beighton, Hackenthorpe, Handsworth, and Woodhouse, which were mentioned in the *Valor Ecclesiasticus*.

By charter **222** (dated 1190–1225), William Barry, lord of Teversal (Nottinghamshire), granted a bovate in his demesne and two tofts and crofts in Stanley, the 'stony clearing' on the Nottinghamshire–Derbyshire boundary. The grant provided sufficient pasture for 300 sheep, 20 cows, a bull, 8 horses with their young, and 16 oxen, on a compact estate that extended to the county boundary at Frankbridge in the north and Biggin Farm in the west. It is now cut in two by the M1 motorway immediately south of Hardwick Hall. Barry's charter refers to a 'land ditch' and to 'the house of the canons', so his grant was not the first in this area. The grange that was clearly necessary to run an estate of this size can be identified with the present Stanley Grange Farm on the western edge of the hamlet (OS ref. SK 459623). Pegge quotes 'the grange at Stanley', held from 1525 by Thomas North on a ninety-year lease, at a rent of 40 shillings, in order to keep 120 sheep.[57] (North also leased the grange at Strawberry Lee and two messuages with two oxgangs of land at Bradway.[58]) In 1537, the grange became

---

[52] *Ibid.*, p. 83.

[53] Addy, *Historical Memorials of Beauchief Abbey*, p. 60. The grant does not appear in the Cartulary, but the *Inspeximus* of 1316 (no. 34) records a substantial gift by Walter the son of Robert of Furneus of three bovates and one acre of land and two tofts in Birley, with a piece of meadow in Beighton and another two acres.

[54] Cameron, *The Place-names of Derbyshire*, II, p. 216.

[55] OS ref. SK 444791.

[56] Pegge, *An Historical Account of Beauchief Abbey*, p. 152. In a survey of 1604, Birley was a compact estate within Beighton, with a sheep walk for 200 sheep (D.V. Fowkes and G.R. Potter (eds), *William Senior's Survey of the Estates of the First and Second Earls of Devonshire, c.1600–28*, Derbyshire Record Society, 13 (1988), p. 1.)

[57] Pegge, *An Historical Account of Beauchief Abbey*, p. 143. Biggin Farm is at SK 445626. This Stanley should not be confused with the one by Dale abbey. The place-name means 'stony clearing'; see J.E.B. Gover, A. Mawer, and F.M. Stenton, *The Place-names of Nottinghamshire* (Cambridge, 1940), p. 136.

[58] Pegge, *An Historical Account of Beauchief Abbey*, pp. 74, 97.

the property of William Bolles, one of the government's receivers of dissolved monasteries.[59]

In 1278 (**70**), Sir Thomas Chaworth allowed the canons to 'enclose their assart where their sheepfold is in the parish of Alfreton with all its woods'. A further grant by Thomas Chaworth (**77**) gave the canons permission 'to enclose their lands, wastes and their grange at the Cotes'. This grange, which probably included a barn to store the tithes of Alfreton, can be identified with Cotespark Farm[60] on the south-eastern edge of Alfreton. It is probable that it was included in the purchases of Sir Francis Leake of Sutton after the Dissolution.

No evidence of a grange has been found at Wymeswold, although the Beauchief canons received considerable grants of land there and, as they were rectors of the church, they would have needed a tithe barn. In 1393 it was reported that the abbey's barn there was full of grain.[61]

Farming and industry

Farming was the mainstay of the abbey's economy. The narrow ridge-and-furrow patterns on the present Beauchief golf course and near Beauchief Hall attest to the importance of arable farming at some late stage in the estate's history, but it is clear from the charters and inventories that the abbey's granges specialized in rearing livestock. A clause in an agreement in 1524 to provide the canon who served as the vicar of Norton with ten 'kye' (dairy cows) insisted that the cows should be marked with the brand ('bryn') of the abbey; this suggests that other cattle at the abbey's granges bore the same mark.[62] The charters contain many references to villeins' services,[63] assarting,[64] enclosure, and common rights. Two charters (**21** and **34**) mention the abbey's park, which was presumably used for rearing deer, and the ponds to the east of the abbey are probably successors to medieval fish ponds. Fairbank's map of 1762 shows 'Beauchief Old Park' as a wood (now Old Park Wood) high on the southern boundary of the estate, and fish ponds by the abbey alongside a field called 'The Damm'.[65] The fine woods that enclosed the Beauchief estate provided both timber and

---

[59] *Ibid.*, p. 67, appendix 10. Bolles also got Felling abbey (Notts).
[60] OS ref. SK 425547.
[61] Addy, *Historical Memorials of Beauchief Abbey*, pp. 145–147.
[62] Sheffield Archives, Norton parish church deeds, 21.
[63] Serfs are referred to in charters **16**, **33**, **46**, **51**, **52**, **53**, and **54**.
[64] Charter **32** mentions 'the ditch of the assart'.
[65] Sheffield Archives, Fairbank collection, BEA 1. See also Sheffield Archives, Fairbank collection, FB 19.

coppiced underwood. Ladies Spring Wood may have been named (like Lady's Cross on the moorland boundary of the grange at Strawberry Lee) from the abbey's dedication to Our Lady; a springwood was a coppice wood and the name was spelt Lady's Spring on the 1762 map. A lease to Nicholas Longford in 1463 exempted 'a spryng that is called Hudclyff banke'.[66]

The Cartulary is not very informative about the working of minerals, but charters **37**, **81**, and **83** show that tenants mined coal on the abbey's estates, while charter **84** suggests that the coal mined in the manor of Alfreton was at Swanwick. No charter mentions lead smelting, but the presence of bole hills in areas where the canons had pastures – for example by their granges at Strawberry Lee and Fulwood and at the northern edge of Norton Park – suggests that they benefited from this lucrative activity. Unfortunately, the everyday accounts of the abbey do not survive. The Beauchief smelting house, which probably stood on the Ecclesall side of the river Sheaf to the north of Hutcliffe Wood, was, of course, a post-Dissolution foundation once water power was used for smelting.[67]

The possessions of the canons included mill sites on the river Sheaf, which are included in a modern survey.[68] The furthest mill upstream was Bradway corn mill (charter **35**),[69] which was leased in 1503 to Roger Barker for forty years. After the Dissolution the mill was granted to Sir Nicholas Strelley; nothing of the mill site survives. The Walk Mill nearby[70] was the Ecclesall fulling mill (charter **116**), erected on the river Sheaf *c*.1280 by the abbey on land given by Sir Ralph of Ecclesall, with leave to turn the course of the river towards the mill. Subsequently, Sir Ralph relinquished all claims on the mill. It was named 'the walke mylne' in 1516 in a lease to John Calton of Totley,[71] but after the Dissolution it became a cutler's grinding wheel. No traces of the mill survive, for the site is occupied by Dore railway station.

Further downstream, the Ecclesall mill at Millhouses[72] was already in existence as the manorial corn mill when it was granted provisionally to the abbey in the mid-thirteenth century by Sir Ralph of Ecclesall (**111**). In return, the canons celebrated Mass at Ecclesall chapel. In 1299 Ralph's son Robert released to the abbey all claims of

---

[66] Jeayes, *Derbyshire Charters*, no. 242; Pegge, *An Historical Account of Beauchief Abbey*, p. 189.
[67] D. Kiernan, *The Derbyshire Lead Industry in the Sixteenth Century*, Derbyshire Record Society, 14 (Chesterfield, 1989), p. 121.
[68] C. Ball, D. Crossley, and N. Flavell (eds), *Water Power on the Sheffield Rivers* (2nd edn, Sheffield, 2006), pp. 148–193.
[69] OS ref. SK *c*.320807.
[70] OS ref. SK 324813.
[71] Sheffield Archives, Beauchief Muniments 1013, fo. 5.
[72] OS ref. SK 336833.

rent from the mill (**119**). In 1529 the abbey still owned 'a milne called Ecclesall Milne lately in the holding of James Oattes', for which a forty-year lease was granted to Thomas Greenwode and family. After the Dissolution it remained part of the Beauchief estate. The site is now occupied by a building that was erected as a steam mill in the nineteenth century. A large weir survives by the children's playground in Millhouses park and the site of the pond can be traced.

The New Mill on the river Sheaf that was granted by Hugh Hauselin of Little Sheffield was another corn mill (**156**). In 1513 the 'New Milne' at Woodseats was leased for sixty years to John Blyth of Norton; after the Dissolution it passed to Robert and William Swyft. There too, or immediately downstream, the canons had built a smithy where the Sheaf flows past Smithy Wood. The lease to Nicholas Longford in 1463, quoted above, exempted 'smythees', and another lease in 1496 allowed Roger Eyre to make charcoal in the abbey's woods at Hutcliffe and by the broad meadow, and to work a bloom hearth by the smithy dam.[73]

The lease in 1463 shows that by then the canons were not directly involved in industrial enterprises within their own grounds, for it referred to 'all lands, etc. within the precincts and bounds of the said Abbey in Beauchief', though with specified exemptions, which included not only the smithies and Hutcliffe Wood but also the walk mill, a barkhouse (to store bark for tanning), and a launderhouse (or wash house), for these were run by other families. Eighty years earlier, a lease from Hugh of Barkhouse to Ralph of Dore and William of Barkhouse specified 'All goods and chattels which he had in the tannery from Beauchief, and all his dues in the tannery'; one of the witnesses was Adam Lawnder.[74] Clearly, these industrial activities had been, to use a modern phrase, 'contracted out' to local families. The Barkers of Dore seem to have acquired their surname from their long association with the barkhouse and tannery.

Charters **7**, **42**, **45**, and **91** relate to the canons' windmill at Coal Aston and the watermill situated near Hazelhurst Farm[75] at the junction of the parishes of Norton, Eckington, and Dronfield, where a tributary flows north–south into the Moss Beck. The canons also had the rents of mills at Beeley and Hathersage (**161–162**, **168**, **173**). The abbey therefore benefited from the usual range of economic activities that were available in the North Midlands during the Middle Ages. The Obituary commemorated Robert Bele, 'our miller', William of

---

[73] OS ref. SK 382811. Jeayes, *Derbyshire Charters*, no. 242. Water-powered bloomeries were in use in England from the fourteenth century onwards.
[74] Sheffield Archives, Bagshawe Collection, 3184.
[75] OS ref. SK 382811.

Radeford, 'called "the tanner", our assistant brother', and Henry the mason of Ecclesall.

The abbey and local society

The Cartulary is a collection of deeds that, for the most part, formally record the grants made to the abbey by holders of property, many of these grants being recurrent. Not all benefactors were knights and lords, as is clearly shown by the entries made in later parts of the Cartulary. The appearance in the Obituary of the names of benefactors whose gifts do not appear in the Cartulary but who were in some cases parishioners in the churches staffed by the abbey is evidence of their desire to give thanks to the canons or to express good will. For example, John Moor of Greenhill donated two silver spoons, William Dolphin of the parish of Eckington gave two marks and seven quarters of wheat, and Michael of Hathersage, who became a brother, gave three wain-loads of lead. The Cartulary sheds only a limited amount of light on what the abbey was asked to do by its friends and patrons. It records agreements with the well-to-do for their burial at the abbey (**7**, **17**, **93**, **122**, **123**, **165**, **166**, **168**, **173**, **174**, **175**), for their commemoration during services (**107**, **111**, **112**) and at Masses for their souls and for the souls of their families (**18**, **22**, **33**, **39**, **40**, **57**, **162**, **191**, **192**), for confraternity (**164**),[76] and for spiritual aid or prayers (**63**). But the Cartulary is clearly not a full record of gifts received or of work undertaken by the canons. The Leake copy of charter **166**, for example, goes further and records, as the Cartulary does not, that around the year 1200, when the abbey was still relatively new, Warin of Beeley made a series of grants to the poor and the sick, to nuns, and to churches spread over a wide area of Derbyshire and Nottinghamshire. Running the parishes of Norton, Alfreton, Edwalton, Wymeswold, and later also Dronfield was clearly important work for the canons, and Pegge records a deed of 1490 by which the abbey appointed Christopher Haslam, a secular chaplain, to instruct boys and novices in singing and grammar at a stipend of 26s 8d a year, with board and lodging at a school in Dronfield.[77]

The Obituary sheds some light on the communal life of the abbey. For example, it records that Sir Roger of Chesterfield 'gave us a new

---

[76] Confraternity, which could be granted to both lay and religious people, brought with it the spiritual benefits, including commemoration after death, that the canons themselves enjoyed. For arrangements within the Premonstratensian order, see Colvin, *White Canons*, pp. 258–259.

[77] Pegge, *An Historical Account of Beauchief Abbey*, pp. 67–68.

vestment of green colour, embroidered with gold, and a hundred silver shillings', that a canon who came from Sheffield gave a vestment costing 20s, that Sir William of Gringley (Nottinghamshire) built a chamber and made a causey by the 'great pool', and that Robert of Edensor, a former prior, bought the great bell and paid for the erection of 'the great belfry' (unfortunately no date for the belfry was given).[78] At various times the visitations record the abbot, sub-prior, circator (who was responsible for discipline), deacon, cellarer, sacristan, novices, acolytes, and licentiates; twenty-six or twenty-seven abbots are known by name.[79] The Obituary also commemorates Sir Henry Stafforth, parson of Treeton, 'our assistant brother, who gave us a silver cup'; Sir Hugh, formerly rector of the church at Handsworth; Sir Richard Oxley, formerly priest of the Guild of the Holy Cross at Chesterfield; and Matilda of Ashover and Margaret of the Brom, two assistant lay sisters.

In the commemoration of Sir Robert Rivers, a former rector of Eckington, the Obituary defined the fraternity of the abbey as:

> that he may be a partaker in all the good things and spiritual benefits which now belong, or which hereafter may belong, to the monastery of the said church, as in masses, psalms, hours, vigils, prayers, fastings, afflictions, disciplines, works, charity, hospitality, and all other works of mercy and spiritual benefits. Adding, moreover, that the day of his anniversary shall be celebrated with a solemn service and a mass in the convent, every year, for ever.

Visitations

The visitations usually reported that all was well.[80] On 28 April 1475, for example, the visitors found brotherly affection, a regularity of discipline beyond all praise, and buildings whose condition was 'everything which could be desired'. Previously, however, at the 20 October 1472 visitation, a complaint was made that 'in the evening,

---

[78] Addy, *Historical Memorials of Beauchief Abbey*, pp. 57, 136.
[79] The abbots are listed in D. Knowles, C.N.L. Brooke, and V.C.M. London (eds), *The Heads of Religious Houses: England and Wales, I, 940–1216* (2nd edn, Cambridge, 1972), pp. 193, 288; D.M. Smith and V.C.M. London (eds), *The Heads of Religious Houses: England and Wales, II, 1216–1377* (Cambridge, 2001), pp. 493–494; Smith, *Heads of Religious Houses, III*, pp. 563–564.
[80] For the visitations of Beauchief and other Premonstratensian houses in the English province by Bishop Richard Redman from 1459 to 1505, see J.A. Gribbin, *The Premonstratensian Order in Late Medieval England* (Woodbridge, 2001); D. Knowles, *The Religious Orders in England, III: the Tudor age* (Cambridge, 1959), pp. 39–51. For Beauchief, with lists of the canons, see F.A. Gasquet (ed.), *Collectanea Anglo-Premonstratensia*, 3 vols, Camden third series, 6, 10, and 12 (London, 1904–1906), I, nos 220–247.

after compline (the last service, at 7 p.m.), the brethren go outside the cloister, stay up so long, and get so much to drink that at midnight, when matins should be said, they cannot keep awake.' Some canons also left the monastery alone, instead of in small groups. In 1500 the visitors ordered that the canons should not be allowed out to 'see common shows' or to visit any inhabited place. Occasionally, individual canons were disciplined. Thus, in 1491 William Widdowson was 'pronounced rebellious' and was suspended.

The most sensational event occurred in 1461, when Abbot John Downham was found guilty of 'solemn perjuries'. He and seven canons 'rose in insurrection with armed men and defensive arms, with swords and with staves and departed the monastery, despising altogether the legal process of our order'. John Swyfte, a Beauchief canon, was appointed abbot in Downham's place. The seven apostate canons eventually returned to the abbey and Downham retired to Wymeswold, where he was commemorated in a window.[81]

The visitation reports also provide some information about the arrangements in the abbey. On 25 May 1488 the visitors noted that 'In this monastery they consume every week 10 bushels of wheat, 16 bushels of oats, and four bushels of barley. They have 20 oxen, 28 sheep, and 12 pigs.' The visitation on 25 August 1498 reported that: 'Owing to the extent of the buildings and the great repairs they are undergoing, the debts of the house are increased, and, at the present time, amount to four score marks [£53 6s 8d].' The visitation on 20 October 1472 mentioned a chantry of eight priests within the abbey, but its founder and purpose are not known. Brief references to other arrangements appear elsewhere. The altar of the Holy Cross is mentioned in charters **18** and **39–41**, the altar of St Katherine in charter **33**, and the altar of St John the Baptist in the Obituary.

Dissolution

The *Valor Ecclesiasticus* of 1535 provides a valuation of the lands, glebe, tithes, and dues belonging to the abbey on the eve of its dissolution. If we accept this record at face value, the abbot and canons appear to have sold off some of their outlying possessions, for there is no

---

[81] Pegge, *An Historical Account of Beauchief Abbey*, pp. 217–218. The inscription read: 'Orate pro anima Johannis Dounham, abbatis de Beauchiffe'. See F. Donald Logan, *Runaway Religious in Medieval England, c.1240–1540* (Cambridge, 1996), pp. 25–34, on the meaning of apostasy as abandonment of the religious life and return to the world.

mention of the properties that had been donated in Nottinghamshire (including, as we have seen, those associated with Edwalton church) nor in those parts of South Yorkshire that lay beyond Hallamshire. On the other hand, the entry for Dronfield parish includes not only properties in the townships of Dronfield, Coal Aston, and Unston, but also some at the minor settlements of Apperknowle, Cowley, and Povey, which are not in the surviving leaves of the Cartulary.

Beauchief abbey was dissolved with the other minor religious houses on 4 February 1537, ten months after the death of the last abbot, John Greenwood, alias Sheffield. The abbey was surrendered 'without giving any trouble or opposition', and Thomas Cromwell's commissioners had found no scandal. The inventory of the copes, vestments, plate, and so forth that was taken on 2 August 1537 is printed in Addy's history.[82]

The abbey and all the land in the Liberty of Beauchief were bought by Sir Nicholas Strelley, who at the time was lord of Ecclesall, and for nearly four hundred years the core of this estate was to remain in the same family.[83] In 1648 Gertrude Strelley, daughter and heiress of the last male of the line, married Edward Pegge of Ashbourne,[84] who used a good deal of the remaining stone to build Beauchief Hall, seven bays wide and three storeys high. The lintel of the main door of the hall is carved with the date 1671 and a Latin inscription. Pegge also made alterations to the tower of the old abbey church in order to form a private chapel, with Nathaniel Baxter, an ejected non-conformist minister, as his chaplain. The interior is still arranged as it was in Pegge's time, with box pews, pulpit, reading desk, clerk's pew, psalm board, and Strelley and Pegge heraldry.[85]

The rest of the abbey's estate was split up and sold to local landowners. Harewood Grange and the Alfreton possessions went to Sir Francis Leake of Sutton, Fulwood Grange to Francis Talbot, 5th earl of Shrewsbury, and Strawberry Lee to Sir Nicholas Strelley. Stanley Grange was acquired by William Bolles, the receiver,

---

[82] *Valor Ecclesiasticus*, III, pp. 172–174. See Addy, *Historical Memorials of Beauchief Abbey*, pp. 123–128 for the 1563 Exchequer Commission, which reported that the chancel of Dronfield church had been neglected for many years both before and after the dissolution of Beauchief abbey, so that the great east window had collapsed and the roof and other windows were in decay. The parsonage house, which had also been the responsibility of the abbey, was 'in great ruin and decay' because it had not been inhabited during the previous sixty years.

[83] G.R. Potter, 'Beauchief abbey after the Dissolution of the Monasteries', *Transactions of the Hunter Archaeological Society*, 11 (1981), pp. 46–51.

[84] R. Meredith, 'Beauchief Abbey and the Pegges', *Derbyshire Archaeological Journal*, 87 (1967), pp. 86–126.

[85] M. Chatfield, *Churches the Victorians Forgot* (Ashbourne, 1979), pp. 155–157; N. Pevsner, *Yorkshire: the West Riding*, revised by E. Radcliffe (Harmondsworth, 1967), p. 476.

Wymeswold passed to Trinity College, Cambridge, and Edwalton to the Cavendish family. The Chesterfield and Brampton properties eventually formed part of the Duke of Portland's estate, the Foljambes got Walton, the Fanshawes bought the Dronfield, Eckington, and Newbold lands, and Sir William West acquired the Staveley, Woodseats, Greenhill, 'Little Lees', and Little Norton properties.

The site of the abbey

In March 1931, Frank Crawford of Beauchief Hall, a local businessman and councillor, gave the site of the abbey to Sheffield City Council. He had previously encouraged the excavations that had been carried out during four successive summers, from 1923 to 1926, by W.H. Elgar, a master at King Edward VII Grammar School, Sheffield, and his pupils.[86] The remains of the church (except the chapel-of-ease), parlour, refectory, chapter house, cloister, and storerooms were uncovered and shown to follow the normal pattern of Premonstratensian foundations. They date from the late twelfth century to the fifteenth century. The present church tower has lost its top storey, which was there when Samuel Buck drew it in 1727. The large west window of the tower (now re-glazed and with its tracery restored) is early fourteenth-century work.[87] The east end of the abbey church is believed to have contained an alabaster altarpiece of the martyrdom of St Thomas of Canterbury, now in the possession of the Foljambe family.[88] A recess in the wall to the north of the altar may have been the tomb of the founder, Robert FitzRanulf. Other benefactors were also buried in the church: for example, at least three members of the Chaworth family were buried before the main altar.[89] The church had a large nave, 78 feet long and 26 feet wide, crossed by transepts of the same width. Several floor tiles from the two chapels to the east of the south transept were well preserved. The remains of a small chantry, and of the newel stair to the dormitory, were found in

---

[86] The results were never fully published. See W.H. Elgar, 'Beauchief Abbey', *Transactions of the Hunter Archaeological Society*, 3 (1929), pp. 162–164.

[87] For architectural details of the church and other built remains see Pevsner, rev. Radcliffe, *Yorkshire: the West Riding*, pp. 475–476; English Heritage, 'Beauchief abbey', http://list.english-heritage.org.uk/resultsingle.aspx?uid=1271291.

[88] Perhaps carved locally during the 1370s. For a colour photograph and description, see J. Alexander and P. Binski (eds), *Age of Chivalry: art in Plantagenet England, 1200–1400* (London, 1987), pp. 210–211, pl. 26; also, but not in colour, in Pegge, *An Historical Account of Beauchief Abbey*, pp. 246–247, pl. ix, and in H. Kirke, 'The Praemonstratensian abbey of Beauchief', *The Reliquary*, 7 (1866–1867), p. 205.

[89] Addy, *Historical Memorials of Beauchief Abbey*, p. 135.

the western part of the transept. The cloisters were sited to the south of the church, with the refectory on the south side of the cloister and the chapter house to the east. The plan of the chapter house consisted of a square and a semi-octagon, with two columns supporting the ribs of the vaulting. A few faint remains of the painting that decorated the columns supporting the chapter house roof and most of the vaulting were found. The two stone coffins containing human bones that were found outside the chapter house doorway were probably those of abbots. Further digging in 1953–1954 by Mr Peter Stiles produced a fine carved head of a mid-fifteenth-century canon and pieces of a Dutch majolica altar vessel of about 1500, both from the vicinity of the south transept.[90]

New investigations in the 1990s showed that the abbey was larger than the walled enclosure suggests and that much more remains to be discovered from modern archaeological techniques of resistivity, surveying, and excavation, as well as from documentary research. Tony Smith used surveying methods and material from the Fairbank papers in Sheffield Archives. Colin Merrony undertook a geophysical survey in April 1993, and he and Rhiannon Harte placed Beauchief in its wider context.[91]

Some of the boundaries of the original estate at Beauchief can still be traced on the ground, but in the south modern housing has encroached at Greenhill and Bradway and to the north similar buildings cover the land between Abbey Lane and Hutcliffe Wood. It is not clear how far the estate extended to the north. The 1762 map shows that Abbey Lane came from Woodseats down the hill to just beyond the abbey but it did not continue north of the river through Ecclesall Woods. Nor was there a route along the river valley through Abbeydale to Totley before the turnpike road was constructed in the early nineteenth century. These busy roads and the railway have destroyed much of the former sense of isolation and peace but, despite the continuous hum of traffic in the background, Beauchief still has much of the character that it possessed in 1789 when Viscount Torrington found 'a most happy situation for beauty and retirement'.[92]

---

[90] Now kept at Weston Park Museum, Sheffield.
[91] A.V. Smith, *Beauchief Abbey: notes on the layout and remains – the abbey and surrounding area* (Sheffield, privately printed, 1993); C.J.N. Merrony, 'More than meets the eye? A preliminary discussion of the archaeological remains of Beauchief abbey and park', in *A Review of Archaeology in South Yorkshire, 1993–1994* (Sheffield, 1994), pp. 60–67; Harte and Merrony, 'Two way traffic'.
[92] C.B. Andrewes (ed.), *The Torrington Diaries*, II (London, 1935), pp. 25–26.

The charters

The Beauchief Cartulary is housed at Sheffield Archives, with the call number MD 3414. It dates from c.1400 and is found on 114 vellum folios, now numbered 1–114. The manuscript is bound in contemporary oak boards that once had a clasp; they measure about 220 mm by 152 mm, the leaves themselves being of a similar measurement although they are unevenly cut. Two preliminary leaves, now numbered II and III, contain fragments of an Anglo-Norman French legal treatise. From a microfilm dated 1953 it appears that there was once also a first leaf, now missing from the manuscript but largely illegible on the microfilm as the result of staining. The charters that follow in the Cartulary are bundled into twelve quires (one missing), some of them with a contemporary signature in the lower margin of the last leaf, as follows:

1. 18 leaves (1 missing): fos 1–17, with the signature *a* at 17v. Between fos 13 and 14 one leaf has been excised without interruption to the text of charter **22**. Fos 7 and 8 have been added with string between 6 and 9 but without causing any break in the text.

    The Cartulary begins on fo. 1 with a header in red: *Previlegia nostri ordinis*. Fos 1–4 contain two documents concerning the whole Premonstratensian order: the papal bull of Lucius III and the circular letter of Abbot Hugh II of Prémontré. Fo. 5r is blank, except for miscellaneous notes written in Latin at a later date and including the confirmation of a debt for £20 owed by one Richard Massye to one Nicholas Dunson. Fo. 5v contains the foundation charter of Robert FitzRanulph (**3**); other Beauchief charters follow, beginning with the *Inspeximus* by King Edward III (**4**) on fo. 6r.

2. 12 leaves: fos 18–29, with the signature *b* at 29v.
3. 12 leaves: fos 30–41, with the signature *c* at 41v.
4. 12 leaves: fos 42–53, with the signature *e* at 53v. This signature is a mistake: there seems to be no interruption in the text of charter **61** between fos 41v and 42r.
5. 12(?) leaves missing through excision.

    Between the quires 4 and 6 (between fos 53 and 54) a whole quire – perhaps of 12 leaves, like its neighbours – has been excised, with a consequent loss of text; only the stubs show. At the bottom of fo. 53v charter **91** lacks the names of all but one witness; fo. 54r begins with a mere fragment of the end of **92**. It is not possible to determine from the confirmations of 1312 (**38**) and 1316 (Appendices II and III) what might have been written on the missing leaves.

6. 12 leaves: fos 54–65, with the signature *d* at 65v. There are no quires signed *f* and *g* but there seems to be no loss of text in charter **114** between fos 65 and 66.
7. 12 leaves: fos 66–77, with the signature *h* at 77v.
8. 8 leaves (2, 1 missing, 1, 1 missing, 3): fos 78–83, with the signature *i* at 83v. A leaf has been excised after 79, and again after 80, without loss of text. There is no quire *j* and there is loss of text from the beginning of the next quire between fos 83 and 84 (charter **158**).
9. 12 leaves (5 missing, 7): fos 84–90, with the signature *k* at 90v. The strings visible between 84 and 85 show that this quire had 12 leaves; only the stubs remain of the first 5 that have been excised. A new charter (**159**) begins at the head of fo. 84r.
10. 8 leaves: fos 91–98, with the signature *l* at 98v.
11. 8 leaves: fos 99–106, with the signature *m* at 106v.
12. 8 leaves: fos 107–114, with no signature at 114v. The final charter (**226**) is unfinished, although, as is sometimes the case elsewhere in the Cartulary, only the witnesses are lacking.

Since each charter in the Cartulary occupies one side of a folio on average (226 charters: 114 folios), some twenty-four charters may have been lost from quire 5. If quires *f*, *g*, and *j* did once exist, and if they comprised twelve folios each, perhaps a further sixty-two charters were included in the Cartulary, but this is not certain. Five leaves have been excised from quire 9, with loss of the text of perhaps another ten charters. Leaves are also missing after folio 114 where the text of the last charter found in the Cartulary (**226**) is unfinished; and, if the Royal Confirmation of 1316 is a guide, the Cartulary may have lost four more charters from here onward. In total the original Cartulary perhaps contained over 270 charters and possibly more than 330. The Concordances in Appendix III also show that some charters confirmed in 1316 are not present in the Cartulary.

More than one Anglicana hand appears to have been at work but the Cartulary seems to be the product of a decision, presumably taken within the abbey, to make a collection of all the available documents that showed its privileges and possessions. The rubricated headings seem to be the work of a single head scribe, who wrote with flourishing ascenders and large rectangles. The initial capital of each entry is given a very simple decoration. Pegge rightly observed that 'There are not many dates in the chartulary [. . .] and the witnesses, towards the end of the volume, are almost perpetually omitted.'[93]

At the beginning of the eighteenth century, the Cartulary was in the possession of a Welsh antiquary, Robert Davies of Llanerch

---

[93] Pegge, *An Historical Account of Beauchief Abbey*, p. ix.

(Denbighshire).[94] Samuel Pegge, the antiquary of Beauchief Hall, used it for his *An Historical Account of Beauchief Abbey* (1801), but he did not publish his transcript, which is now kept in the Library of the College of Arms and which contains many inaccuracies.[95] When Sidney Oldall Addy used the Cartulary for his *Historical Memorials of Beauchief Abbey* (1878), it belonged to Philip Bryan Davies-Cooke, Esq. of Owston, near Doncaster. In the twentieth century, Major P.J. Davies-Cooke of Mold presented the Cartulary to the National Library of Wales, who sold it in 1959 to the Sheffield City Libraries Committee.

Some copies of Beauchief abbey charters appear in other collections and some originals also survive. Four original charters are found among the deeds of Norton parish church, now in Sheffield Archives. They were known to Pegge and to Addy, the latter of whom reproduced their seals in his book.[96] A typewritten calendar of these deeds, made by T. Walter Hall, is available in the Archives. Copies of three of these Norton charters are found in the Cartulary: **41** is a copy of PR2/16; PR2/20A and 20B, both dated 11 November 1312, are the same as **44** and its duplicate **61**, and are themselves duplicates, not indentures or chirographs.[97] Each of these has a small seal with the arms of Thomas Chaworth II. The fourth Beauchief charter, PR2/18, is not found in the Cartulary. It was written, like the others, *c.*1400 and is very comprehensive, being a release and quitclaim to the abbey in free alms by Thomas de Chaworth, knight, of all the lands, rents, mills with watercourses, ponds, ways, suits, services, rights, customs and liberties, tenements, pastures, woods, closes and new enclosures, fishings, easements to such lands, rents, mill, and tenements that had belonged to the abbey within his fees of Norton, Alfreton, and

---

[94] Either Robert Davies (1658–1710) or his son Robert Davies (1685/6–1728); both were antiquaries, as were their ancestors and descendants. See the entry in the *Oxford Dictionary of National Biography*.

[95] Pegge (on whom also see the *Oxford Dictionary of National Biography*) published eight of the charters from the Cartulary, but not fully. These are, in sequence, nos **3**, **4**, **33**, **46**, **37**, **164**–**166**. Pegge, *An Historical Account of Beauchief Abbey*, also printed two documents not included in the Cartulary: a grant by Gilbert of Salmonby, abbot of Beauchief (1236× 1247), to Robert son of Walter of Brampton (p. 226, viid), and an indenture of 1237 made between William, dean of Lincoln, and Gilbert, abbot of Beauchief, concerning lands in Brampton (pp. 227–228, ix). He also used (p. 250) two charters with their seals that were in the possession of Mr John Reynolds, Jr. Reynolds' copies are: 1 = **164** (= British Library, Wolley charter I, 13; copy in Leake 1), 2 = **188** (copy in Leake 12), 3 = **187** (copy in Leake 11), 4: not in the Cartulary (copy of a similar charter in Leake 8), 5 = **183** (copy in Leake 10), 6: not in the Cartulary (= British Library, Wolley charter III, 35; copy of a similar charter in Leake 5).

[96] Pegge, *An Historical Account of Beauchief Abbey*, p. vii; Addy, *Historical Memorials of Beauchief Abbey*, pp. v, 150–151.

[97] Addy, *Historical Memorials of Beauchief Abbey*, pp. 63–64, printed one of these. He also printed PR2/16 (on pp. 61–63).

Wymeswold, and of all charters, deeds, concessions, and muniments that the abbey had received from his ancestors. The witnesses are Sir John of Heriz, Sir Nicholas Wake, Sir William de Staynesby, William and Giles of Meynyle, Robert Sauccheverel, John de Anesley, knights, Robert le Gaunt, John of Brimington, Hugo de canonicis, Hugo de Lynakyr, and others. The seal of Thomas Chaworth – either I or II – is suspended by red laces; its circumscription is not legible. PR2/21 (mentioned above on p. 12) records an agreement made on 3 November 1524 between John, abbot of Beauchief, and Thomas Gylbert, one of the canons, who was vicar and curate of Norton parish church; it shows that the bishop of Coventry and Lichfield, Geoffrey Blythe, had built a chantry house in a croft on the west side of Norton Green.

Another six original copies of grants made to the abbey are known to survive. They are British Library, Harley 83 E 2, Wolley I, 13 (Cartulary **164**), Wolley II, 45 (see **175**), Wolley III, 35 (copied in Leake **5**), Wolley III, 92 (**184**), and The National Archives, CP 25/1/36/2/10 (see **189**). Harley 83 E 2 (Jeayes, *Derbyshire Charters*, no. 2556) is a chirograph confirming a grant, not entered into the Cartulary but made to the abbey in 1280 by Thomas de Camera son of Roger of Birley, of 21d from land in an otherwise unknown place called Dunstorhes. The abbot's brown wax oval seal is attached: the obverse shows a crozier clasped by a hand, with five stars and a crown in the surround, and what remains of the circumscription is ABBATIS DE BELLO-CAPITE; the reverse shows nothing.[98] Three of the witnesses, Adam de Bosco, Robert de Brom, and Roger Hauselin, also appear in the Cartulary and usually together; the others – Henry Wylte, Adam le Blunt,[99] John of Rosinton (Rossington) in Rotherham – do not.

William Dugdale, in his *Monasticon Anglicanum*, printed two charters of Sir Thomas Chaworth I in the possession of the antiquary Samuel Roper of Lincoln's Inn (d. 1658), as well as the general confirmation of

---

[98] Kirke, 'The Praemonstratensian Abbey of Beauchief', p. 202, prints an engraving of this or a similar seal. For an engraving of two oval seals of the abbey, one representing Our Lady and Becket with a half figure below of an abbot with his crozier, the other representing the murder of Becket with another half figure of an abbot, see Pegge, *An Historical Account of Beauchief Abbey*, pl. xii (followed by W. Dugdale, *Monasticon Anglicanum*, ed. J. Caley, H. Ellis, and B. Bandinel, 6 vols (London, 1817–1830), VI, p. 883). The circumscriptions according to Pegge are: SIGILL ABBATIE DE BELLO CAPITE and COM (*recte* E(CCLES)IE?) (SANC)TI THO(ME) MARTIRIS DE BEAVCHEF. For all three seals, the first two not located, the third said to be in the possession of J.H. Hill, solicitor of Hull, see also *Proceedings of the Society of Antiquaries of London*, 17 November 1870 to 3 April 1873, 2nd series, vol. 5, pp. 175–176.

[99] For le Blunt see Jeayes, *Derbyshire Charters*, nos 353, 684, 2491.

the abbey's possessions made by Edward II in 1316.[100] The first of these two Chaworth charters is similar to **18** in the Cartulary; the second is **38**; for the confirmation of 1316, which is not found in the Cartulary, see Appendix II. Folios 357–362v of the British Library manuscript Landsdowne 207B contain excerpts from Beauchief charters made by the antiquary Gervase Holles (1607–1675). These reveal three that are not in the Cartulary. One of them (fo. 359) is an agreement over property, dated 1229, between Robert of Bella Aqua and Amitia, formerly the wife of Nigel de Stokes. Four witnesses are named: one, William de Cressy, appears in the Cartulary (**120, 124**); the others (Nigel de Lisurs, Simon de Crumwell, Robert de Grendun) do not. Another is a lost charter, undated, of Ralph, son of Robert of Ecclesall; Holles names the witnesses (see **111**). A third is the grant of a vill in the thirteenth century by Ralph Musard (see **222**); this is also recorded in the abbey's Obituary and in the Royal Confirmation of 1316 (Appendix II, no. 30).

Jeayes's *Descriptive Catalogue of Derbyshire Charters* (1906) includes summaries of seven of the Wolley charters at the British Library, four Foljambe deeds, and four other documents. Some of these are dated later than the Beauchief Cartulary and are not noticed here. The charters from Glapwell Hall edited by R.R. Darlington include twenty-two charters relating to Beauchief abbey that were unknown to Jeayes; most of these probably come from Darley abbey, which received properties from Beauchief abbey in the thirteenth century.[101] These documents overlap but do not entirely coincide with the charters in the Beauchief Cartulary. The three charters in the Darley Cartulary that relate to Beauchief abbey can all be linked to counterparts in the Glapwell charters. Thomas Tanner, in *Notitia Monastica*, records that the collections of Sir William Haward (*c.*1617–1704) included copies of Beauchief charters that were once in the possession of Peter Le Neve (1661–1729), together with three charters with the seals of the abbey.[102] They have not, however, been identified.

Copies of the twelve Beauchief charters among the Leake family papers at the Derbyshire Record Office (reference D1005 Z/EI) may have been made from originals and include some that are not found in the Cartulary. Like the Glapwell charters, they provide the names

---

[100] Dugdale, *Monasticon Anglicanum*, VI, pp. 883–886. On Roper see the *Oxford Dictionary of National Biography*. For these two Chaworth charters see the notes to **18** and **38**; for the confirmation of 1316 see Appendix II.

[101] R.R. Darlington (ed.), *The Glapwell Charters, Journal of the Derbyshire Archaeological and Natural History Society*, Supplements to vols 56–57 (Kendal, 1957–1959).

[102] T. Tanner, *Notitia Monastica* (reprint with additions, Cambridge, 1782), unnumbered page at *Derbyshire. I, De Bello Capite*; also in the 1744 edition, p. 82. On Sir William Haward and Peter Le Neve see the *Oxford Dictionary of National Biography*.

of witnesses that were truncated in the Beauchief Cartulary and that are now included in the footnotes. Copies of six Beauchief charters, two of them not found in the Cartulary and four of them also copied in the Leake papers,[103] were made in 1777 by John Reynolds, junior, in the course of transcribing a total of thirty-one charters concerning religious houses in Derbyshire. These copies survive in Cambridge University Library, Add. MS 3897, pp. 1–19. Reynolds' exemplars were original charters since five of them still had their seals.

Some earlier antiquaries found their way to the Cartulary itself (*Registrum evidentiarum* or *Registrum chartarum*). In 1581, Robert Glover (a genealogist and from 1570 Somerset Herald) and his friend Thomas Talbot copied from there and from other sources materials to illustrate the history of the Chaworth and other families, such as the Bassets, the Deincourts, and the Furnivals; they are found on fos 44v–90r of the Ashmole manuscript 799 in the Bodleian Library in Oxford. Glover's many journeys had taken him to Derby in 1569.[104] An interest in genealogy also led another sixteenth-century antiquary to turn to the abbey's *Registrum* to reconstruct the descent of the lords of Alfreton and Norton from Ranulph father of Robert: the Oxford manuscript The Queen's College 117 contains on folio 26r–v abstracts of five Beauchief charters (**4**, **7**, **11**, **14**, **64**).[105]

Other documents

Sheffield Archives house other unpublished material relating to Beauchief. A commonplace or note book, which has the call number MD 3500 and consists of 71 folios measuring $6\frac{1}{8}$ x $4\frac{1}{4}$ inches, has

---

[103] **164** (Leake 1), **188** (Leake 12), **187** (Leake 8), **183** (Leake 10), Leake 5.
[104] See W.H. Black, *A Descriptive, Analytical and Critical Catalogue of the Manuscripts Bequeathed unto the University of Oxford by Elias Ashmole* (Oxford, 1845), columns 426–437 for Ashmole 799. Items 70–96 (Black, columns 430–431) summarize the Chaworth and related material. For Beauchief abbey see especially nos 77, 81–83, 96. There is an entry for Robert Glover (1543/4–1588) in the *Oxford Dictionary of National Biography*.
[105] The family tree presented on fos 26–27r is this: (1) Ranulf of Alfreton; (2) Ranulf's two sons, Robert, lord of Alfreton, Norton, and Marnham, the founder of Beauchief abbey, and William, the younger son, who died childless; (3) Robert's son, William, lord of Alfreton in the time of King Richard I; (4) William's daughter, Alicia, and his sons, Robert, lord of Alfreton, Norton, and Marnham, who married Agnes, and Ranulf of Alfreton; (5) Robert's son and heir, Thomas, lord of Alfreton and Norton, who died childless, and Robert's three daughters: Alicia, the eldest daughter and heiress, who married Sir William de Cadurcis, Amitia, the second daughter and heiress who married Robert de Lathum, son of Sir Richard de Lathum, and Letitia, the third daughter and heiress of Sir Thomas of Alfreton, who died childless. According to charter **57**, Robert also had a daughter, Lucy. We are grateful to Professor David Smith for informing us of this find by Professor Nicholas Vincent and to the Librarians of the College, Jonathan Bengston and Amanda Saville, for sending us copies.

explanatory notes on Greek words arranged in alphabetical order, together with notes on theological subjects including the Apostles' Creed.[106] Two dates are given in this small book – 1490 (fo. 55) and 1500 (fo. 1). Deeds relating to property in the locality but not belonging to the abbey, dated 1280–1407, form part of the Bagshawe collection, reference numbers 3174–3185.[107] Some persons named in these deeds also appear in the Cartulary, as do names found in Jeayes, *Derbyshire Charters*. The Norton church deeds include copies of Thomas Chaworth's grants and confirmations, from the early fourteenth century; these are all copied in the Cartulary, and their seals are reproduced by Addy, as mentioned above. The Beauchief muniments, which are mostly post-dissolution, include leases and rentals. Material in the Jackson collection has been published in T.W. Hall and A.H. Thomas, *Descriptive Catalogue of the Charters [...] Forming the Jackson Collection at the Sheffield Public Reference Library* (1914), which lists, with summaries, a number of post-dissolution charters referring specifically to land once in the ownership of Beauchief abbey. Although none of the pre-dissolution charters in the Jackson collection refers to the abbey, a number were issued by one or other of the Chaworths in respect of property in Norton, and some of their witnesses also occur in the Cartulary.[108]

A rare survival among the usual range of monastic archives is the Beauchief Obituary, which was begun in the thirteenth century and continued to the Dissolution. It recorded the names of departed abbots, canons, and benefactors, whose souls were prayed for on fixed days. A short version is kept among the Dugdale manuscripts at the Bodleian Library, Oxford, as MS 39, which formerly belonged to the abbey and which also has a copy of the *Rule* observed by regular canons.[109] The longer version in the British Library (MS Cotton, Caligula A. viii, fos 4–27) was reproduced in translation in chapter III of Addy's history.[110] In the present edition, we have indicated entries in

---

[106] Listed, with a title given in the manuscript of *Explanatio verborum*, in Andrew G. Watson (ed.), *Supplement to the Second Edition* of N.R. Ker (ed.), *Medieval Libraries of Great Britain: a list of surviving books*, Royal Historical Society Guides and Handbooks, 15 (London, 1987), p. 3.

[107] Nearly all of these were printed, not altogether accurately, by S.O. Addy in the *Journal of the Derbyshire Archaeological and Natural History Society*, 3 (1881), pp. 100–106.

[108] For examples, see T.W. Hall and A.H. Thomas, *A Descriptive Catalogue of the Charters [...] Forming the Jackson Collection at the Sheffield Public Reference Library* (Sheffield, 1914), pp. 108–111, 117–123.

[109] *A Summary Catalogue of Western Manuscripts in the Bodleian Library at Oxford* (Oxford, 1937), 2.i, no. 6527. Printed in Tho. Hearnius (ed.), *Johannis [...] Glastoniensis sive historia de rebus Glastoniensibus* ... 2 vols (Oxford 1726), II, appendix 5, pp. 557–566, and in Kirke, 'Praemonstratensian Abbey of Beauchief', pp. 196–202. Samuel Pegge used it in *An Historical Account of Beauchief Abbey*.

[110] Addy, *Historical Memorials of Beauchief Abbey*, pp. 22–60. Cotton, Caligula A. viii, and Landsdowne 207B (mentioned above, p. 30) are among the sources used in listing the abbots

the Obituary that record deaths of benefactors whose names appear in the Cartulary. Gifts made by other benefactors recorded in the Obituary were often of cash or precious metal. Addy also printed (in chapter VI) the surviving documentation from the second half of the fifteenth century of the visitations conducted by senior members of the Premonstratensian order. This information was taken from Ashmole's manuscript 1519 (Bodleian Library) and Peck's manuscript (British Library, Additional MSS 4934). These documents form the basis of chapter IV on the Premonstratensian Canons in Knowles's *Religious Orders in England, III: the Tudor Age* (1959). The Obituary and the visitation reports are important records that complement the Cartulary. Together, they allow us to reconstruct much of the history of this small religious house on the northern border of Derbyshire.

The edition

The only marginal notes in the manuscript that are included in the present edition are those that are clearly written in the same hand as the main body of the text. Other marginal notes, perhaps most of them, were added after the dissolution of the abbey. Our own notes on the text appear at the end of each charter. Square brackets enclose any letters or words that we have added to the transcription and that do not appear in the manuscript; these include expansions of abbreviations and the insertion of words whose omission from the original affects the meaning of the document. The cartulary for the most part lacks punctuation; thus the punctuation in this edition is largely our own. Place-names have been transcribed as written, despite some inaccuracies; however, we have added initial capitals where these are not found in the manuscript. Most but not all of the charters are undated. For these we offer approximate dates, largely based on evidence from other sources. They range from the late twelfth century to the end of the fourteenth, the latest dated charter being from 1382 (**82**).

---

of Beauchief in Knowles, Brooke, and London, *Heads of Religious Houses, I*, p. 193; Smith and London, *Heads of Religious Houses, II*, pp. 493–494; and Smith, *Heads of Religious Houses, III*, pp. 563–564; also in Colvin, *White Canons*, pp. 396–397. The Cotton manuscript is listed in N.R. Ker, *Medieval Libraries of Great Britain: a list of surviving books*, Royal Historical Guides and Handbooks, 3 (2nd edn, London, 1964), p. 8, where Ker also lists one other Beauchief manuscript of the early thirteenth century containing a work (*Adversus Judaeos*) by Petrus Alfonsi, now Cambridge, St John's College, MS 86 (M.R. James, *Descriptive Catalogue of the Manuscripts in the Library of St John's College, Cambridge* (Cambridge, 1913); also available on-line at the college's website).

GLOSSARY

assart: a clearing from woods or waste
bondage: a system whereby land was held for defined services
bovate: an oxgang or the amount of land an ox could plough in a year; one-eighth of a ploughland or carucate
carucate: a unit of taxation in the Danelaw equivalent to eight bovates
chirograph: a formal document, signed and sealed; sometimes copied and sealed twice before separation for each of two parties
curtilage: land on which a dwelling and outbuildings are situated
deforciant: a defendant
demesne: land on a manor that was reserved for a lord's own use
eyre: from the Latin word *iter* (journey); court of justice held by itinerant royal justices in the shires
fee: lordship
feoffaments: the original form of conveyance
free alms: charitable donation
homage: formal acknowledgement of allegiance to a feudal superior
messuage: a dwelling-house and its surrounding property
moiety: half share
multure: a toll on grain ground at a mill
oxgang: *see* **bovate**
reeve: an elected intermediary between a lord and his tenants
rod: a quarter of an acre
seisin: possession of property as distinct from ownership
selions: strips in open fields
soke: land held by free peasants who owed suit of court and other customary dues to the lord of the manor
subinfeudation: the grant of a fief or fee by a chief lord to a sub-tenant on condition of service or payment
syke: a small stream of water, often used as a boundary between lands
tenement: rented property
vill: the smallest unit of local government; a township
villeinage: unfree tenancy of manorial land

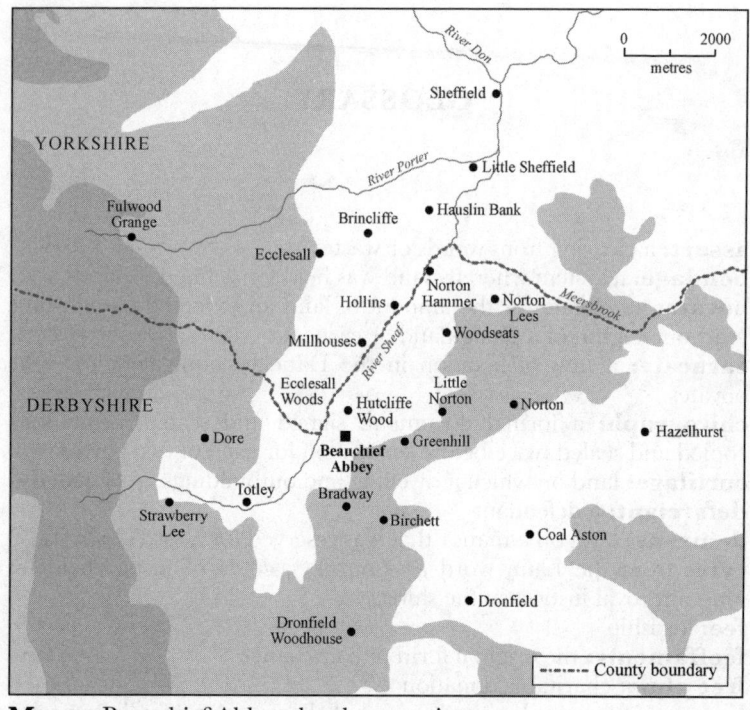

Map 1. Beauchief Abbey: local properties

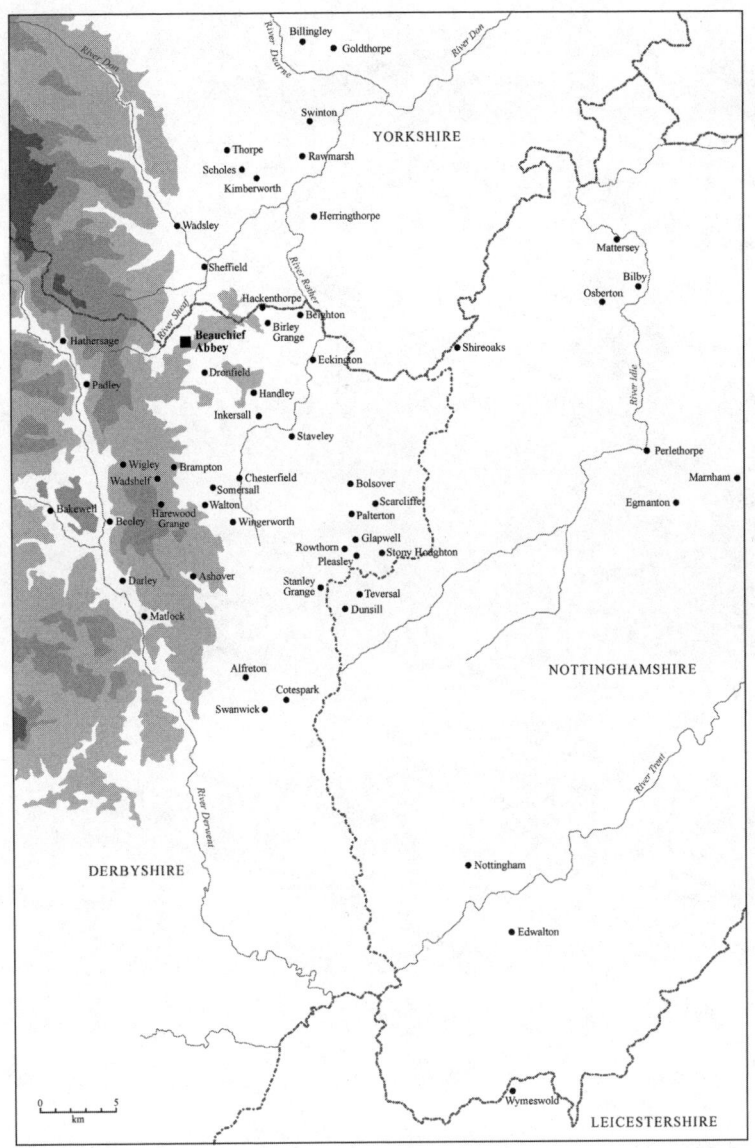

Map 2. Beauchief abbey: properties in Derbyshire, Leicestershire, Nottinghamshire, and Yorkshire

THE BEAUCHIEF ABBEY CARTULARY

[fo. 1r]
　　　　　　　Previlegia nostri ordinis

1. Bull of Pope Lucius III confirming to Hugh, abbot of Prémontré,[1] and the other abbots and canons of the Premonstratensian order, their laws and privileges in perpetuity. 10 March 1184 (by modern reckoning).[2]

Lucius episcopus servus servorum Dei dilectis filiis Hugoni[a] abbati Premonstrat[ens]i et ceteris abbatibus et canonicis Premonstrat[ensis] ordinis, tam presentibus quam futuris, regularem vitam professis inperpetuum.

　In eminenti apostolice sedis specula, licet immeriti, disponente domino constituti, pro singulorum statu solliciti esse compellimur, et ea sincere tenemur amplecti que ad incrementum religionis pertinent[b] et ad virtutum spectant[c] ornatum, quatinus religiosorum quies ab omni sit perturbacione secura et a jugo mundane oppressionis servetur illesa, cum apostolica fuerit tuicione munita. Attendentes itaque quomodo religio et ordo noster,[d] multa refulgens gloria meritorum et gracia redolens sanctitatis palmites suos a mari usque ad mare extenderit, ipsum ordinem et commensales[e] domos eiusdem ordinis apostolice proteccionis presidio duximus confovendas et presenti privilegio[f] muniendas. Ea propter, dilecti in Domino filii, vestris justis postulacionibus benignius annuentes, ad exemplum[g] felicis recordacionis Alexandri pape predecessoris nostri, universas regulares instituciones et disposiciones, quas de communi concensu vel maioris et sanioris partis fecistis, sicut inferius denotatur, auctoritate apostolica roboramus et presentis scripti patrocinio[h] communimus. Videlicet ut ordo canonicus, quemadmodum in Premonstratensi ecclesia secundum beati Augustini regulam et disposicionem recolende memorie Norberti quondam Premonstratensis[i] ordinis institutoris et successorum suorum in candido habitu constitutus esse dinoscitur, per omnes eiusdem[j] ordinis ecclesias perpetuis temporibus inviolabiliter observetur, et eedem penitus observancie, i[i]dem quoque libri qui ad divinum officium pertinent, ab omnibus eiusdem ordinis ecclesiis uniformiter teneantur, nec aliqua ecclesia vel persona ordinis nostri[k] adversus communia ipsius ordinis instituta privilegium aliquod postulare vel obtentum audacter[l] quomodolibet retinere. Nulla eciam ecclesiarum eius quam genuit quamlibet terreni comodi exactionem[m] imponat. Set tantum pater abbas curam de profectu tam abbatis filii quam fratrum domus illius[n] habeat. Et potestatem habeat secundum ordinem corrigendi que in ea noverit corrigenda et illi ei tanquam [fo. 1v] patri reverenciam filialem humiliter exhibeant.[o] Abbas autem Premonstratensis ecclesie, que mater esse dinoscitur aliarum, non solum[p] in ecclesiis illis quas constituit set eciam in omnibus aliis eiusdem ordinis et dignitatem patris obtineat et officium, et ei[q] ab omnibus, tam abbatibus quam fratribus, debita obediencia impendatur.

Preterea omnes abbates ordinis nostri[r] singulis annis ad generale capitulum Premonstratum,[s] post posita omni[t] occasione, conveniant, illis solis exceptis[u] quos a labore vie corporis retardaverit infirmitas; qui tamen idoneum[v] delegare debent[w] nuncium per quem necessitas et causa remoracionis sue capitulo fuerit constitutus. In quo nimirum[x] capitulo presedente abbate Premonstratensi ceterisque confidentibus[y] et in spiritu Dei cooperantibus, de hiis que ad edificacionem animarum, ad instruccionem morum et ad informacionem virtutum atque incrementum regularis discipline spectabunt, sermo diligens habeatur. Porro de omnibus questionibus[z] et querelis, tam spiritualibus quam temporalibus, que in ipso capitulo proposite fuerint, illud teneatur irrefragibiliter[aa] et observetur quod abbas Premonstratensis[ab] cum hiis qui ad sanioris consilii et magis idonei apparuerint juste ac provide judicabit. Sane si abbas[ac] aliquis vestri ordinis infamis vel inutilis aut ordinis sui prevaricator inventus fuerit, et prius per abbatem patrem suum aut per nuncios eius ammonitus suum corrigere et emendare delictum neglexerit, aut cedere, si amovendus fuerit, sponte noluerit, auctoritate generalis capituli deponatur; et depositus sine dilacione ad aliquam ordinis domum in qua, auxilio capituli [fo. 2r] generalis et prece propria, graciam introitus invenire potuerit, revertatur,[ad] in obediencia abbatis, sicut ceteri fratres ipsius domus, firmiter permansurus. Idipsum eciam ullo[ae] tempore, si necesse fuerit et capitulum sine scandalo vel periculo expectari non poterit,[af] per abbatem Premonstratensem et patrem abbatem et alios abbates quos vocaverit fieri licebit. Quod si depositus in se date sentencie contumaciter contrariare temptaverit, tam ipse quam principales eius qui de ordine vestro fuerint in sua contumacia fautores, ab abbate

Premonstratensi[ag] et ceteris abbatibus censura ecclesiastica, donec satisfaciant, coherciantur.

Verum cum aliqua ecclesiarum vestrarum abbate proprio fuerit destituta, sub patris abbatis potestate ac disposicione[ah] consistat, et cum eiusdem consilio qui eligendus fuerit a fratribus eligatur. Electo autem fratres ecclesie statim obedienciam promittant, qui non[ai] quasi absolutus a potestate patris abbatis vel ordinis sui archiepiscopo vel episcopo, in cuius diocesi fuerit, presentetur, plenitudinem officii ab eo percepturus, ita tamen quod, post factam archiepiscopo vel episcopo suo professionem, occasione illa non transgrediatur[aj] instituciones[ak] ordinis sui, nec in aliquo eius prevaricator existat. Si quis eciam ex vobis canonice electus in abbatem, diocesano episcopo semel et iterum per abbates vestri ordinis presentatus, benediccionem ab eo non potuerit optinere, ne ecclesia, ad quam vocatus est, destituta consilio periclitetur, officio et loco abbatis plenarie secundum ordinem fungatur in ea, tam in exterioribus providendis quam in interioribus corrigendis, donec aut interventu generalis capituli vestri aut precepto Romani pontificis seu metropolitani benediccionem suam obtineat.[al] Ceterum si aliqua ecclesiarum vestrarum pastoris solacio destituta, inter fratres de substituendo abbate discordia fuerit vel cissura oborta, et ipsi facile ad concordiam vel unitatem [fo. 2v] revocari nequiverint, pater abbas concilio coabbatum[am] suorum eis[an] idoneam provideat personam, et illi eam sine contradiccione recipiant in abbatem. Quam si recipere contempserint, sentencie subiaceant quam pater abbas cum consilio coabbatum suorum in eos duxerit auctoritate ordinis promulgandam. Si[ap] que autem ecclesie canonicorum alterius ordinis ad ordinem vestrum venerint, ad eam ecclesiam vestri ordinis habeant sine refragacione respectum, in qua vestrum noscuntur ordinem assumpsisse.

Nulla sane ecclesiastica persona [pro chrismate, aut consecrationibus et ordinationibus, aut pro sepultura pretium, aut][aq] pro benedicendo abbate et deducendo in sedem suam palefridum aut aliquid aliud exigere, nullus abbatum vestrorum, eciam si exigatur, dare presumat quia et exigenti et danti nota simoniace pravitatis imminet et periculum. Ad hec quoniam Premonstratensis ecclesia prima mater est omnium ecclesiarum tocius ordinis et patrem super se alium non habet, sicut ad cautelam et custodiam ordinis statutum est per tres primos abbates, silicet de Lauduno et de Floressia et de Cussiaco,[ar] annua visitacio ibidem fiat, et si quid in ipsa domo corrigendum fuerit absque maiori audiencia per eos corrigatur. Quod si abbates in corrigendo tepidus, et fratres sepius moniti incorrigibiles permanserint, ad generale capitulum referatur et, sicut melius visum fuerit, consilio generalis capituli emendetur, et sentencia in hac parte capituli sine retraccione[as] aliqua observetur. Quociens vero ecclesia Premonstratensis sine abbate fuerit, ad prefatos tres abbates eius curia respiciat, et a canonicis ipsius ecclesie, cum eorum consilio, persona in abbatem idonea eligatur, ad consilium suum quattuor aliis abbatibus ad eandem ecclesiam pertinentibus pariter advocatis, quos ipsi canonici providerint advocandos. Liceat quoque unicuique matri ecclesie ordinis vestri, cum consilio abbatis [fo. 3r] Premonstratensis de abbatibus ecclesiarum, que ab ea processisse noscuntur, [sive etiam de alia ejusdem ordinis inferiore Ecclesia sibi][at] quemcumque voluerit,[au] si tamen idoneus fuerit in abbatem assumere. Personam autem de alio ordine nulla ecclesiarum vestrarum sibi eligat in pastorem, nec vestri ordinis aliqua in abbatem monasterii alterius ordinis, nisi de auctoritate Romane ecclesie, ordinetur. Nulli eciam canonicos vel conversos vestros, sine licencia abbatum, recipere aut susceptos liceat retinere.

Si qua vero inter aliquas ecclesias vestri ordinis de temporalibus questio emerserit, non extra ordinem ecclesiastica vel secularis audiencia requiratur, set, mediante Premonstratensi abbate et ceteris quos vocaverit, aut caritative inter eas conponatur aut, auditis utriusque racionibus, eadem controvercia iusto judicio terminetur. Similiter si aliqua in ordine vestro inter prelatos et subiectos suos dissensio vel controversia pro qualibet occasione orta fuerit, nequaquam ecclesiastica aliquave secularis audiencia requiratur, set in ipso ordine consilio et judicio ordinis terminetur.[av] Quia vero singula que ad religionis profectum et animarum salutem ordinastis, presenti abbreviacioni nequiverunt annecti, nos, cum hiis que prescripta sunt, consuetudines vestras, quas inter vos religionis intuitu regulariter statuistis et deinceps, auctore Deo, statuetis, auctoritate apostolica roboramus, et vobis vestrisque successoribus et omnibus qui ordinem vestrum professi fuerint perpetuis temporibus inviolabilitur observandas decernimus.

Ad maiorem quoque ordinis vestri reverenciam et regularis discipline observanciam, vobis, filii abbates, subiectos vestros ligandi et solvendi plenam concedimus facultatem. De cetero, quoniam a strepitu et tumultu seculari remoti, pacem et quietem diligitis, grangias vestras[aw] sicut et atria ecclesiarum a pravorum incursu et violencia libera fore sanctimus, prohibentes ut ibi nullus hominem capere, [fo. 3v] spoliare, verberare seu interficere, aut furtum vel rapinam committere audeat. Ob evitandas vero secularium [virorum][ax] frequencias, liberum sit vobis, salvo jure diocesanorum episcoporum, oratoria in grangiis vestris[ay] constituere et in ipsis vobis et familie vestre divina officia cum necesse fuerit celebrare.

Prohibemus insuper[az] ne aliqua persona, fratres, ordinis vestri audeat ad secularia iudicia provocare, set si quis adversus vos[aaa] aliquid sibi crediderit de jure competere, sub ecclesiastici examine iudicii experiendi habeat facultatem. Preterea presentis scripti auctoritate firmamus ut de novalibus vestris seu de nutrimentis animalium vestrorum nulla ecclesiastica secularisve persona decimas a vobis exigere presumat. Decernimus ergo ut nulli[aab] omnino hominum liceat prefatum monasterium vel ceteras eius abbatias et obediencias temere[aac] perturbare aut earum possessiones auferre, vel ablatas retinere, minuere seu quibuslibet vexacionibus perturbare,[aad] set omnia integra conserventur eorum, pro quorum gubernacione[aae] concessa sunt usibus, profutura omnimodis, salva sedis apostolice auctoritate. Si qua igitur in futurum ecclesiastica secularisve persona, hanc nostre constitucionis paginam sciens, contra eam temere venire temptaverit, secundo terciove commonita, nisi presumpcionem suam[aaf] digna satisfaccione correxerit, potestatis honorisque sui dignitate careat, reamque se divino iudicio existere de perpetrata iniquitate cognoscat, et a sacratissimo corpore ac sanguine Dei et domini redemptoris nostri Jhesu Cristi aliena fiat, atque in extremo examine districte ulcioni subiaceat. Cunctis autem eisdem locis sua jura servantibus sit pax domini nostri Jhesu Cristi, [fo. 4r] quatinus et hic fructum bone accionis percipiant et apud districtum iudicem premia eterne pacis inveniant. Amen.

+Ego Johannes presbiter[aag] cardinalis tituli sancti Marci
+Ego Petrus presbiter cardinalis tituli sancte Susanne
+Ego Laborans presbiter cardinalis sancte Marie transtyberim tituli Calixti
+Ego Pand[ulfus] presbiter cardinalis tituli basilice xii apostolorum
+Ego Lucius Catholice ecclesie episcopus[aah]
+Ego Theodinus Portuensis et sancte Rufine sedis episcopus
+Ego Paulus Prenestinus episcopus
+Ego Jac[inthus] sancte Marie in Cosmidin diaconus cardinalis
+Ego Ardicio diaconus cardinalis sancti Theodori
+Ego Gracianus sanctorum Cosme et Damiani diaconus cardinalis
+Ego Octavianus sanctorum Sergii et Bachi diaconus cardinalis
+Ego Albinus diaconus cardinalis sancte Marie nove

[fo. 4v] Datum Anagnie per manum Alberti sancte Romane ecclesie presbiteri cardinalis et cancellarii vj idus Marcii, indiccione ij, incarnacionis Dominice anno m⁰ c⁰ lxxx⁰iij⁰, pontificatus domini Lucii pape iij anno tercio.

[a] *Hugone.*   [b] *pertinet.*   [c] *spectat.*   [d] *vester,* Migne.   [e] *universas,* Migne.
[f] *presidio.*   [g] *exemplar,* Migne.   [h] *privilegio,* Migne.   [i] *Premonstratunsis.*   [j] *eiudem.*
[k] *vestri,* Migne.   [l] *audeat,* Migne.   [m] *expectationem.*   [n] *illus.*   [o] *exhibebant.*

ᵖ*sosolum.* ᵍ*si.* ʳ*vestri,* Migne. ˢ*premonstrati.* ᵗ*accione* deleted.
ᵘ*exeptis.* ᵛ*idoneum pro se,* Migne. ʷ*debebunt,* Migne.
ˣ *In generali igitur vestro,* Migne. ʸ*considentibus.* ᶻspace; approximately 12 letters erased.
ᵃᵃ*irrefrugabiliter.* ᵃᵇ*Premonstrati.* ᵃᶜ*abbas* repeated and struck through.
ᵃᵈ*ad aliquam [. . .] revertatur. ad domum unde exivit seu ad aliam ejusdem ordinis quam elegerit, sine ulla conditione temporalis commodi revertatur,* Migne 1240A6–8. ᵃᵉ*alio,* Migne.
ᵃᶠ*nequiverit,* Migne. ᵃᵍ*Premonstratenunc.* ᵃʰdispensatione, Migne.
ᵃⁱ*nos.* ᵃʲ*trangrediatur* ᵃᵏ*constitutiones,* Migne. ᵃˡMS here lacks Migne 1240C13–D5.
ᵃᵐ*coabbatam.* ᵃⁿ*eius* with *u* deleted. ᵃᵖIn the MS, two passages appear in reverse order to that in Migne: *Si que [. . .] ordinem assumpsisse* (1241C5–9) and *Ad hec quoniam Premonstratensis ecclesia [. . .] recipere aut susceptos liceat retinere* (1241A2–C3).
ᵃᵠ*pro chrismate [. . .] pretium, aut,* Migne. ᵃʳthe abbots of Laon, Floreffe, and Cuissy.
ᵃˢ*retractatione,* Migne. ᵃᵗ*sive [. . .] sibi,* Migne; *s* with the rest missing.
ᵃᵘ*voluerint,* Migne. ᵃᵛ*Similiter [. . .] terminetur:* lacking in Migne.
ᵃʷ*grangias vestras et curtes,* Migne. ᵃˣ*virorum,* Migne. ᵃʸ*grangiis vestris et curtibus,* Migne.
ᵃᶻ*insuper* (bis). ᵃᵃᵃ*eos.* ᵃᵃᵇ*mulli.* ᵃᵃᶜ*liceat [. . .] temere: liceat ecclesias vestras temere,* Migne.
ᵃᵃᵈ*fatigare,* Migne. ᵃᵃᵉ*gubernatione et sustentatione,* Migne.
ᵃᵃᶠ*presumpcionem suam: reatum suum,* Migne. ᵃᵃᵍ*prisbiter.*
ᵃᵃʰLucius's motto – *Adiuva nos deus salutaris noster* – is written beside this subscription within a double circle, in the centre of which are a cross and the names *sanctus Petrus, sanctus Paulus, Lucius papa tercius.*

[1] Hugh II, abbot of Prémontré 1171–1189, formerly abbot of Cuissy 1160–1165 (N. Backmund, *Monasticon Praemonstratense, id est historia circariarum et canoniarum candidi ordinis praemonstratensis*, 3 vols (Straubing, 1949–1956), II, p. 527 and III, p. 629).
[2] Another version of this letter is printed in J.P. Migne, *Patrologia Latina*, CCI, 1238–1244: *Lucii III Papae Epistolae et Privilegia*, cxxxii. The Beauchief copy has the following arrangement: 1238B–40C13, 1240D6–41A2, 1241C5–9, 1240C13–D5, 1241A2–C3, 1241C10–41D1, 1242B8–C2, 1242B5–8, 1241D8–42A7, 1242D8–12, 1243C6–43D (end). It lacks the following parts found in Migne: 1239C5–15, 1240B6–7 *(vel [. . .] celebrata)*, 1241C3–5 *(sane [. . .] transferre)*, 1241D1–8, 1242A7–B4, 1242C2–D7, 1242D12–43C5. Additions and significant variants found in the Beauchief version are indicated in the apparatus above.

2. Hugh II, abbot of Prémontré, writes to all prelates in the church who know the text of the privilege of Pope Lucius III. The original copy of this bull is to be kept at the mother abbey of the order at Prémontré. Transcripts will be kept in other abbeys belonging to the order, with the seal of the general chapter attached. 10 March 1184 (by modern reckoning)–1189.

Quod privilegium tocius ordinis sit in Premon[stratensi] ecclesia in sequente subscriptura

Reverentissimis dominis et patribus archiepiscopis et episcopis dilectisque in Domino confratribus abbatibus et prepositis ceterisque universis sancte ecclesie prelatis ad quarum pervenerit noticiam transcriptum istud privilegii domini Lucii pape iij, humilis Dei ac domini nostri Jhesu Cristi servus, Hugo Dei paciencia dictus abbas secundus Premonstratensis et abbatum sui ordinis generale capitulum eternam in domino Jhesu salutem. Noverit vestra nobis dilecta in Cristo universitas nos plenum testimonium peribere et in verbo veritatis in commune constanter asserere quod universo generaliter ordini nostro dominus Lucius papa iij^{us}, predecessoris sui felicis memorie Alexandri pape sequtus exemplar, eo per omnia modo indulsit privilegium quo illius in hac carta notatum est transcriptum. Quia vero ipsum privilegium bullatum, bulla ipsius domini pape Lucii, in singulis nostri ordinis domibus esse non potest, in ecclesia Premonstratensi, que aliarum omnium ecclesiarum nostri ordinis mater [est] sciatis illud custodiri, transcriptum vero illius in aliis nostri ordinis abbaciis haberi. Hac autem de causa et ista vobis omnibus scribendo innotescimus et ad corroborandum fidele hoc nostrum testimonium generalis capituli nostri transcripto huic sigillum apponere decrevimus, ut non minus ei fidem adhibeatis quam si ipsum privilegium bullatum in vestra presencia habeatis. Valeat in Cristo dilecta nobis in ipso universitas vestra. Amen.[1]

[1] Fo. 5r is blank except for some later notes, including the record of a debt for £20 owed by one Richard Massye to one Nicholas Dunson.

[CHARTERS OF ROBERT SON OF RANULPH AND HIS FAMILY]

3. Notification to Richard, bishop of Coventry,[1] and to all the sons of holy mother church of the gift in free, pure, and perpetual alms by Robert son of Ranulph to God and St Mary and St Thomas the Martyr,[2] and to the brothers of the Premonstratensian order, for erecting an abbey, of the place called Beauchief in Doreheseles,[3] which is the land contained in the area from Greenhill by Clebern's assart to the assarts of Gervase, Gamel, Hacon, and Gerard, and by the hedge to the brow of the hill called Doreheg, and then down to Roger's assart, and by his hedge beyond the water by the lane to Robert the forester's assart, and then by the road which leads back to Greenhill; of the churches of Norton, Alfreton, Wymeswold, and Edwalton, with all their appurtenances; and of a tenth of all his revenue, for the salvation of the souls of King Henry II and all his sons

and for the salvation of his own soul and those of all his relatives and ancestors. [1173–1176][4]

[fo. 5v]

Ricardo[a] Dei gracia Coventrensi episcopo et omnibus sancte matris ecclesie filiis tam presentibus quam futuris Robertus filius Ran[ulphi] salutem. Sciatis me dedisse Deo et sancte Marie et sancto Thome martiri et fratribus ordinem Premonstratensem professis in liberam, puram et perpetuam elemosinam ad abbathiam construendam locum qui dicitur Beuchef in Doreheseles et quicquid infra metas Doreheseles est, scilicet a Grenhilheg' per sartum Cleberni usque ad sarta Gervasii et Gamelli et Haconis et Gerardi per sepem usque ad[b] cilium montis qui dicitur Doreheg' et ita descendendo per cilium eiusdem montis usque ad sartum Rogeri et sic per sepem eiusdem Rogeri ultra aquam per semitam usque ad sartum Roberti forestarii et sic per viam que ducit usque [ad] predictum Grenhilheg' et quicquid infra metas horum terminorum continetur, et ecclesiam de Nortona cum omnibus pertinenciis suis et ecclesiam de Alvertona cum omnibus pertinenciis suis, similiter ecclesiam de Wimundeswold cum omnibus pertinenciis suis, ecclesiam quoque de Edwaldeston' cum omnibus pertinenciis suis et decimam tocius redditus mei. Hec omnia dedi predictis fratribus pro salute anime Henrici regis secundi et pro salute animarum omnium liberorum suorum et pro salute anime mee et animarum omnium parentum meorum et pro animabus patris mei et matris mee et omnium antecessorum meorum. Teste Albino abbate de Derby,[5] fratre Eustachio de Lileshill', fratre Willelmo de Welbec, Willelmo filio Ran[ulphi], Serlone de Pleseleia,[c6] Matheo de Estona, Rad[ulpho] filio Hugonis, Matheo fratre eius, Willelmo filio et herede Roberti, Adam de Strettona, Odone.

[a] *Ricardus*.   [b] *ad* interlined.   [c] *Preseleia*.

[1] Richard Peche, bishop of Coventry 1161–1182. Derbyshire had been part of the diocese of Lichfield since the seventh century, but in 1102 the see was moved to Coventry. In the early thirteenth century it became known as Coventry and Lichfield. Beauchief lay just inside its northern border.
[2] Thomas Becket was murdered on 29 December 1170 and canonized on 21 February 1173; King Henry II did public penance at Becket's shrine on 12 July 1174.
[3] See the Introduction, p. 4, n. 11. The charter shows that the abbey was erected just beyond several peasant clearances (assarts).
[4] Printed in H.M. Colvin, *The White Canons in England* (Oxford, 1951), pp. 341–342. It is dated as c.1175. Robert son of Ranulph and his gift of four churches occur in the Obituary (9 September).

⁵Albinus, the first abbot of Darley (near Derby), occurs 1151×1176 (D. Knowles, C.N.L. Brooke, and V. London (eds), *The Heads of Religious Houses: England and Wales, I, 940–1216* (2nd edn, Cambridge, 1972), p. 161).
⁶Serlo of Pleasley (for whom see also **182** and R.R. Darlington (ed.), *Cartulary of Darley Abbey*, 2 vols (Kendal, 1945), II, p. 373, n. 2), occurs in the charters of Rufford abbey (Notts) (C.J. Holdsworth (ed.), *Rufford Charters*, 4 vols, Thoroton Society Record Series 29, 30, 32, 34 (Nottingham, 1972–1981), I, p. 72 and nos 99, 118, 132, 133).

4. Inspeximus by Edward I confirming the provisions of the charter in which Robert son of Ranulph gave in free alms to the Premonstratensian order, for erecting an abbey, the place called Beauchief in Doreheseles, which is the land contained in the area from Greenhill by Aldefelde to Twentywellsick, and then down the brook of Twentywellsick to the river Sheaf, and then down to Abbey Brook, and then up Abbey Brook to the ford of the same brook at the road down from Alan's house, and then up this road to Alan's assart, and then to the assarts of Robert and Peter and back up to Greenhill; of the churches of Norton, Alfreton, Wymeswold, and Edwalton; of the mill of Norton; of Hugh's assart near Meersbrook with 1 toft in (Norton) Lees; of 1 toft near Alan's house; of a tenth of all his pannage; and of 2 bovates in Wymeswold from his demesne with 1 toft containing 3 acres, *viz.* on the west 8 selions at Robbewong, 6 selions at Milnhill, 5 selions at Netherbromebergh, 11 selions at Longbenelondichend, 6 selions at Martynhaw, 3 selions at Mykylwaterlandes, 4 selions at Hungerhill, and on the east 4 selions at Cousewellende, 8 selions at Marwaterlandes, 5 selions at Marthegravegate, 9 selions at Kumbardall, 4 selions below the roads, 6 selions to the south of Rikisike, 9 selions at Smaligesikende. [Inspection in 1272–1307 of a charter of c.1180][1]

[fo. 6r]

Edwardus Dei gracia rex Anglie dominus Hibernie et dux Aquit[annie] archiepiscopis, abbatibus, prioribus, comitibus, baronibus, justiciariis, vicecomitibus, prepositis, ministris et omnibus ballivis fidelibus suis salutem. Inspeximus cartam quam Robertus filius Ranulphi fecit Deo et sancte Marie et sancto Thome martiri de Beauchef et abbati ac canonicis ibidem Deo servientibus in hec verba: Ricardo Dei gracia Coventrensi episcopo et omnibus sancte matris ecclesie filiis tam presentibus quam futuris Robertus filius Ranulphi salutem. Sciatis me dedisse Deo et sancte Marie et sancto Thome martiri et fratribus ordinem Premonstratensem professis in liberam et perpetuam elemosinam ad abbaciam construendam locum qui dicitur Beauchef, qui in Doreheseles situs est, silicet a Grenehilheg' per Aldefelde usque ad Quintinewelle et sic descendendo per rivulum prefate Quintinewelle usque ad aquam que dicitur Shava, et per ipsam aquam descendendo usque ad le Broc et per le Broc ascendendo usque ad vadum ipsius le Broc quod est ad viam que descendit de domo Alani et sic ascendendo per ipsam viam usque ad sartum predicti Alani et sic per eius sartum usque ad sarta Roberti et Petri et sic ascendendo usque ad predictum Grenehilheg' et quicquid infra metas horum terminorum continetur. Et ecclesiam de Norton cum omnibus pertinenciis suis et ecclesiam de Alphirton cum omnibus pertinenciis suis, similiter ecclesiam de Wymundeswald cum omnibus pertinenciis suis, ecclesiam quoque de Edwaldeston cum omnibus pertinenciis suis et molendinum de Norton' cum omni multura et omnibus pertinenciis et operibus suis. Ita quod nec ego nec heredes mei [fo. 6v] aliquid aliud molendinum in territorio predicte ville faciemus nec a quoquam exceptis canonicis fieri permittemus. Liceat vero eisdem canonicis alia molendina in territorio predicte ville construere ubicumque voluerint et utile sibi esse perspexerint, et sartum Hugonis juxta Meresbroc cum uno tofto in Leis et unum toftum juxta domum Alani, et totam decimam pannagii tocius terre mee, et duas bovatas terre in Wimundeswald de dumenio meo cum uno tofto continente tres acras terre. Et sciendum est quod sic iacent prefate bovate ex parte occidentali ad Robbe Wong' viij seillinis, ad Milnhill' sex seillinis, ad Nethirbromebereghe quinque seillinis, ad Longbenelondichend' undecim seillinis, ad Martynhaw sex seillinis, ad Mykylwaterlondeshend tres seillinis, ad Hungherhyll quatuor seillinis; ex parte orientali predictum toftum de cultura mea extra villam ad Cousewellende quatuor seillinis, ad Marwaterlandes octo seillinis, ad Marthegravegate quinque seillinis, ad Kumbardall novem seillinis, infra vias quatuor seillinis, ad meridiem de Rikisike sex seillinis, ad Smaligesikende novem seillinis. Hec omnia dedi et concessi, sicut scriptum est, predictis fratribus pro salute Henrici regis secundi et omnium liberorum suorum et pro salute anime et animarum heredum et omnium parentum meorum et pro animabus patris mei et matris mee et uxoris mee et omnium antecessorum meorum. Teste: Albino abbate de Derby, Ad[am] abbate[a] de Wellbec et conventu eiusdem loci,[2] fratre Eustachio de Lilisehill', Waltero decano de Stretton', Willelmo filio Ranulfi, Rogero filio Ranulfi, Johanne de Orreby,[3] Rad[ulph]o filio Hugonis, Matheo fratre suo, Willelmo filio Roberti, magistro Waltero medico, Waltero clerico de Osbertona, Eustachio filio Hugonis, Stephano fratre eius, Adam [fo. 7r] filio Philippi, Gilberto de Bernston', Gilberto de Suctun.

^a *abbatem* with *m* deleted.

[1] Printed in Colvin, *White Canons*, pp. 342–343. The date is given as *c*.1180. Abstract in The Queen's College, Oxford, MS 117, fo. 26r. This charter was confirmed in 1312 (**38**, no. 1) and again in 1316 (Appendix II, no. 1).
[2] Adam, abbot of Welbeck (Premonstratensian), occurs *c*.1180×1194 (Knowles, Brooke, and London, *Heads of Religious Houses*, I, p. 198).
[3] Son of Herbert and Agnes of Orby, the founders of the Premonstratensian priory at Hagnaby (Lincs) in 1175–1176; Hagnaby was also dedicated to St Thomas the Martyr.

5. Gift in free alms by Robert son of Ranulph to Beauchief abbey of 2 bovates in the vill of Wymeswold, one which was Alexander's with a toft and the other which was the widow Lovechild's. The canons quitclaimed to Robert all his demesne which he had previously granted to them at the foundation of their abbey to hold until all the churches of his land were vacant, saving 2 bovates which he gave to them previously as is contained in his great charter which the abbey has from him. [*c*.1180][1]

Carta Roberti filii Ranulphi de duabus bovatis terre in villa de Wymunduswold'

Omnibus sancte matris ecclesie filiis Robertus filius Ranulfi salutem. Sciatis me dedisse^a et hac carta mea confirmasse Deo et sancto Thome martiri de Beauchef et fratribus ibidem Deo servientibus duas bovatas terre in villa de Wymundeswold, unam scilicet que fuit Alexandri cum tofto suo et alteram que fuit Luvechild vidue cum omnibus pertinenciis suis in liberam et perpetuam elemosinam. Et sciendum quod hanc prefatam terram dedi eis eo quod ipsi clamaverunt michi quietum dumenium meum totum exceptis duabus bovatis^b cum pertinenciis suis quas eis prius dederam de ipso dumenio, sicut in magna carta continetur, quam ipsi habent de me quod dumenium prius concesseram eis in fundacione abbacie sue tenend[um] semper donec omnes ecclesie terre mee vacarent ad opus illorum quas eis dedi ad abbaciam construendam, sicut prefata magna carta testatur. Teste: Au. abbate de Welbec,[2] fratre Rogero de Neuhus, fratre Matheo de Wellebec, Rad[ulph]o senescallo, Ricardo diacono, Petro de Herthill, Hacone preposito, Willelmo coco, Adam de Kuctun', Roberto de

Wilicheby, Roberto Ro, Waltero de Suvella, Hugone fratre eius, et multis aliis.

^a*de dedisse.*   ^b*bavatis.*

[1] Printed in Colvin, *White Canons*, p. 343. The date is given as *c.*1180. Colvin writes of this charter: 'It was not only the advowsons of his churches which Robert was giving his canons, but the combined financial interests of patron and rector, and until the rectors in possession died or resigned, the canons would derive little advantage from these pieces of ecclesiastical property. Hence the temporary concession of Robert's demesne at Wymeswold until the churches should fall vacant, and its surrender by the canons when this had taken place' (p. 105). Confimed in 1312 (**38**, no. 2) and again in 1316 (Appendix II, no. 2).
[2] For Adam, abbot of Welbeck *c.*1180×1194, see **4**, n. 2.

6. Gift in free alms by Robert son of Ranulph to Beauchief abbey, for enlarging the site of the abbey, of the place called Brockhurst,[1] *viz.* the area which extends from the ford of Tacheleforde up by the road which leads to Westerley, and through the middle of Westerley eastward through Brockhurst to the road coming up to Brockford, and along it south to Brockford; and of 1 assart which lies between the assart of Hugh son of Albert of Bradway and the land of Gerard of Greenhill next to the Birchitt boundary.[2] [*c.*1180][3]

Carta Roberti filii Ranulfi ad situm largiendum

Omnibus sancte matris ecclesie filiis ad quos presens carta pervenerit Robertus filius Ranulfi salutem in Domino. Sciatis me dedisse et presenti carta confirmasse Deo et sancte Marie et sancto Thome martiri^a de Beauchef et fratribus ibidem [fo. 7v] Deo servientibus ad incrementum et ad situm prefati loci largiendum et ad asiamenta sua facienda locum qui dicitur le Brochirst' a vado scilicet de Tacheleforde ascendendo per viam que vadit usque ad Westerley et sic per medium Vesterlei apud orientem in reccrium per medium le Brochyrst usque ad viam que venit ascendendo usque ad le Brocforde et sic per eandem viam apud meridiem usque Brocforde et quicquid infra metas horum terminorum continetur, et unum sartum quod iacet inter sartum Hugonis filii Alberti de Bradewei in terram Gerardi de Greneill juxta divisam de Bircheved in puram et perpetuam elimosinam pro salute anime mee et patris mei et matris mee et heredum meorum et omnium antecessorum meorum. Hiis testibus: A.[4] abbate de Wellebec, Rad[ulph]o senescallo, Willelmo filio et herede meo, Ricardo diacono,

Petro de Hertil, Roberto fratre suo, Henrico de Schelton', Galfrido fratre suo, Rogero de Fungl', Willelmo de Burton', et pluribus aliis.

^a*matiri*.

[1] A lost place-name meaning a small wood inhabited by badgers.
[2] Upper Birchitt Farm (OS ref. SK 333797) lies south of Bradway, just within the parish of Dronfield.
[3] This charter was confirmed in 1312 (**38** no. 3) and again in 1316 (Appendix II, no. 3).
[4] i.e. Adam (see **4**, n. 2).

7. Gift in free alms by William son of Robert to Beauchief abbey, together with his body, of his mill of Aston.[1] [1190–1220][2]

Carta Willelmi filii Roberti de molendino de Astona

Omnibus sancte matris ecclesie filiis ad quos[a] presens carta[b] pervenerit Willelmus filius Roberti salutem in Domino. Noverit universitas vestra me dedisse et hac carta mea confirmasse Deo et sancte Marie et sancto Thome martiri de Beauchef et fratribus ibidem Deo servientibus cum corpore meo molendinum meum de Hastona cum omni multura sua et omnibus pertinenciis suis in puram et perpetuam elemosinam, libere et quiete, inperpetuum possidendam pro salute anime mee et uxoris mee et heredum meorum et omnium antecessorum meorum. Hiis testibus: Philippo de Huletotes, Serlone de Begleya,[3] Ricardo capellano, Galfrido clerico de Osberton', Petro Hertyll', Roberto fratre suo, Roberto nepote eorum, Hugone de [fo. 8r] Suwel, Rogero de Byrchewde, Rogero de Alfyrton', Henrico Berengervelle, Hugone de Sancdiacre.

^a*quo*. ^bMS has *carta carta carta*.

[1] A windmill at Coal Aston in the parish of Dronfield, not the watermill referred to in **42**; see also **45**.
[2] This is one of two charters in the Cartulary issued by Robert's successor (the other is **11**). Neither Robert's date of death nor that of his son is known. This charter was confirmed in 1312 (**38**, no. 4) and again in 1316 (Appendix II, no. 4). There is an abstract in The Queen's College, Oxford, MS 117, fo. 26r; see also **11** below.
[3] Serlo of Beeley executed a fine connected with his and his father's gifts to the abbey in 1208. He appears as a grantor and a witness – along with other Derbyshire people – in the charters of Rufford abbey (Notts) (Holdsworth, *Rufford Charters*, I, nos 63–64, 98, 112, 113, 124, 126).

8. Gift in free alms by Robert son of William of Alfreton to Beauchief abbey of that land which Elias of Troway[1] held. [1210–1240][2]

Carta Roberti filii Willelmi de Alfretona de quadam terra

Omnibus sancte matris ecclesie filiis ad quos presens carta pervenerit Robertus filius Willelmi de Alfertona salutem. Noverit universitas vestra me dedisse et concessisse et hac presenti carta confirmasse Deo et beate Marie et sancto Thome martiri[a] de Beauchef et fratribus ibidem Deo[b] servientibus illam terram quam Helias de Trowei tenuit de me pro anima patris mei et matris mee tenendam de me et heredibus meis, libere et quiete et pacifice, in puram et perpetuam elemosinam. Hiis testibus: Suone de Heriz,[3] Ricardo de Herthyll', Seylone de Begleya, Roberto capellano de Alfertona, Rad[ulph]o le Poer, Stephano de Byrthewde, et multis aliis.

[a] *matiri.* [b] *Deo* interlined.

[1] In the parish of Eckington (Derbys); OS ref. SK 388797.
[2] The first of seven grants by the founder's grandson entered in the Cartulary. Robert was still alive in 1224 (*Calendar of Close Rolls*, I, p. 611). The charter was confirmed in 1312 (**38** no. 5) and again in 1316 (Appendix II, no. 5).
[3] For the Heriz family, see **26**, n. 4.

9. Gift in free alms by the same Robert son of William of Alfreton to Beauchief abbey, together with his body, of 3 acres by the 24-foot perch[1] on the north of the brook which descends from the abbey to the river Sheaf; and of 1 pound of cumin from the service of Roger of Ridding for the land of Shireoaks.[2] [1210–1240][3]

Alia carta eiusdem Roberti de tribus acris terre

Sciant presentes et futuri quod ego Robertus filius Willelmi de Alfertona dedi et concessi et hac presenti carta mea et sigillo meo confirmavi Deo et ecclesie beati Thome martiris de Bello Capite et canonicis ibidem Deo servientibus tres acras terre cum corpore meo[a] per perticam viginti quatuor pedum mensuratas juxta rivulum, qui descendit ab abbathia ad maiorem rivum de Scheve ex parte aquilonis, et unam libram cimini de servicio Rogeri de Riddyng de terra[b] de Schyrokes in puram et perpetuam elemosinam. Hiis testibus: Rad[ulph]o le Poher, Johanne fratre suo, Rogero de Alretun', Ricardo dispensatore, Thoma de Bradfeld, Thoma Selweyn.

ᵃ*me.*   ᵇMS has *terra de terra.*

¹A perch was more commonly measured at 16½ feet.
²The 3 acres given in the first half of the charter obviously lay in Norton; it is not clear whether the land of Shireoaks was also in Norton or on Robert's Alfreton estate, which contained a hamlet called Riddings. Both Norton and Alfreton adjoin the county boundary and thus the name Shireoaks (which is lost) could have occurred in either place; equally Riddings could be a lost place-name in Norton.
³The charter was confirmed in 1312 (**38**, no. 6) and again in 1316 (Appendix II, no. 7).

10. Gift in free alms by the same Robert son of William of Alfreton to Beauchief abbey of 24 acres by the 24-foot perch with wood in Norton near 3 acres on the north of the brook which descends from the abbey to the river Sheaf.¹ [1210–1240]²

Alia carta eiusdem Roberti filii Willelmi de terra et bosco in Nort'

Sciant presentes et futuri quod ego Robertus filius Willelmi de Alfertun' dedi et concessi et hac presenti carta mea confirmavi [fo. 8v] cum corpore meoᵃ Deo et beato Thome martiri de Bello Capite et canonicis ibidem Deo servientibus viginti quatuor acras terre per perticam viginti quatuor pedum cum bosco insuper crescente in territorio de Norton' juxta tres acras terre que iacent juxta rivum qui descendit ab abbacia usque ad maiorem rivum qui dicitur Scheve versus aquilonem in puram et perpetuam elemosinam. In testimonium autem huius rei scripto presenti sigillum meum apposui. Hiis testibus: Rad[ulph]o rectore ecclesie de Heckyngton', Rad[ulph]o le Poher, Ada capellano de Normanton', Roberto capellano de Alferton', Rogero de Alreton', Ricardo dispensatore, Thoma de Bradfeld', Johanne le Poher, Thoma Selweyn, et aliis.

ᵃ*me.*

¹The woodland evidently lay close to the land given in **9**.
²This charter was confirmed in 1312 (**38**, no. 8) and again in 1316 (Appendix II, no. 8).

11. Confirmation by William son of Robert son of Ranulph to Beauchief abbey of all their possessions and tenements in all his liberties, as his father's charters, which they have, testify. [1185–1200]¹

Omnibusᵃ sancte matris ecclesie filiis Willelmus filius Roberti filii Ran[ulphi] salutem. Sciatis me concessisse et hacᵇ carta presenti confirmasse Deo et sancto Thome martiri et fratribus ordinem Premonstratensem professis apud Beuchef commanent[ibus] omnes possessiones et omnia tenementa in omnes libertates, tam in rebus ecclesiasticis quam in secularibus, in terris cultis et non cultis, in bosco et in plano, in viis et in semitis, in pasturis et in omnibus rebus et tenementis, in liberam et perpetuam elemosinam, ad abbaciam construendam, sicut carte patris mei Roberti, quas de ipso habent, testantur. Teste Adam abbate de Welbec, Roberto filio Ranulfi patre meo, Willelmo filio Ran[ulfi], Rad[ulpho] filio Hugonis, et Matheo fratre suo, Adam de Stretton', Ricardo de Phiniglaia, Adam filio Philippi de Huston', Philippo filio Gerardi de Stirap.

[a]*mnibus.*   [b]*ha.*

[1] One of two charters in the Cartulary executed by the founder's son. Unlike **7**, which appears to have been issued towards the end of William's life, this charter was witnessed by Adam, abbot of Welbeck (who occurs *c.*1180×1194 – see **4**, n. 2), by William's father, Robert, and by William son of Ranulph (who appears to be the grantor's uncle), Ralph son of Hugh, his brother Matthew, and Adam of Stretton, all of whom witnessed the foundation charter of 1173–1176 (**3**), which suggests a slightly earlier date of *c.*1185–1200. Abstract in The Queen's College, Oxford, MS 117, fo. 26v (and see **7** above).

12. Grant by Robert son of William of Alfreton to Roger of Alfreton, for his homage and service, of 6 bovates in the vill of Wymeswold which Ranulph, Robert's brother, gave to Roger; of 2 bovates which Robert gave to the nuns of Campsey Ash;[1] and of 1½ bovates which Ranulph gave to the same nuns with all inhabitants of the same. Roger shall render to Robert one pair of gilt spurs annually. [1210–1240][2]

Sciant[a] presentes et futuri quod ego Robertus filius Willelmi de Alferton' concessi et hac presenti carta mea confirmavi Rogero de Alreton' [fo. 9r] pro homagio et servicio suo sex bovatas terre in villa de Wimundewold' quas Ranulfus frater meus ei dedit, et duas bovatas quas dedi sanctimonialibus de Campesse, et unam bovatam et dimidiam quam Ranulfus frater meus eisdem sanctimonialibus dedit cum pertinenciis et cum omnibus inhabitantibus et cum sequelis suis. Tenendas sibi et heredibus suis vel cui assignare voluerit de me et de heredibus meis in feudo et hereditate, libere et quiete et integre. Reddendo inde annuatim michi et heredibus ad Pascha unum par calcarium deauratorum pro omni servicio et demanda ad me vel ad heredes meos pertinente, salvo forinseco servicio. Ego autem et heredes mei predictas bovatas terre predicto Rogero et heredibus suis vel cui assignare[b] voluerit contra omnes homines warantizabimus. Ut hoc autem ratum permaneat, hoc presenti scripto et sigilli mei munimine confirmavi. Hiis testibus: domino Waltero de Estwett', Rogero de Maressheye, Roberto de Maressheye, Roberto Putrell', Rad[ulpho] le Poher, Johanne clerico de Wimundewold, Henrico de Eadwalton', Thoma de Bradfeld', Ricardo dispensatore, Johanne le Poher, et aliis.

[a] *ciant.*   [b] *n* of *assignare* interlined.

[1] A house of Austin nuns founded *c.*1195 by Theobold de Valoines (W. Page (ed.), *Victoria County History of Suffolk*, II (London, 1907), pp. 112–115). The priory appears to have no connection with Beauchief other than through Robert and his family.
[2] Charter **13** is virtually identical. Robert's gift of two bovates to Campsey is also the subject of **16**, and Ranulph's gift of one and a half bovates is also listed in another of Robert's charters (**15**), as is the service of a pair of gilt spurs yearly. For the later history of the entire nine and a half bovates granted here see **57**–**60**.

13. Grant by Robert son of William of Alfreton to Roger of Alfreton, for his homage and service, of 6 bovates in the vill of Wymeswold which Ranulph, Robert's brother, gave to Roger; of 2 bovates which Robert gave to the nuns of Campsey Ash; and of 1½ bovates which Ranulph gave to the same nuns with all inhabitants of the same. Roger shall render to Robert one pair of gilt spurs annually. [1210–1240][1]

Sciant presentes et futuri quod ego Robertus filius Willelmi de Alferton' concessi et hac presenti carta mea confirmavi Rogero de Alreton' pro homagio et servicio suo sex bovatas terre in villa de Wimundwolde, quas Ranulfus frater meus ei dedit, et duas bovatas, quas dedi sanctimonialibus de Campesse, et unam bovatam et dimidiam, quas Ranulfus frater meus eisdem sanctimonialibus dedit, cum pertinenciis et cum hominibus inhabitantibus et [fo. 9v] cum sequelis suis. Tenendas sibi et assignatis suis et heredibus assignatorum suorum de me et heredibus meis in feudo et hereditate, libere, quiete et integre. Reddendo inde annuatim michi et heredibus meis ad Pascha unum par calcarium deauratorum pro omni servicio et demanda ad me vel ad heredes meos pertinent[ibus], salvo forinseco servicio. Ego autem et heredes mei predictas terras[a] predicto Rogero et assignatis suis et heredibus eorum contra omnes homines et omnes feminas warantizabimus. Ut hoc autem ratum permaneat, hoc presenti scripto et sigilli mei munimine confirmavi. Hiis testibus: domino Waltero de Estweit, Rogero de Mareisheye, Roberto Putrell', Rad[ulpho] le

Poher, Johanne clerico, Henrico de Eadwalton', Thoma de Bradfeld, Ricardo dispensatore, Johanne le Poher, et multis aliis.

^a *terre.*

[1] Virtually identical to **12**, apart from a minor difference in the witness list.

14. Gift in free alms by Robert son of William of Alfreton to Beauchief abbey of 1½ bovates in the vill of Wymeswold which they have of the gift of Ranulph, Robert's brother. [1210–1240][1]

Carta Roberti filii Willelmi de bovata terre in Wymundwold

Sciant presentes et futuri quod ego Robertus filius Willelmi de Alferton' concessi et hac presenti carta mea et sigillo meo confirmavi Deo et ecclesie beati Thome martiris de Bello Capite et canonicis ibidem Deo servientibus unam bovatam terre et dimidiam cum pertinenciis in villa de Wimundewold' in liberam et perpetuam elemosinam, salvo forinseco servicio, quod ad illam terram pertinet illam, scilicet bovatam et dimidiam quam habuerunt ex dono Ran[ulfi] fratris mei. Hiis testibus: Rad[ulpho] le Poher, Johanne fratre suo, Rogero de Alreton', Ricardo dispensatore, Thoma de Bradefeld, Thoma Selweyn.

[1] Abstract in The Queen's College, Oxford, MS 117, fo. 26v.

15. Ratification by Robert son of William of Alfreton of the gift and testament of Ranulph his brother in lands, rents, chattels etc., *viz.* 6 bovates which he gave to Roger of Alfreton, 1½ bovates which he gave to Beauchief abbey, and 1½ bovates which he gave to Campsey Ash from the 9 bovates which Robert gave to him by his charter in the vill of Wymeswold, with 1 pair of gilt spurs to be paid to Robert annually. [1210–1240][1]

[fo. 10r]
Ratificatio Roberti filii Willelmi de Alferton

Omnibus hoc scriptum visuris vel audituris Robertus filius Willelmi de Alferton' salutem. Sciatis me concessisse et ratum et gratum habuisse donum et testamentum domini Ranulfi fratris mei in terris et in redditibus et in catallis et aliis rebus, silicet sex bovatas^a terre cum pertinenciis suis, quas dedit Rogero de Alreton', et unam bovatam terre et dimidiam, quam dedit domui de Beuchef, et unam bovatam et dimidiam cum pertinenciis suis, quam dedit domui de Campesse et sanctimonialibus ibidem Deo servientibus de novem bovatis terre quas ei dederam per cartam meam in villa de Wimundwold. Ita quod nec ego nec heredes mei aliquod de predictis novem bovatis terre exigemus[b] nisi unum par calcarium deauratorum[c] annuatim reddendorum, silicet ad Pascha pro omni servicio et consuetudine et exaccione, salvo forinseco servicio. Et ut hec mea concessio rata et integra permaneat, hoc scriptum sigilli mei apposicione roboravi. Hiis testibus: Willelmo de Huntingfeld', Thoma et Johanne fratribus eius, Willelmo de Pyrhohe, Roberto fratre eius, Roberto filio Brien, Rogero de Alreton', Johanne le Poher, Ricardo dispensatore de Alferton', Thoma Guneton', Willelmo de Westhall', Thoma de Bradfeld', et multis aliis.

[a] *bavatas.* [b] *eigemus.* [c] *deauratarum.*

[1] See **12-13**.

16. Gift in free alms by Robert son of William of Alfreton to the nuns of Campsey Ash of Ralph the reeve of Wymeswold with all his suit and tenement, *viz.* 2 bovates in the vill of Wymeswold which his father held before him. [1210-1230]

Carta Roberti filii Willelmi de Alferton'

Omnibus[a] sancte matris ecclesie filiis ad quos presens scriptum pervenerit Robertus filius Willelmi de Alferton' salutem in Domino. Noverit universitas vestra me intuitu caritatis dedisse et concessisse et hac presenti carta mea confirmasse Deo et ecclesie sancte Marie [fo. 10v] de Campesse et sanctimonialibus ibidem Deo servientibus in puram et perpetuam elemosinam Rad[ulphum] prepositum de Wymundewaut cum tota secta sua et cum toto tenemento suo, silicet cum duabus bovatis terre cum pertinenciis suis in villa de Wimundewaut, quas pater eius ante eum tenuit. Habendum et tenendum inperpetuum libere et quiete, integre, pacifice et honorifice, sine omni calumpnia mei vel heredum meorum, salvo forinseco servicio, scilicet quantum servicium pertinet ad duas alias bovatas terre liberioris terre eiusdem feudi. Et ego et heredes mei warantizabimus predicte domui de Campesse predictum tenementum cum pertinenciis suis contra omnes homines et contra omnes feminas.

Et ut hec mea concessio et donacio rata et integra permaneat, hoc scriptum sigilli mei apposicione corroboravi. Hiis testibus: fratre Stephano abbate de Beuchef,[1] magistro Johanne de Egidio persona de Foxton', Johanne et Roberto capellanis de Campesse, Willelmo de Huntingfeld, Oseberto de Wachesh, Roberto Picot, Roberto Putrell' de Wimundewaut, Johanne clerico, Rogero de Alreton', Johanne le Poher, Ricardo dispensatore, et aliis.

[a]*mnibus*.

[1] Stephen occurs as abbot early in the reign of Henry III and ?1217×1218 (D.M. Smith and V.C.M. London (eds), *Heads of Religious Houses: England and Wales, II, 1216–1377* (Cambridge, 2001), p. 493). A grant by Abbot Stephen to the canons of Darley abbey of all the lands that the abbey of Beauchief had in Glapwell in 1217–1218 by the gift of Simon son of Hugh of Glapwell and others to hold at an annual farm of 22s 6d is printed in Darlington, *Cartulary of Darley Abbey*, II, H 47.

[GIFTS OF SIR THOMAS CHAWORTH I]

17. Confirmation by Sir Thomas Chaworth to Beauchief abbey of all the land which Robert son of William of Alfreton his grandfather gave to them, together with his body, in the vills of Alfreton and Norton. [1247–before 1258][1]

Confirmacio domini Thome Chaworth'

Omnibus ad quos presens scriptum pervenerit dominus Thomas Chaworth salutem in Domino. Noverit universitas vestra me concessisse et hac presenti carta mea confirmasse abbati et conventui de Bello Capite et successoribus suis totam terram cum omnibus pertinenciis, quam Robertus filius Willelmi de Alferton' avus meus dedit eisdem cum corpore suo in villa de Alferton' et de Norton'. Tenendam et habendam sibi et successoribus suis in liberam, puram et perpetuam elemosinam. Et ego Thomas et heredes mei [fo. 11r] predictam terram cum omnibus pertinenciis dictis abbati et conventui et successoribus suis sicut liberam, puram et perpetuam elemosinam warantizabimus, acquietabimus et defendemus inperpetuum. Hiis testibus: Thoma de Leys,[2] Roberto de Oggeston', Willelmo filio eius, Petro Wodhous, Hugone filio eius, Petro de Bircheheved,[3] et aliis.

[1] This is the first in the lengthy series of grants from Thomas Chaworth, who came of age in 1247 and died in 1315. Robert Ogston died in 1258 (Darlington, *Cartulary of Darley Abbey*, I, pp. xl, 17–18).
[2] Norton Lees.
[3] Peter Birchitt witnessed thirteen charters that appear to date from about 1250 to 1280.

18. Gift in free alms by Thomas Chaworth, knight, lord of Norton, to Beauchief abbey, for the maintenance of a canon to commemorate his soul and those of his family annually at the altar of the Holy Cross, of the hamlet of Greenhill in the soke of Norton and of all his serfs in the same hamlet with their lands and families in Greenhill and elsewhere; and of all his serfs in [Norton] Woodseats with their lands there, saving the lands which Thomas of the Wood and William Tinett hold by the river Sheaf. [c.1301][1]

Carta domini Thome Chaworth de Grenhill'

Sciant presentes et futuri quod ego Thomas de Chaworth miles dominus de Norton' dedi, concessi et hac presenti carta mea confirmavi Deo et monasterio beati Thome martiris de Bello Capite religiosis viris abbati et conventui eiusdem loci in liberam, puram et perpetuam elemosinam, pro salute anime mee et patris mei et matris mee uxorum mearum liberorumque meorum, et pro sustentacione unius canonici eiusdem monasterii divina perpetuo celebranda ad altare sancte Crucis in ecclesia de Bello Capite predicta pro anima mea et animabus predictorum et omnium fidelium defunctorum et pro solempni servicio annuatim habendo inperpetuum, sicut pro uno abbate defuncto, totum illud hameletum in soca mea de Norton' quod vocatur Grenhill', sine ullo retenemento, cum omnibus homagiis, wardis, releviis, redditibus, eschaetis, sectis, serviciis tam forinsecis quam aliis quibuscumque, omnium libere tenencium meorum in hameleto de Grenhill' predicto tam presencium quam futurorum cum omnibus approvamentis et aliis pertinenciis suis, et cum omnibus nativis meis in ipso hameleto et cum terris et tenementis que de me tenuerunt in bondagio in eodem hameleto et extra, cum sectis, sequelis, redditibus et serviciis, consuetudinibus et catallis, et omnimodis aliis approvamentis et pertinenciis suis infra hameletum de Grenhyll' [fo. 11v] predictum et extra, sine aliquo retenemento. Dedi eciam Deo et monasterio de Bello Capite predicto et religiosis viris abbati et conventui eiusdem loci omnes nativos meos in les Wodsetes juxta Norton' cum sectis, sequelis, redditibus et serviciis consuetudinibus et eorum catallis ac omnes terras nativas ac tenementa cum omnibus aliis approvamentis et pertinenciis suis, que ipsi vel alii de me tenuerunt infra bundas de les Wodsetes predict' sine aliquo retenemento, salvis michi tamen terris, pratis cum boscis que Thomas de Bosco et Willelmus Tinett de me tenuerunt juxta aquam de Shava. Habendum et tenendum Deo et monasterio predicto ac religiosis viris abbati et conventui predictis et eorum successoribus in liberam, puram et perpetuam elemosinam cum pratis, boscis, pascuis, pasturis, moris, turbariis, quarariis, mineris, marlariis et omnimodis libertatibus, communiis, aysiamentis et aliis approvamentis et pertinenciis suis quibuscumque infra hameletum de Grenhyll' et les Wodsetes predict' et extra tam infra terram quam supra que michi et heredibus vel assignatis meis vel heredibus heredum et assignatorum meorum inde poterint accidere. Et ego predictus Thomas et heredes et assignati mei et eorum heredes omnia predicta homagia, wardas, relevia, redditus, eschaetas, sectas et servicia, tam forinseca quam alia quecumque omnium, libere tenencium meorum predictorum cum omnimodis approvamentis et pertinenciis suis ac eciam omnes nativos meos predictos cum omnibus terris et tenementis predictis et omnimodis eorum sectis, sequelis, redditibus et serviciis consuetudinibus et catallis et omnimodis aliis approvamentis et pertinenciis suis quibuscumque, tam nominatis quam non nominatis, sine aliquo retenemento, Deo et monas[fo. 12r]terio predicto ac religiosis viris abbati et conventui predictis et eorum successoribus in liberam, puram et perpetuam elemosinam contra omnes gentes warantizabimus, acquietabimus et inperpetuum defendemus. In cuius rei testimonium presenti carte sigillum meum apposui. Hiis testibus: dominis Thoma de Furnivall', Ada de Everingham, Waltero de Gousill', Ricardo de Fourneus, Roberto de Eclessale militibus, domino Rogero de Bralisford' rectore ecclesie de Dronnfeld', Willelmo le Brett, Johanne Ayencourt, Rogero le Breton', Simone de Rerisby, Johanne de Bremington', Hugone de Lynacre, et multis aliis.[2]

[1]Compare **28**, **33**, and **40**. W. Dugdale, *Monasticon Anglicanum*, ed. J. Caley, H. Ellis, and B. Bandinel, 6 vols (London, 1817–1830), VI, part 2, pp. 883–884, printed another charter, not found in the Cartulary but similar to **18**, from a copy in the possession of Samuel Roper, the antiquary, of Lincoln's Inn, d. 1658 (on whom see the *Oxford Dictionary of National Biography*). This charter records the gift of Greenhill in free alms for the support of a canon to commemorate the souls of Thomas Chaworth and his family at the altar of the Holy Cross. The beginning and the end of the two charters are identical, as are the witness lists. However, the part of **18** that begins 'Dedi eciam Deo et monasterio de Bello Capite [. . .]' and ends '[. . .] assignatorum meorum inde poterint accidere' is not the same in the Dugdale transcript, where, in place of the grant of the serfs of Woodseats, Thomas here grants the services of Hugh of Little Norton and 12s 8d that the canons and the abbot used to pay him annually in return for holdings in Alfreton and Norton (see also for this **33** and **40**): 'Et totum redditum et servicium Hugonis de Parva Nortona, ep ipsum Hugonem cum tota sequela sua, et cum omnibus catallis suis, et cum toto tenemento suo, quod de me tenuit in bondagio. Dedi etiam et concessi Deo et monasterio de Bello-capite praedicto, et religiosis viris abbati et conventui ejusdem loci, duodecim solidos et octo denarios annui redditus, quos praedicti abbas et conventus mihi reddere solebant pro diversis tenementis, quae de me tenuerunt in Alfreton et Norton. Habendum et tenendum Deo et monasterio praedicto, ac religiosis viris abbati et conventui praedictis, et eorum successoribus, in liberam, puram, et perpetuam elemosinam, cum pratis, boscis, pascuis, pasturis, moris, turbariis, quarariis,

mineris, marlariis, et omnimodis libertatibus, communis, aisiamentis, et aliis approwamentis et pertinentibus suis quibuscumque, infra hameletum de Grenehull praedictum et extra, tam infra terram quam supra, quae mihi et haeredibus meis et assignatis meis vel haeredibus haeredum et assignatorum meorum inde poterunt accidere.' Proper names that are spelt differently are: Grenehull, Adam, Goushull, Furneus, Ecclessale, Braylefforth, Dranefeld, le Bret, de Bincourte, Brinnington, Linacre.

On 1 November 1301, Thomas Chaworth received licence to alienate in mortmain to the abbey for the maintenance of a canon chaplain celebrating divine service there for the souls of Thomas, his wife, Joan, and their ancestors, 10 tofts, 11 bovates, 58 acres of land, 16 acres of wood, and 58s 6d of yearly rent in Alfreton, Norton, Greenhill, Bradway, and Woodseats (*Calendar of Patent Rolls, Edward I: 1292–1301*, p. 616; The National Archives, C 143/35/9 for the preceding inquest *ad quod damnum*). **18** and **22** perhaps represent this estate, since both gifts refer specifically to the maintenance of a chaplain to pray for Thomas's soul and those of his family. Four other charters (**33, 39–41**) also record a gift of premises at Greenhill and elsewhere in Norton for the maintenance of a chaplain to pray at either the altar of St Katherine or that dedicated to the Holy Cross (no dedication is mentioned in **22** or in the licence of 1301). It is possible that these other gifts were also made under the authority of the same licence. See also **47**, a power of attorney dated a few weeks after the licence, which seems likely to be connected with the same business. See, too, **44** and **61**.

[2] Sir Thomas of Furnival III was lord of Hallamshire (which comprised the parishes of Ecclesfield and Sheffield and the chapelry of Bradfield), and of Whiston, 1261–1291. Sir Thomas of Furnival IV succeeded him and died in 1332 (V. Gibbs and H.A. Doubleday (eds), *The Complete Peerage of England, Scotland, Ireland, Great Britain and the United Kingdom*, VI (London, 1926), pp. 580ff; W. Farrer, *Early Yorkshire Charters*, III, Yorkshire Archaeological Society Record Series, extra series (Edinburgh, 1916), p. 3). Sir Adam of Everingham I, lord of Stainborough and Rockley (South Yorks), died in 1286 and was succeeded by his son and namesake, who appears as a witness to deeds in the Monk Bretton cartulary (South Yorks) between 1331 and 1342 (J.W. Walker (ed.), *Abstracts of the Cartularies of the Priory of Monkbretton*, Yorkshire Archaeological Society Record Series 66 (1926), pp. 54, 58, 122). Gousil is an old form of Goxhill (Lincs) (Watts, *The Cambridge Dictionary of English Place-names* (Cambridge, 2004), p. 257); Walter may have been descended from Peter de Gousel who was the founder of the first Premonstratensian house in England, at Newhouse (Lincs); the Gousils were lords of part of the manor of Barlborough. Sir Robert of Ecclesall witnessed the Sheffield town charter in 1297; he was alive in 1329 but died before 1342, the last in his male line (J. Hunter, *Hallamshire: the history and topography of the parish of Sheffield*, ed. A.S. Gatty (London, 1875), pp. 196–197). Roger of Brailsford, rector of Dronfield, witnessed a deed there in 1281 (Staffordshire Record Office, D1229/1/6/1). Sir Thomas of Furnival IV, Sir Adam of Everingham II, Sir William of Gousil, Sir Richard of Fourness, Sir Robert of Ecclesall, Roger of Brailsford, rector of Dronfield church, William the Bret, John of Aynecourt, Roger the Breton, Simon of Reresby, John of Brimington, and Hugh of Linacre form a prominent group of witnesses who appear on a number of occasions in each other's company, although not all together at any one time. Among the charters in which some of them appear together **71** is dated 1301 (William le Bret, Roger Breton) and **38** and **44** (copy in **61**) are dated 1312 (Sir Thomas, Sir Adam, Roger of Brailsford, William le Bret, John of Aynecourt, Roger the Breton, and Hugh of Linacre appear in one or the other). With members of this group the names of Stephen the Eyr and John the clerk of Stubley are also sometimes found; John son of William of Stubley witnessed a deed at Dronfield in 1280 (S. Pegge, *An Historical Account of Beauchief Abbey* (London, 1801), p. 97). John of Aynecourt was descended from Walter of Ancourt, a Norman lord from near Dieppe whose Domesday Book estates were principally in Lincolnshire and Nottinghamshire, and whose son Ralph founded Thurgaton Priory (Notts), to which he gave the benefices of Elmton and Langwith (Derbys); a junior branch held several Derbyshire properties in Scarsdale wapentake until

the male line failed in the mid-fourteenth century (G. Turbutt, *A History of Derbyshire*, 4 vols (Cardiff, 1999) II, p. 483). In **37** (copy in **81**), John of Ayncourt is described as a knight but here and in **33, 38–41, 44, 61** he is not so described, although some other witnesses are; he was recorded at the 1281 Derbyshire eyre (A. Hopkinson (ed.), *The Rolls of the 1281 Derbyshire Eyre*, Derbyshire Record Society 27 (2000), p. 87) and, together with William le Bret, Roger le Breton, Stephen le Eyr, Hugh of Linacre, and John of Stubley, witnessed a grant made to Thomas son of Roger of Gotham by Thomas Chaworth on 3 May 1308 (T.W. Hall and A.H. Thomas, *A Descriptive Catalogue of the Charters . . . Forming the Jackson Collection at the Sheffield Public Reference Library* (Sheffield, 1914), no. 299). Roger the Breton was lord of Calow in the parish of Chesterfield and was recorded at the 1281 Derbyshire eyre, as was William the Bret (Hopkinson, *Derbyshire Eyre*, pp. 30 and 91); other members of the family were lords of Walton in the same parish (Turbutt, *Derbyshire*, II, pp. 496 and 572). John of Brimington served on the jury for Scarsdale wapentake at the 1281 Derbyshire eyre (Hopkinson, *Derbyshire Eyre*, p. 92).

19. Quitclaim by Thomas Chaworth to Beauchief abbey of an annual rent of 3d which John at the new mill[1] pays for a tenement which he holds in the soke of Norton. [1290–1320]

Quieta clamacio Thome Chaworth' de tribus denariatis annui redditus

Universis presens scriptum visuris vel audituris Thomas de Chaworth' salutem in Domino sempiternam. Noverit universitas vestra me remisisse, relaxasse et omnino pro me et heredibus meis quietum clamasse abbati et conventui de Bello Capite in liberam, puram et perpetuam elimosinam, pro salute anime mee et animarum omnium antecessorum et successorum meorum, tres denariatos[a] annui redditus cum pertinenciis, illos scilicet quos Johannes ad novum molendinum pro tenemento quod de me tenuit in soca de Norton' michi reddere consuevit. Ita quod nec ego predictus Thomas nec heredes mei nec aliquis per nos seu pro nobis in dictis tribus denariatis[b] annui redditus cum pertinenciis aliquid jure vel clameum ex nunc quoquomodo habere exigere vel reclamare poterimus inperpetuum. In cuius rei testimonium presenti scripto sigillum meum apposui. Hiis testibus: Willelmo le Brett', Johanne de Ayencourt, Hugone de Linacre, Stephano le Eyr', Johanne de Subbeley, et aliis.[2]

[a] *denarratos*.   [b] *denarratis*.

[1] For the new mill see the Introduction, p. 19.
[2] For these witnesses, see **18**, n. 2.

20. Quitclaim by Thomas Chaworth to Beauchief abbey of an annual rent of 2s from the 4s which they pay him for the land of Robert of the Greaves[1] in the soke of Norton. [1270–1320]

Relaxacio Thome Chaworth' de duobus solidis annui redditus

Pateat universis quod ego Thomas de Chaworth' miles concessi, remisi [fo. 12v] et relaxavi ac omnino pro me et heredibus meis inperpetuum quietum clamavi abbati et conventui de Bello Capite suisque successoribus[a] duos solidos annui redditus cum pertinenciis de quatuor solidis quos michi reddere solebant pro terra Roberti de Greves in soka de Norton'. Ita quod nec ego Thomas nec heredes mei nec aliquis per nos seu nomine nostro aliquid jure vel clameum in dictis duobus solidis cum pertinenciis nec racione eorum habere exigere vel reclamare poterimus inperpetuum. In cuius rei testimonium presenti scripto sigillum meum apposui. Hiis testibus: Thoma de la Wodhous, Petro de Bernes, Johanne de Stubley clerico, Johanne de Byrchehevede, Petro Payne de Norton', et aliis.[2]

[a] *successorbus.*

[1] For Robert of the Greaves see also **22**, **38**, and **48**.
[2] Woodhouse, Barnes, Stubley, and Birchitt are all in Dronfield parish, adjoining Norton. In **42** and **49** Thomas Woodhouse is described as the brother of Richard the marshall of Norton; cf. Richard Marshall of Woodhouse in the Obituary (20 May). In Sheffield Archives, Bagshawe Collection, 3174, Thomas is named as 'clericus de Wodehuses'. Peter de Bernis also witnessed **70** (1278) and **60** (1279). For John the clerk of Stubley see **18**, n. 2.

21. Gift in free alms by Thomas son of William Chaworth to Beauchief abbey of 1 bovate in Norton and 5 acres of assart with a parcel in Norton wood which Adam son of John of the Cliffe[1] held and of Adam himself with all his family and their chattels; of 1 bovate in Bradway and 8 acres of assart in Norton wood which Thomas son of Hugh of the Wood held and of Thomas himself with all his family and their chattels; of ½ bovate in Cockshutt[2] which Winnora held and of Winnora herself with all her family and their chattels; of 1 assart with a toft in Cockshutt which Henry the Bercher[3] held; of 6 acres by the river Sheaf which

Richard of the Moor held; and of 80 acres in Norton wood to the north of the abbey's park.⁴ [1247–1312]⁵

Carta Thome Chaworth' de certis terris et nativis

Omnibus^a Cristi fidelibus hoc scriptum visuris vel audituris Thomas filius Willelmi de Chaworth' salutem in Domino. Noverit universitas vestra me dedisse, concessisse et hac presenti carta mea confirmasse Deo et ecclesie beati Thome martiris de Bello Capite et canonicis ibidem Deo servientibus unam bovatam terre cum pertinenciis quam Adam filius Johannis del Clyfe aliquando tenuit de me in territorio de Norton', et quinque acras assarti cum una parcella in bosco de Norton' quas idem Adam tenuit^b de me, et ipsum Adam cum tota sequela sua et eorum catallis, et unam bovatam terre in territorio de Bradway et octo acras assarti in dicto bosco de Norton' cum omnibus pertinenciis quas Thomas filius Hugonis de bosco tenuit de me, et ipsum Thomam cum tota sequela sua et eorum catallis, et dimidiam bovatam terre cum pertinenciis in Kocschit quam Wynnora tenuit de me, et ipsam Winnoram cum tota sequela sua et eorum catallis, et unum [fo. 13r] assartum cum uno tofto cum pertinenciis in eadem villa quod Henricus le Bercher tenuit de me, et sex acras terre cum pertinenciis iacentes juxta aquam de Scheve quas Ricardus de Mora tenuit de me, et quaterviginti acras terre cum pertinenciis in bosco de Norton' iacentes ex parte aquilonari parci abbatis et conventus de Beauchefe, sicut eisdem sunt assignate et mensurate ad assartandum et seminandum et includendum et ad omnimodum comodum suum inde faciendum. Hec omnia prenominata cum omnibus pertinenciis dedi dicte ecclesie de Beauchef et canonicis ibidem servientibus in liberam, puram et perpetuam elemosinam, libera et quieta ab omnibus secularibus serviciis, sectis, consuetudinibus vel demandis. Et ego Thomas de Chaworth et heredes mei predictas bovatas terre sine aliquo retenemento et predictos tenentes cum tota sequela sua et eorum catallis in predictos quatuorviginti acras terre et dimidiam bovatam terre in Kokechite et predictas sex acras terre juxta Scheve, cum omnibus aliis assartis prenominatis, cum pertinenciis, libertatibus, communiis et asiamentis dictis bovatis et asartis pertinent[ibus], dictis ecclesie et canonicis in liberam, puram et perpetuam elemosinam contra omnes gentes warantizabimus, acquietabimus et defendemus inperpetuum. Hiis testibus: Thoma de Leghys, Thoma de Bramton', Petro de la Wodehous, Hugone filio suo, Petro Byrcheheved, et aliis.

^a *mnibus.*   ^b *tenit.*

¹The cliff rises from the River Sheaf; cf. the present Cliffe Field Road.

²The farm takes its name from a place where woodcocks were trapped. It lies between the site of the abbey and Beauchief Hall.
³A barker or tanner.
⁴The first reference to the abbey's park; cf. the present Old Park Wood.
⁵All the witnesses, apart from Thomas of Brampton, also witnessed **17**, which dates from before 1258. This charter was confirmed in 1312 (**38**, no. 9) and again in 1316 (Appendix II, no. 9).

22. Gift in free alms by Thomas Chaworth, knight, to Beauchief abbey, for the maintenance of a priest to commemorate his soul and those of his family, of an annual rent of 18s which Robert le Redsmyth¹ paid for his tenement in Swanwick near Alfreton; of 1 assart with a toft and croft which Roger the smith held in Birchwood² in the soke of Alfreton; of 1 bovate which Adam of Birchwood held in Birchwood; of the land which Roger the bercher held in the soke of Alfreton; of 1 assart called Robertryddyng bordering on the abbey's assart on the common of (Norton) Lees; of an annual rent of 2s from the tenement which Roger Mons held in Alfreton; of an annual rent of 12d from the tenement which Nicholas Torald held in Alfreton; of 1 bovate which Richard Horegh held in Bradway; and of Robert of the Greaves, his serf, with all his family and their chattels and of the tenement which he held in bondage in the soke of Norton. [c.1301]³

Carta Thome Chaworth de decem et octo solidis annui redditus

Sciant presentes et futuri quod ego Thomas de Chaworth' miles dedi et concessi et hac presenti carta mea confirmavi Deo et ecclesie beati Thome martiris de Bello Capite et abbati et conventui eiusdem loci in liberam, puram et perpetuam elemosinam [fo. 13v]⁴ pro salute anime mee, patris mei, matris mee, uxorum mearumᵃ liberorum meorum et omnium antecessorum meorum, et versus sustentacionem unius canonici sacerdotis divina perpetuo in ecclesiaᵇ predicta pro animabus predictorum celebraturi, decem et octo solidatas annui redditus, quas Robertus le Redsmyth michi reddere consuevit pro tenemento quod de me tenuit in Swanwyke juxta Alfreton' ad festum Michaelis et Annunciacionis beate Marieᶜ cum omnibus pertinenciis et approvamentis et eschaetis suis, et totum illud assartum cum tofto et crofto et pertinenciis suis quod Rogerus faber de me tenuit in Byrchewode in soca de Alfreton', et unam bovatam terre cum pertinenciis quam Adam de Byrchewod de me tenuit in eadem, et totam illam terram cum pertinenciis suis quam Rogerus le Bercher de me tenuit in predicta soca de Alfarton', et totum illud assartum quod vocatur Robertryddyng' buttans de assarto predictorum abbatis et conventus super communam de la Ley cum pertinenciis suis, et duas solidatas annui redditus de tenemento quod Rogerus Mons tenuit in Alferton', et duodecim denariatas[d] annui redditus de tenemento quod Nicholaus Torald de me tenuit in Alferton', et illam bovatam terre cum pertinenciis quam Ricardus Horegh' de me tenuit in Bradway, et Robertum de le Greve nativum meum cum tota sequela sua et omnibus catallis suis,[e] ac totum tenementum cum pertinenciis quod de jure tenuit in bondagio in soca de Norton'. Habendum et tenendum predictis abbati et conventui et successoribus suis in liberam, puram et perpetuam elemosinam cum omnimodis serviciis, approvamentis, sectis curiarum et eschaetis[f] et aliis pertinenciis quibuscumque. Et ego predictus Thomas et heredes mei omnia[g] [fo. 14r] et singula tenementa, redditus et servicia ac nativum predictum cum sequelis suis ac catallis cum omnimodis serviciis, sectis, pertinenciis et eschaetis suis predictis abbati et conventui et eorum successoribus in liberam, puram et perpetuam elemosinam contra omnes gentes warantizabimus, acquietabimus et inperpetuum defendemus. In cuius rei testimonium huic carte sigillum meum apposui. Hiis testibus: Willelmo le Bret, Johanne de Eyncourt, Rogero Breton, Symone de Rerysby, Johanne de Brymington, Hugone de Linacre, Thoma de Leyes, Johanne de Stubbeley, Willelmo de Wynfeld, et aliis.[5]

[a] *meorum.*   [b] *ecllesia.*   [c] *i of Marie interlined.*   [d] *denarratas.*
[e] *suis (bis).*   [f] *h of eschaetis interlined.*   [g] *omnia (bis).*

[1] A copper smith? Traces of copper are found in the New Red Sandstone a few miles further east. No other references have been found for this term; the *OED* does not have an entry. See also **71**.
[2] Cf. Lower Birchwood (OS ref. SK 434544) and Upper Birchwood (OS ref. SK 439547), a mile or so south-west of Alfreton.
[3] For other gifts by Thomas Chaworth for the commemoration of his soul and the souls of his family, see **18**, **33**, **39–41**. This charter was confirmed in 1312 (**38**, no. 10) and again in 1316 (Appendix II, no. 10).
[4] A leaf has been excised between fos 13 and 14 without interruption to the text.
[5] For most of these witnesses, see **18**, n. 2. For appearances together as witnesses of William the Bret, John of Eyncourt, Roger the Breton, John Brimington, and Hugh of Linacre, see **18**, n. 2.

23. Gift in free alms by Thomas Chaworth to Beauchief abbey of the land which Richard of the Moor held in Cockshutt field which lies between the wood belonging to the abbey and the land which Winnora of Cockshutt held of the abbey. [1270–1312][1]

Carta Thome Chaworth' de terra in campo de Kocschete

Omnibus Cristi fidelibus presentem cartam visuris vel audituris Thomas de Chaworth salutem in Domino. Noverit universitas vestra me pro salute anime mee et antecessorum[a] meorum dedisse, concessisse, et hac presenti carta mea confirmasse, abbati et conventui[b] de Bello Capite et eorum sucessoribus in liberam, puram et perpetuam elemosinam totam terram illam quam Ricardus de Mora de me quondam tenuit in campo de Kocschete, iacentem inter boscum dictorum abbatis et conventus et terram quam Wynnora de Kocschete tenuit[c] de eisdem. Tenendum et habendum sibi et successoribus suis libere, quiete et integre cum omnibus pertinenciis, libertatibus et asiamentis, ita quod liceat sepedictis abbati et conventui terram predictam et illam terram quam predicta Wynnora claudere et circumfossare et omnimodum comodum suum inde facere. Et ego dictus Thomas et heredes mei dictam terram cum pertinenciis et asiamentis, [fo. 14v] ut predictum est, dictis abbati et conventui et eorum successoribus in liberam, puram et perpetuam elemosinam contra omnes gentes warantizabimus, acquietabimus et inperpetuum defendemus. In cuius[d] rei testimonium presenti carte sigillum meum apposui. Hiis testibus: Rad[ulph]o[e] de Rerisby, Galfrido de Beghton' clerico, Willemo Matiney, Hugone de Wodhous, Petro de Bernys, Roberto de[f] Graunt, et aliis.[2]

[a] *ancessorum.* [b] *conventi.* [c] *tenuit* interlined. [d] *cuis.*
[e] *Rand[ulph]o* with *n* deleted. [f] Sic; elsewhere, correctly *le.*

[1] Confirmed in 1312 (**38**, no. 11) and again in 1316 (Appendix II, no. 11).
[2] Ralph of Reresby held the manor of Pleasley at the time of the 1281 Derbyshire eyre (Hopkinson, *Derbyshire Eyre*, p. 177). William Matiney also witnessed **70** (1278); Peter de Bernis and Robert le Graunt witnessed **60** (1279). In **213** Robert le Graunt was said to be of Langwith; he was a juror for the wapentake of Scarsdale at the 1281 Derbyshire eyre (*ibid.*, p. 193).

24. Gift in free alms by Thomas Chaworth to Beauchief abbey of 1 toft and croft with buildings which John the smith held in Cockshutt; and of 1 curtilage in the vill of Alfreton near the barn which the canons held in the time of Sir Robert of Lathom. [1247–before 1283][1]

Carta Thome Chaworth' de tofto et crofto in le Kocschit

Omnibus Cristi fidelibus ad quorum noticiam presens scriptum pervenerit Thomas de Chaworth salutem in Domino. Noveritis me pro salute anime mee et omnium antecessorum meorum dedisse, concessisse et hac presenti carta mea confirmasse Deo et ecclesie beati Thome martiris de Bello Capite et canonicis ibidem Deo servientibus, in liberam, puram et perpetuam elemosinam, unum toftum et croftum cum edificiis et pertinenciis suis in le Kocshite, illud scilicet quod Johannes faber de me quondam tenuit, et unum curtilagium in villa de Alferton' juxta horreum dictorum canonicorum, quod quidem tenuerunt tempore domini Roberti de Lathum,[2] prout eisdem[a] infra fossatum assignatur. Tenendum et habendum sibi et successoribus suis in liberam, puram et perpetuam elemosinam inperpetuum. Et ego vero Thomas et heredes mei predictum toftum cum crofto, edificiis et omnibus aliis pertinenciis suis, una cum pretitulato curtilagio, dictis canonicis et successoribus suis contra omnes gentes warantizabimus, acquietabimus et defendemus inperpetuum. In cuius rei testimonium presenti carte sigillum meum apposui. Hiis testibus: domino Gervasio de Barnak,[3] Thoma Foleiambe de Tidiswelle,[4] [fo. 15r] Thoma de Morton' clerico, Hugone de Wodhows, Thoma de Wodhous, Johanne de Birchevede, et aliis.

[a] *s* of *eisdem* interlined.

[1] This charter was confirmed in 1312 (**38**, no. 13) and again in 1316 (Appendix II, no. 13).
[2] Sir Robert of Lathom was the husband of Thomas Chaworth's aunt and, for a short time in the mid-thirteenth century, joint lord in the right of his wife of Alfreton, Norton, etc.; he was also lord of Treeton (South Yorks). See also **66**.
[3] Gervase of Barnak was lord of Treeton (South Yorks) and Beighton (Derbys); he was bailiff of the Forest of the Peak in 1255–1256 (Turbutt, *Derbyshire*, II, p. 567); he witnessed a deed at Bradfield in 1279 (T.W. Hall, *A Descriptive Catalogue of Charters, Copy Court Rolls and Deeds Forming Part of the Wheat Collection* (Sheffield, 1916), p. 4); and was recorded at the Derbyshire eyre in 1281 (Hopkinson, *Derbyshire Eyre*, p. 70); see also **34**, **35**, **43**, **106**, **109**. He was commemorated in the Obituary (27 December) as having confirmed the gift of Sir Robert Fourness, his predecessor as lord of Beighton, of a grange at Birley, a meadow at Beighton, an annual rent of 12s in Le Brome near Rotherham, and common pasture near Padley.
[4] Sir Thomas Foljambe of Tideswell and Wormhill was a forester in the Forest of the Peak who died in 1283 (Turbutt, *Derbyshire*, II, p. 574); he also witnessed **70** (1278) and he was recorded at the 1281 Derbyshire eyre (Hopkinson, *Derbyshire Eyre*, p. 19). He was recorded in the Obituary (January).

25. Gift in free alms by Thomas Chaworth to Beauchief abbey of 1 strip called Eyclyff[1] with the wood growing thereon which lies in length between the land which the abbey holds and the land which Thomas son of John of the wood held and which extends from the abbey's land south to the arable land on the hill, and for which Richard son of Adam formerly paid him 18d annually. [1247–1312][2]

Carta Thome Chaworth' de Eyclyff

Omnibus Cristi fidelibus hoc presens scriptum visuris vel audituris Thomas de Chaworth' dominus de Norton' salutem in Domino. Noveritis me pro salute anime mee et omnium antecessorum et successorum meorum dedisse, concessisse et hac presenti carta mea[a] confirmasse in liberam, puram et perpetuam elemosinam abbati et conventui monasterii sancti Thome martiris de Bello Capite totam illam placeam terre, sine ullo retenemento, que vocatur Eyclyfe, sicut iacet in longitudine inter terram quam idem abbas et conventus tenent et terram quam Thomas filius Johannis de bosco tenet, et dilatat se a terra dictorum abbatis et conventus ascendendo usque ad terram arabilem super collem versus austrum, pro qua eciam placea terre Ricardus filius Adam solvit michi olim decem et octo denarios annuatim. Tenend[um] et habend[um] dictis abbati et conventui et eorum successoribus inperpetuum libere, quiete[b] et integre cum bosco supercrescente et aliis aisiamentis suis in liberam, puram et perpetuam elemosinam, ad assartandum si velint, et omnem comodum suum inde faciendum. Et ego dictus Thomas et heredes mei seu assignati dictam placeam terre cum bosco et aliis aisiamentis suis, ut dictum est, dictis abbati et conventui et eorum successoribus in liberam, puram et perpetuam elemosinam contra omnes gentes warantizabimus, aquietabimus et inperpetuum defendemus. In cuius rei testimonium huic carte sigillum meum apposui. Hiis testibus: Rogero del Clyfe, Thoma de Wodhous, Petro de Bernis, [fo. 15v] Johanne de Birchevede, Willelmo Matiny, Thoma de Heton', Johanne de Stubbeley, et aliis.[3]

[a] *me.*   [b] *quite.*

[1] Perhaps the 'high cliff', a lost place-name.
[2] This charter was confirmed in 1312 (**38**, no. 12) and again in 1316 (Appendix II, no. 14).
[3] Peter de Bernis also witnessed **60** (1279); both he and William Matiney witnessed **70** (1278).

26. Gift in free alms by Thomas Chaworth, knight, to Beauchief abbey of the land called the Qwytekar; of 12 acres in a place called Barsfelde;[1] and of 1 strip which Peter the weaver held near the land of Simon of the Storthes[2] in Alfreton. [1269–1289][3]

Carta Thome Chaworth' de le Qwyteker in Alferton'

Omnibus Cristi fidelibus hoc scriptum visuris vel audituris Thomas de Chaworth miles salutem in Domino sempiternam. Noverit universitas vestra me pro salute anime mee et omnium antecessorum et successorum meorum dedisse, concessisse et hac presenti carta mea confirmasse Deo et beate Marie et ecclesie beati Thome martiris de Bello Capite et abbati et conventui eiusdem loci, in liberam, puram et perpetuam elemosinam, totam illam terram que vocatur le Qwytekar, et duodecim acras terre in loco qui vocatur Berffeld, et illam placeam terre quam Petrus textor de me tenuit juxta terram quondam Simonis del Storthes in territorio de Alferton'. Tenendum et habendum predictis abbati et conventui et eorum successoribus libere, quiete et pacifice, in liberam, puram et perpetuam elemosinam, sine aliqua contradiccione vel inpedimento mei vel heredum meorum, inperpetuum. Ego vero Thomas et heredes mei vel assignati predictam terram cum omnibus pertinenciis suis predictis abbati et conventui et eorum successoribus in liberam, puram et perpetuam elemosinam, ut predictum est, contra omnes gentes warantizabimus, acquietabimus et inperpetuum defendemus. In cuius rei testimonium presenti scripto sigillum meum apposui. Hiis testibus: domino Henrico de Perpount, domino Johanne de Heriz, domino Johanne de Ainisley, domino Willelmo de Steynisby, Roberto le Graunt, Johanne de Brimington', Willelmo Pytte, et aliis.[4]

[1] Whitacre and Barsfield are lost place-names in Alfreton.
[2] An Old Norse word for 'brushwood'; a lost place-name.
[3] Confirmed in 1312 (**38**, no. 14) and again in 1316 (Appendix II, no. 15). Thomas's son and heir, William, who was dead by November 1312 (**44**) and thus predeceased his father, quitclaimed these premises in a charter (**90**) witnessed by at least five of the same witnesses as this one.
[4] Henry Pierrepoint was recorded at Langwith at the 1281 Derbyshire eyre (Hopkinson, *Derbyshire Eyre*, p. 116). John de Heriz, descendant of a Norman family, succeeded his brother Henry as lord of Tibshelf in 1272 or the beginning of 1273 and seems to have died in 1299 (Darlington, *Cartulary of Darley Abbey*, I, p. xxix; Turbutt, *Derbyshire*, II, p. 464); he was recorded at Tibshelf in the 1281 Derbyshire eyre (Hopkinson, *Derbyshire Eyre*, p. 90). William of Stainsby succeeded his father, Jocelin, *c*.1269 and died in 1289 (D. Crook, 'Hardwick before Bess: the origins and early history of the family of Hardwick, of Hardwick, Co. Derby', *Derbyshire Archaeological Journal*, 107 (1987), pp. 45–47); he was a juror of the 1281 Derbyshire eyre (Hopkinson, *Derbyshire Eyre*, p. 193). Robert le Graunt also witnessed **60** (1279) and served on the jury of the 1281 Derbyshire eyre.

27. Gift in free alms by Thomas Chaworth, knight, to Beauchief abbey of 1 assart which Robert Forester once held near the abbey's sheepfold; of 3 acres of arable which Robert of Childre held below the cloister; of 8½ acres which Ranulph of Storthes held and which lie between the land of Samson and the land of Robert Scarlet; and of 5½ acres which Richard Everard once held between the land of Robert Scarlet and the road leading to Birchwood in Alfreton. [1247–1312][1]

Carta Thome Chaworth' de quodam asserto

Omnibus Cristi fidelibus ad [quos] presens scriptum pervenerit Thomas de Cha[fo. 16r]worth miles salutem in Domino sempiternam. Noverit universitas vestra me divino amore et pro salute anime mee antecessorum et successorum meorum dedisse, concessisse et hoc presenti scripto confirmasse Deo et beate Marie et ecclesie beati Thome martiris de Bello Capite, abbati et conventui et eorum successoribus ibidem Deo servientibus, quoddam assertum quod Robertus Forester quondam de me tenuit juxta bercariam dictorum canonicorum, ut iacet in longitudine et latitudine, et tres acras terre arabilis quas Robertus de Childre de me tenuit infra claustrum dictorum canonicorum, et octo acras et dimidiam quas Ranulfus de Storthes de me tenuit et iacent inter terram Sampsonis et terram Roberti Scarlet, et quinque acras et dimidiam quas Ricardus Everard quondam de me tenuit inter terram Roberi Scarlet, et viam ducentem versus Byrchewod in territorio de Alferton. Tenendum et habendum predictis abbati et conventui de Bello Capite et eorum successoribus in liberam, puram et perpetuam elemosinam, sine aliqua diminucione vel impedimento mei vel heredum meorum. Et ego vero dictus Thomas de Chaworth et heredes mei totum dictum assartum cum predicta terra predictis abbati et conventui et eorum successoribus contra omnes gentes warantizabimus, acquietabimus et inperpetuum defendemus. In cuius rei testimonium presenti scripto sigillum meum apposui. Hiis testibus: domino Willelmo de Chaworth', Johanne de Ainesley, Rogero de Somervile, Willelmo de Huffton', Hugone de canonic', Roberto Scerlet, Willelmo forestar, Willelmo Pecke tunc senescallo, Thoma clerico, et multis aliis.[2]

---

[1] Confirmed in 1312 (**38**, no. 15) and again in 1316 (Appendix II, no. 16).
[2] Roger de Somerville also witnessed **60** (1279); Hugo de canonicis and Robert Scarlet also witnessed **70** (1278). Both Roger and Hugh served on the jury of the 1281 Derbyshire eyre for the wapentake of Scarsdale (Hopkinson, *Derbyshire Eyre*, p. 193).

28. Gift in free alms by Thomas Chaworth, lord of Norton, to Beauchief abbey of the land which Thomas of the Wood and William Tynet held in (Norton) Woodseats, saving the lands, meadows, and woods which the same Thomas and William hold by the river Sheaf. [1247–1312][1]

Carta domini Thome Chaworth' infra bundas de Wodsetus

Omnibus Cristi fidelibus hoc presens scriptum visuris vel audituris [fo. 16v] Thomas de Chaworth dominus de Norton' salutem in Domino. Noveritis me dedisse, concessisse et hoc presenti scripto meo confirmasse abbati et conventui de Bello Capite et eorum successoribus in liberam, puram et perpetuam elemosinam totam illam terram cum pertinenciis suis quam Thomas de Bosco et Willelmus Tynet de me tenuerunt infra bundas del Wodsetes cum pertinenciis suis, salvis tamen michi et heredibus meis terris pratis boscis quas iidem Thomas et Willelmus de me tenent juxta aquam de Schava. Tenendum et habendum predictis abbati et conventui et eorum successoribus, libere, quiete, pacifice et integre, in liberam, puram et perpetuam elemosinam, cum omnibus pertinenciis suis. Et ego predictus Thomas et heredes mei predictam terram cum omnibus pertinenciis suis predictis abbati et conventui et eorum successoribus in liberam, puram et perpetuam elemosinam contra omnes gentes warantizabimus, acquietabimus et inperpetuum defendemus. In cuius rei testimonium presenti scripto sigillum meum[a] apposui. Hiis testibus: Johanne Deynecourt, Willelmo le Brect', Rogero Breton', Willelmo Fraunceys', Henrico de Neubolt', Thoma de Leyghes, Johanne de Stubbeley, et aliis.[2]

[a] altered from *sigillo meo.*

[1] Compare **18**, **33**, and **50**. Confirmed in 1312 (**38**, no. 16) and again in 1316 (Appendix II, no. 17). Sir Thomas's great-grandson, Sir Thomas Chaworth III, quitclaimed the premises in 1350 (**50**).
[2] William le Bret and Roger Breton also witnessed **71** (1301).

29. Gift in free alms by Thomas Chaworth, knight, to Beauchief abbey of 1 bovate with tofts, crofts, and buildings which Richard Hore once held in Bradway. [1247–1312][1]

Carta domini Thome Chaworth' de terra in Bradway

Omnibus ad quos presens scriptum pervenerit Thomas de Chaworth miles salutem in Domino sempiternam. Noverit universitas vestra me pro salute anime mee et omnium antecessorum et successorum meorum dedisse, concessisse et hac presenti carta mea confirmasse abbati et conventui de Bello Capite in liberam, puram et perpetuam elemosinam totam illam bovatam terre cum [fo. 17r] toftis, croftis, edificiis et omnibus aliis pertinenciis suis, quam Ricardus Hore quondam de me tenuit in le Bradwey. Tenendum et habendum dictis abbati et conventui suisque successoribus inperpetuum in liberam, puram et perpetuam elemosinam cum omnibus libertatibus, communiis et aisiamentis cum pertinenciis suis ad dictam bovatam terre cum toftis croftis edificiis qualitercumque spectantibus. Et ego predictus Thomas et heredes mei totam predictam bovatam terre cum omnibus pertinenciis suis prenominatis predictis abbati et conventui suis et successoribus inperpetuum contra omnes gentes in liberam, puram et perpetuam elemosinam warantizabimus, acquietabimus et defendemus. In cuius rei testimonium presenti scripto sigillum meum apposui. Hiis testibus: Thoma de le Leghys, Willelmo Matany, Thoma de le Wodhous, Petro de Bernes, Johanne de Byrchevede, et aliis.[2]

[1] Confirmed in 1312 (**38**, no. 17) and again in 1316 (Appendix II, no. 18).
[2] Peter de Bernis also witnessed **60** (1279); both he and William Matiney witnessed **70** (1278).

30. Quitclaim by Thomas Chaworth, knight, to Beauchief abbey of an annual rent of 5s for the land which they held from him in the soke of Norton, which soke was called the land of Robert the fletcher.[1] [1247–1312][2]

Quieta clamacio Thome Chaworth de redditu quinque solidorum

Omnibus ad quos presens scriptum pervenerit Thomas de Chaworth miles salutem in Domino sempiternam. Noverit universitas vestra me dedisse, concessisse et omnino quietum clamasse abbati et conventui de Bello Capite in liberam, puram et perpetuam elemosinam illum annuum redditum quinque solidorum, quem michi solvere consueverunt pro illa terra quam dicti abbas et conventus per quoddam scriptum feofamenti de me tenuerunt in soca de Norton; que[a] quidem soca vocata[b] terra Roberti le fletcher. Ita quod nec ego Thomas nec heredes mei nec assignati aliquod jus vel clameum in predicta terra cum pertinenciis suis amodo vendicare poterimus quoquo jure. In cuius rei testimonium [fo. 17v] presenti scripto sigillum meum apposui. Hiis testibus: Johanne de Brimington, Roberto le

Graunt, Rogero carpentario, Thoma del Wodhous, Petro de Leghys, et aliis.³

ᵃ*que (bis).*   ᵇ*voca.*

¹Maker or seller of arrows.
²Confirmed in 1312 (**38**, no. 18) and again in 1316 (Appendix II, no. 19). For the original gift of land, in which the rent of 5s quitclaimed here was reserved, see **49**.
³Robert le Graunt also witnessed **60** (1279). John of Brimington, Roger the Carpenter, Thomas of Woodhouse, and Peter of Leys together witnessed a grant of land in Norton made by Sir Thomas de Chaworth (printed from a copy then in the possession of Marples and Marples, solicitors in Sheffield, in S.O. Addy, 'A contribution to the history of Norton in Derbyshire', *Journal of the Derbyshire Archaeological and Natural History Society*, 2 (1880), pp. 6–7). The first witness to this charter is William of Folkingham, abbot of Beauchief from at latest 1296 until 1324; his predecessor, abbot Ralph occurs 1282×1283 (Smith and London, *Heads of Religious Houses*, II, p. 494).

31. Gift in free alms by Thomas Chaworth, knight, lord of Marnham, of free and quiet passage at Marnham ferry¹ to the abbot and convent of Beauchief and to all their dependants from all their properties with all their animals, goods, and carriages whenever the need arises and on the best vessel. The ferry men are liable to pay to Thomas ¹/₂ silver mark² if they cause delay. [1247–1312]³

Alia carta domini Thome de Chaworth' militis de libero passagio ad feriam de Marneham

Omnibus ad quos presens scriptum pervenerit Thomas de Chaworth miles dominus de Marnham salutem in Domino sempiternam. Noverit universitas vestra me pro salute anime mee et omnium antecessorum et successorum meorum dedisse, concessisse et hoc presenti scripto meo confirmasse abbati et conventui de Bello Capite suisque successoribus in liberam, puram et perpetuam elemosinam liberum et quietum passagium ad feriam meam de Marnham, tam ipsis quam familie sue, habendum de abbacia predicta et de omnibus aliis locis suis cum omnibus animalibus, rebus ac cariagiis suis aliis quibuscumque et quandocumque opus habuerunt in meliore navigio ferie mee predicte, absque omni exaccione et demanda, libere, quiete inperpetuum. Ita quod feriatores mei et heredes vel assignati mei predictos abbatem et conventum ceterosque familie sue feriandum moram non facient, occasione pecunie sibi non solute vel non solvende,ᵃ sub pena dimidie marce argenti michi et heredibus meis seu assignatis ab ipsis feriatoribus solvenda. Et ego vero predictus

Thomas et heredes mei vel assignati predictum passagium predictis abbati et conventui, ut predictum est, contra omnes gentes in liberam, puram et perpetuam elemosinam warantizabimus, acquietabimus et inperpetuum defendemus. In cuius rei testimonium presenti scripto sigillum meum apposui. Hiis testibus: domino Waltero de Gousehill, domino Johanne [fo. 18r] Buk militibus, Johanne de Vilers in Marnham, Ricardo de Marnham clerico,[b] Thoma de Leys, Thoma de Wodhows, Rogero de Fledeburgh' in Norton', Johanne de Byrcheheved, et aliis.

[a] gap of approximately 5 letters in the MS.   [b] *clerico (bis)*.

[1] Marnham (Notts), by the river Trent; OS ref. SK8169.
[2] A mark was worth 13s 4d.
[3] Confirmed in 1312 (**38**, no. 19) and again in 1316 (Appendix II, no. 20).

32. Gift in free alms by Thomas Chaworth, knight, to Beauchief abbey of 1 strip on the west side of Alfreton Hall. [1247–1312][1]

Carta de una placea terre iacente juxta aulam de Alfreton'

Sciant presentes et futuri quod ego Thomas de Chaworth miles dedi, concessi et hac presenti carta mea confirmavi abbati et conventui de Bello Capite unam placeam terre iacentem ex parte occidentali aule sue in Alferton', sicut illam eis assignavi et dimisi per certas metas de quodam ortulo meo. Tenendum et habendum eisdem abbati et conventui et eorum successoribus inperpetuum in liberam, puram et perpetuam elemosinam, sine ulla contradicione et impedimento heredum et assignatorum meorum. Set et ego predictus Thomas et heredes mei predictam placeam terre predictis abbati et conventui et eorum successoribus in liberam, puram et perpetuam elemosinam contra omnes gentes warantizabimus, acquietabimus et inperpetuum defendemus. In cuius rei testimonium huic scripto sigillum meum apposui. Hiis testibus: Hugone de Wandesley, Waltero de Ufto, Roberto le Graunt, Roberto Scharlet, Hugone de Linacre, Petro de Bernis, Johanne de Bychevede, et aliis.[2]

[1] Confirmed in 1312 (**38**, no. 20) and again in 1316 (Appendix II, no. 21).
[2] Robert le Graunt and Peter de Bernis also witnessed **60** (1279); Peter de Bernis and Robert Scarlet also witnessed **70** (1278).

33. Gift in free alms by Thomas Chaworth, knight, lord of Norton, to Beauchief abbey, for the maintenance of a canon to commemorate his soul and those of his family at the altar of St Katherine, of his hamlet of Greenhill in the soke of Norton with Greenhill Moor, all services of its free tenants, all its lands and tenements held in villeinage, and all his villeins with their families and chattels; and of all lands and tenements which Hugh of Little Norton held in villeinage at Little Norton and (Norton) Woodseats and the same Hugh with his family and their chattels. Also, quitclaim of an annual rent of 12s 8d which the abbey pay him for diverse tenements in Alfreton and Norton. Also, gift in free alms of all lands and tenements held in villeinage in (Norton) Woodseats and all his villeins there with their families and their chattels, saving the lands which Thomas of the wood and William Tinet hold by the river Sheaf. [c.1301][1]

Carta de Grenehill' cum mora eiusdem ville

Sciant presentes et futuri quod ego Thomas Chaworth miles dominus de Norton dedi, concessi et hac presenti carta mea confirmavi [fo. 18v] Deo et monasterio beati Thome martiris de Bello Capite et religiosis viris abbati et conventui eiusdem loci in liberam, puram et perpetuam elemosinam, pro salute anime mee et patris mei et matris mee uxorum mearum liberorumque meorum et pro sustentacione unius canonici eiusdem monasterii divina perpetuo celebrantis ad altare sancte Katerine virginis[a] in ecclesia de Bello Capite predicta, pro anima mea et animabus predictorum et omnium fidelium defunctorum et pro solempni[b] servicio annuatim habendo inperpetuum, sicut pro uno abbate defuncto, totum illud hameletum meum in soca de Norton' quod vocatur Grenehyll', simul cum mora de Grenehyll' et cum homagiis, wardis, releviis, redditibus et ceteris serviciis libere tenencium ibidem, et eciam omnes terras et tenementa que de me tenentur in villinagio in eodem hameleto, et eciam omnes villanos meos ibidem cum eorum sequelis et omnibus catallis suis et cum omnibus pertinenciis suis, tam infra hameletum predictum quam extra qualitercumque spectantibus, sine aliquo retenemento. Dedi eciam Deo et monasterio ac abbati et conventui predictis omnes terras et tenementa que Hugo de Parva Norton' de me tenuit in villinagio de Parva Norton' et Wodesetes et ipsum Hugonem cum tota sequela sua et omnibus catallis suis, sine aliquo retenemento. Remisi eciam relaxavi et quietum clamavi de me et heredibus meis Deo et monasterio ac abbati et conventui predictis duodecim solidatas et octo denariatas[c] annui redditus quas predicti Abbas et conventus michi reddere solebant pro diversis tenementis que de me tenuerunt in Alferton' et Norton'. Preterea dedi, concessi et hac presenti carta mea confirmavi Deo et monasterio [fo. 19r] ac abbati et conventui predictis omnes terras et tenementa cum pertinenciis suis que de me tenentur in villenagio in Wodesetes juxta Norton', et eciam omnes villanos meos ibidem cum totis sequelis suis et omnibus catallis suis sine aliquo retenemento, salvis tamen michi et heredibus meis terris, pratis cum boscis que Thomas de Bosco et Willelmus Tinet de me tenuerunt juxta aquam de Schava. Tenendum et habendum Deo et monasterio ac abbati et conventui predictis eorumque successoribus in liberam, puram et perpetuam elemosinam cum pratis, boscis, pascuis et pasturis, moris, turbariis,[d] quareris, mineris, merleriis et omnimodis libertatibus,[e] communiis et aysiamentis et aliis approvamentis[f] et pertinenciis suis quibuscumque et ubicumque spectantibus, tam infra terram quam supra, inperpetuum. Et ego predictus Thomas et heredes mei omnia et singula prenominata cum omnibus suis pertinenciis prefatis abbati et conventui et eorum successoribus in liberam, puram et perpetuam elemosinam, sicut predictum est, possidenda contra omnes gentes warantizabimus, acquietabimus et inperpetuum defendemus. In cuius rei testimonium presenti carte sigillum meum apposui. Hiis testibus: dominis Thoma de Furnivall', Ada de Everingham, Waltero de Goushill', Ricardo de Furneus', Roberto de Ecclessale militibus, domino Rogero de Braleford rectore ecclesie de Drounfeld', Willelmo le Brect', Johanne de Eyncourt, Rogero le Breton, Symone de[g] Rerisbe, Johanne de Brymington', Hugone de Linacre, et multis aliis.[2]

[a] second *i* of *virginis* interlined.   [b] *solemnpni*.   [c] *denarratas*.   [d] first *r* of *turbariis* interlined.   [e] followed by gap of approximately 7 letters.   [f] followed by another gap of approximately 7 letters.   [g] *le*.

[1] Compare **18, 28, 40,** and **50**. Confirmed in 1312 (**38**, no. 22) and again in 1316 (Appendix II, no. 22). The premises listed here also appear in three charters not recited in 1312 or 1316 (**39–41**) but there (as in the charter printed by Dugdale – see **18**, n. 1) the altar is said to be dedicated to the Holy Cross, not St Katherine; one of the latter group (**40**) contains the original gift of the rent of 12s 8d, which here is quitclaimed. This gift appears to be quite separate from those made in **18** and **22**, which are also to maintain a chaplain to pray for the souls of Thomas and his family, but no particular altar is specified in **22**. This latter gift can perhaps be associated with a mortmain licence of 1301, although it is possible that all the gifts for a chaplain were made under this licence (see **18**, n. 1 and **47**, n. 2: a power of attorney dated a few weeks after the mortmain licence). In the Obituary (24 September), Sir Thomas Chaworth is commemorated, as are his gifts of Greenhill and Woodseats with parcels of land and rent in Alfreton; a Mass is celebrated in perpetuity at the altar of St Katherine and a date is given: 1314.
[2] For these witnesses see **18**, n. 2.

34. Gift in free alms by Thomas Chaworth, knight, to Beauchief abbey of 1 assart in Norton wood north of the abbey's park, lying in length from the road below the park which goes by the ditch of the assart towards Coumbeclyffe to the middle of the river Sheaf and in width from the land which Richard Swappoke once held to the land which the abbey has of the gift of Robert son of William. [1247–1312]

Alia carta domini Thome Chaworth de assarto in bosco de Norton'

Omnibus Cristi fidelibus hoc presens scriptum visuris vel audituris [fo. 19v] Thomas de Chaworth miles salutem in Domino. Noverit universitas vestra me concessisse et hoc[a] presenti scripto meo confirmasse abbati et conventui de Bello Capite in liberam, puram et perpetuam elemosinam totum illud assartum integre cum pertinenciis in bosco de Norton' iacens ex parte aquilonari parci dictorum abbatis et conventus cum tota longitudine sua et latitudine a via, silicet subtus parcum predictum que vadit per fossatum predicti assarti versus le Coumbeclyfe usque ad filum aque de Scheve in longitudine, et a terra quam Ricardus Swappoke aliquando tenuit usque ad terram predictorum abbatis et conventus quam habuerunt ex dono Roberti filii Willelmi in latitudine, sine aliqua diminucione ad includendum, seminandum et omnimodum comodum suum prout expedire viderint autem faciendum. Habendum et tenendum sibi et successoribus suis, ut predictum est, de me et heredibus meis, ita libere et quiete sicut aliqua elemosina liberius ac quiecius potest vel confirmari. Ego vero predictus Thomas et heredes mei predictum assartum cum pertinenciis suis, ut predictum est, sepedictis abbati et conventui eorumque successoribus contra omnes gentes warantizabimus, acquietabimus et ubique defendemus. In cuius rei testimonium huic presenti scripto sigillum meum apposui. Hiis testibus: domino Gervasio de Bernakyl, domino Willelmo de Aubeny, domino Willelmo de Chaworth, domino Rad[ulph]o de Eclessale, Johanne de Vilers', Petro de Byrcheved, Willelmo de Tocham, et aliis.[1]

[a] *ho.*

[1] Gervase of Bernak was alive in 1279 (see **24**, n. 3). Sir Ralph of Ecclesall witnessed a deed at Ecclesfield in 1267 (Hall and Thomas, *Jackson Collection*, p. 6). For Peter Birchitt, see **17**, n. 3.

35. Gift in free alms by Thomas Chaworth to Beauchief abbey of Roger of Bradway, Gilbert of Bradway, Peter at the mill of Bradway,[1] and Emma at the new mill,[2] his serfs, with their chattels, families, services, and all lands which they once held in the parish of Norton with their tofts, crofts, buildings, and other prerogatives. [1247–1312][3]

Alia carta domini Thome Chaworth de nativis

Omnibus Cristi fidelibus hoc presens scriptum visuris vel audituris [fo. 20r] Thomas de Chaworth salutem in Domino. Noverit universitas vestra me dedisse, concessisse et hac presenti carta mea confirmasse Deo et ecclesie beati Thome martiris de Bello Capite et canonicis ibidem Deo servientibus in liberam, puram et perpetuam elemosinam Rogerum de Bradewey, Gilbertum de Bradwey,[a] Petrum ad molendinum de Bradeway, Emmam ad novum molendinum, nativos meos, cum omnibus catallis, sequelis, sectis et serviciis suis, et cum omnibus terris quas de me quondam tenuerunt in parochia de Norton', ac eciam cum toftis, croftis, edificiis, libertatibus, communiis, aysiamentis et omnibus aliis pertinenciis dictis terris qualitercumque pertinentibus,[b] sicuti predicti Rogerus, Gilbertus, Petrus et Emma, nativi mei, illas de me tenuerunt. Tenendum et habendum sibi et successoribus suis in liberam, puram et perpetuam elemosinam. Ego vero Thomas et heredes mei dictos Rogerum, Gilbertum, Petrum et Emmam, cum catallis, sequelis, sectis et serviciis suis, terris, toftis, croftis, edificiis, libertatibus, communiis et aysiamentis predictis, ac omnibus aliis pertinenciis suis, ut predictum est, dictis canonicis et successoribus suis contra omnes gentes warantizabimus,[c] acquietabimus et inperpetuum defendemus. In cuius rei testimonium presentem cartam sigilli mei inpositione[d] roboravi. Hiis testibus: domino Gervasio de Bernak, domino Rad[ulph]o de Eclessale, Thoma Foleiaumbe de Tiddeswell',[4] Willelmo de Gaham,[5] Thoma de Hesilhyrst', Thoma de Wodhous, Johanne de Byrcheved, et aliis.

[a] *Gilbertum de Bradway* interlined. [b] *pertinet.* [c] *ar* of *warantizabimus* interlined. [d] *inposistione.*

[1] In the parish of Norton; OS ref. SK c.320807; for both mills, see the Introduction, pp. 18–19.
[2] Emma of the new mill in Norton may also occur in a case in 1272, in which she and her husband, John de Abbernun, and others were accused of disseising Roger, an earlier abbot of Beauchief, of common right of pasture in Norton (C.E. Lugard (ed.), *Calendar of the Cases for Derbyshire from the Eyre and Assize Rolls (Henry III 1256–1272)* (Barnston, Cheshire, 1938), p. 177). Abbot Roger occurs late in the reign of Henry III/Edward I (Smith and London, *Heads of Religious Houses*, II, p. 494). In 1269 Emma and her husband had been found guilty of

disseising the abbot of Beauchief of 7 acres of common of pasture in one place and 4½ acres in Alfreton (Lugard, *Calendar of the Cases for Derbyshire*, p. 154). For a similar case in 1268–1269 of unjust disseisin of land belonging to the abbot of Beauchief in Nottinghamshire, see **203**, n. 2.

[3] Confirmed in 1316 (Appendix II, no. 25).

[4] Thomas Foljambe also witnessed **70**.

[5] Witnessed a deed at Norton in 1317 (T.W. Hall, *A Descriptive Catalogue of... Ancient Charters and Instruments of Ughill, Waldershelf and Norton Lees* (Sheffield, 1930), p. 11); sometimes recorded as William of Gotham (see **112–113**; given as 'of Gaham' in **43**, **88**, **106**, **111**, **116**); Gaham is an old form of Gotham (Notts); see Watts, *English Place-names*, p. 257.

36. Gift in free alms by Thomas Chaworth, knight, lord of Alfreton, to Beauchief abbey of all the waste lying between the abbey's lands and tenements in the sokes of Alfreton and Norton. The abbey may use any land in Thomas's waste to maintain their ditches and houses and may dig, remove, and quarry whatever they need on Thomas's waste as well as on that of their own lands. They may also enclose and cultivate these wastes. [1247–1316][1]

[fo. 20v]

Carta domini Thome Chaworth' de vasto

Sciant presentes et futuri quod ego Thomas de Chaworth miles, dominus de Alferton, dedi, concessi et hac presenti carta mea confirmavi religiosis viris abbati et conventui de Bello Capite et eorum successoribus in liberam, puram et perpetuam elemosinam totum vastum quod iacet inter terras et tenementa sua que habent infra socas de Alferton et Norton' cum pertinenciis suis, et terram ubicumque eisdem necesse fuerit per totum wastum meum ad fossas suas amplandas et levandas capere, et eciam terram turbas et domos suas emendandas et cooperiendas, et ad omnia alia facienda que sibi fuerint necessaria fodere, capere et cariare,[a] tam de vasto meo quam de vastis infra terras suas iacentibus, sine impedimento mei vel heredum meorum. Tenendum et habendum predictis religiosis abbati et conventui et eorum successoribus in liberam, puram et perpetuam elemosinam cum omnibus pertinenciis suis. Ita quod liceat eisdem religiosis terras suas et vasta infra terras et tenementa sua iacencia claudere, circumfossare et in culturam redigere[b] et omni tempore anni clausa habere. Et ego predictus Thomas et heredes mei omnia predicta, in forma prenotata, predictis religiosis abbati et conventui[c] et eorum successoribus contra omnes gentes warantizabimus, acquietabimus et inperpetuum defendemus. In cuius^d rei testimonium presenti carte sigillum meum apposui. Hiis testibus: domino Henrico de Bralisforde,[2] domino Waltero [fo. 21r] de Gausshyll' militibus, Willelmo Brett', Simone de Grenehyll', Hugone de Linacre, Waltero de Ufton, Roberto Bulmer, et aliis.

^a*carrare.*   ^b*rdigere.*   ^c*coventui.*   ^d*cuus.*

[1] Confirmed in 1316 (Appendix II, no. 26). See also **77**, which is another grant of waste in Alfreton, with the right to enclose both waste and other land belonging to the abbey's grange at Cotes in Alfreton. Simon of Greenhill (whose name probably derived from Greenhill in Alfreton, not Greenhill in Norton) witnessed both charters; the names of other witnesses to **77** place that charter in the last quarter of the thirteenth century, to which this one probably also belongs. See also **18**, n. 2.
[2] (Sir) Henry of Brailsford served on the jury of the Derbyshire eyre in 1281 (Hopkinson, *Derbyshire Eyre*, p. 78) and was a Member of Parliament in 1298 (Turbutt, *Derbyshire*, II, p. 620). He was lord of Wingerworth and of Birchitt and Unstone in the parish of Dronfield (K. Battye, *Unstone: the history of a village* (privately published, 1981), p. 32) and he was recorded in the Obituary (11 July) as 'late patron of the church of Dronfield'.

37. Gift in free alms by Thomas Chaworth, knight, lord of Norton, to Beauchief abbey and its tenants of licence to dig for and carry away coal for their use and profit, provided the tenants have a licence from the abbey to do so, as much in the lands assigned for the support of a chaplain for the Mass of St Mary at Alfreton and the lands held by the abbey as in their own lands and wastes in the sokes of Alfreton and Norton; and of the right to clear the abbey's arable lands and those of their tenants from corn marigolds[1] according to the custom of the sokes of Alfreton and Norton. The abbey may also arrest its tenants and impose damages on them as Thomas and his ancestors used to do. [1247-1316][2]

Carta domini Thome Chaworth' de carbonibus fodendis

Universis Cristi fidelibus ad quos presens scriptum pervenerit^a Thomas de Chaworth miles, dominus de Norton', salutem in Domino sempiternam. Noveritis me pro salute anime mee et omnium antecessorum meorum licenciam dedisse et liberam et licitam potestatem concessisse religiosis viris abbati et conventui de Bello Capite et eorum successoribus in liberam, puram et perpetuam elemosinam ad carbones fodendos, levandos, asportandos et cariandos ad utilitatem et profectum suum et eorum tenencium, tam liberorum quam nativorum, quocienscumque sibi necesse fuerit, si licenciam de predictis abbate et conventu habuerunt, tam in terris ad cantariam misse beate Marie apud Alferton' assignatis et terris tenencium religiosorum predictorum quam in terris suis propriis et vastis inter et infra terras suas iacentibus infra socas de Alferton' et Norton, sine inquietacione vel perturbacione mei vel heredum meorum. Concessi eciam eisdem abbati et conventui quod libere possunt terras suas et terras tenencium, tam liberorum quam nativorum, a goldis mundare per se et suos, secundum consuetudinem in socis de Alferton' et Norton' usitatam, et si defectum in emundacione predicta invenerint quod possint tenentes suos perimire et emendas ab eisdem accipere, sicut ex antiquo per me et antecessores meos con[fo. 21v]sueti fuerant perimiri, ita quod nec ego Thomas nec heredes mei nec aliquis alius per nos seu nomine nostro de huiusmodi emundacione goldarum decetero intromittemus vel intromittent, nec eciam predicti abbas et conventus nec successores sui nec eorum tenentes, si defectus in emundacione goldarum predictarum in bladis suis vel tenencium suorum inveniatur per me vel heredes meos decetero puniantur, graventur seu calumpnientur usque in hiis ab omni fatigacione et inquietacione, sine inpedimento mei vel heredum meorum, in pace inperpetuum remaneant et quieti. In cuius rei testimonium presenti scripto sigillum meum apposui. Hiis testibus: domino Johanne Deyncourt milite, Willelmo de Brett, Rogero Breton', Ada de Rerisby, Rad[ulph]o de eadem, Stephano le Eyr', Hugone de Lynacre, et aliis.[3]

[a] *perverit.*

[1] Gold marigolds (*chrysanthemum segetum*), which were a weed among corn; or possibly charlock.
[2] Confirmed in 1316 (Appendix II, no. 27) and entered again in the Alfreton section of the cartulary (**81**).
[3] John Deyncourt, William le Bret, Roger Breton, and Stephen le Eyr all witnessed the confirmation of 1312 (**38**); all but Stephen also witnessed **71** (1301).

38. General confirmation by Thomas Chaworth, knight, senior lord of Norton, to Beauchief abbey of all grants made by him and his ancestors to the abbey. Made at Norton Tuesday 5 September 1312.[1]

[1; see charter **4**] **The gift in free alms by Robert son of Ranulph, for erecting an abbey, of the place called Beauchief in Doreheseles, which is the land contained in the area from Greenhill by Aldefelde to Twentywellsick, and then down the brook of Twentywellsick to the river Sheaf, and then down to Abbey Brook, and then up Abbey Brook to the ford of the same brook at the road down from**

Alan's house, and then up this road to Alan's assart, and then to the assarts of Robert and Peter and back up to the Greenhill; of the churches of Norton, Alfreton, Wymeswold, and Edwalton; of the mill of Norton; of Hugh's assart near Meersbrook with 1 toft in (Norton) Lees; of 1 toft near Alan's house; of a tenth of all his pannage; and of 2 bovates in Wymeswold from his demesne with 1 toft containing 3 acres, *viz.* on the west 8 selions at Robbewong, 6 selions at Milnehill, 5 selions at Netherbrombergh, 11 selions at Longbenlondeshend, 6 selions at Martynhau, 3 selions at Mikylwaterlondeshendes, 4 selions at Hungurhill, and on the east 4 selions at Mousewelehende, 8 selions at Marwaterlandes, 5 selions at Marthegravegate, 9 selions at Comberdale, 4 selions below the roads, 6 selions to the south of Rykesyk, 9 selions at Smalhengsikeshende.

[2; see 5] **The gift in free alms by the same Robert of 2 bovates in Wymeswold, one which was Alexander's with a toft and the other which was the widow Lovechild's.**

[3; see 6] **The gift in free alms by the same Robert, for enlarging the site of the abbey, of the easements at Brockhurst within the area which extends from the ford at Tacheleford up by the road to Westerley, and through Westerley eastward and right through Brockhurst to the road coming up from Brockford and along it south to Brockford; and of 1 assart lying between the assart of Hugh son of Albert of Bradway and the land of Gerard of Greenhill near the boundary of Birchwood.**

[4; see 7] **The gift in free alms by William son of Robert of the mill of Aston.**

[5; see 8] **The gift in free alms by Robert son of William of the land which Ellis of Troway held.**

[6; see 9] **The gift in free alms by the same Robert of 3 acres by the brook which descends from the north of the abbey to the river Sheaf; and of 1 pound of cumin from the service of Roger of Ridding for the land of Shireoaks.**

[7; not in the cartulary] **The gift in free alms by the same Robert of 60 acres with wood in Alfreton between the land of Suard and Salhinwell.**

[8; see 10] **The gift in free alms by the same Robert of 24 acres with wood in Norton near 3 acres of land lying by the brook which descends from the north of the abbey to the river Sheaf.**

[9; see 21] The gift in free alms by him, Thomas Chaworth, of 1 bovate in Norton and 5 acres of assart with a parcel in Norton wood which Adam son of John of the Cliffe once held and of the same Adam with all his family and their chattels; of 1 bovate in Bradway and 8 acres of assart in Norton wood which Thomas son of Hugh of the wood held and of the same Thomas with all his family and their chattels; of $^1/_2$ bovate in Cockshutt which Winnora held and of the same Winnora with all her family and their chattels; of 1 assart with a toft in Cockshutt which Henry the bercher held; of 6 acres by the river Sheaf which Richard of the moor held; and of 80 acres of land in Norton wood north of the abbey's park.

[10; see 22] The gift in free alms by him, Thomas Chaworth, of the annual rent of 18s which Robert the redsmith paid for the tenement in Swanwick near Alfreton; of 1 assart with a toft and croft which Roger the smith held in Birchwood in the soke of Alfreton; of 1 bovate which Adam of Birchwood held in Birchwood; of all the land which Roger the bercher held in the soke of Alfreton; of 1 assart called Robertryddyng bordering on the abbey's assart on the common of (Norton) Lees; of a rent of 2s from the tenement which Roger Mons held in Alfreton; of a rent of 12d from the tenement which Nicholas Torald held in Alfreton; of 1 bovate which Richard Horegh held in Bradway; and of Robert of the greave, his serf, with all his family and their chattels and of the tenement in the soke of Norton.

[11; see 23] The gift in free alms by him, Thomas Chaworth, of the land which Richard of the moor once held in Cockshutt field which lies between the abbey's wood and the land which Winnora of Cockshutt once held from the abbey.

[12; see 25] The gift in free alms by him, Thomas Chaworth, of the strip called the Cliffe lying in length between the land which the abbey holds and the land which Thomas son of John of the wood held and extending from the abbey's land south to the arable land on the hill.

[13; see 24] The gift in free alms by him, Thomas Chaworth, of 1 toft and croft in Cockshutt which John the smith once held and 1 curtilage in Alfreton near the barn which the abbey held at the time of Robert of Lathom.

[14; see **26**] **The gift in free alms by him, Thomas Chaworth, of the land called the Qwytekere; of 12 acres in Barsfelde; and of the strip which Peter the weaver held near the land of Simon of the Storthes in Alfreton.**

[15; see **27**] **The gift in free alms by him, Thomas Chaworth, of 1 assart which Robert Forester once held near the abbey's sheepfold; of 3 acres of arable which Robert of Childre held below the cloister; of $8\frac{1}{2}$ acres which Ranulph of Storthes held and which lie between the land of Samson and the land of Robert Scarlet; and of $5\frac{1}{2}$ acres which Richard Edward once held between the land of Robert Scarlet and the road leading to Birchwood in Alfreton.**

[16; see **28**] **The gift in free alms by him, Thomas Chaworth, of the land which Thomas of the Wood and William Tynet held in (Norton) Woodseats, saving the lands, meadows, and woods which the same Thomas and William hold by the river Sheaf.**

[17; see **29**] **The gift in free alms by him, Thomas Chaworth, of 1 bovate with tofts, crofts, and buildings which Richard Hore once held in Bradway.**

[18; see **30**] **The gift in free alms by him, Thomas Chaworth, of an annual rent of 5s for the land called the land of Robert the fletcher which they held in the soke of Norton.**

[19; see **31**] **The gift in free alms by him, Thomas Chaworth, of free passage for the animals, goods, and carriages of the abbey at Marnham ferry.**

[20; see **32**] **The gift in free alms by him, Thomas Chaworth, of 1 strip of land on the west side of Alfreton Hall.**

[21; see **60**] **The quitclaim by him, Thomas Chaworth, of the service of gilt spurs which they pay him annually for the land and tenement which they have in Wymeswold of the gift of Roger of Alfreton.**

[22; see **33**] **The gift in free alms by him, Thomas Chaworth, for the maintenance of a canon to commemorate his soul and those of his family at the altar of St Katherine, of his hamlet of Greenhill in the soke of Norton with Greenhill Moor, all services of its free tenants, all its serfs with their lands and tenements held in bondage, their families and chattels; of Hugh of Little Norton with all his family and their chattels and the tenement which he held in bondage at Little Norton; of the rent of 12s 8d which the abbey pays for diverse tenements in Alfreton and Norton; and of all his serfs in Woodseats near Norton with all their**

chattels, families, and lands in Woodseats, saving those which Thomas of the Wood and William Tinet hold by the river Sheaf.

Generalis confirmacio domini Thome Chaworth'

Omnibus sancte matris ecclesie filiis hoc scriptum visuris vel audituris Thomas de Chaworth' miles senior dominus de Norton' salutem in Domino sempiternam. Noverit universitas vestra me cartas, scripta et munimenta donacionum, concessionum et confirmacionum subscriptarum Deo et beate Marie et sancto Thome martiri[a] de Bello Capite ac religiosis viris abbati et conventui eiusdem loci tam per antecessores meos quam per me factarum inspexisse, videlicet donacionis quam Robertus filius Ranulphi per cartam suam fecit Deo et sancte Marie et sancto Thome martiri de Bello Capite ac[b] abbati et canonicis ibidem Deo servientibus in liberam et perpetuam elemosinam ad abbathiam construendam de loco qui dicitur Beauchef qui in Doreheseles [fo. 22r] situs est, silicet a Grenehyllheg' per Aldfeld[c] usque ad Quintynwell' et sic descendendo per rivulum prefate Quintinwell' usque ad aquam que dicitur Shava et per ipsam aquam descendendo usque ad le Brok' et per le Brok' ascendendo usque ad vadum ipsius le Brok' quod est ad viam que descendit de domo Alani et sic ascendendo per ipsam viam usque ad sartum predicti Alani et sic per sartum usque ad sarta Roberti et Petri et sic ascendendo usque ad predictum Grenhilheg' et quicquid infra metas horum terminorum continetur. Et de ecclesia de Norton' cum omnibus pertinenciis suis et de ecclesia de Alferton' cum omnibus pertinenciis suis. Et similiter de ecclesia de Wimundewold cum omnibus pertinenciis suis, et de ecclesia de Edwalton' cum omnibus pertinenciis suis, et de molendino de Norton' cum omni multura et omnibus pertinenciis suis et operibus et de sarto Hugonis juxta Meresbroke cum uno tofto in le Leyges et de uno tofto juxta domum Alani et de tota decima pannagii tocius terre mee et de duabus bovatis terre in Wimundewold de dumenio meo cum uno tofto continente tres acras terre unde octo seliones predictarum duarum bovatarum terre iacent ex parte occidentali ad Robbewong, et sex seliones ad Milnehyll', quinque seliones ad Netherbrombergh', undecim seliones ad Longben londeshend, sex seliones ad Martynhau, tres seliones ad Mikylwaterlondeshendes, quatuor seliones ad Hungurhill' et ex parte orientali predicti tofti de cultura eiusdem Roberti extra villam, ad Mousewelehende quatuor seliones, ad Marwaterlandes [fo. 22v] octo seliones, ad Marthegravegate quinque seliones, ad Comberdale novem seliones, infra vias quatuor seliones, et ad meridiem de Rykesyk sex seliones, ad Smalhengsikeshend novem seliones. Et eciam donacionis et confirmacionis quas idem Robertus per aliam cartam suam fecit Deo et sancto Thome martiri de Beauchef et fratribus ibidem Deo servientibus in liberam et perpetuam elemosinam de duabus bovatis terre in Wymundwolde, una silicet que fuit Alexandri cum tofto suo et altera que fuit Lovechild vidue cum omnibus pertinenciis suis. Et eciam donacionis et confirmacionis quas idem Robertus fecit per aliam cartam suam Deo et sancte Marie et sancto Thome martiri de Beauchef et fratribus ibidem Deo servientibus in puram et perpetuam elemosinam ad incrementum et ad situm prefati loci largiendum et ad aysiamenta sua facienda de loco qui dicitur Brokhyrst, a vado silicet de Tacheleford ascendendo per viam que vadit usque ad Westirley, et sic per medium Westerley apud orientem in rectum per medium le Brokehirste, usque ad viam que venit ascendendo de le Brokforde et sic per eandem viam apud meridiem usque le Brokford, et quicquid infra metas horum terminorum continetur. Et de uno sarto quod iacet inter sartum Hugonis filii Alberti de Bradway et terram Gerardi de Grenhill' juxta divisam de Byrchewode. Et eciam donacionis et confirmacionis quas Wilelmus filius Roberti per cartam suam fecit Deo et sancte Marie et sancto Thome martiri de Beauchefe et fratribus ibidem Deo servientibus in puram et perpetuam elemosinam de molendino de Aston' cum omni multura sua et omnibus pertinenciis. Et eciam donacionis, concessionis et confirmacionis quas Robertus filius Willelmi per cartam suam [fo. 23r] fecit Deo et beate Marie et sancto Thome martiri de Beauchefe et fratribus ibidem Deo servientibus in puram et perpetuam elemosinam de illa terra quam Helias de Trowey tenuit. Et eciam donacionis, concessionis et confirmacionis quas idem Robertus per aliam cartam suam fecit Deo et sancte Marie et ecclesie beati Thome martiris de Bello Capite et canonicis ibidem Deo servientibus in puram et perpetuam elemosinam de tribus acris terre juxta rivulum, qui descendit ab abbathia ad maiorem rivum de Scheve ex parte aquilonis, et de una libra cimini de servicio Rogeri de Riddyng' de terra de Shireokes. Et eciam donacionis, concessionis et confirmacionis quas idem Robertus per aliam cartam suam fecit Deo et beato Thome martiri de Bello Capite et canonicis ibidem Deo[d] servientibus in puram et perpetuam elemosinam de sexaginta acris terre cum bosco insuper crescente in territorio de Alferton' inter terram Suardi et inter Salhinwell'. Et eciam donacionis, concessionis et confirmacionis quas idem Robertus per aliam cartam fecit Deo et beato Thome martiri de Bello Capite et canonicis ibidem Deo servientibus in puram et perpetuam elemosinam de viginti quatuor acris terre, cum bosco insuper crescente in territorio de Norton' juxta tres acras terre que iacent juxta rivulum[e] qui[f] descendit ab abbathia usque ad maiorem rivum qui dicitur Scheve versus aquilonem. Et eciam donacionis, concessionis et confirmacionis quas ego predictus Thomas de Chaworth' per cartam meam feci Deo et ecclesie beati Thome martiris de Bello Capite et canonicis ibidem Deo servientibus in liberam, puram et perpetuam elemosinam de una bovata terre cum pertinenciis quam Adam filius [fo. 23v] Johannis del Clife aliquando tenuit in territorio de Norton', et de quinque acris assarti cum uno parcello in bosco de Norton' quas idem Adam tenuit, et de ipso Ada cum tota sequela sua et eorum catallis et de una bovata terre in territorio de Bradway et de octo acris assarti in dicto bosco de Norton' cum omnibus pertinenciis, quas Thomas filius Hugonis de bosco tenuit, et de ipso Thoma cum tota sequela sua et eorum catallis et de dimidia bovata terre cum pertinenciis suis in Cokshete, quam Winnora tenuit, et de ipsa Winnora cum tota sequela sua et eorum catallis et de uno assarto cum uno tofto cum pertinenciis in eadem villa, quod Henricus le Bercher tenuit, et de sex acris terre cum pertinenciis juxta aquam de Scheve iacentibus, quam Ricardus de mora tenuit. Et de quaterviginti acris terre cum pertinenciis in bosco de Norton', iacentibus ex parte aquilonari parci abbatis et conventus de Beauchef, sicut eisdem sunt assignate et mensurate ad assartandum et seminandum et includendum et ad omnimodum comodum suum inde faciendum. Et eciam donacionis, concessionis et confirmacionis quas per aliam cartam meam feci Deo et ecclesie ac abbati et conventui predictis in liberam, puram et perpetuam elemosinam de decem et octo solidatis redditus, quas Robertus le Redesmit reddere consuevit pro tenemento quod tenuit in Suanwike juxta Alferton', et de toto illo assarto cum tofto et crofto et pertinenciis suis, quod Rogerus faber tenuit in Byrchewod in soca de Alferton', et de una bovata terre cum pertinenciis, quam Adam[g] de Bychewod tenuit in eadem, et de tota illa terra cum pertinenciis quam Rogerus le Bercher tenuit in predicta soca de Alferton', et de [fo. 24r] toto illo assarto quod vocatur Robertridding buttante[h] de assarto predictorum abbatis et conventus[i] super communam de Leye, et de duabus solidatis redditus de tenemento quod Rogerus Mons tenuit in Alferton, et de duodecim denariatis[j] redditus de tenemento quod Nicholaus Thorald tenuit in Alferton', et de illa bovata terre cum pertinenciis quam Ricardus Horegh tenuit in Bradway et de Roberto del Greve nativo cum tota sequela sua et omnibus catallis suis ac toto tenemento cum pertinenciis quod tenuit in bondagio in soca de Norton'. Et eciam donacionis, concessionis et confirmacionis, quas per aliam cartam meam feci[k] eisdem abbati et conventui in liberam, puram et perpetuam elemosinam de tota illa terra quam Ricardus de Mora quondam tenuit in campo de Kocshete, iacenti inter boscum dictorum abbatis et conventus et terram quam Winnora de Kocshete quondam tenuit de eisdem. Et eciam donacionis, concessionis et confirmacionis quas per aliam cartam meam feci eisdem abbati et conventui in liberam, puram et perpetuam elemosinam de tota illa placea terre, sine ullo retenemento, que vocatur Eyclife, sicut iacet in longitudine inter terram quam idem abbas et conventus tenent et terram quam Thomas filius Johannis de bosco tenuit, et dilatat se a terra dictorum abbatis et conventus ascendendo usque ad terram arabilem supra collem versus austrum. Et eciam donacionis, concessionis et confirmacionis quas per aliam cartam meam feci Deo et ecclesie et canonicis predictis in liberam, puram et perpetuam elemosinam de uno tofto et crofto cum pertinenciis in le Kocshete, illud silicet quod Johannes faber quondam tenuit, et de uno [fo. 24v] curtilagio in villa de Alferton' juxta orreum dictorum canonicorum, quod tenuerunt tempore domini Roberti de Lathum, prout eis infra fossatum assignatur. Et eciam donacionis, concessionis et confirmacionis quas per aliam cartam meam feci Deo et beate Marie et ecclesie ac abbati et conventui predictis, in liberam, puram et perpetuam elemosinam, de tota illa terra que vocatur le Qwytekere, et de duodecim acris terre in loco qui vocatur Barsfelde, et de tota illa placea terre quam Petrus textor tenuit, juxta terram quondam Simonis del Storthes in territorio de Alferton'. Et eciam donacionis, concessionis et confirmacionis quas per aliam cartam meam feci Deo et ecclesie ac abbati et conventui predictis, in liberam, puram et perpetuam elemosinam, de quodam assarto quod Robertus Forester quondam tenuit, juxta bercariam dictorum canonicorum, ut iacet in longitudine. Et de tribus acris terre arabilis quas Robertus de Childre tenuit infra claustrum dictorum canonicorum, et de octo acris terre et dimidia quas Ranulphus de Storthes tenuit et iacent inter terram Sampsonis et terram Roberti Sharlete, et de quinque acris terre et dimidia quas Ricardus Edward quondam tenuit inter terram Roberti Scharlet et viam ducentem versus Byrchewod in territorio de Alferton'. Et eciam donacionis, concessionis et confirmacionis quas per aliam cartam meam feci dictis abbati et conventui in liberam, puram et perpetuam elemosinam de tota illa terra cum pertinenciis quam Thomas de bosco et Willelmus Tinet tenuerunt infra bundas de Wodsetes, salvis michi et heredibus meis terris pratis et boscis quas iidem Thomas et Willelmus [fo. 25r] tenent juxta aquam de Scheve. Et eciam donacionis, concessionis et confirmacionis quas per aliam cartam meam feci eisdem abbati et conventui in liberam, puram et perpetuam elemosinam de tota illa bovata terre cum toftis, croftis, edificiis et omnibus aliis pertinenciis suis, quam Ricardus Hore quondam tenuit in le Bradwey. Et eciam donacionis, concessionis et quietaclamacionis quas per aliam cartam meam feci eisdem abbati et conventui in liberam, puram et perpetuam elemosinam de illo annuo redditu quinque solidorum, quem michi solvere annuatim consueverunt pro illa terra que vocatur terra Roberti le fletcher in soca de Norton'. Et eciam donacionis, concessionis et confirmacionis quas per aliam cartam meam feci eisdem abbati et conventui in liberam, puram et perpetuam elemosinam de libero et quieto passagio ad feriam meam de Marnham habendo, tam ipsis quam familie sue de abbathia predicta, et de omnibus aliis locis suis cum omnibus animalibus, rebus ac cariagiis suis aliis quibuscumque et quandocumque opus habuerunt in meliori navigio ferie mee predicte, absque omni exaccione et demanda, libere et quiete. Et eciam donacionis, concessionis et confirmacionis quas per aliam cartam meam feci predictis abbati et conventui in liberam, puram et perpetuam elemosinam de una placea terre iacente ex parte occidentali aule sue in Alferton', sicut illam eis assignavi et divisi per certas metas de quodam ortulo meo. Et eciam relaxacionis et quietum clamacionis quas per scriptum meum feci predictis abbati et conventui et eorum successoribus in liberam, puram et perpetuam elemosinam de toto illo servicio, [fo. 25v] calcarium silicet deauratorum que michi annuatim[1] solvere tenebantur ad Pascha pro tota illa terra et tenementa cum pertinenciis suis que de me tenuerunt in Wimundewold, et que habuerunt de donis Rogeri de Allerton'. Et eciam donacionis, concessionis et confirmacionis quas per aliam cartam meam similiter feci Deo et ecclesie ac abbati et conventui predictis in liberam, puram et perpetuam elemosinam, pro salute anime mee et patris mei et matris mee uxorum mearum liberorumque meorum, et pro sustentacione unius canonici eiusdem loci divina perpetuo celebrantis ad altare sancte Katerine in ecclesia predicta pro anima mea et animabus predictorum omnium et omnium fidelium defunctorum et pro sollempni servicio annuatim habendo inperpetuum, sicut pro uno abbate defuncto, de toto illo hameleto in soca de Norton' quod vocatur Grenehyll', una cum tota mora de Grenehyll' et cum omnibus homagiis, wardis, releviis, redditibus, escaetis, sectis, serviciis tam forincicis quam aliis quibuscumque libere tenencium in hameleto predicto, cum omnibus pertinenciis suis et approvamentis suis de omnibus nativis de eodem hameleto, cum terris tenementisque que de me tenuerunt in bondagio in eodem hameleto et extra, cum sequelis, sectis, redditibus et serviciis, consuetudinibus et catallis, ac omnibus aliis approvamentis et pertinenciis suis infra hameletum predictum et extra, sine aliquo retenemento, et de Hugone de Parva Nortona nativo meo cum tota sequela sua et cum omnibus catallis suis et de toto tenemento quod de me tenuit in bondagio in Perva [fo. 26r] Nortona. Et de duodecim solidatis et octo denariatis redditus quas predicti abbas et conventus michi reddere solebant pro

THE BEAUCHIEF ABBEY CARTULARY

diversis tenementis que de me tenuerunt in Alferton' et Norton'. Et de omnibus nativis meis in le Wodsetes juxta Norton' cum omnibus catallis et sequelis suis. Et de omnibus terris que ipsi nativi, seu alii, de me tenuerunt infra bundas de Wodsetes, sine aliquo retenemento, salvis tamen michi et heredibus meis terris pratis cum boscis que Thomas de bosco et Willelmus Tinet de me tenent juxta aquam de Sheve. Et cartas, scripta ac munimenta predicta rata habens pariter et accepta[m] omnes et singulas donaciones, concessiones et confirmaciones in eisdem cartis, scriptis et munimentis contentas, tam videlicet nominatas quam non nominatas, Deo et beate Marie et predicte ecclesie beati Thome martiris de Bello Capite necnon et abbati et conventui eiusdem loci et eorum successoribus concedo et confirmo omnino de me et heredibus meis quietum clamo in liberam, puram et perpetuam elemosinam inperpetuum possidendo. Propterea volo et concedo quod ego et heredes mei omnes et singulas donaciones et concessiones predictas antedictis abbati et conventui et eorum successoribus contra omnes gentes warantizabimus, acquietabimus et inperpetuum defendemus. Et ut hec mea concessio et confirmacio perpetue firmitatis robur optineant, presens scriptum sigilli mei inposicione roboravi. Hiis testibus: dominis Thoma de Furnivall', Edmundo de Aiencourt, Henrico de Bralesford, [fo. 26v] Laurencio de Chaworth, Roberto de Ecclessall' militibus, domino Rogero de Bralesforde rectore ecclesie de Dronfeld, Willelmo le Brett, Johanne de Aiencourt, Rogero de Bercton', Stephano le Aier', Rogero de Dukmanton', et aliis.[2] Dat' apud Norton' feria tercia proxima post festum sancti Egidii abbatis anno gracie millesimo tricentesimo duodecimo, quod est anno regni domini Edwardi regis filii regis Edwardi sexto.

[a] *a* of *martiri* interlined.   [b] *a.*   [c] first *d* of *Aldfeld* interlined.
[d] *de.*   [e] *l* of *rivulum* interlined.   [f] *que.*   [g] *Adam* interlined.
[h] *buttate.*   [i] *coventus.*   [j] *denarratis.*   [k] *de* deleted.   [l] *annuati.*
[m] *acceppta.*

[1] In this calendar, the charters confirmed have been numbered to facilitate cross-reference with transcripts of the originals located elsewhere in the Cartulary and in the *Inspeximus* of 1316. Thomas is here described as 'the elder' to distinguish him from his grandson and heir apparent, Thomas Chaworth II, who two months later confirmed all the gifts to the abbey made by his grandfather and other ancestors in a charter that states that his father William was then dead (**44**).
[2] For some of the witnesses see **18**, n. 2. Dugdale in *Monasticon Anglicanum*, VI, part 2, p. 884, no. 3, printed another general confirmation of the abbey's possessions in Norton, Alfreton, and Wymeswold which, unlike **38**, does not go into details. The witnesses are: Nicholao Wake, domino Johanne le Heriz, domino Willielmo de Staynisby, dominis Willielmo et Egidio de Meynile, Roberto Sautcheverel, Johanne de Anislay, militibus, Roberto le Grant, Johanne de Brunnigtona, Hugo de canonicis, Hugo de Lynakir, et aliis. Nicholas Wake

was lord of Chesterfield from 1268 (J.M. Bestall, *History of Chesterfield, I: Early and Medieval Chesterfield* (Chesterfield, 1974), p. 105; G.H. White (ed.), *The Complete Peerage of England, Scotland, Ireland, Great Britain and the United Kingdom*, XII, part 2 (London, 1959), p. 299n.). For Sir John de Heriz (d. 1299) and Sir William of Stainsby (d. 1289) see **26**, n. 4. William of Meynill (Langley) was a justice for gaol delivery at the 1281 Derbyshire eyre and Giles of Meynell acted as surety there (Hopkinson, *Derbyshire Eyre*, pp. 20 and 160). Giles of Meynell was a Member of Parliament in 1295 (Turbutt, *Derbyshire*, II, p. 620). Robert le Grant and Hugh de canonicis appear in **60** (1279) and **70** (1278) respectively. Hugh of Linacre appears in **61** (1312). Edmund of Ainecourt claimed free warren at Elmton and Holmesfield at the 1281 Derbyshire eyre (Hopkinson, *Derbyshire Eyre*, p. 123). Sir Thomas Chaworth, who made grants from Greenhill, Woodseats, and Alfreton, is commemorated in the Obituary (24 September).

[GIFTS BY THOMAS DE CHAWORTH I, II, AND III][1]

39. Gift in free alms by Thomas Chaworth, knight, lord of Norton, to Beauchief abbey, for the maintenance of a canon to commemorate his soul and those of his family at the altar of the Holy Cross, of the hamlet of Greenhill in the soke of Norton with all his tenants there with their families, chattels, lands, and services. [c.1301][2]

Carta domini Thome Chaworth de Grenhill'

Sciant presentes et futuri quod ego Thomas de Chaworth miles dominus de Norton' dedi, concessi et hac presenti carta mea confirmavi Deo[a] et ecclesie beati Thome martiris de Bello Capite et religiosis viris abbati et conventui eiusdem loci in liberam, puram et perpetuam elemosinam, pro salute anime mee et patris mei et matris mee uxorum mearum liberorumque meorum et omnium antecessorum et successorum meorum, et pro sustentacione unius canonici divina perpetuo celebrantis ad altare sancte Crucis in ecclesia predicta pro anima mea et animabus predictorum et omnium fidelium defunctorum, totum illud hameletum meum de Grenhill' in soca de Norton', et omnes tenentes meos tam liberos quam nativos cum omnibus catallis et sequelis suis et eorum tenementis, redditibus et serviciis eorumdem, et omnibus aliis eorum provenientibus, homagiis, wardis, releviis, maritagiis, marchetis, auxiliis, recognicionibus, cariagiis, consuetudinibus, sectis curiarum et omnimodis aliis sectis et serviciis, cum moris, marchis et maressis, boscis, planis, viis, semitis, pratis, pascuis et pasturis, turbariis, quareris, mineris et omnimodis aliis como[fo. 27r]ditatibus, libertatibus, communiis et aysiamentis, et omnibus aliis pertinenciis suis quibuscumque que michi et heredibus vel assignatis meis vel heredibus heredum vel assignatorum meorum de predicto hameleto de Grenhyll' et tenentibus et tenementis eorumdem poterunt evenire inperpetuum quoquomodo, sine aliquo retenemento. Tenendum et habendum sibi et successoribus suis libere, quiete, pacifice et integre, in liberam, puram et perpetuam elemosinam, sicut aliqua elemosina liberius et quiecius dari poterit et concedi. Et ego predictus Thomas et heredes et assignati mei et heredes heredum vel assignatorum meorum predictum hameletum de Grenhill' tenentes et tenementa eorumdem cum omnibus pertinenciis suis, sicut predictum est, predictis religiosis abbati et conventui de Bello Capite predicto et eorum successoribus in liberam, puram et perpetuam elemosinam contra omnes gentes warantizabimus, acquietabimus et imperpetuum defendemus. In cuius rei testimonium presenti carte sigillum meum apposui. Hiis testibus: domino Ricardo de Ffourneus, domino Waltero de Gousill', domino Ada de Everingham, domino Rogero le Brett militibus, domino Rogero de Bralisfford rectore ecclesie de Dronfeld, Willelmo le Brett, Johanne de Eynecourt, Rogero le Breton', Simone de Rerisby, Johanne de Brimington, Hugone de Linacre, et aliis.

[a] *De.*

[1] None of the charters under this heading (**39-56**) appears in either the confirmation of 1312 or the *Inspeximus* of 1316. Two (**47** and **48**) and possibly a third (**49**) are charters of Sir Thomas Chaworth I; **44** is a charter of his grandson, Sir Thomas Chaworth II; and **50** is a charter of Sir Thomas Chaworth III, the latter's son.
[2] This charter is the second of four concerned with the maintenance of a priest at the altar of the Holy Cross in the abbey, the other charters being **18**, **40**, and **41**. Sir Thomas Chaworth I made further gifts for the maintenance of a priest to commemorate his soul and those of his family in **22** and in a charter printed by Dugdale (see **18**, n. 1). The gifts were perhaps made *c.*1301, when Sir Thomas obtained a mortmain licence for the same purpose (see **18**, n. 1). The witness lists suggest that **39**, **40**, and **41** also date from about the same time. (cf. **61** and **71**).

40. Gift in free alms by Thomas Chaworth, knight, lord of Norton, to Beauchief abbey, for the maintenance of a canon to commemorate his soul and those of his family annually at the altar of the Holy Cross, of the hamlet of Greenhill in the soke of Norton with all services of free tenants, all serfs with their lands, tenements, and services; of Hugh of Little Norton with his family and their chattels and his rent and service and all his tenement which he holds in bondage;

and of an annual rent of 12s 8d which the abbey pay for diverse tenements in Alfreton and Norton. [*c*.1301][1]

Alia carta domini Thome Chaworth' de Grenhill'

Sciant presentes et futuri quod ego Thomas de Chaworth' miles dominus de Norton' dedi, concessi et hac presenti carta mea confirmavi Deo[a] et monasterio beati Thome martiris de Bello [fo. 27v] Capite et religiosis viris abbati et conventui eiusdem loci in liberam, puram et perpetuam elemosinam, pro salute anime mee et patris mei et matris mee uxorum mearum liberorumque meorum, et pro sustentacione unius canonici eiusdem monasterii divina perpetuo celebrantis ad altare sancte Crucis in ecclesia de Bello Capite predicta pro anima mea et pro animabus predictorum et omnium fidelium defunctorum et pro solempni servicio annuatim habendo inperpetuum, sicut pro uno abbate defuncto, totum illud hameletum meum in soca de Norton' quod vocatur Grenhill' sine ullo retenemento, cum omnibus homagiis, wardis, releviis, redditibus, escaetis, sectis, serviciis tam forinsecis quam aliis quibuscumque omnium libere tenencium meorum in hameleto de Grenhill' predicto, tam presenciorum quam futurorum, cum omnibus approvamentis et aliis pertinenciis suis et cum omnibus nativis meis in ipso hameleto, et cum terris et tenementis que de me tenuerunt in bondagio in eodem hameleto et extra cum sectis, sequelis, redditibus et serviciis consuetudinibus et catallis et omnimodis aliis approvamentis et pertinenciis suis infra hameletum de Grenhill' predictum et extra, sine aliquo retenemento, et totum redditum et servicium Hugonis de Parva Nortona et ipsum Hugonem cum tota sequela sua et cum omnibus catallis suis et cum toto tenemento suo quod de me tenuit in bondagio. Dedi eciam et concessi Deo et monasterio de Bello Capite predicto et religiosis viris abbati et conventui eiusdem loci duodecim solidos et octo denarios annui redditus, quo predicti abbas et conventus michi reddere solebant pro diversis tenementis que de me tenuerunt in Alferton et Norton'. Habendum et tenendum Deo et monasterio predicto ac religiosis viris abbati et conventui predictis et eorum successoribus in liberam, puram et perpetuam elemo[fo. 28r]sinam cum pratis, boscis, pascuis, pasturis, moris, turbariis, quarariis, mineris, marlariis et omnimodis libertatibus, comuniis, aysiamentis et aliis approvamentis[b] et pertinenciis suis quibuscumque infra hameletum de Grenhill' predictum et extra, tam infra terram quam supra, michi et heredibus meis et assignatis meis vel heredibus heredum et assignatorum meorum inde poterunt accidere. Et ego predictus Thomas et heredes mei et assignati mei et eorum heredes omnia predicta homagia, wardas, relevia, redditus, eschaetas, sectas et servicia tam forinseca quam alia quecumque omnium libere tenencium meorum predictorum cum omnimodis approvamentis et pertinenciis suis, ac eciam omnes nativos meos predictos cum omnibus terris et tenementis predictis et omnimodis eorum sectis, sequelis, redditibus et serviciis, consuetudinibus et catallis et omnimodis aliis approvamentis et pertinenciis suis quibuscumque, tam nominatis quam non nominatis, sine aliquo retenemento, Deo et monasterio predicto ac religiosis viris abbati et conventui predictis et eorum successoribus in liberam, puram et perpetuam elemosinam contra omnes gentes warantizabimus, acquietabimus et inperpetuum defendemus. In cuius rei testimonium presenti carte sigillum meum apposui. Hiis testibus: dominis Thoma de Furnivall', Ada de Everingham, Waltero de Goushill', Ricardo de Furneus, Roberto de Ecclessall' militibus, domino Rogero de Bralesford rectore ecclesie de Dronfeld, Willelmo le Brett, Johanne de Ayencourt, Rogero le Breton', Simone de Rerisby, Johanne[c] de Brimington', Hugone de Lynacre, et multis aliis.

[a] *De.*   [b] *apprvamentis.*   [c] Odd abbreviation: *Jhoe [Jhoanne].*

[1] For the date and the witnesses, see **18**, nn. 1 and 2; cf. also **33**, **39**, and **41**.

41. Gift in free alms by Thomas Chaworth, knight, lord of Norton, to Beauchief abbey, for the maintenance of a canon to commemorate his soul and those of his family at the altar of the Holy Cross, of the hamlet of Greenhill in the soke of Norton with all his tenants with their chattels, families, tenements, rents, and services, together with Greenhill Moor. [c.1301][1]

Carta domini Thome Chaworth' de Grenhill'

Sciant presentes et futuri quod ego Thomas de Chaworth' miles dominus de Norton' dedi, concessi et hac presenti carta mea confirmavi [fo. 28v] Deo et ecclesie beati Thome martiris de Bello Capite et religiosis viris abbati et conventui eiusdem loci, in liberam, puram et perpetuam elemosinam, pro salute anime mee et patris mei et matris mee uxorum mearum liberorumque meorum et omnium antecessorum et successorum meorum, et pro sustentacione unius canonici divina perpetuo celebrantis ad altare sancte Crucis in ecclesia predicta pro anima mea et animabus predictorum et omnium fidelium defunctorum, totum illud hameletum meum quod vocatur Grenhill' in soca de Norton' et omnes tenentes meos, tam liberos quam nativos, cum omnibus catallis et sequellis suis, et eorum tenementis, redditibus et serviciis eorumdem et omnibus aliis eorum proventibus, homagiis, wardis, releviis, marchetis, maritagiis, auxiliis, recognitionibus, cariagiis, consuetudinibus, sectis curiarum et omnimodis aliis sectis et serviciis, una cum tota illa mora que vocatur Grenhill' More, sicut plenius iacet per certas divisas, et cum omnibus aliis moris, marchis et marescis, boscis, planis, viis, semitis, pratis, pascuis et pasturis, turbariis, quareriis,[a] mineris et omnimodis aliis comoditatibus, libertatibus, comuniis et aysiamentis et omnibus aliis pertinenciis suis quibuscumque que michi et heredibus vel assignatis meis vel heredum heredibus vel assignatorum meorum de predicto hameleto Grenhyll' et tenentibus et tenementis eorundem poterunt evenire inperpetuum quoquomodo, sine aliquo retenemento. Tenendum et habendum sibi et successoribus suis libere, quiete, pacifice et integre, in liberam, puram et perpetuam elemosinam, sicut aliqua elemosina liberius et quiecius dari poterunt et concedi. Et ego predictus Thomas et heredes et assignati mei et heredes heredum [fo. 29r] vel assignatorum meorum predictum hameletum Grenhill', tenentes et tenementa eorumdem cum pertinenciis suis, sicut predictum est, predictis religiosis abbati et conventui de Bello Capite predictis et eorum successoribus in liberam, puram et perpetuam elemosinam contra omnes gentes warantizabimus, acquietabimus et inperpetuum defendemus. In cuius rei testimonium presenti carte sigillum meum apposui. Hiis testibus: domino Ricardo de Ffurneus, domino Waltero de Goushill', domino Adam de Everingham, domino Rogero le Brett militibus, domino Rogero de Brlisford rectore ecclesie de Dronfelde, Willelmo le Brett, Johanne de Ayencourt, Rogero le Breton', Ada de Rerisby, Petro de Brimington', Hugone de Linacre, et aliis.

[a] *quareris.*

[1] An original copy of this charter is in Sheffield Archives among the deeds of Norton parish church, PR2/16. It was printed by Addy, *Historical Memorials*, pp. 61–63, who omitted the name of Roger le Brett from the witness list and wrote (probably mistakenly) that a seal of green wax was appended with a good impression of the Chaworth arms; there is no seal today. **39** and **40** are similar.

42. Gift in free alms by Thomas Chaworth, knight, to Beauchief abbey of ½ rod near the mill of Aston or Hazlehurst west of the waterway of the mill for transferring the mill from the east of the waterway to the west for the great easement of the mill to be erected in that

place which Roger Pykard held.[1] **The abbey quitclaimed to Thomas 1 rod of arable land which they had in Aston field. [1270–1315]**

Carta domini Thome Chaworth' de molendino de Aston'

Noverint universi hoc presens scriptum visuri vel audituri quod ego Thomas de Chaworth miles dedi, concessi et hac presenti carta mea confirmavi Deo et sancte Marie et ecclesie beati Thome martiris de Beuchef et abbati et conventui eiusdem loci unam dimidiam rodam terre iacentem juxta molendinum suum de Aston' vel Hasilhyrst ex occidentali parte ductus et cursus aque dicti molendini ad transferendum dictum molendinum ab orientali parte dicti cursus aque in occidentalem partem illius ad maius aysiamentum dicti molendini construendi in illa placea quam Rogerus Pykard de me tenuit. Tenendum et habendum dictis abbati et conventui et eorum successoribus ad aisiamentum dicti molendini in eadem placea terre, sicut eis est assignata, [fo. 29v] et mensurata pro voluntate sua transferendi et in feodo[a] meo levandi eo quod hoc dictis abbati et conventui et eorum successoribus a tempore fundacionis dicti monasterii per magnam cartam advoti sui antecessor mei quam vidi et audivi concessum est usitatum et per me confirmatum. Dicti autem abbas et conventus quietum clamaverunt michi et heredibus meis inperpetuum unam rodam terre arabilis quam habuerunt in campo de Aston. Et ego dictus Thomas et heredes mei et assignati dictam placeam terre sicut iacet inter suos rivulos mensurata et assignata dictis abbati et conventui et eorum successoribus in liberam, puram et perpetuam elemosinam cum aysiamentis[b] per vias et semitas infra feodum meum ad dictum molendinum in dicta placea transferendum et construendum et omnimodum comodum suum in ea faciendum[c] contra omnes homines warantizabimus, acquietabimus et inperpetuum defendemus. In cuius rei testimonium presenti carte sigillum meum apposui. Hiis testibus: Ricardo marescallo de Norton', Thoma de Wodhous fratre eius, Petro de Bernis, Johanne de Bircheheved, Hugone de eadem, Roberto le Graunt, Thoma clerico, et aliis.[2]

[a] *fedo.*   [b] *aysiaments.*   [c] *i* of *faciendum* interlined.

[1] Coal Aston mill was originally given to the abbey by William son of Robert (**7**). See also **45** for a windmill at Coal Aston, which was harming the watermill there, and **91** for the abbey's title to the watermill granted by Sir William Chaworth (son of Sir Thomas Chaworth I).
[2] Peter de Bernis and Robert le Graunt also witnessed **60** (1279).

43. Gift in free alms by Sir Thomas Chaworth to Beauchief abbey of 1 strip 40 feet in length and 40 feet in width on the east of 1 toft which the abbey has in Greenhill and which Alice Loole once held of them. [1270–1315]

Alia carta domini Thome Chaworth de terra in Grenhill'

Omnibus hoc scriptum visuris vel audituris dominus Thomas de Chaworth salutem in Domino. Noverit universitas vestra me dedisse, concessisse et hac presenti carta mea confirmasse abbati et conventui de Bello Capite, in liberam et perpetuam elemosinam, unam placeam terre quadraginta pedes in longitudine [fo. 30r] et quadraginta pedes in latitudine continent[em], sicut eisdem assignatur et mensuram ex parte orientali unius tofti quod dicti abbas et conventus habent in Grenhyll', quod iidem ten[ementum] Alicia Loole quondam de eisdem tenere consuevit. Habendum et tenendum in liberam et perpetuam elemosinam ad omnimodum comodum suum inde faciendum inperpetuum. Ego vero Thomas et heredes mei predictam placeam terre dictis abbati et conventui et eorum successoribus contra omnes gentes warantizabimus, acquietabimus et inperpetuum defendemus. In cuius rei testimonium presenti scripto sigillum meum apposui. Hiis testibus: domino Gervasio de Berniak, Willelmo de Gaham,[1] Hugone de la Wodhous, Thoma de Leys, Johanne de Byrcheheved, et aliis.

[1]Witnessed a deed at Norton in 1317 (Hall, *Ancient Charters*, p. 11). Sometimes recorded as William of Gotham; see **35**, n. 5.

44. Confirmation by Thomas Chaworth, knight, son of the late Sir William Chaworth, knight, to Beauchief abbey of all lands, tenements, rents etc. which the abbey had from Sir Thomas Chaworth, his grandfather, and from all his other ancestors in the vills of Wymeswold and Marnham and in the sokes of Norton and Alfreton. Made at Beauchief on 11 November 1312.[1]

Confirmacio domini Thome Chaworth' de omnibus possessionibus nostris

Omnibus ad quorum noticiam hoc presens scriptum pervenerit Thomas de Chaworth' miles filius quondam domini Willelmi de Chaworth militis salutem in Domino sempiternam. Noveritis me concessisse, confirmasse et omnino de me et heredibus meis quietum clamasse inperpetuum religiosis viris abbati et conventui de Bello Capite et eorum successoribus omnes terras et tenementa, redditus, advocaciones ecclesiarum, jura, possessiones ac libertates quascumque, cum omnibus pertinenciis suis, que et quas idem abbas et conventus habent de dono et concessione domini Thome de Chaworth' avi mei ceterorumque antecessorum meorum in villis de Wimundewold in comitatu Leygcestre et Marnham in comitatu Notingham et in socis de Norton' et Alferton' in comitatu Derby. Habendum [fo. 30v] et tenendum in liberam, puram et perpetuam elemosinam. Ita quod nec [ego] predictus Thomas filius Willelmi predicti nec heredes mei nec aliquis per nos seu nomine nostro aliquod jus vel clameum seu calumpniam in prenominatis terris, tenementis, redditibus, advocationibus, juribus, possessionibus ac libertatibus, nec in aliqua parte eorumdem seu eorum pertinenciis, exigere vel vendicare decetero poterimus quoquomodo. In cuius rei testimonium presenti scripto sigillum meum apposui. Hiis testibus: dominis Thoma de Furnivall', Ada de Everingham, Roberto de Wadeslay militibus, domino Rogero de Bralesford rectore ecclesie de Dronfeld, Willelmo le Brett, Johanne de Ayencourt, Hugone Linacre, et aliis. Data apud Bellum Caput in festo sancti Martini episcopi anno gracie millesimo ccc^{mo} duodecimo, quod est anno regni domini Edwardi regis filii regis Edwardi sexto.[1]

[1] This is the only charter in this group which is definitely a deed of Sir Thomas Chaworth II. It was issued two months after his grandfather's general confirmation (**38**), presumably to reinforce that charter. A duplicate of **44** is entered later in the Cartulary as **61**. An original of this charter, with a small seal of green wax on a tag, bearing the Chaworth arms, and listing the same witnesses, survives in Sheffield Archives (Norton parish church deeds, PR2/20A), along with a duplicate that is not an indenture and that also has a small seal, with red and white cords and bearing the Chaworth arms (PR2/20B). Addy, *Historical Memorials*, pp. 63–64, printed one of these. Confirmed in 1316 (Appendix II, no. 52).
[2] For the witnesses see **18**, n. 2; for Robert of Wadsley, who held property in Rotherham, see Holdsworth, *Rufford Charters*, III, p. 535 and nos 989 (12 December 1307) and 990.

45. Gift in free alms by Thomas Chaworth, knight, to Beauchief abbey of the windmill which he built near Aston which was seen to harm the abbey's mill at Aston, with all the suit of multure of Aston, 1 rod for a sufficient place around the mill, and sufficient easement for roads and paths in his fee. Thomas promises to build no more mills in Norton or Aston or the surrounding area. It is permitted for the abbey to transfer the windmill elsewhere in his fee.

It is permitted for Thomas to grind his corn from Norton at the abbey's mill without any toll. [1260–1315][1]

Carta de molendino de Aston'

Sciant omnes tam presentes quam futuri quod ego Thomas de Chaworth miles dedi, concessi et hoc presenti scripto confirmavi abbati et conventui de Bello Capite et eorum successoribus, in liberam, puram et perpetuam elemosinam, molendinum ventriticum quod levavi juxta Aston', ut videbatur ad nocumentum et impedimentum molendini dictorum abbatis et conventus de Aston' et secte multure sue eiusdem ville. Tenendum et habendum dictum molendinum dictis abbati et conventui et eorum successoribus in liberam, puram et perpetuam elemosinam cum tota secta multure de Aston' et cum una roda terre ad placeam sufficientem circa dictum molendinum et cum sufficienti aysiamente [fo. 31r] per vias et semitas in feodo meo ad molendinum. Ita quod nec ego dictus Thomas nec heredes mei seu assignati aliquod aliud molendinum levare poterimus in feodo de Norton' vel de Aston' nec alubi in vicinio ad nocumentum molendinorum dictorum abbatis et conventus, scilicet licebit dictis abbati et conventui et eorum successoribus dictum molendinum ventricium alubi transferre, et scilicet comodum suum in feodo meo collocare, salvo et sine impedimento mei et cuiuscumque alterius, salvis eciam sibi sectis de Norton' et de Aston' molum sua, scilicet quod ego dictus Thomas et heredes mei molemus bladum nostrum et libere faurulie nostre de Norton' sine tolneto multure dande ad molendinum dictorum abbatis et conventus dum ego et heredes mei ibidem perudinaverimus.[a] In cuius rei testimonium presenti scripto sigillum meum apposui. Hiis testibus: domino Thoma Folijambe, Willelmo fratre eius, Petro de Bernis, Thoma de Wodhous, Johanne de Bycheheved, et aliis.[2]

[a] *perhudinaverimus.*

[1] See also **42** and **91**.
[2] Thomas Foljambe witnessed **70** (1278) and Peter de Bernis witnessed **70** (1278) and **60** (1279). William Foljambe was recorded at the 1281 Derbyshire eyre (Hopkinson, *Derbyshire Eyre*, p. 162).

46. Notification by Thomas de Chaworth, knight, lord of Norton, that because he has confirmed all charters, writings, and muniments of gifts, grants, and confirmations of lands, tenements, and church advowsons made by him and his ancestors to Beauchief abbey, he

now wills and grants that if the abbot and convent, their successors, or their men and tenants commit any offence or transgression against him, his heirs, or their men and tenants, then they must answer to him, his heirs, or their men and tenants in his courts of Norton and Alfreton, held at either Norton church if the transgression is committed there or Alfreton church if the transgression is committed there. [1312–1315][1]

Alia carta domini Thome Chaworth' valde necessaria

Universis sancte matris ecclesie filiis ad quos presens scriptum pervenerit Thomas de Chaworth miles dominus de Norton' salutem in Domino sempiternam. Cum nuper habita super hoc deliberacione pleniori cartas, scripta et munimenta donacionum, concessionum et confirmacionum Deo et ecclesie beati Thome martiris de Bello Capite et religiosis viris abbati et conventui ibidem Deo servientibus de terris, tenementis et advocacionibus ecclesiarum, tam per me quam per antecessores[a] meos factarum, diligenter inspexerim, et donaciones, concessiones et confirmaciones [fo. 31v] predictas acceptaverim, et per cartam meam eisdem abbati et conventui et eorum successoribus in liberam, puram et perpetuam elemosinam inperpetuum tenendum confirmaverim, cupiens quod ad honorem Dei et pro salute anime mee et animabus antecessorum et successorum meorum et omnium fidelium defunctorum, predictas donaciones, concessiones et confirmaciones taliter in puram elemosinam factas et concessas absque redaccione in servitutem aliqualiter inviolabiliter observari, ut religiosi predicti devocius, tranquillius et quiecius divinis obsequiis absque mei[b] vel heredum meorum fatigacione seu inquietacione vacare possint graciam facere uberiorem, volo et concedo pro me et heredibus meis quod si contingat deceterum quod absit prefatos abbatem et conventum ac eorum successores seu eorum homines ac tenentes vel eorum aliquem erga me vel heredes meos seu homines et tenentes nostros quoscumque in aliquo delinquere contemptus delictum aliquid transgressiones sive perrales sive reales fuerint perpetrare non propter hoc summoniantur distringantur aut actachientur ad respondendum inde michi aut heredibus meis seu hominibus aut tenentibus nostris in curiis nostris de Norton' et Alferton' seu alibi, set inde sicut[c] emende et correcciones ad ecclesiam de Norton', si in partibus illis, vel ad ecclesiam de Alferton', si in partibus illis, fiat aliqua huiusmodi transgressio et non alibi, et hoc per visum et assensum proborum et legalium virorum de concensu parcium ad hoc electorum, sicut inter vicinum et vicuum et non alio modo. Et ego predictus Thomas et heredes mei predictam libertatem sive [fo. 32r] concessionem prefatis abbati et conventui et eorum successoribus pro se et hominibus ac tenentibus suis utenda warantizabimus et defendemus inperpetuum. In cuius rei testimonium presenti scripto sigillum meum apposui. Hiis testibus: domino Henrico de Bralesford, domino Rogero le Brett militibus, Willelmo le Brett, Rogero Breton', Ada de Rerisby, Stephano le Eyre, Hugone de Linacre, Waltero de Ufton', Johanne de Wyggeley,[2] et aliis.

[a] *ancessores.*   [b] *me.*   [c] *sicut* interlined.

[1] Although not included in the inspection of 1316, this charter seems likely to have been issued by Sir Thomas Chaworth I, sometime between the general confirmation of 1312 (**38**) and his death three years later. The witness list is very similar to **44** and **61**, both of which are dated 1312. Addy, in *Historical Memorials*, Appendix, pp. 144–145, printed a charter similar to **46** that he found in Beauchief Hall (a facsimile appears on the title page), but its whereabouts are now unknown; it lacks three witnesses named in **46**.

[2] John Wigley also witnessed **54**, and he or his namesake witnessed grants of land in Brampton (1310, 1338) and Dore (c.1330) (I.H. Jeayes, *A Descriptive Catalogue of Derbyshire Charters in Public and Private Libraries and Muniment Rooms* (London and Derby, 1906), nos 429, 439, 440, 1019).

47. Letter by the same Thomas Chaworth,[1] lord of Norton, that he has appointed John Tonk as his attorney for placing Beauchief abbey in full and peaceful seisin in all lands and tenants in the sokes of Norton and Alfreton. Made at Norton on Friday 24 November 1301.[2]

Littera eiusdem Thome ad liberandam sesinam

Universis Cristi fidelibus presentes litteras inspecturis vel audituris Thomas de Chaworth miles dominus de Norton' salutem in Domino. Noverit universitas vestra me attornarrasse dilectum virum in Cristo Johannem Tonk ad ponendum abbatem et conventum de Bello Capite in plenam et pacificam sesinam in omnibus terris[a] et tenentibus, tam liberis quam nativis, in soca de Norton' et in soca de Alferton' cum omnibus pertinenciis suis, de quibus habent cartas donacionis mee. In cuius rei testimonium presentibus sigillum meum apposui. Act' et dat' apud Norton' die veneris in crastino sancti Clementis martiris anno Domini m° ccc^{mo} primo et regni regis Edwardi tricesimo.

[a] *terris* interlined.

[1] The headings of **47–50** and **52–53** attribute each of these groups of documents to 'the same Thomas', presumably (in the first group) the Thomas who issued **46** and (in the second group) the Thomas who issued **51**. However, there is some doubt about the identity

because, although **47** is dated 1301, **50** is dated 1350 and was issued by Thomas Chaworth III, great-grandson of Thomas Chaworth I.

[2] This power of attorney must almost certainly be connected with the mortmain licence issued on 1 November 1301, by which Sir Thomas Chaworth I was allowed to alienate a considerable estate in Alfreton and Norton for the maintenance of a chaplain to celebrate divine service in the abbey for his soul and those of his wife, Joan, and their ancestors (*Calendar of Patent Rolls, Edward I, III: 1292–1301*, p. 616). See also **18**, **22**, **33**, and **39–41**.

48. Quitclaim by the same Thomas Chaworth, knight, to Beauchief abbey of Robert of the Greaves in the soke of Norton, his serf, with all his family and their chattels. [1270–1312]

Carta eiusdem Thome de Roberto de le Grevus nativo

Omnes ad quos presens scriptum pervenerit Thomas de Chaworth miles salutem in Domino sempiternam. Noveritis me pro salute anime mee et omnium antecessorum et successorum meorum dedisse, concessisse et omnino pro me et heredibus meis remisisse et quietum clamasse abbati [fo. 32v] et conventui de Bello Capite in liberam, puram et perpetuam elemosinam Robertum in le Greves in soca de Norton', nativum meum, cum tota sequela sua procreata et procreanda et eorum sequelis, cum catallis suis omnibus et omnibus eorum catallis adquisitis et adquirendis. Ita quod nec ego predictus Thomas nec heredes mei nec aliquis pro nobis nec per nos seu nomine nostro in dicto Roberto nec in catallis suis nec in tota sequela sua nec in catallis eorum aliquod jus vel juris clameum decetero habere exigere vel vendicare poterimus quoquomodo racione vel eventu. In cuius rei testimonium presenti scripto sigillum meum apposui. Hiis testibus: Willelmo Matany de Gravesend, Thoma de la Wodhouse, Rogero carpentario de Norton', Petro del Bernes, Johanne de Byrcheheved, et aliis.[1]

[1] William Matiney (on this occasion only) is said to be of Gravesend; he also witnessed **70** (1278). Peter de Bernis also witnessed **70** (1278) and **60** (1279).

49. Grant by the same Thomas Chaworth, knight, to Beauchief abbey of the land which Robert the Fletcher[1] once held which lies between the land which William son of Sunun holds and that which Adam of the Cliffe once held to the west on the river Sheaf and to the east on the Fulsyk with the strip which the same Robert held on the other

part of the Fulsyke. The canons shall render to Thomas 5s annually. [1260–1315]

Alia carta eiusdem Thome de terra quam Robertus Forst' quondam tenuit

Omnibus Cristi fidelibus hanc presentem cartam visuris vel audituris Thomas de Chaworth miles salutem in Domino. Noveritis me dedisse, concessisse et hac presenti carta mea confirmasse abbati et conventui de Bello Capite totam illam terram cum pertinenciis et provenientibus suis quam Robertus le fletcher quondam de me tenuit, iacentum inter terram quam Willelmus filius Sunune tenet ex una parte et terram quondam Ade del Clyfe ex altera parte versus occidentem super aquam de Shava et versus orientem super le Fulsyk, cum illa placea terre quam idem Robertus tenuit ex altera parte del Fulsyke. Tenendum et habendum dictis abbati et conventui et eorum successoribus libere, quiete et integre. Reddendo inde annuatim dum dictam terram tenere voluerint michi [fo. 33r] et heredibus meis quinque solidos argenti ad duos anni terminos annuatim, scilicet ad festum Annunciacionis sancte Marie Virginis duos solidos et sex denarios et ad[a] festum sancti Michaelis duos solidos et sex denarios pro omnibus serviciis, sectis tam curiarum quam aliarum rerum, et pro omnibus consuetudinibus et demandis que per me vel heredes meos vel quoscumque alios de predicta terra exigi poterit nec teneantur dicti abbas[b] vel conventus vel eorum successores juramentum fidelitatis facere michi vel heredibus meis vel cuicumque alii set tantum dictum annuum redditum solvere. Et ego Thomas et heredes mei dictam terram integre cum pertinenciis et vesturis et proventibus suis ad claudendum et clausam tenendum dictis abbati et conventui et eorum successoribus pro dicto redditu contra omnes gentes warantizabimus, acquietabimus et inperpetuum defendemus. In cuius rei testimonium presenti carte sigillum meum apposui. Hiis testibus: domino Ran[ulpho] vicario[c] de Norton', Ricardo marescallo,[d] Thoma fratre eius, Thoma de Wadiswyke clerico, Petro de Bernis, Johanne de Byrcheheved, Willelmo Matyne, et aliis.[2]

[a] *af.*   [b] *abbas* interlined.   [c] *vicareo*.   [d] *carescallo* (see **56**).

[1] Robert the Fletcher appears from the heading also to have been known as Robert Forst.
[2] Richard the Marshall's brother was Thomas of Dronfield Woodhouse (see **42** and **20**, n. 2). Peter de Bernis witnessed both **70** (1279) and **60** (1278). William Matiney also witnessed **70** (1278).

50. Quitclaim by the same Thomas Chaworth,[1] lord of Norton, to Beauchief abbey of the land, meadows, and wood which Thomas of the Wood and William Tynet once held in (Norton) Woodseats, saving those lands which they held by the river Sheaf, as is more fully found in the charter of Sir Thomas Chaworth his great-grandfather. Made at Norton on Wednesday 7 April 1350.

Relaxacio eiusdem Thome de quodam bosco in le Wodesetes

Noverint universi me Thomam de Chaworth dominum [de] Norton' remisisse, relaxasse et omnino de me et heredibus meis quietum clamasse inperpetuum abbati et conventui de Bello Capite et eorum successoribus totum jus meum et clameum quod habeo, habui seu aliquo modo habere potero, in tota illa terra prato et bosco cum pertinenciis que Thomas de bosco et Willelmus Tynet quondam tenuerunt in le Wodesetes, salvis michi et heredibus meis terris, pratis et boscis que iidem [fo. 33v] Thomas et Willelmus tenuerunt juxta aquam de Schava, prout in carta domini Thome de Chaworth proavi mei eisdem abbati et conventui confecta plenius continetur. Ita quod nec ego dictus Thomas nec heredes mei aliquid decetero juris vel clamei in predictis terra, prato et bosco cum omnibus pertinenciis suis ut predictum est quoquomodo versus dictum abbatem et conventum seu eorum successores exigere clamare vel vendicare poterimus inperpetuum. In cuius rei testimonium presenti scripto quiete clamacionis sigillum meum apposui. Hiis testibus: domino Johanne Basset,[2] Rogero de Paddeley, Henrico Daate, Waltero de Elmeton', Ada de Gotham,[3] et aliis. Dat' apud Norton' die marcurii proximo post festum sancti Ambrosii anno Domini m° ccc^{mo} quinquagesimo.

---

[1] Sir Thomas Chaworth III, the great-grandson of Sir Thomas Chaworth I who gave these premises to the abbey sometime before 1312.
[2] In 1398 this John Basset, knight, or his namesake, sold to the abbey for £20 seventy acres of pasture in Birchitt, just beyond the southern border of their estate (H.J.H. Garratt (ed.), *Derbyshire Feet of Fines, 1323–1546*, Derbyshire Record Society 11 (Chesterfield, 1985), p. 69); see also **218**.
[3] Adam of Gotham witnessed a grant of land in Norton by Sir Thomas Chaworth on 17 September 1352 (printed from a copy in the possession of Marples and Marples, solicitors in Sheffield, but not dated correctly, in Addy, 'A contribution to the history of Norton in Derbyshire', pp. 7–8; Jeayes, *Derbyshire Charters*, no. 1776).

51. Quitclaim by Thomas Chaworth,[1] knight, to Beauchief abbey of William Picard in the soke of Norton, his serf, with all his family and their chattels. [1290–1320]

Carta domini Thome Chaworth de Willelmo Picard'

Omnibus ad quos presens scriptum pervenerit[a] Thomas de Chaworth miles salutem in Domino sempiternam. Noveritis me pro salute anime mee et omnium antecessorum et successorum meorum dedisse, concessisse et omnino pro me et heredibus meis remisisse et quietum clamasse abbati et conventui de Bello Capite in liberam, puram et perpetuam elemosinam Willelmum Picard in soca de Norton', nativum meum, cum tota sequela sua procreata et procreanda et eorum sequelas, cum omnibus catallis suis et omnibus eorum catallis adquisitis et adquirendis. Ita quod nec ego predictus Thomas nec heredes mei nec aliquis pro nobis nec per nos seu nomine nostro in dicto Willelmo nec in catallis suis nec in tota sequela sua nec in catallis eorum aliquod jus vel juris clameum decetero habere exigere vel [fo. 34r] vendicare poterimus quoquomodo racione vel eventu. In cuius rei testimonium presenti scripto sigillum meum apposui. Hiis testibus: Willelmo le Brett, Johanne Deyncourt,[b] Rogero Breton', Johanne Brimigton', Hugone de Linacre, Thoma de Leys, Johanne de Stubley, et aliis.[2]

[a] *perverit.* [b] *Deyncorut.*

[1] For Thomas Chaworth see **47**, n. 1.
[2] William le Bret, John Deyncourt, and Roger Breton all witnessed **71** (1301). William, John, and Hugh of Linacre witnessed **44** and **61** (both of 1312); see also **18**, n. 2.

52. Quitclaim by the same Thomas Chaworth, knight, to Beauchief abbey of John the swane son of Adam of Greenhill, his serf, with all his family and their chattels. [1260–1315]

Alia carta eiusdem Thome de Johanne le Swayne

Noverint universi hoc presens scriptum visuri vel audituri quod ego Thomas de Chaworth miles dedi, concessi et omnino quietum clamavi abbati et conventui de Bello Capite in liberam, puram et perpetuam elemosinam Johannem le Swane filium Ade de Grenehyll', nativum meum, cum tota sequela sua et omnibus catallis suis presentibus et futuris. Ita quod nec ego predictus Thomas nec[a] heredes mei nec aliquis alius per nos seu pro nobis aliquod jus vel clameum in predicto Johanne vel in sequela sua seu catallis eorum nomine nativitatis debiti servitutis vel consuetudinis deinceps exigere vel vendicare poterimus. In cuius rei testimonium huic presenti scripto sigillum meum apposui. Hiis testibus: Rogero de Fletburgh, Petro de Bernis,[1] Johanne de Byrcheheved, Thoma de Wodhous, Thoma de Leys, et aliis.

[a] *ne.*

[1] Peter de Bernis also witnessed **70** (1278) and **60** (1279).

53. Quitclaim by the same Thomas Chaworth, knight, lord of Norton, to Beauchief abbey of Roger son of Richard the squire of Norton, once his serf, with all his family and their chattels. [1260–1315]

Alia carta eiusdem Thome de Rogero filio Ricardi Swyere

Omnibus Cristi fidelibus hoc presens scriptum visuris vel audituris Thomas de Chaworth miles dominus de Norton' salutem in Domino sempiternam. Noveritis me pro salute anime mee et omnium antecessorum et successorum meorum dedisse, concessisse et hoc presenti scripto meo omnino quietum clamasse abbati et conventui de Bello [fo. 34v] Capite et eorum successoribus vel assignatis in liberam, puram et perpetuam elemosinam Rogerum filium Ricardi le Squyer' de Norton', quondam nativum meum, cum tota sequela sua et catallis. Ita quod nec ego predictus Thomas nec heredes mei vel assignati nec aliquis per nos vel nomine nostro aliquod jus vel clameum in predicto Rogero et sequela sua vel catallis amodo exigere vel vendicare poterimus inperpetuum. In cuius rei testimonium presenti scripto sigillum meum apposui. Hiis testibus: Johanne de Brimington', Hugone de Tokysforth', Thoma de Wodhous, Petro de Bernis,[1] Johanne de Stubley, Johanne de Bircheheved, Rogero carpentario, et aliis.

[1] Peter de Bernis also witnessed **70** (1278) and **60** (1279).

54. Quitclaim by Thomas Chaworth, knight, lord of Norton, to Beauchief abbey of Thomas Gory of the soke of Norton, his serf, with all his family and their chattels. [1280–1320]

Carta domini Thome Chaworth' de Thoma Gory, nativo de soka de Norton'

Omnibus ad quos presens scriptum pervenerit Thomas de Chaworth' miles, dominus de Norton, salutem in Domino sempiternam. Noveritis me pro salute anime mee et omnium antecessorum et successorum meorum dedisse, concessisse et omnino pro me et heredibus meis remisisse et quietum clamasse abbati et conventui de Bello Capite et eorum successoribus, in liberam, puram et perpetuam elemosinam, Thomas Gory de soka de Norton', nativum meum, cum tota sequela sua procreata et procreanda et eorum sequela, cum omnibus catallis suis adquisitis et adquirendis. Ita quod nec ego predictus Thomas nec heredes mei nec aliquis alius, per nos seu pro nobis vel nomine nostro, aliquod jus vel clameum in predicto Thoma Gory vel in sequela sua seu catallis eorum decetero habere, exigere vel vendicare poterimus quoquomodo. In cuius rei testimonium presenti [fo. 35r] scripto sigillum meum apposui. Hiis testibus: Johanne de Ayencourt, Rogero Breton', Stephano le Eyr', Hugone de Linacre, Johanne Wyggeley, Johanne Broune de Aston', Willelmo de Haselberg', et aliis.[1]

[1] John Deyncourt and Roger Breton also witnessed **71** (1301). For John Wigley, see **46**, n. 2.

55. Quitclaim by Thomas Chaworth, knight, to Beauchief abbey of Thomas, Hugh, and John sons of Adam at the spring in Greenhill, his serfs, with all their families and their chattels. [1260–1320]

Carta domini Thome de Chaworth de Thoma, Hugone et Johanne filiis[a] Ade ad fontem in Grenhil

Universis hoc scriptum visuris vel audituris Thomas de Chaworth miles salutem in Domino sempiternam. Noverit universitas vestra me pro salute anime mee et omnium antecessorum meorum dedisse, concessisse et pro me et heredibus meis inperpetuum quietum clamasse abbati et conventui de Bello Capite Thomam, Hugonem [et] Johannem, filios Ade ad fontem in Grenehill, nativos meos, cum tota sequela sua et cum omnibus catallis suis ubicumque inventis, tam presentibus quam futuris. Ita quod nec ego Thomas nec heredes mei nec aliquis per nos seu nomine nostro aliquid jus[b] vel clameum in dictis Thoma, Hugone [et] Johanne vel in sequela sua vel in catallis suis, ut predictum est, decetero exigere vel nobis vendicare poterimus quoquomodo. In cuius rei testimonium presenti scripto sigillum meum apposui. Hiis testibus: Johanne de Brimigton', Hugone de Linacre, Johanne de Stubbeley clerico, Petro del Bernis, Rogero del Grene in Norton', et aliis.[1]

[a] *Johannem filium.* [b] *jur.*

[1] Peter de Bernis also witnessed **70** (1278) and **60** (1279). John of Brimington, Hugh of Linacre, and John the clerk of Stubley appear together as witnesses in **22**.

56. Gift in free alms by Thomas Chaworth, knight, to Beauchief abbey of William son of Richard the squire, his serf, with all his chattels, family, land, and tenement in the soke of Norton; and of the annual rent of 6d which William the cook paid for his tenement in the soke of Norton. [c.1269–1289]

Carta domini Thome Chaworth' de Willelmo filio Ricardi le Squier'

Omnibus Cristi fidelibus hanc presentem cartam visuris vel audituris Thomas de Chaworth miles salutem in Domino sempiternam. Noverit universitas vestra me pro salute animarum Rose et Alicie uxorum mearum dedisse et concessisse et hac presenti carta mea con[fo. 35v]firmasse abbati et conventui de Bello Capite eorumque successoribus, in liberam, puram et perpetuam elemosinam, Willelmum filium Ricardi lesquier, nativum meum, cum omnibus catallis suis et tota sequela sua cum terra[a] et tenemento toto que de me tenuit in soka de Norton' cum pertinenciis, una cum servicio sex denariorum annui redditus cum pertinenciis et escaetis quos Willelmus cocus michi solvere solebat pro tenemento quod de me tenuit in dicta soca de Norton'. Tenendum et habendum dictis abbati et conventui et eorum successoribus cum pertinenciis, communiis et aisiamentis in liberam, puram et perpetuam elemosinam. Et ego dictus Thomas et heredes mei seu assignati dictum Willelmum nativum, cum catallis et sequela sua et cum tota terra et tenemento cum pertinenciis quod de me tenuit, ut dictum est, una cum servicio dicti Willelmi coci et heredum suorum pro dicto tenemento quod de me tenuit dictis abbati et conventui et eorum successoribus in liberam, puram et perpetuam elemosinam pro salute animarum dictarum uxorum mearum contra omnes gentes warantizabimus, acquietabimus et ubique defendemus. In cuius rei testimonium presenti carte sigillum meum apposui. Hiis testibus: domino Willelmo de Staynesby, Rogero de Somervile, Roberto le Graunt, Willelmo Pyce, Ricardo marescallo,

Willelmo filio Matyne, Petro de Bernis, Johanne de Bircheheved, et multis aliis.[1]

^a *terram.*

[1] William of Stainsby succeeded his father, Jocelin, as lord of Stainsby *c.*1269 and died in 1289 (Crook, 'Hardwick before Bess', pp. 45–47). Roger de Somerville, Robert le Graunt, and Peter de Bernis all witnessed **60** (1279).

[WYMESWOLD]

57. Grant by Roger of Alfreton to Beauchief abbey of 9$^{1}/_{2}$ bovates in the vill of Wymeswold with all tenants and their families. The canons shall render to the lord of the fee 1 pair of gilt spurs annually. The abbey will maintain a canon to celebrate Mass for Roger's soul and those of his family forever. [1210–1240][1]

Carta Rogeri de Alfreton' de terra in villa de Wymundwold

Omnibus ad quos presens scriptum pervenerit Rogerus de Alreton' salutem in Domino. Noveritis me dedisse et hac presenti carta mea confirmasse Deo et ecclesie beati Thome martiris [fo. 36r] de Beuchefe et canonicis ibidem Deo servientibus, pro salute anime mee et pro animabus Roberti filii Willelmi et Ranulfi fratris sui et Luce filie dicti Roberti et pro animabus omnium advocatorum meorum, novem bovatas terre et dimidiam in villa de Wymundewold cum omnibus tenentibus et eorum sequelis et cum omnibus libertatibus et aliis pertinenciis et aisiamentis dicte terre infra villam et extra pertinentibus. Habendas et tenendas inperpetuum liberas, quietas ab omni seculari servicio et exaccione michi vel heredibus meis pertinentibus. Reddendo inde annuatim domino feodi unum par calcarium deauratorum et faciendum forinsecum servicium quantum ad tantam terram pertinet, sicut continetur in cartis donatorum meorum quas dictis canonicis tradidi. Abbas vero et conventus dicte domus de Beuchef ad peticionem meam concesserunt michi caritative quod ipsi sustinebunt unum canonicum celebrantem missam pro anima mea et pro animabus omnium predictorum advocatorum meorum inperpetuum. Et ut ista mea donacio rata et stabilis permaneat, hanc cartam sigillo meo signatam eis confeci in testimonium. Insuper cartas donatorum meorum quas penes se habent eis tradidi. Hiis testibus: Rogero de Osberton', Roberto

Putrell', Thoma de Leys, Henrico de Birchewod, Stephano Manluel, Thoma de Bradefeud, et aliis.

[1] For the earlier history of this estate, which Robert son of William of Alfreton gave to Roger of Alfreton, see **12–16**. Roger's death and benefaction are recorded in the Obituary (1 January); Masses to be celebrated at the altar of the Holy Cross.

58. Notification that Thomas Chaworth is held to make warranty forever to Beauchief abbey for all lands in Wymeswold which Roger of Alfreton gave to them and for 1 pair of gilt spurs to be paid to him annually. [1247–1279][1]

Carta domini Thome Chaworth ad waranciam[a] faciendam

Omnibus[b] hoc presens scriptum visuris vel audituris Thomas de Chaworth' salutem in Domino. Noverit universitas vestra me teneri pro me et heredibus meis ad waranciam[c] faciendam inperpetuum [fo. 36v] abbati et conventui de Bello Capite et successoribus suis de tota terra cum pertinenciis in villa et in territorio de Wimundewold, quam Rogerus de Alerton' dedit eisdem abbati et conventui et pro uno pare calcarium deauratorum michi et heredibus meis annuatim ad Pascha solvendorum, sicut continentur in carta feofamenti quam predicti abbas et conventus habent de predicto Rogero de Alreton'. In cuius rei testimonium presenti scripto pro me et heredibus meis sigillum meum apposui. Hiis testibus: domino Willelmo de Chaworth, Willelmo Putrell' de Wymundewold, Roberto forestario, Hugone de Wodhous, Petro de Bircheheved, et aliis.

[a] *woranciam.* [b] *mnibus.* [c] *woranciam.*

[1] Dated after Thomas came of age in 1247 and before he executed **60** in 1279.

59. Quitclaim by Robert Putrell to Beauchief abbey of the church of Wymeswold which Robert son of Ranulph gave to them. [1180–1189][1]

Quieta clamacio Roberti Putrell' de ecclesia de Wymundwold

Omnibus sancte matris ecclesie filiis ad quos presentes littere pervenerint Robertus Putrell' salutem in eo qui est vera salus. Noverit universitas vestra me concessisse et presenti scripto confirmasse et quietum clamasse totum jus quod michi vendicabam in ecclesia de Wymundeswold et in omnibus pertinenciis suis Deo et sancte Marie et sancto Thome martiri de Beauchef et fratribus ibidem Deo servientibus, quam eis Robertus filius Ranulfi dedit, ad quem jus patronatus prefate ecclesie pertinebat in liberam et perpetuam elemosinam, pro salute anime mee et patris mei et matris mee et heredum meorum et omnium antecessorum meorum. Teste Turstino de Geredon' et M. de Ritford et A. de Welbec abbatibus, A. priore de Wyrkesop, R. priore de Sclelford, magistro Vicario, magistro Gervasio de Kenlingworth, magistro[a] Willelmo Norm', magistro Lisiardo, magistro Petro de [fo. 37r] Dancastr', Galfrido clerico de Sulcholm, T. de Lond', Willelmo et Galfrido filiis suis.[2]

[a] *magistro* interlined.

[1] For the original grant, see **3** and **4** above. According to a confirmation recorded in the *matricula* of Hugh of Wells, bishop of Lincoln 1209–1235, the appropriation of the church of Wymeswold to Beauchief abbey had taken place thirty-five years earlier, when Hugh of Avallon (St Hugh) had been bishop, 21 September 1186×16 November 1200 (W.P.W. Phillimore (ed.), *Rotuli Hugonis de Welles*, Canterbury and York Society, I, Diocese of Lincoln, I (London, 1909), p. 255; D.M. Smith (ed.), *English Episcopal Acta, IV, Lincoln 1186–1206* (London, 1986), no. 18). Robert Putrell of Cotes (Leicestershire) witnessed two charters *c.*1200 at Cotes and Hoton and granted land in Hoton and Prestwold to the abbey of St Evroul (Normandy); each of these places lies immediately south-west of Wymeswold (D. Postles, *The Surnames of Leicestershire and Rutland* (Oxford, 1998), pp. 106, 126).
[2] Thurstan, abbot of Garendon (Cistercian, Leics), d. 1189 (Knowles, Brooke, and London, *Heads of Religious Houses*, I, p. 135). Matthew, abbot of Rufford (Cistercian, Notts), *c.*1174–*c.*1201 (*ibid.*, p. 141). For Adam, abbot of Welbeck, see **4**, n. 2. A. prior of Worksop (Augustinian, Notts), 1188×1191 (*ibid.*, p. 190). Remigius (?Raymond), prior of Shelford (Augustinian, Notts), occurs 1173 (*ibid.*, p. 183). Mr Vicarius: perhaps Mr Vacarius, the civil lawyer and ecclesiastical administrator in the province of York who, as a canon of Southwell (Notts), witnessed charters and was involved in business concerning the abbeys of Welbeck (1191–1198) and Rufford (*c.*1190). He still held a prebend at Norwell (Notts) in 1191. See R.W. Southern, 'Master Vacarius and the beginning of an English academic tradition', in J.J.G. Alexander and M.T. Gibson (eds), *Medieval Learning and Literature: essays presented to Richard William Hunt* (Oxford, 1976), pp. 257–286, esp. pp. 283–285. Unlikely to be Vacarius, chaplain to the precentor of Lincoln cathedral 1197–1203 (William of Blois, bishop 1203–1206) and canon *c.*1200–after *c.*1212. This Vacarius, perhaps a nephew of Mr Vacarius, is almost invariably named *Vacarius capellanus, canonicus*, or *concanonicus*; in one instance, his name too is spelt Vicarius. See Smith, *English Episcopal Acta, IV*, nos 230, 243, 251, 298–299; C.W. Foster and K. Major (eds), *The 'Registrum Antiquissimum' of the Cathedral Church of Lincoln*, IX, Lincoln Record Society 62 (1958), p. 76; IV, Lincoln Record Society 32 (1937), p. 161; X, Lincoln Record Society 67 (1973), pp. 65–66; also Southern, 'Master Vacarius', pp. 284, n. 1 and 285. Mr Gervase of Kenlingworth: probably Kenilworth (Warwicks), which has an early spelling *Kenelyngworth* (Watts, *English Place-names*, p. 340). Mr William Norm': perhaps Mr William Normannicus (the Norman). T. de Lond': perhaps London or Londonthorpe (Lincs).

60. Quitclaim by Thomas Chaworth, knight, to Beauchief abbey of the service of gilt spurs which they are held to pay annually at Easter for the land and tenement which they have in Wymeswold of the gift of Roger of Alfreton. Made on 1 November 1279.[1]

      Quieta clamacio domini Thome Chaworth' de servicio
                    calcarium deauratorum

Omnibus sancte matris ecclesie filiis hoc presens scriptum visuris vel audituris Thomas de Chaworth miles salutem in Domino. Noveritis me pro salute anime mee et omnium antecessorum meorum relaxasse et omnino quietum clamasse de me et heredibus meis seu assignatis inperpetuum abbati et conventui de Bello Capite et eorum successoribus, in liberam, puram et perpetuam elemosinam, illud servicium totum calcarium scilicet deauratorum que michi annuatim solvere tenebantur ad Pascha pro tota illa terra et tenemento cum pertinenciis suis que de me tenuerunt in Wymundeswold et que habuerunt de dono Rogeri de Alferton'. Ita quod nec ego predictus Thomas nec heredes mei seu assignati nec aliquis alius per nos seu pro nobis aliquod jus vel clameum in predicto servicio calcarium deauratorum vel in dicto tenemento nec aliquod aliud servicium, sectam, consuetudinem vel demandam de dicto tenemento exigere, vendicare vel demandare poterimus inperpetuum. In cuius rei testimonium presenti scripto sigillum meum apposui. Act' et dat' ad festum Omnium Sanctorum anno regni regis Edwardi filii Henrici regis septimo. Hiis testibus: domino Waltero de Kibuf', domino Willelmo de Matynesby, Galfrido de Becton clerico, Rogero de Somervyle, Roberto le Graunt, Petro de Bernys, et multis aliis.

[1] Confirmed in 1312 (**38**, no. 21) and again in 1316 (Appendix II, no. 51). See **57**, n. 1, concerning the earlier history of this service.

[CHARTER OF SIR THOMAS CHAWORTH II]

61. Confirmation by Thomas Chaworth, knight, son of the late Sir William Chaworth, knight, to Beauchief abbey of all lands, tenements, rents etc. which they have by the gift of Thomas Chaworth, his grandfather, or other of his ancestors in the vills of Wymeswold and Marnham and in the sokes of Norton and Alfreton. Made at Beauchief 11 November 1312.[1]

      Quieta clamacio domini Thome Chaworth'

Omnibus ad quorum noticiam hoc presens scriptum pervenerit Thomas [fo. 37v] de Chaworth' miles filius quondam domini Willelmi de Chaworth' militis salutem in Domino sempiternam. Noveritis me concessisse, confirmasse et omnino de me et heredibus meis quietum clamasse inperpetuum religiosis[a] viris abbati et conventui de Bello Capite et eorum successoribus omnes terras et tenementa, redditus, advocaciones ecclesiarum, jura, possessiones ac libertates quascumque, cum omnibus pertinenciis suis, que et quas iidem abbas et conventus habent de dono et concessione domini Thome de Chaworth' avi mei ceterorumque antecessorum meorum in villa de Wymundewold in comitatu Leygcestr' et Marnham in comitatu Notinham, et in sokis de Norton' et Alfreton' in comitatu Derby. Habendum et tenendum in liberam, puram et perpetuam elemosinam. Ita quod nec ego predictus Thomas filius Willelmi predicti nec heredes mei nec aliquis per nos seu nomine nostro aliquod jus vel clameum seu calumpniam in prenominatis terris, tenementis, redditibus, advocacionibus, juribus, possessionibus ac libertatibus, nec in aliqua parte eorumdem seu eorum pertinenciis exigere vel vendicare decetero poterimus quoquomodo. In cuius rei testimonium presenti scripto sigillum meum apposui. Hiis testibus: dominis Thoma de Furnival, Ada de Everingham, Roberto de Waddesley militibus, domino Rogero de Bralisford rectore ecclesie de Dronfeld, Willelmo le Brett, Johanne de Ayencourt, Hugone de Linacre, et aliis. Dat' apud Bellum Caput in festo sancti Martini episcopi anno gracie m⁰ ccc⁰ duodecimo, quod est anno regni domini Edwardi regis filii regis Edwardi sexto.

[a] *rligiosis.*

[1] This is another copy of **44**.

[WYMESWOLD]

62. Quitclaim by Stephen of Nevil to Beauchief abbey of an annual rent of 1 pair of gilt spurs for the tenement which they hold in Wymeswold. Stephen must make suit every 3 weeks at the court of Leicester for the abbey, as much for the tenement which they hold in Wymeswold from the fee that was once Robert son of William's as for the

tenement which Stephen holds of the same fee in the same vill. [c.1279?][1]

[fo. 38r]

Quieta clamacio Stephani Nevel de redditu calcarium deauratorum

Omnibus Cristi fidelibus presens scriptum visuris vel audituris Stephanus de Nevil salutem in Domino sempiternam. Noverit universitas vestra me dimisisse, relaxasse et omnino quietum clamasse pro me et heredibus meis inperpetuum abbati et conventui de Bello Capite et eorum successoribus totum jus et clameum ac eciam omnes demandas quas exigere consuevi, vel qualitercumque exigere seu habere potero, in annuo redditu unius paris calcarium deauratorum cum omnibus pertinenciis suis racione tenementi quod tenent in Wymundewold. Ita siquidem quod nec ego nec heredes mei nec aliquis pro me vel per me in predictis calcaribus cum pertinenciis suis aliquod jus vel clameum nec eciam aliquod aliud servicium nec demandas aliquas racione predictorum calcarium vel tenementi pretitulati decetero exigere, clamare vel vendicare poterimus inposterum. Propterea ego Stephanus et heredes mei tenemur ad faciendam sectam de tribus septimanis in tres septimana ad curiam Leycestrie pro predictis abbate et conventu et eorum successoribus, tam pro tenemento quod dicti abbas et conventus tenent in Wymundewold de feodo, quod fuit quondam Roberti filii Willelmi, quam pro tenemento quod ego teneo de eodem feodo in eadem villa. Ita quod ego et heredes mei teneamur decetero ad defendendum et warantizandum sepedictos abbatem et conventum et eorum successores de predicta secta, ut supra dictum est, inperpetuum. In quorum testimonium hoc presens scriptum sigilli mei munimine roboravi. Hiis testibus: domino [fo. 38v] Thoma Chaworth', domino Nicholao de Boby, Johanne de Vilers, Johanne Putrell' de Wimundewold, Galfrido filio Stephani de Westwold, Ricardo de Leke, Johanne de Siwoldby, Roberto de Belgrave, Arnaldo de Wimundewold, Rogero clerico[a] de eadem, et aliis.

[a] *clerco.*

[1] This appears to be part of the same transaction as **60**.

63. Quitclaim by William Jorrs to Beauchief abbey of the church of Wymeswold which Robert son of Ranulph gave them. The abbey granted to William at the end of his life the spiritual succour that it would give to one of the canons. [*c*.1180–1194][1]

Quieta clamacio Willelmi Jorrs de ecclesia de Wymunwold

Omnibus sancte matris ecclesie filiis Willelmus de Jorrs salutem. Noverit universitas vestra me concessisse et presenti scripto confirmasse et quietum clamasse totum jus quod michi vendicabam in ecclesia de Wimundeswold Deo et sancte Marie et sancto Thome de Beuchef et fratribus ibidem Deo servientibus quam eis Robertus filius Ranulfi dedit, ad quem jus patronatus prefate ecclesie pertinebat, in liberam et perpetuam elemosinam pro salute anime mee et patris mei et matris mee et omnium antecessorum meorum. Et sciendum quod prefati abbas et canonici concesserunt michi spirituale beneficium in extremis vite mee sicut uni canonicorum nostrorum. Hiis testibus: A. abbate de Wellebec, Johanne capellano de Wymundwold, Willelmo filio Ranulfi, Willelmo filio Roberti, Rad[ulpho] filio Hugonis, Henrico clerico de Horchent, Roberto de Torp, Roberto Andegavensi, Reginaldo de Insula, Herardo de Bernest, Roberto de Jorr, Ivene de Prestwolde, Rad[ulpho] filio Radulfi, Henrico de Bergervile, Odone filio Rad[ulphi], Ada de Strett', et aliis.

[1]The church of Wymeswold was included in Robert's first foundation charter (3). The appearance of Adam, abbot of Welbeck (occurs 1180×1194) provides an approximate date; see 4, n. 2.

64. Confirmation by Alice daughter of William son of Robert of Alfreton of the gift of Ranulph, her brother, *viz*. of 1½ bovates which her brother Ranulph gave to Beauchief abbey; of 1½ bovates which he gave to the nuns of Campsey Ash in free alms; and of 6 bovates which he gave to Roger of Alfreton from the 9 bovates which he had in the vill of Wymeswold of the gift of their first-born brother Robert son of William. Roger shall render to Robert 1 pair of gilt spurs annually. [1210–1225][1]

Quieta clamacio Alicie filie Willelmi

Omnibus sancte matris ecclesie filiis presentibus et futuris Alicia [fo. 39r] filia Willelmi filii Roberti de Alreton' salutem in Domino. Noveritis me pro salute anime mee et pro salute anime Ran[ulfi] fratris mei cuius heres sum concessisse et presenti carta mea confirmasse et quietum clamasse pro me et heredibus meis inperpetuum donum Ranulfi fratris mei, scilicet unam bovatam terre et dimidiam cum pertinenciis suis quam dedit domui de Beuchef, et unam bovatam terre et dimidiam cum pertinenciis suis quam dedit domui de Campesse in perpetuam elemosinam, et sex bovatas terre cum pertinenciis suis quas dedit Rogero de Alreton' et heredibus suis de novem bovatis terre quas habuit in villa de Wimundewold de dono primogeniti fratris nostri Roberti filii Willelmi de Alferton'. Reddendo de predictis novem bovatis terre annuatim unum par calcarium deauratorum predicto Roberto filio Willelmi et heredibus suis, scilicet ad Pascha pro omni servicio et consuetudine et exaccione, salvo forinseco servicio. Ita quod nec ego nec aliquis heredum meorum aliquid in predicta terra clamare poterimus, hanc concessionem et quietam clamacionem sigillo meo corroboravi. Hiis testibus: Roberto filio Willelmi de Alferton', Johanne et Roberto capellanis de Campesse, Ran[ulpho] de Jorr, Roberto Putrell', Johanne clerico, Roberto filio Brien', Johanne le Poer, Ricardo dispensatore de Alferton', Thoma de Gunetune, Willelmo de Westhall', Thoma del Bradfeld, Thoma de Peke, et multis aliis.

[1] This charter was perhaps executed about the same time as Alice's brother Robert confirmed Ranulph's gifts from the family's Wymeswold estate (**15**; and see **12–16** for other Wymeswold charters of the same period). It is also entered in the Alfreton section of the cartulary (**76**), apparently because the scribe believed (almost certainly wrongly) that part of the estate lay in that manor. There is an abstract of Alice's charter in The Queen's College, Oxford, MS 117, fo. 26v. (See also **7** above.)

65. Grant by Abbot William[1] and the convent of Beauchief to Robert Ladde, clerk of Burton, for his homage and service, of 1 toft and croft which Robert son of John held in Wymeswold with 1 selion in the field of Wymeswold on Woldhyll. Robert shall render to the abbey 4s annually. It is not permitted for Robert to sell, give, demise, or assign the said land, or any part of it, without the abbey's consent or to carry parts of it elsewhere. [1210–1230]

Carta abbatis et conventus de Bello Capite

Sciant presentes et futuri quod nos frater Willelmus abbas de Bello Capite et eiusdem loci connventus dedimus, concessimus et hac presenti [fo. 39v] carta nostra confirmavimus Roberto Ladde clerico de Burton', pro homagio et servicio suo, illud toftum et croftum cum edificiis quod Robertus filius Johannis de nobis tenuit in Wymundwold cum una selione in campo eiusdem iacente super Woldhyll'. Tenendum et habendum predicto Roberto et heredibus suis libere, bene et pacifice. Reddendo inde annuatim nobis et successoribus nostris quatuor solidos sterlingorum, videlicet ad festum Pent[ecostes] duos solidos et ad festum sancti Martini duos solidos pro omnibus aliis serviciis, salvis foraneis serviciis et sectis curiarum nostrarum, nec licebit predicto Roberto vel alicui heredum suorum predictum tenementum vel aliquam eius partem cuicumque alii sine assensu et voluntate nostra expressa vendere, dare, dimittere, invadiare vel assignare nec terram de predicto tofto vel tenemento cariare vel asportare alibi quam super terram quam de nobis tenent seu tenebunt et edificia in statu quo ea susceperunt vel meliori sustinebunt et defectus si qui ibi fuerint cum predictum tenementum quocumque casu dimiserunt sumptibus suis propriis emendabunt per consideracionem duorum legalium virorum pro voluntate predictorum abbatis et conventus ad hoc elegendorum, quod si contingat servicium de predicto tenemento debita et consueta per unum annum integrum aretro fore nec districcionem sufficientem in eodem posse inveniri quo minus predictum servicium poterit competenter infra predictum annum levari, licebit nobis et successoribus nostris comodum nostrum facere de predicto tenemento, sine impedimento et contra[fo. 40r]diccione predicti Roberti et heredum suorum, vel cuiuslibet alterius ex parte ipsorum nec volere poterit[a] in hac parte aliqua inpetracio a curia domini regis contra hanc formam inter nos invitam. Et nos predicti abbas et conventus predictum tenementum predicto Roberto et heredibus suis pro predictis serviciis contra omnes gentes forma prescripta warantizabimus. In cuius rei testimonium huic presenti scripto sigillum nostrum apposuimus. Hiis testibus: Galfrido filio Stephani, Roberto de Warnwike, Johanne Ingram, Johanne filio Ade le Spenser, Roberto Blanckaim clerico,[b] et aliis.

[a] *poterit* interlined.   [b] *clerco.*

[1] Abbot William occurs early in the reign of Henry III (Colvin, *White Canons*, p. 396; Smith and London, *Heads of Religious Houses*, II, p. 493).

[AGREEMENT BETWEEN SIR THOMAS CHAWORTH I AND ROBERT OF LATHOM]

66. Agreement made between Sir Thomas Chaworth and Sir Robert of Lathom. Thomas granted to Robert the marriage-right of whichever of his sons was his heir, or

if they should all predecease him then of whichever of his daughters were unmarried on the day that his last son and heir dies. So that Thomas's heir is married to Joan, Robert's daughter, or to another of his legitimate daughters if the said Joan should die before the said marriage is contracted. If Thomas or any of his heirs oppose this agreement then Thomas grants that Robert should have all the lands and tenements which Nicholas of Lathom, kinsman of Thomas, once gave him and which came to Joan of Lathom, Nicholas's mother, by hereditary right, *viz.* those lands in Alfreton, Norton, Osberton,[1] Edwalton, Wymeswold, Tokeby,[2] and elsewhere which Thomas has demised to Robert of Lathom[3] on his death by a chirograph made between them, so that they be held by Robert and his heirs borne by Joan, his wife, daughter of Adam of Milum. [1247–1310]

Convencio inter dominum Thomam Chaworth' et
Robertum Lathum

Hec est convencio facta inter dominum Thomam Chaworth ex una parte et dominum Robertum de Lathum ex altera, videlicet quod predictus Thomas dedit et concessit dicto Roberto maritagium heredis sui, videlicet cuiuscumque ex filiis suis qui pro tempore heres suus fuerit. Si vero contingat quod omnes filii dicti Thome infata quod absit decesserint, idem Thomas concedit dicto Roberto maritagium filiarum suarum, videlicet illarum que non fuerint maritate die quo ultimus filius suus heres obierit, ita quod liceat dicto Roberto maritare ipsum heredem qui pro tempore fuerit ad Johannam filiam[a] suam vel ad aliam si quam habuerit ex uxore sua legitime procreatam. Si dicta Johanna infata quod absit decesserit antequam matrimonium inter heredem dicti Thome et dictam Johannam legitime fuerit contractum. Si vero contingat quod dictus Thomas vel quicumque ex filiis suis vel ex filiabus suis qui pro tempore heres suus fuerit vel aliquis per suam procuracionem contra donacionem et concessi[fo. 40v]onem dicti maritagii venire presumpserit, ita quod illud maritagium per eorumdem procreacionem seu defectum non valeat perduci ad effectum, sicut predictum est, sive dictus Robertus de Lathum fuerit mortuus sive vivus idem Thomas concedit pro se et heredibus suis et presenti scripto confirmat quod dictus Robertus de Lathum habeat et teneat omnes terras et tenementa cum omnibus pertinenciis suis, sine aliquo retenemento, que Nicholaus de Lathum cognatus ipsius Thome quondam sibi dedit per cartam suam, que sibi descendebant jure hereditario de hereditate Johanne de Lathum quondam matris ipsius Nicholai, videlicet in Alferton', Norton', Osberton', Edwalton', Wymundwold, Tokeby et omnibus aliis locis, sine aliquo retenemento. Et eciam cum omnibus feodis militum predicte hereditati dicte Johanne de Lathum pertinentibus quas terras et que tenementa dictus Thomas dimisit dicto Roberto de Lathum ad terminum vite per cirographum inter eos exinde confectum. Tenenda et habenda dicto Roberto et heredibus suis de Johanna filia Ade de Millum uxore sua procreatis libere et quiete de capitalibus dominis feodi, ut in dominicis, serviciis, homagiis, wardis, releviis, dotibus cum contigerint et cum omnibus escaetis que predictis terris et tenementis quocumque modo possunt pertinere, sine aliquo retenemento. In cuius rei testimonium hoc presens scriptum mutua sigillorum suorum apposicione corroboraverunt.[b] Hiis testibus: domino Rogero tunc abbate de Bello Capite, domino Rogero [fo. 41r] de Eynecourt, domino Galfrido Barry,[4] domino Roberto de Watynhow, Henrico de Birchewod, Ran[ulpho] de Wandesley, Rogero de Somervile,[5] Waltero de Ufton, et aliis.

[a] *f* struck through.   [b] *corroberaverunt.*

[1] Three miles east of Worksop.
[2] Tugby (Leics).
[3] For Robert of Lathom, see also **23**.
[4] For Sir Geoffrey Barry (fl. 1244), see **203**, n. 2.
[5] Roger de Somerville was still alive in 1279 (**60**).

[ALFRETON]

67. Gift in free alms by Thomas Chaworth, knight, to Beauchief abbey of 1 assart with a toft and croft and houses built on it which Roger the smith of Birchwood once held in the soke of Alfreton. [*c*.1278][1]

Carta domini Thome Chaworth' de assarto in soka de Alferton'[a]

Omnibus Cristi fidelibus hoc scriptum visuris vel audituris Thomas de Chaworth miles salutem in Domino sempiternam. Noveritis me pro salute anime mee et omnium antecessorum et successorum meorum dedisse, concessisse et hoc presenti scripto meo confirmasse Deo et ecclesie beati Thome martiris de Bello Capite et abbati et conventui eiusdem loci, in liberam, puram et perpetuam elemosinam, totum illud assartum cum tofto, crofto et domibus superedificatis quod Rogerus faber de Byrchewod quondam de me tenuit in soka de Alferton'. Tenendum et habendum dictis abbati et conventui et eorum successoribus cum omnibus pertinenciis suis, libertatibus, communiis et aysiamentis in liberam, puram et perpetuam elemosinam inperpetuum. Ita quod predicti abbas et conventus possunt predictum assartum pro voluntate sua in toto vel in parte licite claudere et circumfossare. Et ego dictus Thomas et heredes mei totum dictum assartum cum tofto, crofto et domibus superedificatis, cum omnibus pertinenciis suis, libertatibus, communiis et aysiamentis, ut predictum est, predictis abbati et conventui et eorum successoribus in liberam, puram et perpetuam elemosinam contra omnes gentes warantizabimus, acquietabimus et inperpetuum defendemus. In cuius rei [fo. 41v] testimonium presenti scripto sigillum meum apposui. Hiis testibus: Hugone de canonicis, Willelmo de Somerwile, Egidio de Gossale, Roberto Scarlett, Willelmo Scarlett, et aliis.[2]

[a] Corrected from *Nortona*.

[1] This charter and **68** were probably executed about the same date as **70** (1278), since all three were witnessed by Robert and William Scarlet. The premises conveyed here reappear in **22** (which may date from *c*.1301), in which a yearly rent of 18s from premises in Swanwick, the subject of **71** (1301) and **69** (1324), is also mentioned.
[2] Hugh de canonicis also witnessed **70** (1278). Giles of 'Gossale' is presumably the Giles of Rossale who witnessed **74** (1304) and, together with Robert Scarlet, **72** and **73**.

68. Quitclaim by Thomas Chaworth, knight, to Beauchief abbey of Agnes of Birchwood widow of Roger the smith of Birchwood and all her family and their chattels. [*c*.1278][1]

Carta domini Thome Chaworth de relicta Rogeri fabri

Noverint universi presens scriptum visuri vel audituri me Thomam de Chaworth militem concessisse et omnino pro me et heredibus meis inperpetuum quietum clamasse abbati et conventui de Bello Capite et eorum successoribus totum jus meum et clameum quod habui seu habere potero in Agnete de Byrchewod, relicta quondam Rogeri fabri de Byrchewod, et in tota sequela sua et in catallis suis et in catallis sequele sue. Ita quod nec ego dictus Thomas nec heredes mei nec aliquis alius nomine nostro seu per nos aliquid juris vel clamei in dicta Agnete, nec in sequela sua nec in catallis suis nec in catallis sequele sue, in posterum habere, exigere seu reclamare poterimus quoquomodo racione vel eventu. In cuius rei testimonium presenti scripto sigillum meum apposui. Hiis testibus: Hugone de Ulgerthorpp',[2] Hugone de canonicis, Waltero de Ufton', Roberto Scarlet, Willelmo Scarlet, et aliis.

[1] For the date see **67**, n. 1.
[2] For Hugh of Ulkerthorpe, see **74** (1304).

69. Notification by Beauchief abbey that Richard the redsmith of Swanwick has been paying them 18s annually for the tenement which he holds in Swanwick in the soke of Alfreton, but that due to the affection they have for him they now grant to Richard, Emma his wife, and Thomas their son that they shall now pay 13s 4d annually for the same tenement for as long as they live.[1] Made at Beauchief on 6 January 1324.

Scriptum abbatis de Bello Capite

Omnibus ad quorum noticiam hoc presens scriptum pervenerit abbas et conventus de Bello Capite salutem in Domino sempiternam. Noverit universitas vestra quod licet Ricardus le redsmyth' de Swanwyke nobis reddere consuevit decem et octo solidos annuatim [fo. 42r] pro tenemento quod tenet in Swanwyk in soka de Alfreton', ex affeccione quam habemus erga predictum Ricardum concessimus eidem Ricardo et Emme uxori sue et Thome filio suo quod ipsi ad totam vitam suam nobis et successoribus nostris singulis annis pro tenemento predicto annuatim solvant tresdecim solidos et iiij^{or} denarios ad duos anni terminos, videlicet in festo sancti Michaelis Archangeli sex solidos octo denarios et in festo Annunciacionis beate Marie Virginis sex solidos et octo denarios, cum aliis serviciis inde debitis et consuetis. In cuius rei testimonium sigillum nostrum presenti scripto apposuimus. Hiis testibus: Rogero de Ufton', Roberto de Swanwyk, Willelmo le Waleys, Henrico de Lancroft',[2] Willelmo Cissore, et aliis. Dat' apud Bellum Caput predictum die Epiphanie Domini anno Domini m° ccc° vicesimo tercio.

[1] This reduction in rent in 1324 followed a series of national harvest failures and livestock disasters.
[2] Henry witnessed **73** as Henry of Longcroft (the modern name of a farm in South Wingfield); he also witnessed **87** (1299) and **71** (1301).

70. Grant by Thomas Chaworth, knight, to Beauchief abbey of licence to enclose their assart where their sheepfold is in the parish of Alfreton with all its woods. Made in 1278.

Carta ad circumfossandum et claudendum apud Alfreton' omni tempore anni

Noverint universi hoc presens scriptum visuri vel audituri quod ego Thomas de Chaworth miles dedi, concessi et confirmavi abbati et conventui de Bello Capite et eorum successoribus inperpetuum licenciam liberam et legitimam potestatem quod possint assartum suum ubi barcaria eorum sita est in parochia de Alferton' cum toto bosco suo circumfossare, claudere et omni tempore anni clausum habere et omnimodum comodum suum inde facere, sine nocumento et calumpnia mei heredum meorum et omnium nativorum meorum in dicta parochia. In cuius rei testimonium presenti scripto [fo. 42v] sigillum meum apposui. Act' et dat' anno Domini m° cc° lxx° octavo. Hiis testibus: domino Thome Foleiambe, Hugone de canonicis, Roberto Scarlet', Willelmo fratre eius, Willelmo Colt,[1] Petro de Bernis, Willelmo Matyny, et aliis.

[1] Described as 'of Alfreton' in the 1281 Derbyshire eyre (Hopkinson, *Derbyshire Eyre*, p. 122).

71. Quitclaim by Walter of Ufton[1] to Thomas Chaworth of an annual rent of 20s of which 2s are paid annually by same Thomas and 18s are paid annually by Robert the redsmith in the soke of Alfreton. Made at Beauchief on Sunday 26 November 1301.

Carta viginti solidorum redditus in parochia de Alfreton'

Pateat universis me Walterum de Ufton' pro me et heredibus meis concessisse et quietum clamasse inperpetuum domino Thome de Chaworth' et heredibus suis et assignatis suis totum jus meum et clameum quod habui, habeo vel habere potero in illis viginti solidatis annui redditus de quibus percipere solebam singulis annis duos solidos per manus ipsius domini Thome et decem et octo solidos de Roberto le redsmyth in soka de Alferton', quondam tenente dicti domini Thome, qui quidem predictus Robertus ad integralem solucionem dictorum decem et octo solidorum annui redditus faciend[am] michi per quoddam scriptum per dictum dominum Thomam assignabatur. Ita quod nec ego Walterus nec heredes mei nec aliquis pro nobis seu per nos aliquid juris vel clamei in dictis viginti solidatis annui redditus inperpetuum habere, exigere vel reclamare poterimus quoquomodo nec in aliqua parte ipsius redditus. In cuius rei testimonium presenti scripto sigillum meum apposui. Hiis testibus: Willelmo le Brett, Johanne Deyncourt, [fo. 43r] Rogero Breton', Willelmo Bulmer, Henrico de Lancroft,² et aliis. Act' et dat' apud Bellum Caput die Dominica in crastino sancte Katerine virginis anno regni regis Edwardi tricesimo.

¹Now Uftonfields in the parish of South Wingfield (K. Cameron, *The Place-names of Derbyshire*, 3 vols (Cambridge, 1959), II, p. 336).
²For Henry of Longcroft, see **69**, n. 2.

72. Gift in free alms by Walter of Ufton to Beauchief abbey of an annual rent of 10s in the soke of Alfreton of which 2s are paid annually by Thomas Chaworth and 8s are paid annually by Robert the redsmith. [1270–1320]¹

Carta Walteri de Ufton' de decem solidatis redditus in soka de Alfreton'

Universis presens scriptum visuris vel audituris Walterus de Ufton' salutem in Domino sempiternam. Noverit universitas vestra me dedisse, concessisse et hoc presenti scripto meo confirmasse abbati et conventui de Bello Capite et eorum successoribus, in liberam, puram et perpetuam elemosinam, decem solidatos annui redditus in soka de Alferton' de quibus dicti abbas et conventus annuatim percipient per manus domini Thome de Chaworth' et heredum suorum in festo Annunciacionis beate Marie duodecim denarios et de tenemento Roberti le redsmyth' per manus ipsius Roberti et heredum suorum quatuor solidos vel de quocumque dictum tenementum tenente in soka de Alferton' et in festo sancti Michaelis de domino Thome de Chaworth' duodecim denarios, et de tenemento dicti Roberti quatuor solidos. Tenendum et habendum dictis abbati et conventui et eorum successoribus in liberam, puram et perpetuam elemosinam de me et heredibus meis inperpetuum. Et ego dictus Walterus et heredes mei predictos decem solidatos annui redditus predictis abbati et conventui eorumque successoribus [fo. 43v] in liberam, puram et perpetuam elemosinam contra omnes gentes inperpetuum warantizabimus, acquietabimus et inperpetuum defendemus. In cuius rei testimonium presenti scripto sigillum meum apposui. Hiis testibus: Hugone de Ulgerthorpp', Hugone de canonicis, Egidio de Rossale, Roberto Scharlett, Willelmo Colt, et aliis.²

¹See also **73**.
²Hugh of Ulkerthorpe and Giles of Rosasale also witnessed **74** (1704). The place-name Ulkerthorpe is now known as Oakerthorpe in the parish of South Wingfield (Cameron,

Place-names of Derbyshire, II, pp. 335–336). Hugo de canonicis, Robert Scarlet, and William Colt also witnessed **70** (1278).

73. Quitclaim by Walter of Ufton to Sir Thomas Chaworth of an annual rent of 10s of which 2s are paid annually by the said Thomas and 8s are paid annually by Robert the redsmith in the soke of Alfreton. [1270–1320][1]

Quieta clamacio Walteri de Ufton' de decem solidatis annui redditus

Pateat universis me Walterum de Ufton' pro me et heredibus [meis] concessisse, remisisse ac omnino quietum clamasse inperpetuum domino Thome de Chaworth' et heredibus suis vel assignatis suis totum jus meum et clameum quod habui vel habere potui seu potero in illis decem solidatis annui redditus, quorum duos solidos singulis annis percipere solebam per manus ipsius domini Thome et octo solidos de Roberto de Redsmyth' in soka de Alferton', quondam tenente dicti domini Thome. Qui quidem predictus Robertus ad integralem solucionem dictorum decem solidorum annui redditus faciend[am] michi per quoddam scriptum per dictum dominum Thomam assignabatur. Ita quod nec ego Walterus nec heredes mei nec aliquis pro nobis seu per nos aliquid juris vel clamei in dictis decem solidatis annui redditus inperpetuum habere, exigere vel reclamare poterimus quoquomodo, nec in aliqua parte ipsius redditus. In cuius rei testimonium presenti scripto sigillum meum apposui. Hiis testibus: Ranulpho de Swanwyke, [fo. 44r] Roberto Scharlett, Egidio de Rossale, Henrico de Longcr[o]ft,[2] Willelmo Colt, et multis aliis.

[1] See also **72**.
[2] For Henry of Longcroft see **69**, n. 2.

74. Grant in the form of a chirograph by Thomas the forester of Alfreton to Beauchief abbey, for the term of 14 years from 11 November 1304, of 1 strip of land with the adjacent meadow in Somercotes called Wyntersedecrofte; of 1 strip of wood in Somercotes called Tomelingreve; and of 2 acres of meadow, one called the Bentt and the

other lying between the Qwythengrenes and bordering on Herewise, for a term of 14 years beginning at the feast of St Martin [11 November] 1304.

Dimissio Thome forestarii de placea terre que vocatur Wyntersedecrofte iacente in territorio de Somercote

Universis Cristi fidelibus presens scriptum visuris vel audituris Thomas dictus forestarius de Alferton' salutem in Domino. Noverit universitas vestra me concessisse et ad terminum dimisisse religiosis viris abbati et conventui de Bello Capite unam placeam terre cum prato adiacente in territorio de Somercote, que vocatur Wyntersedecrofte, et unam placeam bosci in eodem territorio, que vocatur Tomelingreve, et duas [acras] prati, quarum una vocatur le Bentt et alia iacet juxta le Qwythengrenes et abbuttat super Herewise, cum omnibus pertinenciis suis, usque ad terminum quatuordecim annorum proximo sequentium plene completorum, termino incipiente in festo sancti Martini in yeme anno domini m° ccc° quarto. Habendum et tenendum predictis religiosis abbati et conventui libere, quiete, pacifice et integre cum omnibus libertatibus, pasturis, communiis et aysiamentis dictis placeis terre, bosci et prati pertinentibus usque ad finem predictorum quatuordecim annorum plene completorum. Et sciendum est quod ego predictus Thomas volo et concedo quod non liceat michi vel heredibus meis assignatis predictas placeas terre, bosci et prati alicui dare, vendere vel assignare infra terminum prenominatum sine licencia et voluntate abbatis et conventus. [fo. 44v] Et ego predictus Thomas et heredes mei dictam dimissionem et concessionem, ut predictum est, predictis religiosis abbati et conventui usque ad finem termini predicti plenarie completi contra omnes gentes warantizabimus, acquietabimus et inperpetuum defendemus. In cuius rei testimonium huic presenti scripto[a] cirographato utriusque partis presentis sigilla alternatim sunt appensa. Hiis[b] testibus: Hugone de Ulkerthorp', Egidio de Rossale, Rogero de Swanwyk, Petro de Alferton', Johanne de Aula de eadem,[1] et aliis.

[a] *scripto* interlined.   [b] *H* struck through.

[1] Alfreton Hall; see also **87**.

75. Gift in free alms by John Sergant of Alfreton to Beauchief abbey of 8 selions in Alfreton in the place called Crokesbero lying on the south side of the road which goes to Ufton.[1] [1210–1240]

Carta Johannis Seriant de Alfreton' de octo selionibus cum pertinenciis

Omnibus sancte matris ecclesie filiis tam presentibus quam futuris Johannes Sergant de Alferton' salutem in Domino. Noverit universitas vestra me divine pietatis intuitu dedisse, concessisse et hac presenti carta mea confirmasse Deo et ecclesie beati Thome martiris de Beuch' et canonicis ibidem Deo servientibus octo selliones terre cum pertinenciis in territorio de Alferton', scilicet in loco qui vocatur Crokesbero iacentes juxta viam que vadit versus Ufton' ex parte meridiana in liberam, puram et perpetuam elemosinam pro salute anime mee et omnium antecessorum et heredum meorum. Et sciendum quod ego Johannes et heredes mei warantizabimus et acquietabimus predictas octo selliones terre cum pertinenciis prenominatis canonicis de Bello [fo. 45r] Capite contra omnes homines inperpetuum. Hiis testibus: Rogero de Ridding,[2] Roberto filio eius, Rogero de Hollerton', Alexandri de Byrchewod, Rad[ulpho] de Qwynfeld, et aliis multis.

[1] This may be either the modern Wingfield Road or the path that runs west from the end of Church Street to Ufton Fields. Crokesbero is a lost minor place-name.
[2] Roger of Ridding is also mentioned in 9, dated 1210–1240.

76. Quitclaim by Alice daughter of William son of Robert of Alfreton of the gift of Ranulph, her brother, *viz.* of 1½ bovates which her brother Ranulph gave to Beauchief abbey; of 1½ bovates which he gave to the nuns of Campsey Ash in free alms; and of 6 bovates which he gave to Roger of Alfreton from the 9 bovates which he had in the vill of Wymeswold of the gift of their eldest brother Robert son of William. Roger shall render to Robert 1 pair of gilt spurs annually. [1210–1240][1]

Carta Alicie filie Willelmi de Alfreton' de certis bovatis terre de Alfreton' et Wymudwold

Omnibus sancte matris ecclesie filiis presentibus et futuris Alicia filia Willelmi filii Roberti de Alferton' salutem in Domino. Noveritis me pro salute anime mee[a] et pro salute anime Ranulfi fratris mei, cuius heres sum, concessisse et presenti carta mea confirmasse et quietum clamasse pro me et heredibus meis inperpetuum donum Ranulfi fratris mei, scilicet unam bovatam terre et dimidiam cum pertinenciis suis quam dedit domui de Beuchef, et unam bovatam terre et dimidiam quam dedit domui de Campesse in perpetuam elemosinam, et sex bovatas terre cum pertinenciis suis quas dedit Rogero de Alreton' et heredibus suis de novem bovatis terre quas habuit in villa de Wymundewold de dono fratris nostri primogeniti Roberti filii Willelmi de Alferton'. Reddendo de predictis novem bovatis terre annuatim unum par calcarium deauratorum predicto Roberto filio Willelmi et heredibus suis, scilicet ad Pascha pro omni servicio et consuetudine et exaccione, salvo forinseco servicio. Ita quod nec ego nec aliquis heredum meorum aliquid in predicta terra clamare poterimus, hanc concessionem et quietam clamacionem sigillo meo corroboravi. [fo. 45v] Hiis testibus: Roberto filio Willelmi de Alferton', Johanne et Roberto capellanis de Campesse, Ran[ulpho] de Jorr, Roberto Putrell', Johanne clerico, Roberto Brien, Johanne le Poer, Ricardo dispensatore de Alferton', Thoma de Gunetun', Willelmo de Westhall', Thoma de Bradfeld, Thoma del Pek, et multis aliis.

[a] *mee* interlined.

[1] This appears to be a copy of **64**. Despite the heading, all the lands in the charter were almost certainly in Wymeswold.

77. Gift in free alms by Thomas Chaworth, knight, lord of Alfreton, to Beauchief abbey of all the waste which lies between the lands and tenements which they have in the soke of Alfreton. The canons are permitted to enclose their lands, wastes, and their grange at the Cotes.[1] [1270–1320]

Carta domini Thome de Chaworth' de vasto et de aliis terris in soka de Alfreton'

Sciant presentes et futuri quod ego Thomas de Chaworth' miles, dominus de Alferton', dedi, concessi et hac presenti carta mea confirmavi religiosis viris abbati et conventui de Bello Capite et eorum successoribus, in liberam, puram et perpetuam elemosinam, totum vastum quod iacet inter terras et tenementa sua que habunt infra sokam de Alferton' cum omnibus pertinenciis suis. Tenendum et habendum predictis religiosis abbati et conventui et eorum successoribus in liberam, puram et perpetuam elemosinam cum omnibus pertinenciis suis. Ita quod liceat eisdem religiosis terras suas et vastum inter terras et tenementa sua iacencia que ad eosdem pertinent et ad grangiam suam de le Cotes claudere, circumfossare et omni tempore anni clausa habere. Et ego predictus Thomas et heredes mei omnia ista predicta in forma prenotata dictis religiosis abbati et conventui et eorum [fo. 46r] successoribus contra omnes gentes warantizabimus, acquietabimus et inperpetuum defendemus. In cuius rei testimonium presenti carte sigillum meum apposui. Hiis testibus: Simone de Grenhyll', Willelmo de Somervile, Willelmo Fraunceys, Hugone de Ulkerthorpe, Reginaldo de Holins, et aliis.[2]

[1] Now represented by Cotespark Farm, Alfreton.
[2] William of Somerville witnessed **67**, dated c.1278, which also allowed the canons to enclose land in Alfreton. Hugh of Ulkerthorpe witnessed **74** (1304).

78. Gift in free alms by Thomas Chaworth, knight, to Beauchief abbey of an annual rent of 8s to be taken from Robert the redsmith for the tenement which he holds in the soke of Alfreton. [1270–1320][1]

Carta domini Thome Chaworth' de octo solidatis annui redditus

Omnibus hoc scriptum visuris vel audituris Thomas de Chaworth' miles salutem in Domino sempiternam. Noverit universitas vestra me dedisse, concessisse et hoc presenti scripto meo confirmasse abbati et conventui de Bello Capite in liberam, puram et perpetuam elemosinam octo solidatos annui redditus cum pertinenciis, percipiendos annuatim de Roberto le reedsmyth' et heredibus suis pro tenemento quod tenet in soka de Alferton' ad duos anni terminos, videlicet ad Annunciacionem beate Marie quatuor solidos et ad festum sancti Michaelis quatuor solidos. Tenendum et habendum dictis abbati et conventui suisque successoribus in liberam, puram et perpetuam elemosinam inperpetuum. Et ego dictus Thomas et heredes mei predictos octo solidatos annui redditus cum pertinenciis predictis abbati et conventui suisque successoribus in liberam, puram et perpetuam elemosinam contra omnes gentes inperpetuum warantizabimus, acquietabimus et defendemus. In cuius rei testimonium presenti [fo. 46v] scripto sigillum meum apposui. Hiis testibus: domino Johanne de Heryz milite, Hugone de Ulgerthorpp', Simone de Grenhill' clerico, Egidio de Rosale, Roberto Scharlet, et aliis.[2]

[1] See **72–73** for the earlier history of this rent.
[2] Hugh of Ulkerthorpe witnessed **74** (1304) and Robert Scarlet witnessed **70** (1278).

79. Quitclaim by Thomas Chaworth, lord of Alfreton, to Beauchief abbey of the land in Thorteley[1] in the soke of Alfreton which they hold by the assignment of John of Abru[...]. [1290–1320]

Carta Thome de Chaworth' de terra de Thortley in soka de Alfreton'

Omnibus ad quorum noticiam presens scriptum pervenerit Thomas de Chaworth', dominus de Alferton', salutem in Domino sempiternam. Noveritis me concessisse, confirmasse et omnino pro me et heredibus meis quietum clamasse abbati et conventui de Bello Capite et eorum successoribus in liberam, puram et perpetuam elemosinam totam illam terram in Thorteley in soca de Alferton' quam iidem abbas et conventus tenuerunt ex assignacione Johannis de Abru[...] cum omnibus pertinenciis suis, libertatibus, communiis et aysiamentis. Tenendum et habendum predictis abbati et conventui et eorum successoribus in liberam, puram et perpetuam elemosinam, libere, quiete, pacifice et integre inperpetuum. Et ego predictus Thomas et heredes mei predictam terram cum omnibus pertinenciis suis predictis abbati et conventui et eorum successoribus in liberam, puram et perpetuam elemosinam warantizabimus, acquietabimus et contra omnes gentes defendemus inperpetuum. In cuius rei testimonium presenti scripto sigillum meum apposui. Hiis testibus: Hugone de Ulkerthorpp, Waltero de Oftona, Willelmo Fraucys, Henrico [fo. 47r] de Langcroft, Willelmo le Wyte, et aliis.[2]

[1] A lost place-name (Cameron, *Place-names of Derbyshire*, I, p. 190).
[2] Hugh of Ulkerthorpe witnessed **74** (1304); Henry of Longcroft witnessed **87** (1299), **71** (1301), and **69** (1324); William White witnessed **87** (1299).

80. Gift in free alms by Thomas Chaworth, knight, to Beauchief abbey of the land with a toft, croft, and buildings which Roger the bercher once held in bondage in the soke of Alfreton. The canons shall render to Thomas 6s 8d annually. [1290–1330]

Carta domini Thome de Chaworth' de terra in Alfreton' sokon

Sciant presentes et futuri quod ego Thomas de Chaworth' miles dedi, concessi et hoc presenti scripto confirmavi abbati et conventui de Bello Capite totam illam terram, cum tofto et crofto, edificiis[a] et omnibus pertinenciis suis, quam Rogerus le Bercher quondam de me tenuit in bondagio in soka de Alferton'. Tenendum et habendum dictis abbati et conventui eorumque successoribus in liberam, puram et perpetuam elemosinam. Reddendo inde annuatim michi et heredibus meis sex solidos viij denarios ad duos anni terminos, silicet ad festum Annunciacionis beate Marie iij solidos iiij^{or} denarios, et ad festum sancti Michaelis iij solidos iiij denarios, pro omnibus secularibus serviciis, fidelitatibus, sectis, curiis, consuetudinibus et demandis. Et ego dictus Thomas et heredes mei totam predictam terram cum tofto, crofto et edificiis, cum omnibus pertinenciis suis, predictis abbati et conventui eorumque successoribus pro predicto servicio contra omnes gentes warantizabimus, acquietabimus et inperpetuum defendemus. In cuius rei testimonium presenti scripto sigillum meum apposui. Hiis testibus: domino Johanne de Heryz, Willelmo de Somervile, Hugone de Ulgerthorpp', Waltero de Hofton', Rogero de Swanewyc, Henrico de Langcroft, Wilelmo le Wyte, et multis aliis.[1]

[a] *di* of *edificiis* interlined.

[1] Hugh of Ulkerthorpe and Roger of Swanwick witnessed **74** (1304). For Henry of Longcroft and William White, see **79**, n. 2.

81. Gift in free alms by Thomas Chaworth, knight, lord of Alfreton, to Beauchief abbey and its tenants of licence to dig for and carry away coal for their use and profit, provided the tenants have a licence from the abbey to do so, as much in the lands assigned for the support of a chaplain for the celebration of the Mass of St Mary at Alfreton and the lands held by their tenants as in their own lands and wastes in the sokes of Alfreton and Norton; and of the right to clear the abbey's arable lands and those of their tenants from corn marigolds according to the custom of the sokes of Alfreton and Norton. The abbey may also arrest its tenants and impose damages on them as Thomas and his ancestors used to do. [1247–1316][1]

[fo. 47v]

Carta domini Thome de dando licenciam ad carbones fodendos in soka de Alferton'

Universis Cristi fidelibus ad quos presens scriptum pervenerit Thomas de Chaworth miles, dominus de Alferton, salutem in Domino sempiternam. Noveritis me pro salute anime mee et omnium antecessorum et successorum meorum licenciam dedisse et liberam et licitam potestatem concessisse religiosis viris abbati et conventui de Bello Capite et eorum successoribus in liberam, puram et perpetuam elemosinam ad carbones fodendos, levandos, asportandos et cariandos ad utilitatem et profectum suum et eorum tenencium quocienscumque sibi necesse fuerit, tam in terris ad cantariam misse beate Marie apud Alferton' assignatis et terris tenencium religiosorum predictorum quam in terris suis propriis et vastis inter et infra terras suas iacentibus infra socas de Alferton' et Norton', sine inquietacione vel perturbacione mei vel heredum meorum. Concessi eciam eisdem abbati et conventui quod libere possint terras suas et tenencium suorum a goldis mundare, secundum consuetudinem in socis de Alferton' et Norton' usitatam[a] per se et suos et si defectum in mundacione predicta invenerint quod possint tenentes suos punire, sicut ex antiquo puniri fuerat consuetum, sine inpedimento et calumpnia mei vel heredum meorum. In cuius rei testimonium presenti scripto sigillum meum apposui. Hiis testibus: domino Johanne de Ayencourt milite, Willelmo le Brett, Rogero Breton', Ada de Re[fo. 48r]risbe, Rad[ulpho] de eadem, Stephano le Eyer, Hugone de Linacr', et aliis.

[a] *uisitatam.*

[1] Copy of **37**; see the note there for dating evidence.

82. Quitclaim by John Wolaton to Beauchief abbey of a certain meadow and 3½ acres of arable in the Ridding which Richard Bars once held from the abbey. Made at Watnall[1] on Friday 1 August 1382.

Quieta clamacio Johannis Wolaton' de terra in le Ryddyng

Noverit universi per presentes me Johannem Wolaton' remisisse, relaxasse et omnino pro me et heredibus meis quietum clamasse abbati et conventui de Bello Capite et eorum successoribus omnem jus et clameum juris quod habui, vel habere potero, in quondam prato ortulo et[a] tribus[b] acris terre et dimidia arabilibus in le Riddyng que Ricardus Bars quondam tenuit de predictis abbate et conventu. Ita quod nec ego nec heredes mei nec aliquis nomine nostro aliquod jus vel clameum juris in predictis prato ortulo et tribus[b] acris et dimidia terre arabilibus cum pertinenciis suis decetero exigere vel vendicare poterimus, set ab omni accione juris simus exclusi per presentes in futurum. In cuius rei testimonium presentibus sigillum meum apposui. Hiis testibus: Willelmo de Aderley, Nicholao de Bakewell', Rad[ulpho] Bercher,[2] et aliis. Dat' apud Watenaw die veneris in festo sancti Petri quod dicitur ad vincula anno regni regis Ricardi secundi post conquestum sexto.

[a] *d* struck through.   [b] *trbus.*

[1] Between Nottingham and Eastwood.
[2] Perhaps Ralph Barker of Dore; see **218**.

83. Letter by Robert of Radclyffe, abbot of Beauchief,[1] and his convent that since Thomas Chaworth, lord of Alfreton, granted them an annual rent of 13s 4d for the term of 40 years to be taken from his manor of Alfreton,[2] the abbey has granted to Thomas the coal mine in the parish of Alfreton. If, however, the mine provides no coals in the said 40 years or if Thomas does not mine the coals or take the profits then the said annual rent shall cease. Made at Alfreton on Saturday 23 October 1367.

Carta Roberti de Adclyff abbatis de Beucheff

A touz yceaux qe cestes lettres verront ou orront Robert de Radclyfe abbe de Beuchef et le covent de mesme le lieu salutz en Dieu. Sachetz qe come mons[ieur] Thomas de Chaworth seignur de Alferton' nous[a] eit done et grante un annuite de tressze soldz et quatre deneres a terme [fo. 48v] quarantz anz a prendre de son manoir de Alferton', come plus pleynement[b] apiert par son fayt eut a nous faite. Nient purtant nous le avanditz abbe et covent veloms et grantoms par ycestes pur nous et pur noz successoures qe sil avigne qe la minere des carbons le dit mons[ieur] Thomas en le paroche Dalfirton' faile issuit qe nuls carbons illeoqes puissent estre gaignes deinz les qarant anz avanditz, ou a quele hure qe ne plese au dit monsieur Thomas faire ascuns carbons estre mines et gaignes el paroche avandit qadonqes la dite annuite de tressze soldz et quatre[c] deneres cesse, et le fait le ditz mons[ieur] Thomas del annuite avandit a nous fait de tote perde sa force et escase pur null. En tesmoignance de quele chose a ycestes endentures les parties avanditz entrechaungeablement ont mis leurs seals. Done a Alfirton' le samadi prochein apres la feste de seint

Luk Evangeliste lan du regne le roi Edward tierce apres le conquest quarantisme premere.

^a*mous.*   ^b*y* of *pleynement* interlined.   ^c*u* of *quatre* interlined.

[1] See Smith and London, *Heads of Religious Houses*, II, p. 494 and D.M. Smith (ed.), *Heads of Religious Houses: England and Wales, III, 1377–1540* (Cambridge, 2008), p. 563.
[2] See **85**, executed the day before this letter was written.

84. Indenture made between Thomas Chaworth, knight, lord of Alfreton, on the one part and Robert of Radclyfe, abbot of Beauchief,[1] and his convent on the other to resolve a disagreement between them concerning the payment of tithe for coal in Swanwick and elsewhere in the parish of Alfreton. [*c*.1367][2]

Indentura inter Thomam Chaworth' et abbatem de Beucheff

Ceste endenture fait entre mons[ieur] Thomas de Chaworth' chivalere, seignur de Alferton', dune part, et sieur Robert de Radclyfe, abbe de Beuchefe, et le covent de meisme la [fo. 49r] place persones del esglice de Alferton' daltre part, tesmogne qe come debat et plee estoit entre eaux mew et comense sur disme des carbons de meer en Swanwyk et aillours deinz les boundes et les limites del paroch' del dit esglise de Alferton', levandit abbe et covent disantz et affermantz soi avoir par comune ley de seint esglise et auxint par comune usage de pays. Et lavandit mons[ieur] Thomas disant qil ne null' de ses auncestres unqes paierent dismes des carbons deinz meisme la paroch' par quoi^a usage ne title de prescripcion ne puist prendre effect en lui de yceo, par quoi au dirrain par comune assent des amis et par counseil dampartz a Alferton' le dimaigne prochein apres la Chaundelur' lan du regne le roi Edward tierce apres le conquest qarantisme premere en la presence sieur Robert Rivers parsone del esglise de Ekyngton', William de Wakebrigge, Johan at Well', Richard de Ufton', et altres. Pur ceo qe null' certangte del cleym ne de la demande labbe et covent sur la demaunde des dismes avandit nest un qore fait ne aviggez en null court mes, pur bone conscience et unite et amour entre les avanditz mons[ieur] Thomas et labbe et covent faire et engrosser ils sont apesetz et acordetz en manere qeu suit. Cest assavoir qe pur le disme carbon [fo. 49v] deinz le paroche avandit lavandit mons[ieur] Thomas grantera pur lui et ses heires al avandit abbe et covent et loures successours tressze soldz et quatre deneres annuelment aprendre de son manoir de Alferton', par auxi bone seurte com le consail labbe et covent saveront ordeigner a durer tanqe le carbon de meer illeoqes puise estre trove et gaigne sur le soil le dit mons[ieur] Thomas. Et auxint soit gaigne en la paroch avandit issuit totes veires qe si en apres ne soit aviggez en null court de seint esglise qe disme de carbon de meer ne doit estre done ne paye du drott ou qe si comune opinuon des gentz apris de la ley de seint esglise soit qe lavandit disme de carbon ne doit estre paye du droit. Par quoi lavandit mons[ieur] Thomas ou ses heires volent cesser del payment del avandit mark qe cele payment del mark avandit ne soit trette pris ne alegge payment del disme del carbon en mayntenance del title labbe et covent et contre la defens le dit mons[ieur] Thomas ou seis heirs. Et a touz ceaux covenantz lealment tenir et parfournir lavandit mons[ieur] Thomas soi oblige et ses heires. Et sil defaile en les covenant avandit de payer al avandit abbe et covent et lours successoures vint livres. Et lavandit abbe et covent obligent soi et lours successoures a tenir les cove[fo. 50r]nantz avanditz, et sils defailent en les covenantz avanditz de paier au dit mons[ieur] Thomas et a ses heires vint livres. En tesmoignance de qeles choses a ycestes endentures les parties avanditz entrechaungeablement ont mis leurs seals.

[a] *u* of *quoi* interlined.

[1] See Smith and London, *Heads of Religious Houses*, II, p. 494 and Smith, *Heads of Religious Houses*, III, p. 563.
[2] Presumably executed at the same time as **83** and **85**.

85. Grant by Thomas Chaworth, knight, lord of Alfreton, to Beauchief abbey of an annual rent of 13s 4d for the term of 40 years to be taken from his manor of Alfreton. Made at Alfreton on Friday 22 October 1367.[1]

Carta domini Thome Chaworth' de tribus[a] solidis et iiij[or] denariis

A touz yceaux qe cestes lettres veront ou orront Thomas de Chaworth chivalere, seignur de Alferton', salutz en Dieu. Sachetz moi avoir done et grante a Robert de Radclyfe abbe de Beuchefe et al covent de meisme le lieu et a lours successours une annuite de tressze soldz et quatre deneres a terme de qarant anz a prendre de mon manoir de Alfirton' a les festes de la Nativite de nostre Seignur et seint Johan le Baptistre par owels porcions. Et ieo voil et grante par ycestes qe si la dit annuite de tressze soldz et qatre deneres soit a derere, en partie ou en tote, apres null des termes avanditz qadonqes bien lise au dit abbe et a ses successoures a destreindre pur la rent avandit durant le terme de quarant anz avanditz, et cele destres retenir tanqe gres li soit fait de la dite annuite ensemblement et les arrerages. En tesmoignance de quele chose a ycestes jai mis mon seal. Don a Alferton' le vendredi prochein apres la feste de seint Luk le [fo. 50v][b] Evangeliste lan du regne le roi Edward tierce apres le conquest quarantisme premere.

[a]The rubric here says 3s, despite all other references in this and **83** and **84** being to 13s.
[b]Folio heading: *Relaxacio domini Thome Chaworth*.

[1]The grant mentioned in **83**, executed the following day.

86. Thomas Chaworth, knight, abandons any claim against the abbot for harm or trespass. Made at Norton on Wednesday 7 April 1350.

Relaxacio domini Thome Chaworth

Conne chose soit a totes gentz moi Thomas de Chaworth' chivalere avoir relesse a Robert de Ratclife abbe de Beuchefe et au covent de meisme le lieu chescun maniere accion personel et a tous les hommes et servantz du dit abbe chescun manier accion du trespas a moi fait par reson dastune debat qad estee einz ces houres parentre le dit abbe et moi du comensement de monde tanqe a iour de la confeccion de cestes. En tesmoignance de qele choise a yceste escript ay mys mon seal. Escript a Norton' en le conte de Derby le meskerdy prochein apres la feste de seynt Dambrose en lan du regne le roi Edward le tierce puys le conquest Dengletere vynt et quarte.

87. Quitclaim by Thomas Chaworth, knight, lord of Alfreton, to Beauchief abbey and all their tenants in the soke of Alfreton of all the common pasture called the Lee.[1] Made at Alfreton on 29 September 1299.

Carta domini Thome Chaworth de comuna pasture

Pateat universis per presentes quod ego Thomas de Chaworth' miles, dominus de Alferton', dedi, concessi et hac presenti carta mea omnino quietum clamavi pro me et heredibus meis vel assignatis abbati et conventui de Bello Capite et omnibus aliis qualitercumque tenentibus de soka de Alferton' [fo. 51r] totam illam communiam pasture que dicitur le Leye. Ita quod nec ego dictus Thomas nec heredes mei vel assignati seu aliquis alius nomine nostro predictam communiam pasture arrare, assartare vel frussare decetero poterimus quoquomodo. In cuius rei testimonium presenti sigillum meum est appensum. Hiis testibus: Henrico de Langcroft,[2] Roberto de Grenhill', Willelmo Bulmer, Willelmo le Wyte, Johanne de aula,[3] et aliis. Dat' apud Alferton' in festo sancti Michaelis anno Domini m° cc° nonagesimo nono.

[1] The place-name survives in Flowery Leys Lane, a turning off High Street in Alfreton.
[2] For Henry of Longcroft see **69**, n. 2.
[3] Alfreton Hall; see also **74**.

88. Quitclaim by Thomas Chaworth, knight, to Beauchief abbey of Adam Hutun son of Eudes Leneire, once his serf, with all his family and their chattels. [1250–1320].

Quieta clamacio domini Thome Chaworth Ada filio Ede Leneire[a]

Omnibus Cristi fidelibus presens scriptum visuris vel audituris Thomas de Chaworth miles salutem in Domino. Noveritis me dedisse et penitus quietum clamasse et hoc presenti scripto confirmasse de me et heredibus meis abbati et conventui de Bello Capite et successoribus suis Adam Hutun filium Ede Leneir', quondam nativum meum, cum tota sequela sua et omnibus catallis suis. Ita quod nec ego nec heredes mei nec aliquis per me vel pro me inperpetuum aliquod jus vel clameum in dicto Ada cum tota sequela sua et omnibus catallis suis aliquomodo exigere, vendicare vel calumpniare poterimus. In cuius rei testimonium huic presenti scripto sigillum meum apposui. Hiis testibus: Thoma de Bramton', Willelmo de Gaham, Petro de Byrchehed, Thomas de Wadescayf, [fo. 51v] Roberto le Blount, Thoma de Wodhous, Thoma de Leys, et multis aliis.

[a] Or *Leveire*.

89. Quitclaim by Alexander son of Alexander of Birchwood to Beauchief abbey of the wood and land in Alfreton, which his lord Robert son of William gave to them in free alms together with his body. [1225–1240][1]

Quieta clamacio Alexandri de Birchewode de quondam bosco et terra in Alferton'

Omnibus Cristi fidelibus hoc scriptum visuris vel audituris Alexander filius Alexandri de Byrchewod salutem in Domino. Noverit universitas vestra me divini amoris intuitu relaxasse et quietum clamasse de me et heredibus meis Deo et beate Marie et ecclesie beati Thome martiris de Bello Capite et canonicis in eadem ecclesia servientibus totum jus et clameum quod habui vel habere potero in bosco et in terra in territorio de Alferton', quam dominus meus Robertus filius Willelmi dedit eisdem canonicis cum corpore suo in puram et perpetuam elemosinam, liberam et quietam et solutam ab omni seculari servicio et exaccione de me et heredibus meis inperpetuum pro salute anime mee et omnium antecessorum et heredum meorum. Et ut hec mea relaxacio et quieta[a] clamacio firma et stabilis futuris temporibus perseveret, presens scriptum sigilli mei inpressione roboravi. Hiis testibus: Roberto tunc capellano de Alferton', Rad[ulpho] de Bredun', Nicholao de Meenil, Roberto de Kelesehold, et aliis.

[a] *quita.*

[1] Robert was still alive in 1224 (*Calendar of Close Rolls*, I, p. 611).

[CHARTERS OF SIR WILLIAM CHAWORTH, SON AND HEIR APPARENT OF SIR THOMAS CHAWORTH I]

90. Quitclaim by Sir William Chaworth son and heir of Sir Thomas Chaworth to Beauchief abbey of 1 strip called the Qwytekar in Alfreton with 12 acres in Barsfelde and the strip which Peter the weaver held near the land of Simon of the Storthes in Alfreton; of everything of which the abbey is seized in the fees of Norton, Alfreton, and Wymeswold; and of all charters, enfeoffments, gifts, grants, quitclaims, and muniments which the abbey has from him or his ancestors. [1269-1289][1]

Quieta clamacio domini Willelmi Chaworth' de le[a] Qwytekar

Omnibus sancte matris ecclesie filiis hoc scriptum visuris [fo. 52r] dominus Willelmus de Chaworth miles, filius et heres domini Thome de Chaworth, salutem in Domino sempiternam. Noverit universitas vestra me pro salute anime mee et omnium antecessorum et successorum meorum concessisse et confirmasse et omnino quietum clamasse Deo et beate Marie et ecclesie beati Thome martiris de Bello Capite et abbati et conventui illius loci eorumque successoribus, in liberam, puram et perpetuam elemosinam, totam illam placeam terre que vocatur le Qwytekar in territorio de Alferton' cum duodecim acris terre in loco qui dicitur Barffeld et cum illa placea terre, quam Petrus textor tenuit juxta terram Simonis del Storthes in territorio eiusdem ville, ac omnes terras, redditus, molendina cum sitibus suis, cursibus aquarum, stagnis, viis et semitis, sectas, sequelas, servicia, possessiones, consuetudines, jura et libertates, tam laici feodi quam beneficiorum ecclesiasticorum, ac omnia tenementa cum pratis, boscis, clausis et non clausis, pasturis, piscariis et omnibus eorum proventibus pertinenciis, communiis et aysiamentis, quibus omnibus predictis cum pertinenciis suis predicti abbas et conventus loci predicti vestiti sunt et seysiti infra feoda de Norton', Alferton' et Wymundeswold. Concedo etiam et confirmo ac quietum clamo pro me et heredibus meis seu assignatis sepedictis abbati et conventui et eorum successoribus in liberam, puram et perpetuam elemosinam omnes cartas, feofamenta, donaciones, concessiones, quietasclamaciones et omnia munimenta [fo. 52v] que dicti abbas et conventus habent de antecessoribus meis, vel de me ipso, ut hoc scriptum solum cum necesse fuerit pro omnibus aliis munimentis suis sibi sufficiat inperpetuum. Et ego predictus Willelmus et heredes mei ac assignati omnes terras, redditus, beneficia ecclesiastica[b] et eorum jura, molendina, sectas, sequelas, servicia, possessiones, consuetudines et libertates, ac omnia tenementa cum pratis, boscis, stagnis, piscariis, communiis et omnimodis aysiamentis suis, proventibus et pertinenciis, ut predictum est, quibus predicti abbas et conventus vestiti sunt et seysiti infra feoda predicta, eisdem abbati et conventui et eorum successoribus in liberam, puram et perpetuam elemosinam contra omnes gentes warantizabimus, acquietabimus et ubique inperpetuum defendemus. In cuius rei testimonium presenti scripto sigillum meum apposui. Hiis testibus: domino Henrico de Perpoynt, domino Johanne de Heryz, domino Johanne de Anesley, domino Ran[ulpho] de Wandesley, domino Willelmo de Steynesby, domino Egidio de Yeynyll', Johanne de Brimigton', Roberto de Rerysby, Waltero de Ufton', Roberto Scharlett, et aliis.[1]

[a] *le* inserted. [b] *eccliastica ecclesiastica.*

[1] This is in part a confirmation of one particular charter of William's father's (**26**), which was among those confirmed in September 1312 (**38**, no. 14), and at least five of the witnesses listed here also witnessed his father's gift, suggesting that the two were executed about the same date. At the same time, William gave a general confirmation of the abbey's title to all their possessions on his family's estates and of all the muniments that the canons had from him or his family. William's only other charter in the Cartulary (**91**) is similar in structure. Both this charter and **26** can be dated quite closely from the appearance of William of Stainsby, who succeeded his father, Jocelin, *c.*1269 and died in 1289 (Darlington, *The Cartulary of Darley Abbey*, I, p. xxix). He and Robert of Reresby together witnessed Leake **5** (see Appendix I).
[2] Giles of Yeynll is probably the same as Giles of Meynell (**38**, n. 2), from Meynell Langley in south Derbyshire. Robert Scarlet also witnessed **70** (1278).

91. Confirmation by William Chaworth, knight, son and heir of Sir Thomas Chaworth, to Beauchief abbey of everything that they have in the fees of Thomas his father and others of his ancestors at Norton, Alfreton, and Wymeswold of the gift, sale, or grant of his father or other of his ancestors; and of all charters, feoffments, gifts, quitclaims, grants, and muniments which the abbey has from his father or other of his ancestors; and of the new mill in Norton and the mill of Aston or Hazlehurst. [1270–1312][1]

Confirmacio domini Willelmi Chaworth'

Omnibus sancte matris ecclesie filiis hoc presens scriptum visuris vel audituris Willelmus de Chaworth miles, filius et heres domini Thome de Chaworth, salutem in Domino sempiternam. [fo. 53r][a] Noverit universitas vestra me, divine pietatis intuitu ac pro salute anime mee et omnium antecessorum meorum, concessisse et confirmasse Deo et beate Marie et ecclesie beati Thome martiris de Bello Capite et abbati et conventui illius loci eorumque successoribus inperpetuum, in liberam, puram et perpetuam elemosinam, omnes terras redditus, sectas, sequelas, servicia, possessiones et libertates, tam laici feodi quam beneficiorum ecclesiasticorum, ac omnia tenementa cum pratis, boscis, pasturis, stagnis et piscacionibus, et omnibus eorum proventibus, pertinenciis, communiis et aysiamentis, quas et que terras, redditus, beneficia ac tenementa, cum aliis que prenotata sunt abbas et conventus monasterii predicti habent in feodo dicti domini Thome, patris mei et aliorum antecessorum meorum, apud Norton', Alferton' et Wymundewold ex dono vendicione vel concessione patris mei predicti vel aliquorum antecessorum meorum vel advocatorum dicti monasterii. Concedo insuper et confirmo pro me et heredibus meis seu assignatis abbati et conventui predicti monasterii et eorum successoribus inperpetuum omnes cartas, feofamenta, donaciones, quietasclamaciones, concessiones et omnia et singula munimenta, in liberam, puram et perpetuam elemosinam, que et quas dicti abbas et conventus habent a patre meo vel ab aliquo antecessorum nostrorum. Concedo ad hec et confirmo eisdem abbati et conventui et eorum successoribus, in liberam, [fo. 53v] puram et perpetuam elemosinam, molendinum in soca de Norton' et dicitur novum molendinum et molendinum de Aston' sive de Hasilhyrst cum cursibus aquarum ad dicta molendina et sectis et operibus suis et terra in feodo antecessorum meorum juxta predicta molendina vicinius capienda ad opera dictorum molendinorum et stagnorum suorum, sine omni impedimento mei vel heredum meorum et tenencium seu assignatorum meorum, set non de terra arabili aut prato dummodo alia vasta terra ibidem in vicinis possit inveniri. Volo insuper et concedo ut intra terras suas et assartas dominicas in soka de Norton' et Alferton' possint dicti abbas et conventus et eorum successores ac servientes fodere, querere et cariare turbariam, quareriam, marleriam, minam quamcumque et carbones marinos cum hec et huiusmodi invenerint, set quod sibi viderint expedire, sine omni impedimento mei vel heredum meorum seu assignatorum. Et ut predicti abbas et conventus et eorum homines et tenentes in feodis de Norton' et Alferton' habeant inperpetuum liberum aysiamentum per semitas et vias eundi, equitandi et cariandi, sine omni impedimento mei vel heredum meorum seu assignatorum, et ceteri[b] tenentes de predictis feodis huiusmodi aysiamentum habuerint. In cuius rei testimonium presenti scripto sigillum meum apposui. Hiis testibus: domino Thoma.[2]

[a] At head of folio (in a different script): *Pateat universi per presentes me Georg' Ottley de Pytchford.*
[b] *seteri.*

[1] See **90**, n. 1.
[2] This charter breaks off here at the end of the fourth quire; the next quire has been completely excised and only the stubs remain.

[SCHOLES AND THORPE HESLEY]

92. Fragment of a gift in free alms concerning Scholes. [1190–1220][1]

[fo. 54r] suis hominibus predictas terras et tenentibus in omnibus locis et pascuis tocius communionis mee de Schales, in puram et perpetuam elemosinam, libere et quiete ab omni seculari exaccione inperpetuum, possidendam pro salute anime mee et uxoris mee et heredum meorum et omnium antecessorum meorum. Hiis testibus: Ricardo et Jardano capellanis de Norton', Willelmo filio Roberti, Petro Hertyll', Roberto filio Henrici, Hugone fratre suo, Hugone de Hulecotes, Henrico de Bereng', Rogero de Fimeleya de Schales, et aliis.[2]

[1] Charters **92**–**98** cannot be dated precisely but they all date from before Idonea of Leyburn's quitclaim of 1296 (**99**). Donations were made by three generations of this family: Robert,

Hugh, and Richard (who was alive in 1296) (**99**). They each relate to properties within the Honour of Tickhill.

[2] The earlier part of this fragment was probably copied at the end of the quire that has been excised between fos 53 and 54. It belongs to a charter that was perhaps the first in the group that comprises **92**–**98**; see the list of witnesses in **7**, which includes Peter Harthill, Henry Berengerville, and Richard the chaplain.

93. Gift in free alms by Hugh son of Robert of Scholes to Beauchief abbey, together with his body, of 1 croft with buildings which Robert his nephew once held in Scholes, so that Robert and his heirs shall hold the croft from the abbey forever. Robert shall render to the canons 12d annually. [1230–1280]

Carta de Scoles in Halumschire[1]

Omnibus sancte matris ecclesie filiis presentibus et futuris Hugo filius Roberti de Schales salutem in Domino. Noverit discretio vestra me divine pietatis intuitu dedisse et hac mea presenti carta confirmasse Deo[a] et ecclesie sancti Thome martiris de Beuchef et canonicis ibidem Deo servientibus cum corpore meo totum croftum cum edificiis et cum omnibus aliis pertinenciis, scilicet quod Robertus, nepos meus, aliquando de me tenuit in predicta villa de Schales, cum omnibus libertatibus, comuniis et aysiamentis ad predictam villam pertinentibus, in liberam, puram et perpetuam elemosinam, pro salute anime mee et patris mei et matris mee et omnium antecessorum et heredum meorum. Ita tamen quod predictus Robertus et heredes eius prenominatum croftum de supradictis canonicis de Beuchef pro homagio et servicio suo inperpetuum teneant. Reddendo [fo. 54v] inde annuatim predictis canonicis duodecim denarios duobus terminis, scilicet sex denarios ad festum sancti Martini et sex denarios ad Pent[ecosten] pro omni seculari servicio et demanda. Hiis testibus: domino Rad[ulpho] de Eclessall', Thoma Barbot,[2] Willelmo filio Hugonis, Rad[ulpho] clerico de Wyntwrth', Thoma de Merkesbourgh', Willelmo de Maddehou,[3] Osberto Thakall', Johanne serviente de Kymbyrwrth', Willelmo clerico de Shales, et aliis.

[a] *Dee.*

[1] Scholes actually lay in the lordship of Kimberworth, just beyond the Hallamshire border.
[2] Barbot Hall, Greasbrough.
[3] Meadow Hall, Kimberworth.

94. Gift in free alms by Hugh son of Robert of Scholes to Beauchief abbey of the land which Siggrit daughter of Henry of Scholes once held in Scholes; and of 1 portion of meadow which lies between Siggrit's land and the land of Hugh son of William with a toft and croft. [1230–1280]

Alia carta de Scoles

Omnibus sancte matris ecclesie filiis presentibus et futuris Hugo filius Roberti de Schales salutem in Domino. Noverit universitas vestra me divine pietatis intuitu dedisse, concessisse et hac mea presenti carta confirmasse Deo et ecclesie sancti Thome martiris de Beuchef et canonicis in[a] eadem ecclesia Deo servientibus totam terram quam Siggrit filia Henrici de Schales de me aliquando tenuit in territorio de Schales et unam dalam que iacet inter terram eiusdem Sigerit et terram Hugonis filii Willelmi cum tofto et crofto et omnibus libertatibus, communiis et aysiamentis predicte terre pertinentibus, in liberam, puram et perpetuam elemosinam, pro salute anime mee et omnium antecessorum et heredum meorum. Ita quod predicta Sigerit et heredes sui in omnibus et per omnia de omni servicio suo et homagio predictis canonicis de Beuchef, sicut dominis suis omnino inperpetuum sint responsuri. Hiis testibus: Simone [fo. 55r] capellano de Wrteley, Nicholao de Wrteley et Nicholao filio suo,[1] Rad[ulph]o filio Roberti de Eclessall', Jeremia de Leysers, Roberto de Wyntworth', Willelmo filio Hugonis de eadem villa, Stephano de Areley, et aliis.

[a] *et.*

[1] Several lords of Wortley and Aston (South Yorks) in the thirteenth and fourteenth centuries bore the personal name Nicholas.

95. Quitclaim by Richard son of Hugh of Scholes to Beauchief abbey of the homage and service of Robert son of Gilbert of Perlethorpe[1] for the land which he held in the vill of Scholes. [1260–1296]

Alia carta de Scoles

Omnibus Cristi fidelibus hoc scriptum visuris vel audituris Ricardus filius Hugonis de Schales salutem in Domino. Noverit universitas vestra me divine pietatis intuitu dedisse et quietum clamasse de me et heredibus meis inperpetuum, pro salute anime mee, Deo et ecclesie sancti Thome martiris de Beuchef et canonicis ibidem Deo servientibus, homagium et totum servicium quod Robertus filius Gilberti de Peverelthorpe michi debebat pro terra quam de me tenuit in villa de Schales. Ita quod idem Robertus et heredes sui de predicto homagio et servicio dictis canonicis de Beuchef amodo inperpetuum intendant et respondeant in omnibus predicte terre pertinentibus. Hiis testibus: magistro Roberto tunc temporis officiali de Westhing, Johanne Dorli, Rermero persona de Treton', Henrico[a] de Merkesburo, Willelmo filio Hugonis, Rogero filio Reynes de Aldewark, et aliis.[2]

[a] *Hnre*.

[1] North of Ollerton (Notts).
[2] Treeton, Mexborough, and Aldwark all lie within a few miles of Scholes.

96. Quitclaim by Thomas son of Robert of Masbrough[1] to Beauchief abbey of the land which Robert his brother sold him in the vill of Scholes. Robert son of Gilbert of Perlethorpe shall render to the canons 12d annually. [1260–1300]

Alia carta de Skoles

Sciant presentes et futuri quod ego Thomas filius Roberti de Merkesburo dedi et quietum clamavi, pro amore Dei et salutem anime mee, de me et heredibus meis inperpetuum, Deo et ecclesie [fo. 55v] sancti Thome martiris de Beuchef et canonicis ibidem Deo servientibus, totum jus et clameum quod habui, vel habere potui, in terra quam Robertus, frater meus, michi vendidit in villa de Schales. Ita quod dicti canonici de Beuchef annuam firmam suam, videlicet duodecim denarios de manu Roberti filii Gilberti de Peverelthorpe ad duos terminos, scilicet ad Pent[ecosten] et ad festum sancti Martini, annuatim percipiant. Et ut hec mea donacio et quieta clamacio stabilis et firma futuris temporibus perseveret, eam tam sigilli mei inpressione quam testium subscripcione roboravi. Hiis testibus: magistro Roberto tunc tempore officiali de Westthind, Johanne Dorli, Remero persona de Treton, Henrico de Merkesburo, Willelmo filio Hugonis, et aliis.

[1] On the west bank of the River Don, by Rotherham.

97. Grant by Hugh of Scholes son of Robert to Robert son of Alice his nephew, for his homage and service, of all the land which Cecily his aunt once held in Scholes. Robert, who gave Hugh ½ silver mark for this grant, shall render to him 12d annually. [1230–1280]

Carta Hugonis de Scoles

Sciant presentes et futuri quod ego Hugo de Schales filius Roberti concessi et dedi et hac presenti carta mea confirmavi Roberto filio Alicie, nepoti meo, et heredibus suis, pro homagio suo et servicio et pro dimidia marca argenti quam michi dedit in gersuma,[a] totam terram quam Cecilia, matertera mea, quondam tenuit in Schales. Habendam et tenendam de me et heredibus meis sibi et heredibus suis in feudo et hereditate, libere, quiete et in pace, cum comunis et libertatibus et omnibus aliis aysiamentis infra villam et extra ad predictam terram pertinentibus. Reddendo inde annuatim michi et heredibus meis duodecim denarios, silicet sex [fo. 56r] denarios ad Pent[ecosten] et sex denarios ad festum sancti Martini, pro omnibus secularibus serviciis et exaccionibus et demandis. Et ego Hugo et heredes mei warantizabimus predictam terram cum pertinenciis predicto Roberto et heredibus suis contra omnes homines inperpetuum. Hiis testibus: Ada de Wyntworth' capellano, Rad[ulpho] de Eclessale, Thoma Beryb', Roberto filio Willelmi, Willelmo filio Hugonis, et aliis.

[a] *gersum.*

98. Grant by Robert the clerk of Masbrough to Richard son of Hugh of Scholes, for his homage and service, of 1 croft with buildings and a garden which Ellis the carpenter once held in the vill of Scholes. Richard, who gave Robert 20s for this grant, shall render to him 13d annually. [1250–1296]

Carta Thome filii clerici de Merkesbord

Sciant presentes et futuri quod ego Thomas filius Roberti, clerici de Merkesbord, concessi et dedi et hac presenti carta mea confirmavi Ricardo filio Hugonis de Schales, pro homagio suo et servicio et pro viginti solidis argenti quos michi dedit in gersumma,[a] totum illud croftum cum edificiis et gardino et cum omnibus pertinenciis, sine aliquo retenemento, quod scilicet Helyas carpentarius quondam tenuit in villa de Schales. Habendum et tenendum de me et heredibus meis sibi et heredibus suis in feudo et hereditate, libere, quiete et in pace, cum communiis et libertatibus et omnibus aliis aisiamentis ad predictam terram pertinentibus. Reddendo inde annuatim michi et heredibus meis decem et tres denarios, scilicet sex denarios et obulum ad Pent[ecosten] et sex denarios et obulum ad festum sancti Martini, pro omnibus serviciis et demandis. Et ego Thomas et heredes mei warantizabimus predictum croftum cum edificiis et omnibus aliis pertinenciis predicto Ricardo et heredibus suis contra omnes homines inperpetuum. Hiis testibus: domino Johanne [fo. 56v] Delly, Thoma Barbot, Willelmo de Reynes, Willelmo filio Roberti de Wyntworth', Roberto de Wdehous, Hugone de eadem, Stephano de Berley, Hugone de Tancreslay, Willelmo de Maddehou, Rad[ulpho] clerico, et multis aliis.

[a] *gersummam.*

99. Quitclaim by Idonea of Leyburn,[1] lady of Kimberworth, to William of Folkingham, abbot of Beauchief,[2] and his successors of all the lands and tenements which his predecessors entered into by feoffment of the ancestors of Richard of Scholes and of other tenants or their ancestors in Thorpe[3] and Scholes which are of the fee of her manor of Kimberworth. Made at Kimberworth on Tuesday 10 April 1296.

Quieta clamacio Ydone domine de Kymbreworth de certis terris in Thorp et Scoles

A touz ceus qe cestes lettres verrount ou orrount Idoigne de Leyborne, dame de Kymbreworth', saluz en Dieu. Sachez qe frere Williem de Fowyngham, abbe de Beuchef, et pleinement moun gre fet pur leutres en toutes les terres e touz les tenemenz oue les apurtinaunces en les queus les predecessoures le dit abbe entrerent par les feffemonz des auncestres Richard des Eschales et des autres tenaunz ou de lour auncestres en Thorp et en Eschales, qe sorunt du fee de moun maneire de Kymbreworth'. Parqoi jeo voil e graunt pur moi et pur mes eirs qe le dit abbe et ses successours a touz jours soient quites e en pees de toutes maneres de demaundes e de grevaunces qe nous les enpurrirouns fere par ley de terre par cele acher soun eines par nous ne par nos baillifs a nul jour ne soient destreinz ne en nul manere grevez par la cheisoun avauntdit. En tesmoignaunce de ceste chose a cestes lettres ai mis moun seal. Don a Kymbreworth le marsdy preschein apres la feste seint Ambrose Levest' lan du [fo. 57r] regne le roi Edwarde fiz le roi Henri vintisme quart.

[1] Lady of Kimberworth from 1265 to 1334 (J. Hunter, *South Yorkshire: the history of the deanery of Doncaster*, 2 vols (London, 1826–1831), II, p. 27).
[2] See Smith and London, *Heads of Religious Houses*, II, p. 494; Leake **8** and **9** (see Appendix I).
[3] Thorpe Hesley (South Yorks) adjoins Scholes.

100. Quitclaim by Richard son of Edward of Scholes to Beauchief of all lands, rent, and tenement which they have in Thorpe and Scholes and elsewhere by the gift of Richard his father and others of his ancestors; and of all charters, feoffments, gifts, grants, quitclaims, and muniments which they have from Richard his father and his other ancestors. [1280–1320]

Quieta clamacio Ricardi filii Edwardi de Schales de omnibus terris et tenementis nostris in Thorp et Schales

Pateat universis me Ricardum filium Edwardi de Schales concessisse et confirmasse ac omnino pro me et heredibus meis inperpetuum quieta clamasse abbati et conventui de Bello Capite omnes terras, redditus ac tenementa que dicti abbas et conventus habent in Thorp' et Schales et in omnibus aliis locis de dono et concessione Ricardi, patris mei, et antecessorum meorum. Habendum et tenendum dictis abbati et conventui suisque successoribus inperpetuum in liberam, puram et perpetuam elemosinam, cum omnibus pertinenciis suis, libertatibus, comuniis et aysiamentis, cum wardis, releviis, escaetis et omnimodis aliis pertinenciis ac serviciis de dictis terris, redditibus ac tenementis cum pertinenciis qualitercumque provenientibus.[a] Ita quod nec ego Ricardus nec heredes mei nec aliquis per nos seu nomine nostro aliquid juris vel clamei in dictis terris, redditibus ac tenementis, nec in eorum tenentibus nec in aliquibus pertinenciis suis, nominatis vel non nominatis, habere, exigere vel reclamare poterimus quoquomodo[b] inperpetuum. Concedo eciam et confirmo ac pro me et heredibus meis inperpetuum quietum clamo predictis abbati et conventui suisque successoribus in liberam, puram et perpetuam elemosinam omnes cartas, feofamenta, donaciones, concessiones, quietas clamaciones ac munimenta que habent de predicto Ricardo, patre meo, et de antecessoribus meis, plene et integre in suo robore predictis abbati et conventui suisque successoribus [fo. 57v] inperpetuum volitura. Et ego dictus Ricardus et heredes mei predictas terras, redditus ac tenementa cum omnibus suis pertinenciis prenominatis, necnon cartas, feofamenta, donaciones, concessiones, quietas clamaciones ac munimenta predicta per hanc meam concessionem confirmacionem ac quietamclamacionem predictis abbati et conventui suisque successoribus, pro quadam summa pecunie michi soluta in grossomma,[c] contra omnes gentes inperpetuum in liberam, puram et perpetuam elemosinam warantizabimus, acquietabimus et defendemus. In cuius rei testimonium presenti scripto sigillum meum apposui. Hiis testibus: Stephano de Belewe,[1] Johanne de Wyntwrth clerico, Willelmo sub via de eadem, Ricardo filio Henrici de Thorpp', Ricardo fabro de eadem, et aliis.

[a]*ve* of *provenientibus* interlined.   [b]*ququomodo*.   [c]*grossumma*.

[1] Stephen de Belheu or Bella Aqua paid the lay subsidy of 1297 at Ecclesfield and Rawmarsh and witnessed deeds at Rawmarsh in 1305 (T.W. Hall, *A Descriptive Catlaogue of Miscellaneous Charters and Other Documents Relating to the Districts of Sheffield and Rotherham* (Sheffield, 1916), p. 7) and at Worsbrough in 1318 (Walker, *Cartularies of Monkbretton*, p. 127).

101. Gift in free alms by Richard of Scholes to Beauchief abbey of an annual rent of 5s 7½d in the vill of Thorpe near Scholes, of which Hugh Bridde pays 2s 5½d annually for 1 assart in Thorpe lying between Richard's wood and common of Thorpe bordering at one end on the watercourse of Thorpe and at the other end on the land of Laurence the smith, and Henry son of Laurence pays 2s 6d annually for 1 assart in Thorpe lying between Richard's wood and the field of Woodseats and bordering at one end on the common of Thorpe and the other end extending towards Scholes, and Ralph the cobbler pays 8d annually for ½ assart called Ladyriddyng in Thorpe. [1280–1320]

Carta Ricardi de Scoles de quinque solidis vij d et ob.

Omnibus hoc scriptum visuris vel audituris Ricardus de Scoles salutem in Domino sempiternam. Noverit universitas vestra me dedisse, concessisse et hac presenti carta mea confirmasse abbati et conventui de Bello Capite et eorum successoribus in liberam, puram et perpetuam elemosinam quinque solidos septem denarios et obulum annui redditus in villa de Thorp' juxta le Scoles annuatim percipiendos, videlicet de Hugone Bridde et heredibus suis duos solidos et quinque denarios et obulum ad duos anni terminos, scilicet ad festum sancti Martini in yeme quindecim denarios et ad festum Pentecost[es] quindecim denarios [fo. 58r] et obulum pro uno assarto quod de me quondam tenuit in eadem villa de Thorp, iacens inter boscum meum et comunam de Thorp' buttans ad unum[a] caput super ductum aque de Thorp' et ad aliud super terram Laurencii fabri. Et de Henrico filio Laurencii et de heredibus suis duos solidos et sex denarios ad terminos predictos pro uno assarto quod de me quondam tenuit in eadem, iacens inter boscum meum et campum de Wodsetes et buttans ad unum caput super comunam de Thorp tendit ad aliud versus le Scoles. Et de Rad[ulpho] sutore et heredibus suis octo denarios ad Assumpcionem beate Marie Virginis pro uno dimidio assarto quod de me quondam tenuit in eadem et vocatur Ladyriddyng' cum omnibus pertinenciis, libertatibus, homagiis, wardis, releviis, eschaetis cum omnibus aliis serviciis que de predictis terris et earum tenentibus aliquomodo peterunt[b] provenire. Tenendum et habendum sibi et successoribus suis libere, quiete [et] integre. Ego vero dictus Ricardus et heredes mei predictos quinque solidos septem denarios et obulum annui redditus fideliter de predictis terris et earum tenentibus annuatim percipiendos, cum omnibus pertinenciis, libertatibus, homagiis, wardis, releviis, eschaetis cum aliis serviciis, ut predictum est, dictis abbati et conventui et eorum successoribus in liberam, puram et perpetuam elemosinam contra omnes gentes warantizabimus, acquietabimus et inperpetuum defendemus. In cuius rei testimonium presenti scripto sigillum meum apposui. Hiis testibus: domino Rad[ulpho] de Eclessall', Henrico de Tynislove, Willelmo de Mundisder, Willelmo[c] de Wyntworth, Nicholao de Wodhous, et aliis.[1]

[a] *unam.*   [b] *e* of *peterunt* interlined.   [c] *Wilelmo.*

[1] Henry de Tinsley witnessed a deed in 1301 and died *c.*1319 (Hunter, *South Yorkshire*, II, p. 32); William de Wentworth witnessed deeds at Kilnhurst in 1304 and Rawmarsh in 1305 (Hall, *Miscellaneous Charters*, pp. 7, 10); Nicholas de Woodhouse paid the lay subsidy of 1297 at Handsworth.

102. Quitclaim by Nicholas son of John of Rotherham to Richard of Scholes of 1 bovate which John his father bought in Thorpe which William son of Richard of Dore holds. [1280–1320]

Quieta clamacio Nicholai filii Johannis

[fo. 58v]
Omnibus[a] hoc scriptum visuris vel audituris Nicholaus filius Johannis de Roderham salutem in Domino. Noveritis me concessisse et omnino quietum clamasse Ricardo de Schales et heredibus seu assignatis suis totum jus et clameum quod habui, vel habere potui, in illa bovata

terre cum pertinenciis quam Johannes, pater meus, de eo emit in Thorp, quam Wilelmus filius Ricardi de Dore tenet. Tenendum et habendum dicto Ricardo heredibus vel[b] assignatis suis seu cuicumque dare, vendere vel alienare voluerit, libere, quiete et integre. Ita quod nec ego Nicholaus nec heredes mei in predicto tenemento aliquod jus vel clameum exigere poterimus. In cuius rei testimonium hoc presenti scripto sigillum meum apposui et insuper feofamentum quod Johannes, pater meus, de eo Ricardo habuit, eidem Ricardo liberavi et tradidi in testimonium veritatis. Hiis testibus: Thoma Barbot, Willelmo de Mundisder, Henrico Lecard, Johanne del Stede,[1] Henrico Lecard, Johanne de Wyresdale, Roberto le Seller' de Roderham, et aliis.

[a] *mnibus.*   [b] *ve.*

[1] Stead Farm, Hoyland (South Yorks).

103. Quitclaim by Richard son of Hugh of Scholes to John of Rotherham, clerk, of 1 bovate in Thorpe which Richard son of William of Thorpe held, saving the assart which lies in the field of Schales. John, who gave Richard son of Hugh 3 silver marks for this grant, shall render to him 1 rose annually. [1280–1320]

Carta Ricardi filii Hugonis de Schales de terra in Thorp

Sciant presentes et futuri quod ego Ricardus filius Hugonis de Schales concessi, vendidi et de me et heredibus meis inperpetuum quietum clamavi Johanni de Roderham clerico et heredibus vel assignatis suis et eorum heredibus pro tribus marcis argenti quas michi dedit illam bovatam terre cum omnibus pertinenciis suis in Thorp', quam Ricardus filius Willelmi de Thorp de me quondam tenuit, excepto illo assarto quod iacet in campo de Schales quod retineo. Habendam et tenendam eisdem Johanni vel assignatis suis quibuscumque et [fo. 59r] eorum heredibus libere, quiete et integre. Reddendo inde annuatim michi et heredibus meis unum florem, qui vocatur rosa, infra quindecim dies post Nativitatem beati Johannis Baptiste pro omni servicio, consuetudine et demanda, salvo servicio capitali domino pertinente. Et ego et heredes mei warantizabimus predictam terram cum omnibus aysiamentis tante terre in Thorp' pertinentibus et aliis pertinenciis suis dicto Johanni et heredibus vel assignatis suis et eorum heredibus per predictum servicium contra omnes homines inperpetuum et de omnibus demandis acquietabimus. Ut autem hec mea vendicio robur firmitate perpetue optineat, presens scriptum sigilli mei munimine corroboravi. Testibus: Willelmo filio Roberti de Wyntworth', Roberto de Wodhous, Hugone de Wyndhyll', Willelmo filio Willelmi de Wyntwrth', Henrico de Stede, Stephano de Herlay, Henrico filio suo, Ada de Berne, et multis aliis.

[SWINTON]

104. Quitclaim by Walter brother of Daniel butler of King John to William son of Daniel, his brother, of lands and tenures including mills. William gave Walter 2½ bovates and 1 curtilage in Swinton and 1 meadow in Swinton. [1199–1216][1]

Quieta clamacio Walteri fratris Danielis pincerni domini regis

Sciant presentes et futuri quod ego Walterus, frater Danielis pincerni domini regis Johannis, quietum clamavi pro me et pro meis heredibus totum jus et clameum siquod habui vel[a] habere potui in[b] terris et tenuris, tam in molendinis quam in omnibus aliis tenementis, absque ullo retenemento, ad opus meum vel heredum meorum Willelmo filio Danielis, fratris mei prenominati, tanquam heredi ipsius Daniel de sua legitima sponsa genito. Et pro hac quieta clamacione dedit michi prefatus Willelmus duas bovatas terre et dimidiam et unum curtilagium in villa de Suinthon et unum pratum in territorio [fo. 59v] de Swynnthon', sicut continetur in carta quam habeo de predicto filio et heredi dicti Daniel. Hiis testibus: Willelmo Basset, Ermemot de Wenham', Ada de Hertehyll', Ricardo Peche, Roberto tunc decano de Derleia,[2] Ricardo de Eddeshover', Willelmo de Derleia, Roberto le Archer', Johanne de Derl, Willelmo le Dagge, magistro Rad[ulpho] de Tideswell', Willelmo de Sancto Johanne, et aliis.[3]

[a] *ve.* [b] *et.*

---

[1] For the abbey's estate in Swinton, see also **109**. Swinton formed part of the Honour of Tickhill.
[2] See **176** for a grant by Robert, dean of Darley, to Ralph of Fallinge.
[3] All the witnesses are from Derbyshire, though the grant relates to a South Yorkshire estate. William Basset was described as 'of Langwith' in the Obituary (17 May; 'Langwad' in the shorter version); see also **222**, n. 4. Adam of Harthill was one of the knights who perambulated the royal forest of Derbyshire in 1225 (Turbutt, *Derbyshire*, II, p. 584). Richard

of the Peak was recorded in the Obituary in February. Robert the archer was an hereditary officer in the Forest of the Peak (*ibid.*, II, p. 571).

[SCHOLES]

105. Gift in free alms by Hugh son of Ralph of Scholes to Beauchief abbey of an annual rent of 12d from Henry son of Thomas of Bradwell.[1] **[1270–1320]**

Omnibus[a] in Cristo presentibus et futuris Hugo filius Radulfi de Schales salutem in Domino. Noveritis me dedisse et concessisse et hac presenti carta mea confirmasse Deo et ecclesie beati Thome martiris de Beuchef et canonicis ibidem Deo servientibus duodecim denarios annuatim inperpetuum, percipiendos duobus terminis de firma Henrici filii Thome de Bradwella et heredum suorum, scilicet ad festum sancti Martini vj denarios et in die Pent[ecostes] sex denarios, in puram et perpetuam elemosinam, pro salute anime mee et patris mei et matris mee et omnium antecesssorum et heredum meorum. Hiis testibus: Adam capellano de Roderham, Rad[ulpho] de Ecclessall', Hugone de Waddesley,[2] Roberto de Wyntwrth, Roberto de Wodhous, Willelmo filio Hugonis, Rad[ulpho] clerico, et aliis.

[a] *mnibus*.

[1] Bradwell near Castleton (Derbyshire) seems to be the only candidate for this name.
[2] Hugh of Wadsley witnessed **32, 114, 130, 132, 145, 149**, and **156**, all of which can be dated between 1250 and 1320 and mostly 1270–1320.

[GOLDTHORPE, SWINTON, AND BILLINGLEY]

106. Gift in free alms by William son of Andrew of Hooton to Beauchief abbey of an annual rent of 20s from his tenants in Goldthorpe,[1] **which William Daniel his late grandfather gave to Andrew his father on his marriage to Leticia, William's mother. [1280–1316]**[2]

Omnibus[a] ad quos presens scriptum pervenerit Willelmus filius Andree de Hotune salutem in Domino. Noverit universitas vestra me dedisse, concessisse et hac presenti carta mea confirmasse Deo [fo. 60r] et ecclesie beati Thome martiris de Bello Capite et canonicis ibidem Deo servientibus viginti solidatas redditus ad duos anni terminos, scilicet ad Pascha decem solidatas et ad festum sancti Michaelis decem solidatas de tenentibus meis in Golthorp' percipiendas, sicut Willelmus Daniel, quondam avus meus, dedit Andree, patri meo, in liberum maritagium cum Leticia, matre mea, cum omnibus eschaetis proventibus que me vel heredes meos de predictis tenentibus quocumquemodo contingere possent. Tenendum et habendum in liberam, puram et perpetuam elemosinam. Et ego Willelmus et heredes mei totum predictum redditum Deo et ecclesie et dictis canonicis, sicut predictum est, in liberam, puram et perpetuam elemosinam warantizabimus, acquietabimus et defendemus inperpetuum. In cuius rei testimonium presenti scripto sigillum meum apposui. Hiis testibus: domino Thoma de Beleuu, domino Gervasio de Bernak, Adam de Normanvile, Radulfo de Sefeud clerico, Willelmo de Wyntwrth', Willelmo de Gahame,[3] Ricardo de Gaham fratre eius, Rogero de Berche, et aliis.[4]

[a] *mnibus.*

[1] Originally just a single farm within the Honour of Tickhill between Barnsley and Doncaster, in the early twentieth century Goldthorpe grew into a populous coal-mining town. See Hunter, *South Yorkshire*, I, pp. 386–387. The nearest Hootons are Hooton Pagnell and Hooton Roberts.
[2] This charter was confirmed in 1316 (Appendix II, no. 35). The gift was confirmed in **110**. Successive generations of the Daniel family were foresters in the Campana ward of the Forest of the Peak. They held land in Tideswell, Taddington, Priestcliffe, and Wormhill (Turbutt, *Derbyshire*, II, p. 573).
[3] Gaham is an old form of Gotham (Notts); see **35**, n. 5.
[4] Deeds were witnessed by Thomas Belheu at Swinton in 1290 (Hall, *Miscellaneous Charters*, p. 5); Adam de Normanville at Kilnhurst in 1306 (*ibid.*, p. 101); William Wentworth at Rawmarsh in 1305 (*ibid.*, p. 7); William de Gotham at Norton in 1317 (Hall, *Ancient Charters*, p. 11). For Gervase de Bernak see **24**, n. 3.

107. Gift in free alms by Richard son of William Daniel of Tideswell to Beauchief abbey of an annual rent of 20s from his tenants of Goldthorpe so that the canons will perform a service for him on the St Martin's day after his death. [1280–1320][1]

Omnibus[a] ad quos presens scriptum pervenerit Ricardus filius Willelmi Daniel de Tyddeswell' salutem in Domino. Noverit universitas vestra me dedisse, concessisse et hac presenti carta mea confirmasse Deo et ecclesie beati Thome martiris de Bello Capite et canonicis ibidem Deo servientibus viginti solidatas [fo. 60v] redditus annuatim de tenentibus meis de Golthorp percipiendas, cum omnibus eschaetis proventibus que me vel heredes meos de predictis tenentibus quocumquemodo contingere possent, scilicet duodecim solidatas ad illuminare beate Marie sustentandum et octo solidatas ad pitanciam conventus die sancti Martini loco anniversarii mei, ita quod eodem die post obitum meum plenarium pro me in conventu fiet servicium. Tenendas et habendas in liberam, puram et perpetuam elemosinam. Et ego Ricardus et heredes mei totum predictum redditum dictis ecclesie et canonicis, sicut predictum est, in liberam, puram et perpetuam elemosinam warantizabimus, acquietabimus et defendemus inperpetuum. Hiis testibus: domino Willelmo le Latemer', domino Rad[ulpho] de Normanvile, Willelmo le Breton,[2] Roberto filio Rogeri de Oldewerk, Ricardo de Flincham, et aliis.

[a] *mnibus.*

[1] This grant was recorded in the Obituary (7 November) as '12s to sustain the lamp of the Blessed Mary, and 8s for a pittance to the convent'.
[2] William le Bret witnessed **71** (1301) and **61** (1312).

108. Gift in free alms by William son of Daniel of Tideswell[1] to Beauchief abbey of an annual rent of 12s from his farm in the vill of Goldthorpe to be paid by him at Beauchief. William has subjected himself and his heirs to the jurisdiction of the archdeacon of Derby in case any of them fails to pay the said rent. [1250–1290]

Carta Willelmi filii Danielis de Tyddeswel de redditu xij^{cim} solidorum[a]

Omnibus Cristi fidelibus hoc presens scriptum visuris vel audituris Willelmus filius Danielis de Tyddeswell' salutem in Domino. Noverit universitas vestra me divine pietatis intuitu dedisse, concessisse et hac presenti carta mea confirmasse Deo et beate Marie et sancto Thome martiri de Bello Capite et canonicis ibidem Deo servientibus, pro salute anime mee uxoris mee, liberorum meorum et omnium antecessorum et heredum meorum, in liberam, puram et perpetuam elemosinam redditum duodecim solidorum de firma [fo. 61r] mea in villa de Golthorp' per manum meam et heredum meorum annuatim apud Beuchefe duobus terminis percipiendum, scilicet sex solidos infra octavas sancti Michaelis et sex solidos infra octavas Pasche. Et sciendum quod spontanea voluntate subieci me et heredes meos jurisdictioni archidiaconi Derbeye quod si aliquando ego vel heredes mei predictum redditum duodecim solidorum supradictis terminis fideliter et plene non solverimus ad solucionem, tam principalis debiti quam pene quadraginta denariorum, in quolibet termino per censuram[b] ecclesiasticam appellacione remota et absque omni reclamacione laici feudi nos compellet. Et ego et heredes mei warantizabimus hunc redditum duodecim solidorum predictis canonicis contra omnes homines inperpetuum. Hiis testibus: Roberto de Blida persona de Austreton',[2] Ricardo capellano de Schefeld, Ricardo de Edemsowir', Rogero de Alreton', Eustachio clerico domini de Schefeld,[3] Andrea de Hoton', Roberto clerico de Totinley', et aliis.

[a] *densolidorum.*   [b] *cinsuram.*

[1] The grantor is presumably the father of the grantor in **107**.
[2] Misterton (see **132**); Blida is Blyth.
[3] Eustachius Clericus paid the lay subsidy of 1297 at Handsworth. See also **130**, **132**, and **133**.

109. Gift in free alms by John son of Richard Daniel[1] to Beauchief abbey of an annual rent of 11s in Swinton and in Billingley, *viz.* **4s annually from Thomas of Bella Aqua[2] for a tenement in Swinton, 3s 6d annually from Hugh Bauzan for a tenement in Billingley, and 3s 6d annually from Henry Fraunc for a tenement in Billingley. [1270–1316][3]**

Carta Johannis filii Ricardi Daniel de redditu undecim solidorum

Omnibus hoc scriptum visuris vel audituris Johannes filius Ricardi Daniel salutem in Domino sempiternam. Noverit universitas vestra me pro salute anime mee et antecessorum meorum dedisse, concessisse et hac presenti carta mea confirmasse Deo et ecclesie sancti Thome de Bello Capite et canonicis ibidem Deo servientibus undecim solidos annui redditus [fo. 61v] in Swynton' et in Bylynglay, videlicet de Thoma de Bella Aqua et heredibus suis quatuor solidos per annum pro tenemento quod de me tenet in Swynton'. Et de Hugone Bauzan et heredibus suis tres solidos [et] sex denarios per annum pro tenemento quod de me tenet in Bylinglay. Et de Henrico Fraunc' et de heredibus suis tres solidos et sex denarios pro tenemento quod de me tenet in eadem villa. Tenendum et habendum eisdem canonicis et suis successoribus in puram et perpetuam elemosinam libere, quiete, pacifice et integre cum homagiis, releviis et eschaetis et omnibus suis pertinenciis vel que quoque jure pertinere potuerint inperpetuum. Et ego Johannes et heredes mei predictis canonicis et eorum successoribus predictum redditum annuum, sicut superius dictum est, contra omnes gentes warantizabimus inperpetuum. Et ut hec mea donacio et concessio pura et perpetua sit, presens scriptum sigilli mei munimine roboravi in testimonium veritatis. Hiis testibus: domino Rad[ulph]o de Eccleshall', domino Gervasio de Bernak, Thoma de Mounteny, Thoma Doylly, Thoma Foleiambe, Willelmo filio Andree de Hoton, Willelmo Foleiambe, Henrico de Eynneslawe, Roberto de Wombewell, et multis aliis.[4]

[1] John is commemorated and this gift is recorded in the Obituary (7 November).
[2] Hunter, *South Yorkshire*, II, pp. 46–47 notes that the family of de Bella Aqua or Bellew, lords of Bolton-on-Dearne, were landowners in Rawmarsh (South Yorks), where the Chaworths also held land, and in neighbouring Swinton and Billingley. A Sir Thomas de Bella Aqua and his gift of 10 marks to the abbey occur in the Obituary (30 June).
[3] Confirmed in 1316 (Appendix II, no. 36).
[4] For Gervase de Bernak see **24**, n. 3. Thomas de Mounteney of Cowley and Shirecliffe (Hallamshire) paid the lay subsidy of 1297 at Ecclesfield and witnessed deeds there in 1298 and 1307 (Hall, *Miscellaneous Charters*, p. 212); he was alive in 1325 (Hunter, *Hallamshire*, p. 227). Thomas Foljambe also witnessed **70** (1278). Henry of Eynneslawe is presumably Henry of Tinsley, as Tynneslawe was an old spelling of the place-name. Robert de Wombwell was lord of Wombwell in 1316 (Hunter, *South Yorkshire*, II, p. 123).

110. Confirmation by Robert of Hooton son of William of Hooton (Roberts) to Beauchief abbey of the rent and service which the canons have in Goldthorpe of the gift of William his father. [1290–1330][1]

Carta Roberti de Hoton' de toto redditu in Goldthorp

Omnibus Cristi fidelibus ad quos presens scriptum pervenerit Robertus de Hoton, filius Willelmi de Hoton under e haghe, salutem in Domino sempiternam. Noveritis me pro me et heredibus meis concessisse, confirmasse, relaxasse et omnino quietum clamasse [fo. 62r] Deo et ecclesie beati Thome martiris de Bello Capite et canonicis ibidem Deo servientibus in liberam, puram et perpetuam elemosinam totum jus et clameum quod habui vel habere potui, habeo vel habere potero, in toto redditu et servicio quod dicti canonici habent in Golthorpe ex dono predicti Willelmi, patris mei. Ita quod nec ego dictus Robertus nec heredes mei nec aliquis alius per nos seu nomine nostro aliquod jus vel clameum dictis redditu et servicio cum omnibus eschaetis, proventibus et omnibus aliis appendiis et pertinenciis suis exigere, vendicare seu calumpniare poterimus quoquomodo, set ab omni peticione, vendicacione jure et demanda quo ad predicta per istud festum inperpetuum simus exclusi. Et ego dictus Robertus et heredes mei totum predictum redditum et servicium cum omnibus pertinenciis suis predictis canonicis in liberam, puram et perpetuam elemosinam contra omnes gentes warantizabimus, acquietabimus et inperpetuum defendemus. In cuius rei [testimonium] presentibus sigillum meum est appensum. Hiis testibus: domino Edmundo de Wasteneys, Roberto de Ecclessall', Willelmo Clarell' militibus, domino Rogero rectore medietatis ecclesie de Roderham, Thoma le Breton', Willelmo le Wavasur', Ricardo de Loversall', Willelmo de Sapirton', Petro del Roydes, et aliis.[2]

[1] For the original gift see **106**.
[2] Edmund de Wasteneys, lord of Todwick (South Yorks), was recorded in 1323 and 1331 (Hunter, *South Yorkshire*, II, p. 159). Sir William Clarel of Aldwark and Rawmarsh paid the lay subsidy of 1297 at Rawmarsh and was recorded in 1310 and 1322 (*ibid.*, pp. 52–53). William le Vavasour was lord of Denaby (South Yorks) in 1316; his *inquisition post mortem* was held in 1323 (*ibid.*, I, p. 395).

[ECCLESALL, SHEFFIELD, AND DRONFIELD]

111. Gift in free alms by Ralph son and heir of Robert of Ecclesall to Beauchief abbey, for the maintenance of a canon with a clerk to celebrate in the chapel of Ecclesall,[1] for the maintenance of the said chapel, and for the maintenance of the canons who say a daily prayer at the end of each chapter for the souls of his family, of his mill of Ecclesall[2] with a pond, waterway, and all suits and multure, saving multure of his house in Ecclesall and fishing in the mill pond, until he or his heirs provide the canons with an annual rent of 6 silver marks in exchange for the said mill. The canons are permitted to take timber from Ralph's wood in Ecclesall[3] for repairing the mill and its land. In snow and floods the canons may celebrate Mass for the souls of his family at Beauchief. They must not send to Ecclesall chapel any canon whom he does not like. If anything happens to the chapel of Ecclesall the canons must maintain a canon or secular chaplain in the church of Sheffield.[4] If the canons wish to withdraw the said chantry

then they shall be excommunicated and lose the said mill. Chirograph. [1250–1290]

Carta Radulphi de Ecclessale de molendino eiusdem

Omnibus Cristi fidelibus presentem cartam visuris vel audituris Radulfus, filius et heres Roberti de Ecleshall', salutem in Domino. Noverit universitas vestra me dedisse, concessisse et hac [fo. 62v] presenti carta mea confirmasse Deo et ecclesie beati Thome martiris de Bello Capite et canonicis ibidem Deo servientibus, pro salute anime mee et Cecilie uxoris mee et omnium antecessorum et successorum meorum, in liberam, puram et perpetuam elemosinam ad pietantiam dictorum canonicorum totum molendinum meum de Ecleshall', sine aliquo retenemento, cum stagno et cursu aque, cum libero introitu et exitu, et cum omnibus sectis molendini et multure et omnibus pertinenciis, libertatibus, aysyamentis, operibus stagni, et cum omnibus profectibus dicto molendino qualitercumque pertinentibus, pro sustentacione unius canonici cum clerico divina celebranti in capella de Ecclesshall et pro sustentacione dicte capelle in omnibus, tam in opere domus quam in divino servicio misse propriis sumptibus dictorum canonicorum, et ad sustentacionem dictorum canonicorum, qui singulis diebus unam oracionem Dominicam dicent ad exitum capituli pro anima patris mei et animabus omnium fidelium defunctorum. Et quod predicti canonici habeant liberum introitum et exitum per medium curie mee et per medium terre mee ad dictam capellam serviendum et sustinendum. Tenendum et habendum dictis canonicis et successoribus suis integre, quiete, sine contradiccione aliqua mei vel heredum meorum, in liberam, puram et perpetuam elemosinam quousque dictis canonicis vel successoribus suis annuum redditum sex marcarum argenti in excambio pro predicto molendino in aliquo certo loco ego vel heredes mei sufficienter providerimus, salva tamen michi et heredibus meis [fo. 63r] multura domus mee de Ecleshall' et piscaria stagni sine aliquo dampno molendini vel multure faciendo. Liceat eciam dictis canonicis capere meremium in bosco meo de Eccleshall ubi melius sibi viderint expedire, quocienscumque necesse fuerit, ad dictum molendinum reparandum et terram loco propinquiori ad stagnum proficiendum per visum forestariorum meorum. Et sciendum est quod cum dictis canonicis alio certo loco de predicto annuo redditu sex marcarum per me vel heredes meos fuerit satisfactum dictum molendinum cum pertinenciis suis omnibus michi et heredibus meis quiete revertetur. Ego vero Rad[ulfus] et heredes mei predictum molendinum cum stagno et cursu aque et omnibus pertinenciis suis, ut predictum est, dictis canonicis et successoribus suis pro sustentacione dictorum capelle capellani et clerici in liberam,[a] puram et perpetuam elemosinam contra omnes gentes warantizabimus et defendemus. Preterea sciendum est quod in tempore tempestatis magne inundacionis aquarum et nivis licebit dictis canonicis missam pro animabus supradictis in ecclesia de Bello Capite celebrare, et non mittent aliquem canonicum ad dictam capellam quem ego vel heredes mei habebimus odiosum. Et si dicta capella quod absit aliquo casu deficerit predicti canonici tenentur sustinere unum canonicum vel capellanum secularem in ecclesia de Schefeld divina celebrantem. Et si contingat quod dicti canonici per aliquam procuracionem vel concessionem alicuius[b] possint vel velint predictam cantariam[c] a dicta [fo. 63v] capella usque ad abbathiam vel alibi retrahere obligant [se] excommunicari ab universa ecclesia catholica et ut dictum molendinum omnino amittant. In horum omnium testimonium presenti carte cyrografate partes huic inde sigilla sua apposuerunt. Hiis testibus: domino Thoma de Furnivall', domino Rad[ulpho] de Wrtelay, Rad[ulpho] de Schefeld clerico, Willelmo de Gaham, Thoma de Leys, Thoma de Wodhous, et multis aliis.[5]

[a] *libera.*   [b] *alicus.*   [c] *predictam cantariam predictam.*

[1] This chapel fell out of use after the Dissolution but was rebuilt in the 1620s. The church of All Saints, Ecclesall, is its successor.
[2] OS ref. SK 336833; see the Introduction, pp. 18–19. The Sheffield suburb of Millhouses takes its name from this mill.
[3] Ecclesall Woods, on the opposite bank of the river Sheaf to Beauchief, remain intact.
[4] Ecclesall was a chapel-of-ease within the parish of Sheffield.
[5] For Thomas of Furnival see **18**, n. 2. In the Excerpts made by Gervase Holles (1607–1675) from Beauchief charters (British Library, Lansdowne MS 207B, fos 359–362v at fo. 359), names of witnesses are copied from another, unknown charter of Ralph, son of Robert of Ecclesall: 'Dominus Thomas de Furnivale, Dominus Gervasius de Bernaby, Dominus Robertus de Munteney testes cartae Radulphi filii Roberti de Ecklisale'. Gervase of Bernaby may be the same person as Gervase de Bernak; see **24**, n. 3. For other Sheffield charters, see **130–138**, **147–150**, and **156–157**.

112. Agreement made between Ralph son of Robert of Ecclesall on the one part and Beauchief abbey on the other. Ralph gave his mill of Ecclesall to Beauchief abbey in free alms with its pond, waterway, and all suits and multure, saving multure of his house in Ecclesall and fishing in the mill pond, as long as they provide the annual rent of 4 silver marks. The canons were permitted to take timber from Ralph's wood in Ecclesall for repairing the mill and its land. The canons will take 4 marks or its value in multure annually with all of the residue of the multure to go to Ralph. When the canons are so paid the mill will revert

back to Ralph. The canons are held to Ralph for the said 4 marks and ¹/₂ mark assigned in Attercliffe[1] to maintain a canon to celebrate in the chapel of Ecclesall for the souls of his family except in stormy weather and floods. They must not send to Ecclesall chapel any canon whom he does not like. If anything happens to the chapel of Ecclesall the canons must maintain a canon or secular chaplain in the church of Sheffield. If the canons wish to withdraw the said chantry then they shall be excommunicated and lose the said mill. Chirograph. [1250–1280]

Convencio facta inter Rad[ulphum] filium Roberti de Ecclessale ex parte una et abbatem de Bello Capite ex parte altera

Omnibus Cristi fidelibus presens scriptum visuris vel audituris Rad[ulphus] filius Roberti de Eccleshall' salutem in Domino. Noverit universitas vestra quod ita convencio inter me ex parte una et abbatem et conventum de Bello Capite ex altera, videlicet quod ego Rad[ulphus] pro me et heredibus meis dimisi,[a] concessi et hoc presenti scripto meo confirmavi dictis abbati et conventui pro salute anime mee et Cecilie uxoris mee et animabus patris et matris mee et omnium antecessorum meorum totum molendinum meum de Eccleshall' in puram et perpetuam elemosinam, cum stagno et cursu aque et cum omnibus pertinenciis et sectis multure ad dictum molendinum qualitercumque contingentibus. Tenendum et habendum, integre et libere, prout ego umquam liberius tenui vel aliquo jure tenere potui, sine aliqua contradiccione mei vel heredum meorum, quousque predictis abbati et conventui annuum redditum quatuor marcarum argenti in aliquo loco certo providere competent, salvo tamen michi et heredibus [fo. 64r] meis multura domus mee de Ecleshall' et piscatura stagni et aque dicti molendini sine omni dampno vel nocumento molendini vel multure faciendo. Liceat eciam dictis abbati et conventui capere meremium in bosco meo de Eccleshall' ubicumque sibi viderint expedire, quociens opus fuerit, ad dictum molendinum perficiendum et terram loco propinquiori ad stagnum perficiendum, per visum forestariorum meorum. Et sciendum est quod predicti abbas et conventus percipient annuatim quatuor marcas vel valorem in multura de dicto molendino per visum unius legalis hominis ex parte predicti Rad[ulphi] et heredum suorum et totum residuum dicte multure solvent dicto Rad[ulpho] et heredibus suis per visum eiusdem hominis. Et sciendum est quod cum predictis abbati et conventui de dicto annuo redditu in loco certo, ut predictum est, per me vel heredes meos fuerit competenter provisum dictum molendinum, sine omni contradiccione vel calumpnia dictorum abbatis et conventus michi et heredibus meis quiete revertetur. Et ego predictus Rad[ulphus] et heredes mei predictum molendinum dictis abbati et conventui in liberam, puram et perpetuam elemosinam vel alibi eisdem de predicto annuo redditu quatuor marcarum, ut supradictum est, per me vel heredes meos provisum fuerit contra omnes gentes warantizabimus, acquietabimus et ubique defendemus. Preterea sciendum est quod predicti abbas et conventus tenentur dicto Rad[ulpho] et heredibus suis pro prenominatis quatuor marcis et una dimidia marca assignata in Attyrclyfe ad sustinendum unum canonicum divina [fo. 64v] celebrantem in capella de Eccleshall' pro animabus superius nominatis inperpetuum, excepto tempore tempestatis et magne inundacionis aquarum et nivis emergent[arum]. Ita scilicet quod dicti abbas et conventus non mittent aliquem canonicum ad dictam capellam que predictus Rad[ulphus] vel heredes sui habebunt odiosum. Et si dicta capella quod absit aliquo casu deficerit, predicti abbas et conventus teneantur ad sustentandum dictum canonicum vel capellanum secularem in ecclesia de Schefeld celebrantem. Et si contingat quod abbas et conventus per aliquam procuracionem vel concessionem alicuius possint vel velint predictam cantariam a predicta capella usque ad abbathiam de Bello Capite vel alibi retrahere, obligant se excommunicari ab universa ecclesia Catholica et ut dictum annuum redditum omnino amittant. In horum omnium testimonium huic presenti scripto cyrographato utraque pars sigillum suum hinc inde alternatim apposuit. Hiis testibus: domino Thoma de Furnivall', domino Rad[ulpho] de Wrtlay, Ran[ulpho] clerico de Schefeld, Petro de Byrcheheved, Thoma del Wodhous, Willelmo del Gotham, et aliis.[2]

[a]*dimsi*.

[1]The eastern township of the parish of Sheffield. Ralph of Ecclesall was succeeded as lord of Ecclesall by his son Robert, then by his grandson Ralph and great-grandson Robert, all of whom are named in this Cartulary, but who are sometimes difficult to distinguish in the absence of dates.
[2]For Thomas of Furnival III see **18**, n. 2; for Peter Birchitt see **17**, n. 3.

113. Gift in free alms by Ralph son of Robert of Ecclesall to Beauchief abbey of all the land with a toft, croft and buildings which Richard son of Jordan of Attercliffe held in the vill of Attercliffe and of the same Richard with all his family and their chattels. [1250–1280]

Carta Rad[ulphi] filii Roberti de Ecclessale de Ricardo filio Jordani de Atterclyff

Omnibus Cristi fidelibus presentem cartam visuris vel audituris Rad[ulphus] filius Roberti de Eccleshall' salutem in Domino. Noveritis me pro me et heredibus meis dedisse, concessisse et hac presenti carta mea confirmasse Deo et beate Marie et ecclesie beati Thome martiris de Bello Capite et canonicis ibidem Deo servientibus [fo. 65r] in liberam, puram et perpetuam elemosinam totam terram cum tofto, crofto et edificiis quam Ricardus filius Jordani de Atterclyfe de me tenuit in villa et territorio de Atterclyfe, cum prato, bosco et omnibus pertinenciis, sine aliquo retenemento, infra villam et extra, et dictum Ricardum cum tota sequela sua et omnibus catallis suis. Tenendum et habendum dictis canonicis et successoribus suis inperpetuum, cum omnibus eschaetis, wardis, releviis, homagiis racione dicte terre qualitercumque provenientibus. Ita quod nec ego nec heredes mei nec aliquis pro me vel per me aliquod jus vel clameum in dicta terra cum pertinenciis omnibus et dicto Ricardo cum sequela sua et catallis suis decetero vendicare vel calumpniare aliquomodo poterimus. Et ego dictus Rad[ulphus] et heredes mei totam predictam terram cum tofto et crofto, prato et bosco, et omnibus aliis pertinenciis et dictum Ricardum, cum tota sequela sua et omnibus catallis suis, sicut predictum est, dictis canonicis et eorum successoribus in liberam, puram et perpetuam elemosinam contra omnes gentes warantizabimus, acquietabimus et defendemus inperpetuum. In cuius rei testimonium presenti carte sigillum meum apposui. Hiis testibus: domino Thoma de Furnivall', domino Rad[ulpho] de Wrtelay, Ran[ulpho] de Acton', Rad[ulpho] de Schefeld clerico, Petro de Byrchehed, Willemo de Gotham, Roberto Auselyn, Rogero de Holyns, et aliis.[1]

---

[1] For Thomas of Furnival III see **18**, n. 2; for Peter Birchitt see **17**, n. 3; for Roger de Hollins see **152**. Robert Hauselin witnessed a deed at Sheffield in 1267 (Hall, *A Descriptive Catalogue of Sheffield Manorial Records*, III (Sheffield, 1934), p. 136); see **128**, n. 2.

114. Gift in free alms by Ralph son of Robert of Ecclesall to Beauchief abbey of 1 toft in the vill of Sheffield with houses which Robert the clerk of Hooton once held. [1250–1280]

Carta Rad[ulphi] filii Roberti de Ecclessale de tofto in Schefeld

Omnibus presentibus et futuris Rad[ulphus] filius Roberti de Eccleshall' salutem in Domino. Noverit universitas vestra me dedisse et con[fo. 65v]cessisse et hac presenti carta confirmasse Deo et ecclesie sancti Thome martiris de Beuchef et canonicis ibidem Deo servientibus unum toftum in villa de Schefeld cum domibus et pertinenciis suis, quod Robertus, clericus de Hoton', de me aliquando tenuit in puram et perpetuam elemosinam, pro salute anime mee et patris mei et matris mee et Sarre uxoris mee et omnium antecessorum et heredum meorum. Hiis testibus: Roberto senescallo,[1] Hugone de Wadeslay, Ricardo filio Arturi, Roberto filio Wydonis de Wadeslay,[2] Suainio le Buliona,[3] et aliis.

[1] See also **120** and **124**.
[2] See also **144**, dated 1260–1310.
[3] Sweyn of Boulogne?

115. Gift in free alms by Ralph son of Robert of Ecclesall to Beauchief abbey of 1 toft and all his land in the vill of Dronfield by inheritance after the death of Robert son of Roger of Dronfield. The canons must render service for the said lands to the lords of the fee.[1] [1250–1280]

Carta Rad[ulphi] filii Roberti de Ecclessale de terra in Dronfeld

Omnibus Cristi fidelibus hoc presens scriptum visuris vel audituris Rad[ulphus] filius Roberti de Eccleshall' salutem in Domino. Noverit universitas vestra me dedisse, concessisse et hac presenti carta mea confirmasse, in domo de Bello Capite, abbati et conventui et eorum successoribus, in liberam, puram et perpetuam elemosinam, ad pitanciam conventualem, toftum et totam terram quam habui vel aliquomodo habere potui in villa et territorio de Dronefeld, racione hereditatis per discessum Roberti filii Rogeri de Dronfeld cum omnibus pertinenciis suis, libertatibus, communiis et aysiamentis in bosco, prato, pastura, wardis, releviis, eschaetis dictis tofto et terre pertinentibus, pro quadam convencione inter nos cyrographata, videlicet sustinendi capella de Eccleshall' in omnibus, sicut scriptum inter nos confectum testatur. Tenendum et habendum predictis abbati et conventui et successoribus suis de me et heredibus meis [fo. 66r] in liberam, puram et perpetuam elemosinam, faciendo inde servicium dominis feodi quod ad illam terram pertinet. Ego vero Radulfus et heredes mei predictum toftum cum terra et pertinenciis suis omnibus, ut predictum est, dictis abbati et conventui et eorum successoribus contra omnes gentes warantizabimus et defendemus inperpetuum. In cuius rei testimonium presenti carte sigillum meum apposui. Hiis testibus: domino Thoma de Chaworth', Jordano de Apetoft, Thoma de Leys, Thoma de Wodhous, Petro de Bycheheved, et aliis.[2]

[1] This property is now occupied by The Grange and the former Henry Fanshawe grammar school.
[2] Thomas de Leys and Peter Birchitt witnessed **17**; for Peter Birchitt see **17**, n. 3; for Thomas de Woodhouse see **20**, n. 2.

116. Gift in free alms by Ralph son of Robert of Ecclesall to Beauchief abbey of 1 fulling mill[1] to be erected next to the river of Sheffield[2] and licence to turn the river of Sheffield from its course towards the mill. The canons shall render to Ralph ⅓ of the mill's profits annually. [1270–1320]

Carta Radulphi filii Roberti de Ecclessale de molendino fullonico

Omnibus Cristi fidelibus presens scriptum visuris vel audituris Rad[ulphus] filius Roberti de Eccleshall' salutem in Domino. Noveritis me pro salute anime mee et antecessorum meorum dedisse, concessisse et hoc presenti scripto confirmasse abbati et conventui de Bello Capite locum competentem in terra mea juxta aquam de Schefeld ubi melius sibi viderint expedire ad molendinum unum fulonicum faciendum et construendum ad comodum illorum et meum et licenciam tornandi aquam de Schefeld de solito cursu suo ad dictum molendinum et in terra dictorum abbatis et conventus fuerit constructum et factum. Tenendum et habendum dictis abbati et conventui et successoribus suis in liberam, puram et perpetuam elemosinam. Reddendo inde michi et heredibus meis terciam partem tocius comodi et profectus provenientis de dicto molendino annuatim. Et sciendum est quod [fo. 66v] dicti abbas et conventus invenient duas partes sumptus et ego et heredes mei inveniemus terciam partem ad dictum molendinum faciendum et sustinendum in omnibus. Et ego Rad[ulphus] et heredes mei predictum locum et dictam licenciam tornandi dictam aquam, sicut predictum est, in omnibus dictis abbati et conventui et successoribus suis pro tercia parte comodi et profectus provenientis ad dictum molendinum in liberam, puram et perpetuam elemosinam warantizabimus, acquietabimus et defendemus. In cuius rei testimonium presenti scripto sigillum meum apposui. Hiis testibus: Roberto de Oldwerk, Ran[ulpho] senescallo de Schefeld, Rad[ulpho] de Schefeld clerico, Rad[ulpho] Hauselyn', Roberto fratre suo,

Willelmo de Gaham, Hugone de Wdehous, Thoma de Leys, Johanne filio Petri de Byrcheheved, et aliis.[3]

[1] The Walk Mill, OS ref. SK 324813; see the Introduction, p. 18.
[2] The river Sheaf.
[3] Robert Hauselin was a witness to **113**, dated to 1250–1280; William de Gaham was a witness in 1317 (**43**, n. 1); Thomas de Leys and Peter Birchitt witnessed **17**; for Peter Birchitt see **17**, n. 3. This is the only occasion on which John Birchitt is described as the son of Peter, a frequent witness in the second half of the thirteenth century.

117. Gift in free alms by William son of Gamel of Ecclesall to Beauchief abbey of an annual rent of 12d to be paid by him. [1270–1310]

Carta Willelmi filii Gamel de Ecclessale de redditu xij^{cim} denariorum

Omnibus Cristi fidelibus presentibus et futuris Willelmus filius Gamel de Eccleshall' salutem in Domino. Noverit universitas vestra me divine pietatis intuitu dedisse, concessisse et hac presenti carta mea confirmasse Deo et beate Marie et sancto Thome martiri de Beuchef et canonicis ibidem Deo servientibus redditum duodecim denariorum, in liberam, puram et perpetuam elemosinam, pro salute anime mee et omnium antecessorum meorum, de manu mea et heredum meorum annuatim ad Assumpcionem beate Marie inperpetuum percipiendum. Hiis testibus: Jordano capellano[a] de Schefeld, Hugone Hauselin,[1] Wilelmo de Wggill',[2] Hugone de Brom, [fo. 67r] Radulfo de Simiterio,[b] et multis aliis.

[a] *cappellano* with first *p* struck through.   [b] for *Cimiterio* as in **118**.

[1] The Hauselins were the principal tenants of the lords of Ecclesall. They lived at Hauslin Bank (later Machin Bank) in the hamlet of Little Sheffield, close to the abbey, on the opposite bank of the river Sheaf. The name was Norman French in origin, denoting a householder below the level of a lord of a manor: see Hey, *Historic Hallamshire* (Ashbourne, 2002), p. 67. For Hugh see also **118, 130–133, 149, 156**, and **158**, in which some of the witnesses appear in other documents that can be dated from 1267 to 1297.
[2] Ughill (South Yorks).

118. Gift in free alms by Hugh Hauselin of Little Sheffield to Beauchief abbey of an annual rent of 12d to be paid by him. [1270–1310]

Confirmacio Hugonis Hauselin de redditu duodecim denariorum

Omnibus ad quos presens scriptum pervenerit Hugo Hauselin de Parva Schefeld salutem in Domino. Noverit universitas vestra me divine pietatis intuitu dedisse, concessisse et hac presenti carta mea confirmasse Deo et beate Marie et ecclesie beati Thome martiris de Beuchef et canonicis ibidem Deo servientibus redditum duodecim denariorum, in liberam, puram et perpetuam elemosinam, pro salute anime mee et omnium antecessorum meorum, de manu mea et heredum meorum annuatim ad Assumpcionem beate Marie Virginis inperpetuum percipiendum. In cuius rei testimonium presenti scripto sigillum meum apposui. Hiis testibus: Jordano capellano de Schefeld, Willelmo capellano eiusdem ville, Radulfo de Cimiterio, Johanne de Langlay,[a] Thoma de Bosco,[1] et aliis.

[a] *g* of *Langlay* interlined.

[1] Thomas de Bosco witnessed a deed in Sheffield prior to 1290 (T.W. Hall, *A Descriptive Catalogue of Early Charters Relating to Lands In and Near Sheffield* (Sheffield, 1938), p. 2).

119. Quitclaim by Robert of Ecclesall, knight,[1] son and heir of Sir Ralph of Ecclesall, to Beauchief abbey of an annual rent of 2 marks from the mill of Ecclesall.[2] The canons shall have any writings or muniments mentioning the said rent. Made at Beauchief on Wednesday 3 June 1299.

Relaxacio Roberti de Ecclesall' militis

Pateat universis me Robertum de Eccleshall' militem, filium et heredem domini Rad[ulphi] de Eccleshall', relaxasse et omnino quietum clamasse, pro me et heredibus meis vel assignatis, religiosis viris abbati et conventui de Bello Capite et eorum successoribus inperpetuum omnes acciones, calumpnias et demandas quas habui, vel habere potui, in duabus marcis annui redditus, racione molendini de Eccleshall' seu alia occasione vel contractu quocumque per me ab eisdem religiosis aliquando petitis. Ita quod nec ego dictus Robertus nec heredes mei nec aliquis[a] alius [fo. 67v] nomine nostro in predictis duabus marcis aliquod jus clameum vel calumpniam exigere vel vendicare decetero poterimus inperpetuum quoquomodo. Volo eciam et concedo quod si aliqua scripta vel munimenta de predictis duabus marcis mencionem faciencia penes quascumque personas inveniantur pro cassis, vanis et irritis futuris temporibus habeantur. In cuius rei testimonium presentibus litteris sigillum meum apposui. Dat' apud

Bellum Caput die marcurie proximo ante festum Pentecostes anno regni regis Edwardi vicesimo septimo.

^a*aliquis* repeated and deleted.

¹See **18**, n. 2.
²See **111** and **112** for the rent, previously stated as either 6 or 4 marks, payable out of Ecclesall mill.

[MATTERSEY]

120. Agreement in the form of a chirograph made between Ralph of Ecclesall and William of Cressy.[1] **Ralph has granted to William all his land of Mattersey**[2] **and its tenants, saving religious men, for a term of 20 years. William, who gave Ralph 11 silver marks for this grant, shall render to him 13s annually and to the lords of the fee 6s annually for the said term of 20 years. If William builds anything on the said land to the value of 100s or less Ralph is held to answer to William for his expenses. Made on 29 September 1227.**

Sciant[a] omnes presentes et futuri hanc convencionem esse factam anno gracie m° cc° xxvij° ad festum beati Michaelis etc. presens inter Rad[ulphum] de Eccleshall' et Willelmum de Cresse, scilicet quod Rad[ulphus] concessit, dimisit[b] et hoc presenti cirographo confirmavit prefato Willelmo de Cressy et heredibus suis vel eius assignatis totam terram suam de Mareshey, tam de dominico suo quam de omnibus libere tenentibus, tam infra villam quam extra, in omnibus locis et in omnibus liberis, communiis et aysiamentis predicte terre pertinentibus, sine aliquo retenemento. Tenend[am] et habend[am] sibi et heredibus suis vel eius assignatis, exceptis viris religiosis de prenominato Rad[ulpho] et heredibus eius et suis assignatis, a predicto festo beati Michaelis usque ad finem viginti annorum. Reddendo inde annuatim prefatis Rad[ulpho] et heredibus suis vel suis assignatis tres [fo. 68r] decim solidos argenti, scilicet sex solidos et sex denarios[c] ad Pentecosten et sex solidos et sex denarios ad festum sancti Dionisii, pro omnibus serviciis, exceptis sex solidis annuatim persolvendis dominis feudi eisdem terminis, salvo forinseco et salva warda. Et sciendum est quod si predictus Willelmus vel[d] heredes eius vel eius assignati in predicta terra aliquid edificaverint ad valenciam centum solidorum, vel ad minus, Rad[ulphus] prenominatus vel heredes eius vel sui assignati tenentur respondere Willelmo vel heredibus eius vel eius assignatis de eius expensa et sumptu in fine viginti annorum per visum et consideracionem proborum hominum et legalium et predictam terram cum omnibus pertinenciis suis supra dictis Willelmo et heredibus eius vel eius assignatis contra omnes homines warantizare. Pro hac autem concessione et dimissione dedit sepedictus Willelmus prefato Rad[ulpho] premanibus xj marcas argenti de gersuma[e] et tam Rad[ulphus] quam Willelmus hanc convencionem firmiter et legale affidaverunt tenendam et presentibus scriptis sigilla sua in testimonium posuerunt. Hiis testibus: Willelmo et Reginaldo abbatibus de Wellebec et de Rupe, Roberto et Willelmo prioribus de Wyrkesop' et de Blida, Jordano Foliot, Rogero de Maresay, Reginaldo de Glewit, Roberto de Scefeld senescallo, Thoma de Sancto Quintino, Galfrido de Hoddyshac, Rad[ulpho] de Auverse, Henrico filio Rogeri, et aliis.[3]

[a] *ciant.* [b] *dimsit.* [c] *denaris.* [d] *vel* interlined. [e] *gersume.*

[1] For William of Cressy, see **124** and the Introduction, p. 3. The Cressys were a Norman family who held land in Nottinghamshire and at High Melton (South Yorks); see Hunter, *South Yorkshire*, I, pp. 363–364; Holdsworth, *Rufford Charters*, I, no. 264 and note.
[2] North-east of Blyth (Notts).
[3] The witnesses included the abbots of Welbeck and Roche, the priors of Worksop and Blyth, and Thomas of St Quentin, from near the mother house of the Premonstratensian order. Reginald of 'Glewit' perhaps appears in **124** as Reginald of Colwick (Notts). 'Auverse' is perhaps Auvers-sur-Oise, not far from St Quentin.

121. Confirmation by Robert son of Ralph of Ecclesall to Beauchief abbey of all the land which his father gave them, together with his body, in the territory of Mattersey according to the charter which they have from him. The canons shall render to Robert 6s annually. [1227–1260][1]

[fo. 68v]

Omnibus[a] sancte matris ecclesie filiis presentibus et futuris Robertus filius Rad[ulphi] de Ecclesball' salutem in Domino. Noverit universitas vestra me pia devocione et mera voluntate concessisse et hac presenti carta confirmasse Deo et ecclesie sancti Thome martiris de Bello Capite et canonicis ibidem Deo servientibus in perpetuam elemosinam totam terram cum omnibus pertinenciis et libertatibus quam pater meus dedit supradicte ecclesie de Bello Capite cum corpore suo in territorio de Mareshay in omnibus et per omnia, secundum tenorem carte quam habent de patre meo. Tenendam et habendam de me et heredibus meis inperpetuum libere et quiete, honorifice et pacifice. Reddendo inde annuatim michi et heredibus meis sex solidos argenti, scilicet tres solidos ad Pentecosten et tres solidos ad festum sancti Martini pro omni seculari servicio et demanda ad me et ad heredes meos pertinente, salvo forinseco[b] servicio. Ego vero et heredes mei warantizabimus predictis canonicis de Bello Capite totam prenominatam terram cum pertinenciis contra omnes homines. Hiis testibus: Ricardo et Johanne tunc capellanis de Ecclesfeld, Nicholao de Wrtelay, Henrico de Tankyrslay, Rad[ulpho] de Normanvil, Thoma de Barboth, Helia de Eccleshall', Rogero filio Reyneri, et aliis.

[a]*mnibus.* [b]*forinceco.*

[1] Later than **120** (1227), which records the original gift of this estate. The witnesses to **121-123** are the same in all three charters. Robert had previously been associated in a confirmation of the gift by his father (**123**); Robert son of Ralph of Ecclesall was the grandfather of Sir Robert of Ecclesall.

122. Gift in free alms by Ralph son of Robert of Ecclesall to Beauchief abbey, together with his body, of all his land of Mattersey with all its wood. [1227–1260]

Carta Radulphi filii Roberti de Ecclessale de terra de Mareshey

Omnibus sancte matris ecclesie filiis ad quos presens carta [fo. 69r] pervenerit Radulphus filius Roberti de Eccleshall' salutem in Domino. Noverit universitas vestra me divine pietatis intuitu dedisse et concessisse et hac presenti carta confirmasse Deo et beate Marie et ecclesie sancti Thome martiris de Beuchef' et canonicis ibidem Deo servientibus cum corpore meo totam terram meam de Mareshey, infra villam et extra villam, cum toto bosco superexistente et cum omnibus pertinenciis, libertatibus et communiis, pascuis et pasturis, pratis et piscariis, et omnibus aysiamentis ad predictam terram pertinentibus. Tenendam libere, quiete et pacifice, solutam et quietam ab omni seculari servicio et demanda de me et heredibus meis in perpetuam elemosinam, pro salute anime mee et omnium antecessorum et heredum meorum, salvo tamen servicio dominorum predicti feodi de Mareshay et forensi servicio. Et sciendum quod ego Rad[ulphus] et heredes mei totam predictam terram cum omnibus predictis pertinenciis prenominatis canonicis de Beuchef' contra omnes homines warantizabimus. Hiis testibus: Ricardo et Johanne tunc capellanis de Ecclesfeld, Nicholao de Wrtelay, Henrico de Tankyrley, Rad[ulpho] de Normanvil, Thoma Barboth, Helia de Eccleshall', Rogero filio Reineri, et multis aliis.

123. Confirmation by Ralph son of Robert of Ecclesall, with the consent of Robert his son and heir, to Beauchief abbey, together with his body, of all his land of Mattersey with all its wood. The canons shall render to the canons of Marshey[1] 6s annually. [1227–1260]

Confirmacio de terra de Mareshey

Omnibus sancte matris ecclesie filiis ad quos presens carta pervenerit Rad[ulphus] filius Roberti de Eccleshall' salutem in Domino. Noverit universitas vestra me assensu et voluntate Roberti filii mei et heredis dedisse et concessisse et hac mea presenti [fo. 69v] carta confirmasse Deo et beate Marie et ecclesie sancti Thome martiris de Beuchef' et canonicis ibidem Deo servientibus cum corpore meo totam terram meam de Mareshey, infra villam et extra villam, cum toto bosco superexistente et cum omnibus pertinenciis, libertatibus et communiis, pasturis, pratis et piscariis et in omnibus aysiamentis ad predictam terram pertinentibus. Tenendam de me et heredibus meis libere et quiete et pacifice in perpetuam elemosinam, pro salute anime mee et omnium antecessorum et heredum meorum, solutam et quietam ab omni seculari servicio et demanda, salvis tamen canonicis de Marshey sex solidis argenti duobus terminis percipiendis, scilicet tres solidos ad Pentecost[en] et tres solidos ad festum sancti Dionisii, et salvo forinseco servicio. Et ego predictus Rad[ulphus] et heredes mei iamdictis canonicis de Beuchef totam predictam terram, cum toto bosco superexistente, cum omnibus pertinenciis, contra omnes homines warantizabimus. Hiis testibus: Ricardo et Johanne tunc capellanis de Ecclesfeld, Nicholao de Wrtelay, Henrico de Tankyrlay, Rad[ulpho] de Normanvil, Thoma Barboth', Helia de Eccleshall', Rogero filio Reineri, et aliis.

[1] Mattersey priory, a small Gilbertine house, founded in 1185.

124. Agreement in the form of a chirograph made between Ralph of Ecclesall and William of Cressy. Ralph granted to William all his land of Mattersey and its tenants, saving religious men, for a term of 20 years. William, who gave Ralph 11 silver marks for this grant, shall render to him 13s annually and to the lords of the fee 6s annually for the said term of 20 years. If William

builds anything on the said land to the value of 100s or less Ralph is held to answer to William for his expenses. Made on 29 September 1227.[1]

De quadam convencione facta inter Rad[ulphum] de Ecclessale et Willelmum Cressy

Sciant omnes presentes et futuri hanc convencionem esse factam anno gracie m° cc° xxvij ad festum beati Michaelis, tunc presens inter Rad[ulphum] de Eccleshall' et Willelmum de Cressy, scilicet quod Rad[ulphus] concessit, dimisit et hoc presenti cirographo con[fo. 70r]firmavit prefato Willelmo de Cressy et heredibus suis vel eius assignatis totam terram suam de Mareshay, tam de dominco suo quam de omnibus libere tenentibus, tam infra villam quam extra, in omnibus locis et in omnibus liberis, communiis et aysiamentis predicte terre pertinentibus, sine aliquo[a] retenemento. Tenendam et habendam sibi Willelmo et heredibus suis vel eius assignatis, exceptis viris religiosis, de prenominato Rad[ulpho] et heredibus eius et suis assignatis a predicto festo beati Michaelis usque ad finem viginti annorum. Reddendo inde annuatim prefatis Rad[ulpho] et heredibus eius vel suis assignatis tresdecim solidos argenti, scilicet sex solidos et sex denarios ad Pentecost[en] et sex solidos et sex denarios ad festum sancti Dionisii pro omnibus serviciis, exceptis sex solidis persolvendis dominis feudi eisdem terminis, salvo forinseco et salva warda. Et sciendum est quod si predictus Willelmus vel heredes eius vel eius assignati aliquid in predicta terra edificaverint ad valenciam centum solidorum vel ad minus, Rad[ulphus] prenominatus vel heredes eius vel sui assignati tenentur respondere Willelmo vel heredibus eius vel eius assignatis de expensa et sumptu in fine viginti annorum, per visum et consideracionem proborum hominum et legalium, et predictam terram cum omnibus pertinenciis suis sepedictis Willelmo et heredibus eius vel eius assignatis contra omnes homines warantizare. Pro hac autem concessione et dimissione dedit sepedictus Willelmus prefato Rad[ulpho] premanibus xj marcas argenti de gersuma et tam Rad[ulphus] quam Willelmus hanc convencionem firmiter et legaliter affidaverunt tenendam et presentibus scriptis sigilla sua in testimonium [fo. 70v] apposuerunt. Hiis testibus: Willelmo et Reginaldo abbatibus de Welbec et Rupe, Roberto et Gilberto prioribus de Wyrkesop' et de Blida, Jordano Foliot, Rogero de Mareshay, Reginaldo de Colewic', Roberto de Schefeld senescallo, Thoma de Sancto Quintino, Galfrido de Hoddishac, Rad[ulpho] de Avers, Henrico filio Rogeri, et multis aliis.

[a] *alquo.*

[1] A copy of **120**, with some discrepancies in the witness lists.

125. Notification by Ralph of Ecclesall to the sheriff of Nottinghamshire and his bailiffs, barons, and all free men that he has given to Beauchief abbey all his land of Mattersey. He sent to the sheriff and his men Ellis his steward to present the canons' proctor for placing the said land in full seisin. [1250–1280][1]

Littera Radulphi de Ecclessale de terra de Mareshey

Viris venerabilibus et amicis in Cristo carissimis vicecomiti de Notingh[am] et eiusdem comitatus ballivis, baronibus[a] et liberis universis Rad[ulphus] de[b] Ecclesshall' salutem in Domino. Universitati vestre significo quod instinctu compunctus[c] divino dedi et carta mea confirmavi Deo et ecclesie beati Thome martiris de Bello Capite et canonicis in eadem ecclesia Deo famulantibus totam terram meam de Mareshey cum omnibus pertinentiis[d] pro amore Dei et salute anime mee. Et memorandum est quod mitto ad vos presencium latorem Heliam, senescallum meum, ad presentandum eorumdem canonicorum procuratorem et eidem[e] coram vobis de dicta terra cum pertinenciis ex parte mea, silicet cum carta et firma de eadem terra proveniente plenariam seysinam faciendam. Quare universitatem vestram precor humiliter quatinus si placet, dictum senescallum meum benigne admittatis et hiis que ex parte mea coram vobis fecerit favorem prebeatis et testimonium cum necesse fuerit perhibeat. Valete in Domino.

[a] *barronibus.* [b] *de* interlined. [c] *compuctus.* [d] *pertinentibus.* [e] *eid.*

[1] This charter is later than **120** and was perhaps executed about the same time as **122**, but in the absence of witnesses it is not certain which of the two Ralphs of Ecclesall this was.

[BRINCLIFFE]

126. Grant by Robert son of Hugh of Little Sheffield to Beauchief abbey of an annual rent of 1d which William his brother pays for the land which Adam the carter[i] holds in Brincliffe[2] and of the homage of the same Adam. [1250–1280]

Carta de denario annui redditus[a]

Omnibus Cristi fidelibus presens scriptum visuris vel audituris [fo. 71r] Robertus filius Hugonis de Parva Schefeld salutem in Domino.

Noveritis me pro salute anime mee et antecessorum meorum dedisse, concessisse et hoc presenti scripto confirmasse Deo et beate Marie et ecclesie beati Thome de Bello Capite et abbati et conventui ibidem Deo servientibus unum denarium annui redditus quem Willelmus, frater meus, tenebatur michi solvere pro terra quam Adam carectarius tenet in Brendeclive, una cum homagio eiusdem. Ita quod nec ego nec aliquis ex parte mea vel heredum meorum vel assignatorum aliquod jus vel clameum decetero in dicto denario annui redditus aliquomodo vendicare vel calumpniare poterimus. In cuius rei testimonium huic presenti scripto sigillum meum apposui. Hiis testibus: Rad[ulpho] clerico de Schefeld, Jordano capellano de Schefeld, Roberto de Oldewerk, Thoma de Leghes, Petro del Wodhous, Petro de Byrchehede, Ranulfo vicario de Nortona, et aliis.

[a] *Carta de Parva Schefeld et Bro juxta Schefeld* marginated.

[1] See also **128, 140, 141, 149**.
[2] A hamlet in the sub-manor of Ecclesall; Brincliffe is a prominent escarpment in Sheffield.

127. Gift in free alms by William son of Hugh Hauselin of Little Sheffield to Beauchief abbey of an annual rent of 3s for 1 bovate with a toft in Brincliffe which Adam the carter[1] once bought and held. [1250–1280]

Carta de tribus solidatis annui redditus

Omnibus Cristi fidelibus hoc presens scriptum visuris vel audituris Willelmus filius Hugonis Hauselin de Parva Schefeld salutem in Domino. Noverit universitas vestra me dedisse, concessisse et hac presenti carta mea confirmasse, pro salute anime mee et antecessorum meorum, Deo et beate Marie et ecclesie beati Thome martiris de Bello Capite, [fo. 71v] abbati et canonicis ibidem Deo servientibus, tres solidatos annui redditus [pro] una bovata terre cum tofto in Brendclive, quam Adam carectarius quondam emit et de me tenuit, ad duos anni terminos percipiendos, videlicet ad Annunciacionem beate Marie in Marcio decem et octo denarios et ad Assumpcionem beate Marie decem et octo denarios, apud Bellum Caput. Habend[os] et tenend[os] de me et heredibus meis in liberam, puram et perpetuam elemosinam, sicut aliqua elemosina liberius dari vel teneri potest, cum homagiis et serviciis, sectis, wardis, releviis, eschaetis, sectis[a] et omnibus pertinenciis dictis abbati et canonicis in liberam, puram et perpetuam elemosinam contra omnes homines warantizabimus, defendemus [et] acquietabimus. Ut hec mea donacio, concessio et confirmacio rata et stabilis inperpetuum permaneat, huic presenti scripto sigillum meum apposui. Hiis testibus: Rad[ulpho] clerico de Schefeld, Roberto de Oldewerk, Adam de Wandell', Thoma de Leys, Petro de Byrchehede, Ran[ulpho] vicario de Nortona, et aliis.²

ᵃ *sectis* interlined.

¹ See also **149**, which records the gift by Hugh Hauselin to his son William of the homage and service of Adam the carter, valued at 3s a year.
² Thomas de Leys and Peter Birchitt witnessed **17**; for Peter Birchitt see **17**, n. 3.

128. Grant by Adam of Brincliffe, carter, to William of Brincliffe of 4 acres in Brincliffe lying on the west of the acre which he sold to Robert Hauselin and bordering at one end on the syke which lies on the east of Adam's land and at the other end on the road which goes from the house of Robert Hauselin to Brincliffe. William, who gave Adam a sum of money for this grant, shall render to him 4d annually. [1250–1290]¹

Carta Ade de Brendclyff

Sciant presentes et futuri quod ego Adam de Brendclive carectarius dedi, concessi et hac presenti carta mea confirmavi Willelmo de Brendclive et cuicumque et quocumque tempore dare, assignare vel legare voluerit quatuor acras terre cum pertinenciis in territorio de Brendclive, sicut iacent insimul ex occidentali parte illius acre terre quam vendidi Roberto [fo. 72r] Hauselin ibidem, et buttat unum caput super siccum quod carrit versus orientem in terra mea et aliud super viam que vadit de domo Roberti Hauselin versus Brendclyf, pro una pecunie summa, quam predictus Willelmus michi dedit premanibus. Tenend[as] et habend[as] de me et heredibus meis dicto Willelmo et cuicumque in quocumque tempore dare assignare voluerit libere, quiete integre et hereditarieᵃ cum omnibus pertinenciis ad predictam terram pertinentibus. Reddendo inde annuatim michi et heredibus meis quatuor denarios argenti, scilicet medietatem ad festum sancti Martini in yeme et medietatem ad Pentecost[en], pro omni servicio seculari, exaccione et demanda. Et ego predictus Adam et heredes mei predictam terram cum pertinenciis predicto Willelmo, sicut predictum est, warantizabimus et contra omnes homines, pro predicto redditu, inperpetuum defendemus. Ut hec mea donacio et concessio rata et stabilis permaneat, presenti scripto inpressionem sigilli mei apposui. Hiis testibus: Roberto Hauselin, Rogero fratre eius, Robert del Brom,

Reynero de Schefeld clerico, Rogero de Holyns, Rad[ulpho] clerico, et aliis.²

[a] *hereditatre.*

¹ See **113** and **118**.
² Robert Hauselin and Robert del Brom (Broom Hall, Ecclesall) witnessed a deed at Sheffield in 1267 (Hall, *Manorial Records*, III, p. 136). Robert de Brom also witnessed the confirmation of a grant from Thomas de Camera, son of Roger of Birley, to Beauchief abbey in 1280 (British Library, Harley Charters, 83, E. 2; Jeayes, *Derbyshire Charters*, no. 2556); see also **141**. Roger Hauselin paid the lay subsidy of 1297 at Sheffield.

129. Grant by Robert of England to Adam of Sheffield, cook,¹ and Ellen his wife of all that land with wood and meadow which he bought from Roger son of Juliana the carter in the fee of Brincliffe which lies between the land of William of Little Sheffield on the east and the road which leads from Robert's house to Brincliffe on the west, and the land of the prior of Worksop² on the north and common pasture on the south. He also granted them an annual rent of 2½d from Beatrice wife of Robert Hauselin. Adam and Ellen, who gave Robert a certain sum of money for this grant, shall render to Beauchief abbey 8d annually. [1290–1310]

Carta Roberti de Englond[a]

Sciant presentes et futuri quod ego Robertus de Engeland dedi, concessi et hac presenti carta mea confirmavi Ade de Schefeld dicto coco et Elene, uxori sue, et eorum heredibus vel eorum assignatis totam illam terram, cum bosco et prato, quam emi de Rogero filio Juliane cartarii in feudo de Brendclyfe, sicut [fo. 72v] inter terram Willelmi de Parva Schefeld ex parte orientali et viam que ducit de domo mea versus le Brendclyf ex parte occidentali et terram prioris de Wyrksop' ex parte boriali et communam pasturam ex parte australi. Preterea dedi et concessi predictis Ade et Elene et eorum heredibus vel eorum assignatis duos denarios et obulum annualis redditus, recipiendos de Betricia uxore Roberti Hauselin et heredibus suis ad duos anni terminos, videlicet unum denarium et quadrantem ad Annunciacionem beate Marie et unum denarium et quadrantem ad Assumpcionem beate Marie Virginis pro quadam summa pecunie, quam predicti Adam et Elena michi dederunt premanibus. Tenendum et habendum predictis Ade et Elene et eorum heredibus vel eorum assignatis cum omnibus pertinenciis, libertatibus, aysiamentis predicte terre cum prato et bosco adiacentibus et predictis duobus denariis annualis redditus cum eschaetis adiacentibus in feudo et hereditate, libere, quiete et pacifice. Reddendo inde annuatim pro me et heredibus meis Deo et beato[b] Thome martiri de Bello Capite octodecim denarios argenti ad duos anni terminos, videlicet medietatem ad Annunciacionem beate Marie et aliam medietatem ad Assumpcionem beate Marie Virginis pro omnibus serviciis et demandis. Et ego vero predictus Robertus et heredes mei warantizabimus et defendemus predictam terram cum prato et bosco adiacentibus et predictos duos denarios et obulum annualis redditus cum eschetis predictis Ade et Elene et eorum heredibus vel eorum assignatis et contra omnes inperpetuum acquietabimus. In cuius rei testimonium hanc presentem cartam [fo. 73r] inpressione sigilli mei roboravi. Hiis testibus: Rogero Hauselin, Willelmo de Parva Schefeld, Ricardo de Hele, Willelmo de Mora, Johanne del Clife, Willelmo Hauselin, Thoma de bosco de Schefeld, Ricardo Corbard de eadem, et aliis.[3]

[a] *Nota* marginated.   [b] *beati*.

[1] Adam the cook paid the lay subsidy of 1297 at Sheffield and witnessed a deed there in 1290 (Hall, *Early Charters*, p. 2). He is referred to in the Obituary (3 May) as 'our assistant brother'.
[2] Worksop priory was founded *c*.1120 by William de Lovetot, lord of Hallamshire, and his wife, Emma.
[3] The lay subsidy of 1297 was paid in Sheffield by Roger Hauselin, Willelmo de Parva Schefeld, Ricardo de Hele, Willelmo de Mora, and Willelmo Hauselin. Thomas de Bosco witnessed a deed in Sheffield in 1290 (Hall, *Early Charters*, p. 2). Richard Corbard was perhaps the Richard Torkard of Sheffield who witnessed the contemporary charters **151** and **155**.

[SHEFFIELD]

130. Gift in free alms by Simon son of Roscelin of Bromp to Beauchief abbey of an annual rent of 4s from him and his tenants who hold the bovate which was Alexander's which Simon bought from Hugh Hauselin.[1] **[1270–1320]**[2]

Carta Symonis filii Roscilini de Bromp' de redditu quatuor solidorum

Omnibus sancte matris ecclesie filiis presentibus et futuris Simon filius Roscilini de Bromp' salutem in Domino. Noverit universitas vestra me divine pietatis intuitu dedisse et hac presenti carta confirmasse Deo et sancte Marie et ecclesie sancti Thome martiris de Beuchef et canonicis in eadem ecclesia Deo servientibus, pro salute anime mee et patris mei et matris mee et omnium antecessorum et heredum meorum, redditum[a] quatuor solidorum in puram et perpetuam elemosinam annuatim inperpetuum percipiendum de me et heredibus meis sive eorum assignatis et tenentibus qui illam bovatam terre tenuerint que fuit Alexandri quam emi de Hugone Hauselin'. Et sciendum quod hiis terminis reddetur predictus redditus, scilicet in Purificacione beate Marie duos solidos et ad festum sancti Petri advincula duos solidos. Et ut hec mea donacio et confirmacio firma et stabilis futuris temporibus perseveret, presens scriptum tam sigilli mei inpressione quam testium subscriptione roboravi. Hiis testibus: Hugone de Wadisleya, Rogero de Alreton', Hugone Hauselin', Eustachio clerico,[3] Waltero de Kanrenn, Hugone de Bromp', et aliis.

[a] *reditum.*

[1] For Hugh Hauselin see also **118, 126, 149, 156,** and **158**.
[2] For other Sheffield charters see **111–119** *passim,* **147–150,** and **156–157**.
[3] See **108**.

131. Quitclaim by Hugh Hauselin of Little Sheffield to Beauchief abbey of Richard son of Thoke, his serf, with all his movable chattels. The canons gave Hugh 6s for this quitclaim. [1270–1320]

[fo. 73v]

Omnibus[a] Cristi fidelibus hoc presens scriptum visuris vel audituris Hugo Hauselin de Parva Schefeld salutem in Domino. Noverit universitas vestra me manumisisse et liberum et absolutum dimisisse de me et heredibus meis inperpetuum Ricardum filium Thoke hominem, meum nativum, cum omnibus suis catallis mobilibus, abbati et canonicis de Bello Capite pro sex solidis argenti, quos idem abbas et canonici michi pro predicta manumissione[b] et libertate premanibus dederunt. Ut hec mea quietaclamacio et libertatis concessio firmitatis robur optineat, eam tam sigilli mei inpressione quam testium subscriptionem munivi. Hiis testibus Roberto filio Qwith' de Wadel', Willelmo de Alreton', Thoma de bosco, Hugone filio Godolfi, Rad[ulpho] de Cimiterio, et aliis.

[a] *mnibus.* [b] *manumisissione.*

132. Quitclaim by Hugh Hauselin to Beauchief abbey of Richard le Sergaunt, his serf, with all his family and their chattels. [1270–1320]

Quieta clamacio Hugonis Hauselin de Ricardo Sergaunt nativo

Omnibus ad quos presens scriptum pervenerit Hugo Hauselin salutem in Domino. Noveritis me dedisse et hac presenti carta mea liberum et quietum clamasse Deo et ecclesie beati Thome martiris de Beuchef de me et heredibus meis Ricardum le Sergaunt, nativum meum, cum tota sequela sua et cum omnibus catallis suis, et cum omnibus dicto Ricardo pertinentibus. Ita quod nec ego nec heredes mei aliquod jus vel clameum in dicto Ricardo vel sequela vel catallis aliqua racione vel occasione nobis de[fo. 74r]cetero vendicare poterimus. Et ego Hugo et heredes mei dictum Ricardum cum sequela sua et cum omnibus predictis dicte[a] ecclesie de Beuchef et canonicis ibidem Deo servientibus contra omnes homines warantizabimus inperpetuum. Hiis testibus: domino Roberto persona de Mystyrton' tunc temporis senescallo,[1] Eustachio persona de Handeswrth, Hugone de Waddesley, Henrico filio Godulfi, Laniclo filio eius, et aliis.

[a] *de.*

[1] Robert the parson of Misterton was described in **108** as 'of Blythe'. As the Honour of Tickhill was known alternatively as the Honour of Blyth, Robert may have been the seneschal (originally a French term for the chief officer) of the honour 'at that time'.

133. Gift in free alms by Hugh Hauselin to Beauchief abbey of all the land with wood and pasture which Richard le Sergaunt once held in the vill of Ecclesall. [1280–1320]

Carta Hugonis Hauselin de terra in villa de Ecclessale

Omnibus ad quos presens scriptum pervenerit Hugo Hauselin salutem in Domino. Noveritis me dedisse et hac presenti carta mea confirmasse Deo et ecclesie beati Thome martiris de Beuchef totam terram illam, cum bosco et pastura et omnibus libertatibus, aisiamentis dicte terre pertinentibus, quam Ricardus le Sergaunt aliquando de me tenuit in villa de Eccleshall'. Tenendam et habendam de me et heredibus meis in liberam, puram et perpetuam elemosinam. Et ego Hugo et heredes mei totam prenominatam terram cum pertinenciis dicte ecclesie de Beuchef warantizabimus, acquietabimus et defendemus, sicut liberam et puram elemosinam contra omnes homines inperpetuum. In cuius rei testimonium huic scripto sigillum meum apposui. Hiis testibus: domino Roberto de Eccleshall', Eustachio persona de Handsworth',[a]

Roberto le Breton', Hugone del Brom, Rogero de Oldewerk', et aliis multis.[1]

[a] *d* of *Handsworth'* corrected from an *s*.

[1] Eustachius paid the lay subsidy of 1297 at Handsworth. Robert le Breton witnessed Sheffield's town charter in 1297 as seneschal of Hallamshire (Hunter, *Hallamshire*, p. 39) and a deed at Kilnhurst (South Yorks) in 1306 (Hall and Thomas, *Jackson Collection*, p. 10).

134. Grant by Walter the baker of Sheffield to William the tanner[1] of Sheffield of 1 rod bordering on Ulkelwell at one end and on the land of Henry son of William the tanner on the other, and as it lies in length and width between the land of Brun Gerard and the land of Richard Scyvel. William, who gave Walter 26d for this grant, shall render to the chief lords one 1 halfpenny at Christmas and three 3 farthings on 24 June. [1250–1310]

[fo. 74v]

Sciant[a] presentes et futuri quod ego Walterus pistor de Schefeld dedi, concessi et hac presenti carta mea confirmavi Willelmo tannatori de Schefeld unam rodam terre buttantem super Ulkelwell' ad unum caput et ad aliud super terram Henrici filii Willelmi tannatoris, sicut iacet in longitudine et latitudine inter terram Brun Gerard' et terram Ricardi Scyvel, absque omni retenemento pro viginti sex denariis, quos dictus Willelmus dedit michi premanibus in gersumma. Tenend[am] et habend[am] de me et heredibus meis sibi et heredibus suis vel assignatis suis et eorum heredibus libere, quiete pacifice, in feudo et hereditate. Reddendo inde annuatim capitalibus dominis unum obulum ad Natale Domini et tres quadrantes ad Nativitatem beati Johannis Baptiste pro omnimodis serviciis, sectis et demandis. Ego vero dictus Walterus et heredes mei dictis Willelmo et heredibus suis vel assignatis suis et eorum heredibus ubicumque et quandocumque dare vel assignare voluerint, totam dictam terram cum omnibus pertinenciis suis contra omnes homines et feminas warantizabimus, acquietabimus et defendemus inperpetuum. In huius rei testimonium huic scripto sigillum meum dignum duxi apponendum. Hiis testibus: Ada de bosco, Lambekyn Gamell' filio Cerlon', Simone Frende, Raynero Bullon', et aliis.[2]

[a] *ciant*.

[1] William of Radeford, 'called "the tanner", our assistant priest', was commemorated in the Obituary (16 January).

²Adam de Bosco ('of the wood') witnessed deeds in Sheffield in 1267 (Hall, *Manorial Records*, III, p. 136) and 1290 (Hall, *Early Charters*, p. 19) and paid the lay subsidy of 1297 there. See **135, 136, 139–141, 143, 147, 148, 154**. In **154** he is described as the brother of Thomas de Bosco (see **118**). In the reign of Henry III Adam de Bosco, Reyner de Bullone (Boulogne?), and Simon Frend witnessed another deed (Hall, *Early Charters*, p. 5).

135. Grant by Walter the baker of Sheffield to William the tanner of Sheffield of ½ acre on Brocolfclive lying beyond Horepittes,¹ one end of which lies as far as the syke below Brocolfclive and next to the land of Gamel son of Solon; and of 1 rod of land, one head of which lies on Urkelwelsike and the other on the croft of the pelterer. William, who gave Walter a certain sum of sterling for this grant, shall render to the chief lords of the fief 3d and 3 farthings annually. [1250–1310]

Carta Walteri pistoris

Sciant presentes et futuri quod ego Walterus pistor de Schefeld dedi, concessi et hac presenti carta mea confirmavi [fo. 75r] Willelmo tannatori de eadem, pro quadam summa sterlingorum michi data premanibus, in territorio de Schefeld dimidiam acram terre super Brocolfclive[a] iacentem ultra Horepittes et caput iacet usque ill' Syke sub Brocolfclive et iacet juxta terram Gamil' filii Solon', et unam rodam terre de qua unum caput latet super Urkelwelsike et aliud caput super croftum pelliparii, cum omnibus pertinenciis et aysiamentis et libertatibus ad tantam terram, infra villam et extra, pertinentibus. Tenendam et habendam de me et heredibus meis sibi et heredibus suis[b] sive assignatis libere, quiete, pacifice et hereditarie.[c] Reddendo inde annuatim capitalibus dominis tres denarios et tres quadrantes ad duos terminos, scilicet ad Natale Domini et ad Nativitatem sancti Johanne Baptiste pro omnibus serviciis, secularibus consuetudinibus et demandis. Et ego vero predictus Walterus et heredes mei predicto Willelmo et heredibus suis sive assignatis predictas terras, cum omnibus pertinenciis predictis, contra omnes homines et feminas warantizabimus et inperpetuum defendemus. Ut hec mea donacio et concessio rata sit et stabilis permaneat, in testimonium huius rei huic presenti scripto sigillum meum apposui. Hiis testibus: Adam de bosco, Simone Frend, Gamil' filio Solon', Hugone [L]unt, Petro de Pecto, Willelmo Pid', Ricardo Walteroc, et aliis multis.²

[a]First *o* of *Brocolfclive* interlined.   [b]*suis* repeated with the second deleted.   [c]*hereditare*.

¹Pitsmoor, north Sheffield (A.H. Smith, *Place-names of the West Riding of Yorkshire* (Cambridge, 1961), I, p. 212).
²Adam de Bosco and Simon Frend also witnessed **134**. William Pidd witnessed a deed at Grenoside (Hallamshire) in 1267 (Hall, *Miscellaneous Charters*, p. 209); he also witnessed **148**.

136. Grant by Hugh the smith to Richard son of Gerard of ½ acre lying between Gosedyrtker and the land of Reyner of Bullon; of 1 rod lying between the land which Walter the baker held; and of the road which leads to Hulkelwell. The canons shall render to Hugh 1 pair of white gloves annually. [1250–1310]

Carta Hugonis le Smyth'

Sciant presentes et futuri quod ego Hugo Smyth dedi, con[fo. 75v]cessi et hac presenta carta mea confirmavi Ricardo filio Gerardi dimidiam acram terre iacentem inter Gosedyrtker et terram Reyneri de Bullon' et unam rodam terre iacentem in longitudine inter terram quam Walterus pistor quondam tenuit et viam que ducit ad Hulkelwell'. Tenend[as] et habend[as] de me et heredibus meis sibi et heredibus suis libere, integre et hereditarie[a] cum omnibus pertinenciis ad predictam terram pertinentibus. Reddendo inde annuatim michi et heredibus meis unum par albarum cirotecarum ad Natale pro omni servicio et demanda, salvo servicio capitalium dominorum. Et ego vero predictus Hugo et heredes mei predictam terram cum pertinenciis predicto Ricardo et heredibus suis sive assignatis warantizabimus et contra omnes homines inperpetuum defendemus. In cuius rei testimonium huic presenti scripto inpressione sigilli mei apposui. Hiis testibus: Adam de bosco, Ricardo de Lavendere, Gamel' filio Gerlon', Reynero de Bullon', Ricardo coco, et aliis.

[a] *herditare.*

[RAWMARSH]

137. Gift in free alms by Adam of Saint Mary[1] to Beauchief abbey of an annual rent of 2s which Hugh the cook pays for a toft in Halches[2] and for an assart which Adam gave to them. [1190–1227]

[fo. 75v]

Carta Ade de Sancta Maria de redditu duorum solidorum

Omnibus qui hoc scriptum viderint vel audierint Adam de Sancta Maria salutem. Noverit universitas vestra me dedisse, concessisse et hac mea carta confirmasse Deo et ecclesie sancti Thome martiris de Bello Capite et canonicis ibidem Deo servientibus redditum duorum solidorum quos Hugo cocus solebat reddere michi pro uno tofto in Halches et uno sarto [fo. 76r] que ego dedi eidem. Tenend[um] et habend[um] in liberam, puram et perpetuam elemosinam pro salute anime mee et omnium antecessorum et successorum meorum, scilicet duodecim denarios ad Pascha et duodecim denarios ad festum sancti Michaelis. Hiis testibus: Ricardo abbate de Welbec,[3] Matheo eiusdem loci canonico, Willelmo de Rennes, Johanne filio Suani, Rogero de Kuken',[4] Thoma de Wetecroft, Ricardo capellano de Ramareis, Petro de Kylnehyrst, et aliis.

[1] The Saint Mary family formerly held a knight's fee in Rawmarsh, which they subinfeuded from the Deincourts. An Adam of Saint Mary was the eldest son of Paganus, a lord who flourished in the 1160s and who bestowed the tithes of Rawmarsh on Welbeck abbey (Hunter, *South Yorkshire*, II, p. 146), but the one named seems to be a later, unrecorded Adam.
[2] Upper Haugh, Rawmarsh (Smith, *Place-names of the West Riding*, p. 175).
[3] Richard was recorded as abbot of Welbeck between 1196 and 1215; his successor, William, was recorded in 1227.
[4] Cuckney (Notts).

138. Gift in free alms by the same Adam of Saint Mary to Beauchief abbey of an annual rent of 2s which Hugh the cook pays for a toft in Halches and for an assart which they hold. [1190–1227][1]

Alia carta eiusdem Ade

Sciant presentes et futuri quod ego Adam de Sancta Maria dedi, concessi et hac presenti carta mea confirmavi pro salute anime mee et omnium antecessorum et heredum meorum Deo et ecclesie sancti Thome martiris de Bello Capite et canonicis ibidem Deo servientibus, in liberam, puram et perpetuam elemosinam, redditum duorum solidorum quos Hugo cocus et heredes sui michi reddere solebant pro uno tofto in Halches et uno sarto que de me tenuerunt. Et sciendum quod assignavi heredibus[a] eiusdem Hugonis ad prefatos duos solidos iamdictis canonicis duobus terminis annuatim inperpetuum reddendos,[b] scilicet duodecim denarios ad Pascha et duodecim denarios ad festum sancti Michaelis. Hiis testibus: domino Ricardo abbate de Welbec, Matheo eiusdem loci canonico, Ricardo capellano de Romareis, Willelmo de Rennes, Johanne filio Swani, Rogero de Kukeneya, Thoma de Wetecroft, Petro de Kylnshyrst, et multis aliis.

[a] *heredes.*   [b] *rededendos* with second *e* deleted.

[1] Almost identical to **137** apart from the reference to Hugh's heirs and the statement that they held the premises of Adam, instead of Hugh being given them.

[BRINCLIFFE]

139. Quitclaim by Roger son of Peter of Bradfield to Robert of England of a moiety of land with a toft, croft, and buildings at Brincliffe which came to him after the death of Juliana daughter of Adam the carter, his mother. Robert gave Roger a certain sum of money for this grant. [1280–1320][1]

[fo. 76v]

Omnibus[a] hoc scriptum visuris vel audituris Rogerus filius Petri de Bradefeld salutem in Domino sempiternam. Noverit universitas vestra me concessisse ac pro me et heredibus meis inperpetuum quietum clamasse Roberto dicto de England et heredibus suis vel suis assignatis quibuscumque pro quadam summa pecunie michi soluta premanibus, totum jus et clameum quod habui vel habere potui seu aliquotiens habere potero in illa medietate terre cum tofto, crofto, edificiis et omnibus ac omnimodis aliis pertinenciis suis, apud le Brendclif que michi contigit ibidem post discessum Juliane filie Ade carectarii, matris mee. Ita quod nec ego Rogerus nec heredes mei nec aliquis alius pro nobis vel per nos seu nomine nostro aliquid juris vel clamei in dicta medietate terre predicte cum pertinenciis ex nunc habere, exigere vel reclamare poterimus, quoquomodo colore vel caucela. In cuius rei testimonium presenti scripto sigillum meum apposui. Hiis testibus: domino Daniele cappellano de Schefeld, Adam de bosco in eadem, Roberto Hauselin, Rogero fratre suo, Roberto Hasard, et multis aliis.[2]

[a] *mnibus.*

[1] For other transactions relating to the same premises, see **126–129**, **141**, and **151**.
[2] Daniel Capellanus and Roger Hauselin paid the lay subsidy of 1297 at Sheffield.

140. Quitclaim by the same Roger son of Peter of Bradfield to the same Robert of England of the land with a toft, croft and buildings which Adam the carter held at Brincliffe. [1280–1320][1]

Quieta clamacio Rogeri filii Petri de Bradfeld

Omnibus hoc scriptum visuris vel audituris Rogerus filius Petri de Bradefeld salutem in Domino sempiternam. Noverit universitas vestra me concessisse ac pro me et heredibus meis inperpetuum quietum clamasse Roberto dicto de Engeland [fo. 77r] et heredibus suis vel assignatis quibuscumque totum jus meum et juris clameum quo habui, vel habere potui seu aliquotiens habere potero, in tota illa terre cum tofto, crofto et edificiis et cum omnibus aliis pertinenciis, libertatibus, comunis et aysyamentis ad dictam terram qualitercumque spectantibus, quam Adam carectarius quondam tenuit apud le Brendclyf. Ita quod nec ego Rogerus nec heredes mei nec aliquis pro nobis seu per nos vel nomine nostro aliquod jus vel juris clameum in dicta terra cum tofto, crofto, edificiis et omnibus ac omnimodis pertinenciis suis, nominatis et non nominatis, ex nunc habere, exigere vel reclamare poterimus inperpetuum quoquomodo. In cuius rei testimonium presenti scripto sigillum meum apposui. Hiis testibus: Adam de bosco in Schefeld, Rogero Hauselin, Roberto fratre suo, Roberto Hasard, Johanne Freende, et aliis.

[1] Possibly executed to reinforce the quitclaim in **139**, which concerns only a moiety of the premises and which follows the grant in **141**.

141. Grant by the same Roger son of Peter of Bradfield to the same Robert of England of a moiety of land with a toft, croft, and buildings which Adam the carter held at Brincliffe and which moiety came to him after the death of Juliana his mother, daughter of the aforesaid Adam. Robert, who gave Roger a certain sum of money for this grant, shall render to Beauchief abbey 3s annually. [1280–1320][1]

Alia carta eiusdem Rogeri

Notum sit omnibus presens scriptum visuris vel audituris quod ego Rogerus filius Petri de Bradfeld dedi, concessi et hac presenti carta mea confirmavi Roberto dicto de Engeland totam illam medietatem illius terre, cum tofto, crofto, edificiis et omnibus ac omnimodis aliis pertinenciis suis, quam Adam carectarius tenuit apud le Brendclyf, que quidem medietas michi contigit post decessum Juliane, matris mee, filie predicti Ade. Tenendam et habendam dicto Roberto et heredibus suis vel suis assignatis quibuscumque [fo. 77v] libere, quiete, pacifice et integre inperpetuum, cum omnibus libertatibus suis, comunis et aysiamentis et omnibus ac omnimodis aliis pertinenciis ad dictam medietatem terre cum pertinenciis qualitercumque spectantibus. Reddendo inde annuatim ecclesie beati Thome martiris de Bello Capite tres solidos ad duos anni terminos, videlicet ad Annunciacionem beate Marie decem et octo denarios et ad Assumpcionem eiusdem decem et octo denarios pro omnibus secularibus serviciis, exaccionibus, consuetudinibus et demandis, salvo forinseco servicio, ad tantam terram pertinentibus. Et ego dictus Rogerus et heredes mei totam predictam medietatem terre cum tofto, crofto, edificiis et omnibus ac omnimodis aliis pertinenciis suis, nominatis et non nominatis, predicto Roberto et heredibus suis vel suis assignatis quibuscumque in forma predicta contra omnes gentes warantizabimus, acquietabimus et defendemus inperpetuum, pro servicio antedicto. Pro hac autem donacione et confirmacione dedit michi predictus Robertus quamdam summam pecunie premanibus in gersumma. In cuius rei testimonium presenti scripto sigillum meum apposui. Hiis testibus: Ada de bosco in Schefeld, Roberto Hauselin, Rogero fratre suo, Johanne Freend, Roberto Hasard, Willelmo del Holyns, et aliis.[2]

[1] The initial sale of the premises to which the quitclaim in **139** relates.
[2] Witnesses listed here also witnessed the confirmation by Thomas de Camera, son of Roger of Birley, of a grant to Beauchief abbey in 1280 of rent of 21d from land in Dunstorthes (British Library, Harley Charters 83 E. 2). To this is attached a brown wax oval seal of the abbot of Beauchief. Summary in Jeayes, *Derbyshire Charters*, no. 2556; see also **128**. The location of Dunstorthes is unknown.

[WADSLEY]

142. Quitclaim by Richard son of Richard Costenoth to Beauchief abbey of 1 toft in the vill of Wadsley[1] which they have by the gift of his father. [1250–1280]

Quieta clamacio Ricardi Costnozth' de uno tofto in Wadisley

Omnibus hoc scriptum visuris vel audituris Ricardus filius Ricardi Costenocht salutem in Domino. Noverit universitas vestra me concessisse et quietum clamasse de me et heredibus meis Deo, abbati et conventui de Beuchef unum toftum cum pertinenciis in villa de Wadisl', quod habent de dono Ricardi, patris mei. Ita quod nec ego nec heredes mei nec aliquis per nos in dicto tofto cum pertinenciis decetero aliquid jus vel clamium nobis vendicare poterimus. In cuius rei testimonium hoc presens scriptum sigilli mei impressione roboravi. Hiis testibus: Ricardo de Hanel, Ricardo de Aston', Petro de Byrcheheved, Hugone Hauselin, Radulfo clerico[a] de Schefelde, et aliis.[2]

[a] *clerco.*

[1] In the parish of Ecclesfield.
[2] For Peter Birchitt see **17**, n. 3; for Hugh Hauselin see **117**, n. 1.

143. Grant in the form of a chirograph by Beauchief abbey to Ralph the clerk of Sheffield of 1 toft with a strip which Richard Costenoth gave them below the wood of Wadsley. Ralph shall render to Beauchief abbey 8d annually. [1250–1310]

[fo. 78r]

Carta de una placea terre Ricardi Costenot sub bosco de Wadesley

Omnibus Cristi fidelibus ad quos presens scriptum pervenerit abbas et conventus de Bello Capite salutem in Domino. Noveritis nos dedisse, concessisse et hac presenti carta nostra confirmasse Rad[ulpho] de Schefeld clerico et heredibus suis vel assignatis illud toftum cum placea et cum omnibus pertinenciis suis quod Ricardus Costenot nobis dedit sub bosco de Wadesley. Tenendum et habendum de nobis et successoribus nostris sibi et heredibus suis vel assignatis libere et quiete, bene et in pace, sine aliquo retenemento inperpetuum. Reddendo inde annuatim nobis et successoribus nostris octo denarios ad duos anni terminos, scilicet ad festum sancti Martini in yeme quatuor denarios et ad Pentecosten quatuor denarios, pro omni seculari servicio, exaccione vel demanda. Nos autem et successores nostri dictum toftum cum placea et cum omnibus pertinenciis suis, sicut predictum est, predicto Rad[ulpho] de Schefeld clerico et heredibus suis vel assignatis contra omnes homines warantizabimus, acquietabimus et defendemus inperpetuum. In cuius rei testimonium huic presenti scripto, in modum cirographi confecto, alternatim sigilla sua apposuerunt. Hiis testibus: Willelmo de Arnehall', Adam de Byrchehede, Adam de bosco de Schefeld, Roberto del Brom', Reynero clerico de Schefeld, et aliis multis.[1]

[1] William of Arnehall was perhaps of Darnall (Sheffield). For Adam de Bosco, see **134**. Robert de Brom (see also **128**) witnessed a deed in Sheffield in 1267 (Hall, *Manorial Records*, III, p. 136) and in Whiston in 1283 (A.S. Scott-Gatty, 'Records of the Court Baron of the manor of Sheffield', *Transactions of the Hunter Archaeological Society*, 1:3 (1914), p. 258).

144. Gift in free alms by Robert son of Robert Wyden of Wadsley to Beauchief abbey of 1 toft in the vill of Wadsley which Richard Costenoth held from Robert's father; and of a piece of land to the north of the toft which Robert the mason held. [1260–1310]

Carta Roberti filii Roberti Wyden de Wadesley[a]

Omnibus ad quos presens scriptum pervenerit Robertus filius Roberti [fo. 78v] Wyden de Wadesley salutem in Domino. Noverit universitas vestra me dedisse, concessisse et hac presenti carta mea confirmasse abbati et conventui de Bello Capite et successoribus suis, in liberam, puram et perpetuam elemosinam, unum toftum in villa de Wadesley, quem Ricardus Costenoth tenuit de Roberto, patre meo, in eadem villa, et unam aliam placeam iuxta illum toftum versus aquilonem, quem Robertus cementarius aliquando tenuit cum omnibus pertinenciis, communis et aysiamentis. Tenendum et habendum bene et quiete illis et successoribus suis in liberam, puram et perpetuam elemosinam. Et ego dictus Robertus et heredes mei predictum toftum et predictam placeam cum omnibus pertinenciis dictis abbati et conventui et successoribus suis, sicut predictum est, contra omnes homines warantizabimus, acquietabimus et defendemus inperpetuum. Hiis testibus: domino Willelmo de Camora, Henrico de Spina,[1] Thoma Brom', Thoma de Staington', Petro de Byrchehed, et multis aliis.

[a] *Iⁱ filii Reginaldi* written beneath rubric in different hand.

[1] Henry de Spina ('thorn tree') witnessed deeds in Bradfield in 1279 (Hall, *Wheat Collection*, p. 5) and 1290 (Hall, *Early Charters*, p. 17).

145. Gift in free alms by Wido son of Roger of Wadsley, with the consent of Robert his son and heir, to Beauchief abbey of an annual rent of 10d from Robert son of Osbert of Wadsley and of the homage and service which the same Robert made to him for a toft, croft, and all the land which he held. [1260–1310]

Carta Wydonis filii Rogeri de Waddesley de redditu
decem denariorum

Omnibus sancte matris ecclesie filiis ad quos presens carta pervenerit Wido filius Rogeri de Waddesley salutem in Domino. Noverit universitas vestra me assensu et voluntate Roberti filii mei et heredis dedisse, concessisse et hac mea presenti[a] [carta] confirmasse Deo et sancte Marie et sancto Thome martiri de Beauchefe et canonicis ibidem Deo servientibus, in liberam, puram et perpetuam elemosinam, pro salute anime mee et omnium [fo. 79r] antecessorum et heredum meorum, decem denarios de Roberto filio Osb[erti] de predicta villa singulis annis in die Assumpcionis beate Marie percipiendos, et homagium et servicium quod idem Ricardus[b] michi solebat facere pro tofto et crofto et pro tota terra quam de me aliquando tenuit, secundum tenorem carte quam habet de me. Hiis testibus: Rad[ulpho] de Eccleshall', Hugone de Wadesleya, Willelmo filio Dolfini, Thoma de Stalint', Henrico filio Rogeri de Wadesleya, Willelmo de Camora,[1] et aliis.

[a] *presenta.*   [b] *sic* for *Robertus.*

[1] Also witnessed **144**.

146. Grant by Richard Costenoth to Beauchief abbey of 1 toft in the vill of Wadsley which he held from Robert son of Wido. The canons shall render to Richard one 1 arrow annually. [1250–1280]

Carta Ricardi Costenoth de uno tofto in villa de Waddeslay

Omnibus hoc scriptum visuris vel audituris Ricardus Costenoth' salutem in Domino. Noverit universitas vestra me dedisse, concessisse et hac presenti carta mea confirmasse Deo et ecclesie beati Thome martiris de Beuchefe unum toftum cum omnibus pertinenciis in villa de Wadesley, quod tenui de Roberto filio Widonis in eadem villa. Tenendum et habendum libere et quiete. Reddendo inde annuatim, pro me et heredibus meis, unam sagittam dicto Roberto et heredibus suis in die Natalis Domini pro omni servicio. Et ego Ricardus et heredes mei predictum toftum cum omnibus pertinenciis abbati et conventui pro predicto servicio contra omnes homines warantizabimus inperpetuum. In cuius rei testimonium huic presenti scripto sigillum meum apposui. Hiis testibus: Ricardo de Hanley, Ricardo de Aston', Petro de Byrchehed, Hugone Hauselin', Rad[ulpho] clerico de Schefeld, et aliis.

[BROCKHOLECLIFF]

147. Grant by William the merchant of Sheffield to Margaret, daughter of Walter the shepherd, of ¹/₂ acre in Brokeholeclyff[1] **lying between the land of Walter and the land which Roger of the alder-grove held. Margaret, who gave William 10s for this grant, shall render to the chief lord 2¹/₂d annually. [1250–1310]**

Carta de Brokeholeclyff

[fo. 79v]

Sciant presentes et futuri quod ego Willelmus marcator de Schefeld dedi, concessi et hac presenti carta mea confirmavi Margarete, filie Walteri pastoris, unam dimidiam acram terre iacentem in Brokeholeclyfe inter terram dicti Rogeri[a] et terram quam[b] Rogerus de Alneto quondam tenuit, pro decem solidis quos predicta Margareta dedit michi premanibus. Tenendum et habendum de me et heredibus meis sibi et heredibus suis sive assignatis suis libere, quiete, integre et hereditarie[c] cum omnibus pertinenciis ad predictam terram pertinentibus. Reddendo inde annuatim capitali domino duos denarios et obulum, silicet medietatem ad Nativitatem sancti Johannis Baptiste et medietatem ad Natale Domini pro omni servicio seculari, exaccione vel demanda michi vel heredibus meis pertinentibus. Et ego vero predictus Willelmus et heredes mei predictam terram cum pertinenciis predicte Margarete et heredibus suis sive assignatis suis warantizabimus et contra omnes homines inperpetuum defendemus. In cuius rei testimonium presens scriptum sigillo meo roboravi. Hiis testibus: Ada de bosco, Ricardo Lavender, Gamel[lo] filio Serlonis, Reynero de Bullon', et multis aliis.[2]

[a] *sic* for *Walteri*.   [b] *Walterus* deleted.   [c] *hereditare*.

[1] Brocco Bank, in the lordship of Ecclesall.
[2] For Adam de Bosco and Reyner de Bullon, see **134**, n. 2. Gamel Serle witnessed a deed at Sheffield in 1290 (Hall, *Early Charters*, p. 1); see also **148**.

148. Grant by Simon son of Henry son of Gunnild of Sheffield to William the tanner of his dross-corn next to William's tenement with a certain part of land as the boundaries are placed. William, who gave Simon a certain

sum of sterlings for this grant, shall render to him a 1 rose annually. [1250–1310]

Carta Symonis filii Henrici filii Gunnulde de Schef'

Sciant presentes et futuri quod ego Simon filius Henrici filii Gunnilde de Schefeld dedi, concessi et hac presenti carta mea confirmavi Willelmo tannatori quadam summa [fo. 80r][1] sterlingorum michi data premanibus, meum cural[lum] iuxta tenementum suum, et quamdam partem terre usque metas positas, cum omnibus pertinenciis, aisiamentis et libertatibus a predicto cural[lo] et partem terre predicte pertinentibus. Tenendum et habendum de me et heredibus meis sibi et heredibus suis sive assignatis libere, quiete, pacifice et hereditarie.[a] Reddendo inde annuatim michi et heredibus meis ad Nativitatem sancti Johannis Baptiste unum florem rose pro omni seculari servicio, consuetudine et demanda. Et ego vero predictus Simon et heredes mei prefato Willelmo et heredibus suis sive assignatis predictum cural[lum] et partem terre predicte, cum omnibus pertinenciis predictis, contra omnes homines et feminas warantizabimus et defendemus inperpetuum. Ut mea donacio et concessio rata sit et stabilis permaneat, huic presenti scripto in testimonium huius rei sigillum meum impressione roboravi. Hiis testibus: Ada de bosco, Simone Frend, Ricardo Walterot, Hugone Kent, Gamil[lo] filio Serlonis, Petro de Pecco, Willelmo Pid', Reginaldo de Bulon', Waltero pistore, et multis aliis.[2]

[a] *hereditare.*

[1] A leaf has been excised from the MS after fo. 79 but without interruption to the text.
[2] For Adam de Bosco, Simon Frend, and Reyner Bullon, see **134**; Richard Walterot and William Pidd, **135**; Gamel son of Serle, **134–136**, **147**.

149. Grant by Hugh Hauselin to William his son, for his homage and service, of the homage and service of Adam the carter, *viz.* **3s. William will give Hugh 1d annually for this grant. [1270–1320]**[1]

Carta Hugonis Hauselin

Sciant presentes et futuri quod ego Hugo Hauselin dedi, concessi et hac presenti carta confirmavi Willelmo filio meo, pro homagio et servicio suo, et pro uno denario michi et heredibus meis annuatim solvendo die Natalis Domini pro omni servicio homagium et servicium Ade de Charet' et heredum suorum, vicelicet octodecim denarios [fo. 8ov] ad festum sancte Marie in Marcio et octodecim ad Assumpcionem eiusdem Virginis. Et ego Hugo Hauselin et heredes mei warantizabimus predictum homagium et servicium prenominato Willelmo et heredibus suis contra omnes homines inperpetuum. Et ut[a] hec donacio mea et concessio rata permaneat et inconcussa, presentem cartam sigilli mei impressione roboravi. Hiis testibus: Roberto de Eccleshal', Hugone de Wadesley, Johanne de Midop', Germ[ano] de Mortumleg', Waltero de Campo Remigii, Eustachio clerico, Ada de Waddesley, et aliis multis.[2]

[a] *ut* interlined.

[1] See **127**, which records William's gift to Beauchief of the 3s mentioned here. For his father, Hugh, see **118**, **130–133**, **156**, and **158**.
[2] For Eustachius, see **108**, n. 3. Adam de Wadsley witnessed a deed at Ecclesfield in 1267 (Hall and Thomas, *Jackson Collection*, p. 6) and another at Bradfield in 1279 (Hall, *Wheat Collection*, p. 4).

150. Gift in free alms by William of Hollins[1] to Beauchief abbey of 1 piece of land, arable, meadow, and wood, lying between the land of Richard son of Adam the cook of Sheffield and le Botheclyfesyke and bordering at the west end on the road which leads from William's house to Sheffield and at the east end on Richard's land. [1280–1320]

Carta Willelmi Holyns de una placea terre prati et bosci[a]

Sciant presentes et futuri quod ego Willelmus del Holins dedi, concessi et hac presenti carta mea confirmavi religiosis viris abbati et conventui de Bello Capite, in liberam, puram et perpetuam elemosinam, unam placeam terre arabilis, prati et bosci cum pertinenciis, sicut iacet inter terram Ricardi filii Ade coci de Schefelde et le Botheclyfesyke, et abbuttat ad unum caput versus occidentem super viam que ducit de domo mea versus Schefeld et ad aliud capud versus orientem super terram predicti Ricardi. Habendum et tenendum predictis religiosis abbati et conventui et eorum successoribus in liberam, puram et perpetuam elemosinam, libere, quiete, pacifice et integre, cum omnibus libertatibus, communis et aysiamentis et cum omnibus aliis pertinenciis suis. Et ego predictus Willelmus et heredes mei predictam placeam terre arabilis prati et bosci cum omnibus pertinenciis suis predictis religiosis abbati et conventui et eorum successoribus [fo. 81r][2] in liberam, puram et perpetuam elemosinam contra omnes gentes warantizabimus, acquietabimus et inperpetuum defendemus. In cuius rei testimonium huic presenti scripto sigillum meum apposui.

Hiis testibus: Rogero Hauselin, Thoma de bosco de Schefeld, Adam coco de eadem, Lamberto tinctore de eadem, Willelmo Hauselin', et aliis.[3]

[a] *bossi. una pla* written under the rubric, with the final *a* left half-formed, presumably for *placea*.

[1] For William of Hollins and his son Roger, see also **152–155**.
[2] A leaf has been excised after fo. 80 but without interruption to the text.
[3] Roger and William Hauselin, Adam the cook, and Lambert Tinctor (dyer) paid the lay subsidy of 1297 at Sheffield. Adam witnessed deeds in Sheffield in 1304–1305 (Hall, *Early Charters*, pp. 5 and 7). Lambert Tinctor witnessed deeds there in 1290 (*ibid.*, p. 2), 1304, and 1338 (Hall, *Ancient Charters*, pp. 5 and 13). Thomas de Bosco witnessed deeds there in 1290 (Hall, *Early Charters*, p. 2), 1304 (*ibid.*, p. 5), and 1315 (*ibid.*, p. 8).

[BRINCLIFFE]

151. Gift in free alms by Robert of England to Beauchief abbey of an annual rent of 6d in Brincliffe[1] from a 1 toft, croft, and acre lying between the land of Adam the cook of Sheffield and his meadow, and which Robert bought from Agnes his daughter, with power of distraint. [1280–1320]

[fo. 81r]

Carta Roberti Englond de sex denariatis annui redditus

Omnibus hoc scriptum visuris vel audituris Robertus de Englange salutem in Domino sempiternam. Noverit universitas vestra me dedisse, concessisse et confirmasse ac omnino pro me et heredibus meis inperpetuum quietum clamasse abbati et conventui de Bello Capite capitalibus dominis meis in liberam, puram et perpetuam elemosinam sex denariatos annui redditus[a] cum pertinenciis in le Brendclyf ad Annunciacionem beate Marie Virginis et ad Assumpcionem eiusdem annuatim per equalem[b] porcionem percipiendos, de uno tofto et crofto et una acra terre iacentes inter terram Ade coci de Schefeld et pratum eiusdem Ade in territorio de Brendclife, que emi de Agnete filia mea in virginitate sua. Set si ad terminos statutos ad redditum levandum districcio in dicto tenemento inveniri non poterit, concedo per me et heredes meos ut, quociens necesse fuerit, per omnem terram meam pro redditu antedicto liberam distringendi habeant potestatem. Ego vero predictus Robertus et heredes mei predictos sex denariatos annui redditus cum pertinenciis predictis abbati et conventui suis et successoribus in forma predicta tenendos, habendos, levandos contra omnes gentes inperpetuum warantiza[fo. 81iv]bimus, acquietabimus et defendemus. In cuius rei testimonium presenti scripto sigillum meum apposui. Hiis testibus: domino Daniele de Schefeld capellano, Ada coco de eadem, Thoma de bosco, Lamberto tinctore, Ricardo Torkard, Thoma le Seriaunt, et aliis.[2]

[a] *reditus.*   [b] *equam.*

[1] For other Brincliffe charters, see **126–129** and **139–141**.
[2] Richard Torkard paid the lay subsidy of 1297 at Sheffield. See **150** for other witnesses.

[HOLLINS]

152. Gift in free alms by Roger son of William of Hollins to Beauchief abbey of 1 toft with gardens in Hollins[1] which he had after the death of his father. [1300–1340]

Carta de quodam tofto in le Holyns[a]

Omnibus Cristi fidelibus hoc presens scriptum visuris vel audituris Rogerus filius Willelmi del Holyns salutem in Domino sempiternam. Noveritis me dedisse, concessisse et presenti scripto confirmasse religiosis viris abbati et conventui de Bello Capite et eorum successoribus, in liberam, puram et perpetuam elemosinam, totum illud toftum cum gardinis et omnibus pertinenciis suis in le Holyns, quod habui post decessum Willelmi, patris mei, adeo integre, sicut ipse tenuit tempore mortis sue. Habendum et tenendum predictis religiosis et eorum successoribus in liberam, puram et perpetuam elemosinam libere, quiete, pacifice et integre, cum omnibus libertatibus, communis et aysiamentis dicto tofto pertinentibus. Et ego predictus Rogerus et heredes mei predictum toftum cum gardinis et omnibus aliis pertinenciis suis predictis religiosis et eorum successoribus in liberam, puram et perpetuam elemosinam contra omnes gentes warantizabimus, acquietabimus et inperpetuum defendemus. In cuius rei testimonium presenti scripto sigillum meum apposui. Hiis testibus: Lamberto tinctore de Schefeld, Willelmo Spynke de Parvo Schefeld, Roberto del Clyff, Thoma del Gotham, et aliis.[2]

[a] Marginated: *Carte del Holt et Holyns.*

[1] Hollins was known alternatively as Holt House, situated on the north bank of the river Sheaf, within the parish of Sheffield, to the east of Millhouses (Smith, *Place-names of the West Riding*, I, p. 199).

²For Lambert Tinctor, see **150**, n. 3. Thomas de Gotham witnessed a deed at Norton in 1324 (Hall, *Ancient Charters*, 1935, p. 12) and a lease of land in Dore on 24 July 1325 (Jeayes, *Derbyshire Charters*, no. 1018).

153. Quitclaim¹ by the same Roger son of William of Hollins in the soke of Ecclesall in Hallamshire to Beauchief abbey of the same toft with gardens which they have by the gift of his father in Hollins. [1300–1340]

Quieta clamacio de supradicto tofto

[fo. 82r]

Omnibus hoc scriptum visuris vel audituris Rogerus filius Willelmi de Holyns in soca de Ecclessall' in Halumschyre salutem in Domino. Noveritis me remisisse, relaxasse et omnino pro me et heredibus meis quietum clamasse religiosis viris abbati et conventui de Bello Capite et eorum successoribus totum jus quod habui vel habere potui vel habeo seu habere potero in toto illo tofto, cum gardinis et omnibus aliis pertinenciis suis, quod iidem religiosi habent ex dono et concessione Willelmi de Holyns, patris mei predicti, in le Holyns predict[o]. Ita quod nec ego nec heredes mei, nec aliquis alius nomine nostro, aliquod jus vel clameum in predicto tofto cum gardinis et aliis pertinenciis suis decetero exigere vel vendicare poterimus quoquomodo. In cuius rei testimonium presenti scripto sigillum meum apposui. Hiis testibus: Lamberto tinctore de Schefeld, Willelmo Spynk de Parva Schefeld, Roberto del Clyfe, Thoma del Gotham, et aliis.²

¹The quitclaim following the gift made in **152**.
²The witnesses are the same as in **152**.

154. Quitclaim by the same Roger son of William of Hollins in the soke of Ecclesall in Hallamshire to Beauchief abbey of the tenement which they have by the gift of his father in Hollins. [1300–1316]¹

Quieta clamacio Rogeri filii Willelmi de Holyns de quodam tenemento

Omnibus hoc scriptum visuris vel audituris Rogerus filius Willelmi del Holyns in soca de Ecclessall' in Halumschyre salutem in Domino.

Noveritis me remisisse, relaxasse et omnino pro me et heredibus meis quietum clamasse religiosis viris abbati et conventui de Bello Capite et eorum successoribus totum jus et clameum quod habui vel habere potui seu habeo vel habere potero in toto illo tenemento cum pertinenciis, quod iidem religiosi habent ex dono et concessione Willelmi de Holyns, patris mei predicti, [fo. 82v] in le Holyns predict[o]. Ita quod nec ego nec heredes mei, nec aliquis alius nomine nostro, aliquod jus vel clameum in predicto tenemento cum pertinenciis decetero exigere vel vendicare poterimus quoquomodo. In cuius rei testimonium presenti scripto sigillum apposui. Hiis testibus: domino Roberto de Ecclessall', Rogero Hauselin, Willelmo Hauselin, Adam de Schefeld coco, Thoma de bosco in Schefeld, Ade fratre eius, Stephano le Joesu, et aliis.[2]

[1] Confirmed in 1316 (Appendix II, no. 55).
[2] For Roger and William Hauselin, see **129**, n. 3; Adam of Sheffield cook, **150**, n. 3; Thomas de Bosco, **118**, n. 1; Adam de Bosco, **134**, n. 1.

155. Gift in free alms by William of Hollins to Beauchief abbey of an annual rent of 1d which Adam son of Richard the ditcher paid for the tenement which he held in William's field. [1290–1310]

Carta Willelmi de Holyns de redditu unius denarii

Sciant presentes et futuri quod ego Willelmus de Holyns dedi, concessi et hac presenti carta mea confirmavi abbati et conventui de Bello Capite et eorum successoribus in liberam, puram et perpetuam [elemosinam] quemdam annuum redditum unius denarii, quem Adam filius[a] Ricardi le Sykere michi reddere consuevit pro tenemento quod de me tenuit in campo meo cum omnibus pertinenciis suis. Tenendum et habendum dominis abbati et conventui et eorum successoribus in liberam, puram et perpetuam elemosinam, libere,[b] quiete, pacifice et integre, cum omnibus pertinenciis suis, libertatibus, profectibus, escaetis et proventibus, communis et aysiamentis omnimodis dicto redditui pertinentibus. Et ego prefatus Willelmus et heredes mei predictum annuum redditum unius denarii cum omnibus pertinenciis suis predictis abbati et conventui et eorum successoribus in liberam, puram et perpetuam elemosinam warantizabimus, acquietabimus et contra omnes gentes inperpetuum defendemus. In cuius rei testimonium presenti carte sigillum meum est appensum. Hiis testibus: Thoma de Schefeld, Ada dicto coco de eadem, [fo. 83r] Thoma de bosco de eadem, Ricardo Torkerd de eadem, Rogero Hauselin, et multis aliis.[1]

[a] *filius (bis).* [b] *libire.*

[1] Thomas de Sheffield witnessed Sheffield's town charter in 1297. The other witnesses paid the lay subsidy there in the same year.

[LITTLE SHEFFIELD]

156. Gift in free alms by Hugh Hauselin of Little Sheffield[1] to Beauchief abbey of the formation of a dam for their mill called the New Mill[2] in his field of Holleford. It is permitted for the canons to lead the water of the Sheaf for their own profit through the middle of his alder-grove in the south part of the same field, saving arable land. [1270–1320]

Carta Hugonis Hauslen' de Parva Schefeld de stagno faciendo

Sciant presentes et futuri quod ego Hugo Hauslen' de Parva Schefeld dedi, concessi et hac presenti carta mea confirmavi Deo et ecclesie beati Thome martiris de Bello Capite et canonicis ibidem Deo servientibus formacionem stagni molendini sui quod vocatur novum molendinum in cultura mea de Holleford. Ita quod liceat eisdem canonicis ducere aquam Scheve ad libitum et comodum suum per medium alnetum meum in parte meridiana eiusdem culture de Holleford extra terram arabilem, in liberam, puram et perpetuam elemosinam, pro salute anime mee et Juliane uxoris mee et heredum meorum. Et ut hec mea donacio, concessio et confirmacio stabilis et inconcussa futuris temporibus perseveret, eam tam sigilli mei inpressione[a] quam testium subscripcione roboravi. Hiis testibus: Nicholao de Worthel', Henrico de Tankyrleys, Johanne de Mydehop', Johanne constabilario de Schefeld, Hugone de Waddesley, et multis aliis.

[a] *inppressione.*

[1] Little Sheffield was a hamlet in Ecclesall, immediately south of Sheffield. For other gifts by Hugh to the abbey see **118, 131–132, 149,** and **158**.
[2] The site was later occupied by Norton Forge, also known as Norton Hammer Wheel (C. Ball, D. Crossley, and N. Flavell (eds), *Water Power on the Sheffield Rivers* (2nd edn, Sheffield, 2006), p. 169); see the Introduction, p. 19.

157. Quitclaim by William the merchant of Sheffield to Beauchief abbey of 1 strip called the Mylneclyff which he held from William of Hollins. [1280–1320]¹

Quieta clamacio Willelmi mercatoris de Schefeld de placea terre que vocatur le Mylneclyff

Universis presens scriptum inspecturis Willelmus mercator de[a] Schefeld salutem in Domino sempiternam. Noverit universitas vestra me dedisse, concessisse et omnino quietam clamasse pro me et heredibus meis abbati et conventui de Bello Capite [fo. 83v] totam illam placeam terre que vocatur le Mylneclyff, quam nuper tenui de Willelmo del Holyns, sicut iacet in longitudine et latitudine. Ita quod nec ego Willelmus nec heredes mee nec aliquis nomine nostro in dicta placea terra vel in aliqua eius parte aliquod jus vel clameum inposterum vendicare poterimus quoquo jure. In cuius rei testimonium presenti scripto sigillum meum apposui. Hiis testibus: Rogero Hauselin', Roberto fratre eius, Roberto del Brom', Ada clerico de Schefeld, Johanne Frend, et multis aliis.

[a] *de (bis).*

¹ See 150.

[ECCLESALL]

158. Grant by Roger son of Hugh Hauselin to Beauchief abbey of an annual rent of 5s which Roger of Hollins paid for a certain bovate which he held in the vill of Ecclesall. [1250–1280]

Carta [Rogeri filii] Hugonis Hauselin de quinque solidatis annui redditus

Omnibus ad quos presens scriptum pervenerit Rogerus filius Hugonis Hauselin salutem in Domino. Noveritis me dedisse, concessisse et hac presenti carta mea confirmasse abbati et conventui de Bello Capite et successoribus suis quinque solidatas redditus, quas Rogerus del Holyns solebat reddere michi per annum pro quadam bovata terre, quam tenuit de me in villa de Ecclessall', cum wardis, releviis et omnibus aliis escaetis, que me vel heredes meos de predicto redditu et de predicto tenemento quocumque modo contingere possint.

Tenend[as] et habend[as] illis et successoribus suis in liberam, puram et perpetuam elemosinam. Et ego predictus Rogerus et heredes mei totum predictum reditum cum omnibus aliis pertinenciis, sicut predictum est, predictis abbati et conventui et successoribus suis contra omnes homines warantizabimus, acquietabimus et defendemus inperpetuum. Hiis testibus: Roberto de Oldewerk', Willelmo Brom', Roberto Hauselin', Ricardo de Flin.[1]

[1] For Roger of Aldwark, see **116**, **126**, and **127**; for Robert Hauselin, see **113**, **116**, **128**, **139–141**, and **157**; for Richard of Flintham, see **107**. The rest of this charter and probably also the text of other charters is missing, owing to the excision of five leaves.

[TOTLEY]

159. Grant by William of Dronfield and Agnes his wife to Beauchief abbey of common pasture at Strawberry Lee[1] for goats and other animals, according to what is contained in a charter the canons have from the lord William de Menul.[2] [1250–1290]

[fo. 84r]

Universis sancte matris ecclesie filiis ad quos presens scriptum pervenerit Willelmus de Dronefeld et Agnes uxor eius salutem in Domino. Noverit universitas vestra nos concessisse et hac presenti carta nostra confirmasse Deo et beate Marie et ecclesie beati Thome martiris de Bello Capite et canonicis Premonstrensi ordinis ibidem Deo servientibus communem pasturam apud Streberiley de capris de ceteris animalibus, secundum quod continetur in carta quam habent de domino Willelmo del Menul. Hanc vero concessionem et confirmacionem warantizabimus eisdem canonicis quamdiu dominium nostrum ibi durat. Hiis testibus: Johanne del Beyle, Waltero de Lyndesay, et pluribus aliis.

[1] A grange in Totley, OS ref. SK 285799; see the Introduction, p. 14, and **161** and **163**.
[2] Sir William de Meynell was alive in 1274 (Turbutt, *Derbyshire*, II, p. 520). In the 1160s Robert de Meynell acquired the manor of Langley, part of which became known as Meynell Langley, and the family retained this possession until the death of Sir Ralph de Meynell in 1389 (*ibid.*, p. 488).

[CHESTERFIELD]

160. Gift in free alms by Hugh Wake[1] to Beauchief abbey of free right of purchase and sale in his vill of Chesterfield and throughout the entire wapentake of Scarsdale, with free entry, exit, and passage, and free from all tolls and custom.[2] [1233–1241][3]

Carta Hugonis Wak de libertate emendi et cariandi

Omnibus sancte matris ecclesie filiis ad quos presens scriptum pervenerit Hugo Wak salutem[a] in Domino. Noverit universitas vestra me caritatis intuitu et pro salute anime mee et pro animabus patris et matris mee et omnium antecessorum et successorum meorum concessisse et hac presenti carta mea confirmasse Deo et ecclesie beati Thome martiris de Beaucheff et fratribus ibidem Deo servientibus liberam empcionem et vendicionem in villa mea de Chesturfeld, tam in domo quam in foro, et per totum wapintak de Scarusdale, cum libero introitu et exitu et cariagio, absque omni tolneto et consuetudine. Hanc vero concessionem et confirmacionem feci in liberam, puram et perpetuam eis elemosinam. Et ego et heredes mei [fo. 84v] totam prescriptam concessionem et confirmacionem predictis fratribus de Beaucheff warantizabimus contra omnes homines inperpetuum. Hiis testibus etc.

[a] *saltem.*

[1] Hugh Wake succeeded William Brewer the younger as lord of Chesterfield in 1233 and died in 1241 (Bestall, *History of Chesterfield*, I, p. 59). **195** is a virtually identical grant of the same privileges to the canons.
[2] i.e. the canons did not have to pay market tolls in Chesterfield or the wapentake of Scarsdale, which covered north-east Derbyshire.
[3] For other Chesterfield deeds, see **192–202**.

[HATHERSAGE]

161. Gift in free alms by Matthew of Hathersage[1] to Beauchief abbey of an annual rent of 1 mark from his mill at Hathersage; and of common of pasture on Hathersage Moor for all their livestock at their granges of Fulwood[2] and Strawberry Lee, *viz.* **from Fulwood to Burbage Brook,[3] and then down to Hyggehou,[4] and there down to Lightokford, and then down to (Nether) Padley,[5] and then up to Lady's**

Cross,[6] and then up by the boundaries[7] of Totley and Dore to the boundaries of Hallamshire. [1220–1270]

Carta Mathei de Haversegge de una marcata redditus[a] de molendino de Haversegge

Omnibus etc. Matheus de Haversegge salutem in Domino. Noverit universitas vestra me dedisse, concessisse et hac presenti carta mea confirmasse Deo et ecclesie beati Thome martiris de Bello Capite et canonicis ibidem Deo servientibus in liberam, puram et perpetuam elemosinam, pro salute anime mee et omnium antecessorum meorum et successorum, unam marcatam redditus de molendino meo de Haversegge annuatim per manum meam et heredum meorum vel illorum qui dictum molendinum[b] tenuerint ad Purificacionem beate Marie Virginis, sine aliqua contradictione, cavillacione vel impedimento, apud Haversegge percipiendam. Preterea[c] dedi et concessi dictis canonicis de Bello Capite comunam pasture ubique super moram meam de Haversegg' infra metas subscriptas ad omnia averia sua levancia vel cubancia apud grangiam suam de Fulwode et de Streberiley, tam ad oves quam ad cetera animalia qualia, dicti canonici apud dictam grangiam de Fulwode et grangiam de Streberiley ponere voluerint, videlicet de Fulwode usque ad caput de Burbache, et sic descendendo usque ductum aque de Burbache usque ad Hyggehou et de Hyggehou descendendo usque ad Lightokford et de Lightokford usque Paddeley et de Paddel' ascendendo[d] usque ad Levedicros et sic de le Levedicros ascendendo per divisas de [fo. 85r] Totinley et de Dore usque ad metas de Halumschire. Hanc autem marcatam redditus et comunam pasture cum pertinenciis super moram meam de Haverseg', infra metas predictas, dedi dictis canonicis in liberam, puram et perpetuam elemosinam, soluta et quieta ab omnibus secularibus serviciis, sectis, consuetudinibus et demandis. Et ego dictus Matheus et heredes mei etc. Hiis testibus etc.

[a] *redditu.*   [b] *melendinum.*   [c] final *e* of *Preterea* interlined.   [d] *ascendedo.*

[1] Matthew of Hathersage obtained a grant of free warren in 1249 (*Calendar of Charter Rolls, Henry III*, 1226–1257, p. 345). He was a witness to **167** and was remembered in the Obituary (2 March). A Matthew of Hathersage or a Sir Matthew of Hathersage (d. 1259) appear in Holdsworth, *Rufford Charters*, nos 69 and 79 as a witness or as witnesses to grants made by Ralf Musard I or II, both of whom appear in the Royal Confirmation of 1312 (Appendix II below, nos 30–33).
[2] This is the first reference to the grange at Fulwood.
[3] Burbage Brook takes its name from the prehistoric site known as Carl Wark; it flows east of the earthwork down into Padley Gorge.

⁴Higger Tor, OS ref. SK 256819.
⁵OS ref. SK 250782.
⁶OS ref. SK 274782. The Lady Cross is dated 1263 in Cameron, *Place-names of Derbyshire*, II, p. 265, on the basis of the lost Potter transcript of this document (see Foreword above, p. vii), but no date is given here.
⁷The Totley boundary is marked by the wooden pole at SK 267791. Totley and Dore lay just inside Derbyshire. Hallamshire comprised the parish of Sheffield and the parish of Ecclesfield with its chapelry of Bradfield.

162. Confirmation by Simon of Goosehill¹ to Beauchief abbey of an annual rent of 1 mark which Matthew of Hathersage gave them from his mill in Hathersage, one moiety of which Simon's mother Matilda, sister and one of the heirs of Matthew, gave to him by her charter. The canons will receive ½ mark from the moiety of the mill and from 1 bovate which Simon son of Matthew holds in villeinage in Hathersage, with power of distraint. The canons will say 1 annual Mass for the soul of Matilda, Simon's mother, for this grant. [1250–1290]

Carta Symonis Gousill' de eodem

Omnibus etc. Symon de Gousill' salutem. Noveritis me concessisse et confirmasse Rad[ulpho] abbati de Bello Capite et canonicis ibidem Deo servientibus donum et concessionem Mathei de Haversegge, que quondam fecit abbati de Bello Capite et canonicis eiusdem loci, de una marcata redditus de quodam molendino aquatico in Haversegge, cuius medietatem Matilda mater mea, soror et una heredum predicti Mathei, michi per cartam suam contulit. Ita quod predictus Rad[ulphus] abbas et successores sui inperpetuum recipiant dimidiam marcatam de predicta medietate predicti molendini et de una bovata terre, quam Symon filius Mathei de me tenet in villenagio in eadem, per manum meam et heredum meorumᵃ et aliorum quorumque predicta tenementa tenencium ad festum sancti Martini in hyeme apud Haversege. Si vero contingat quod predicta dimidia marcata redditus, sive aliqua pars eius, temporibus futuris aretro fuerit, volo et concedo pro me et heredibus meis et assignatis meis quod predictus abbas et successores sui libere possint facere districciones in predictis tenementis in quorumcumque manibus futuris temporibus predicta tenementa devenire contigerint, et predictas districciones retinere [fo. 85v] quousque predicta dimidia marcata redditus plenarie eisdem fuerit persoluta. Pro hac autem concessione predictus abbas et eiusdem loci conventus concesserunt predicto Symoni quod ipsi decetero singulis annis celebrari facient pro anima Matildis Gousil, matris mee, in die aniversarii sui unam missam inperpetuum. In cuius rei testimonium etc. Hiis testibus etc.

[a] *meum.*

[1] Simon of Goosehill (Goxhill, Lincs) served on the High Peak jury at the 1281 Derbyshire eyre and claimed a free chase on his land at Hathersage (Hopkinson, *Derbyshire Eyre*, pp. 180 and 193). According to Pegge (*Beauchief Abbey*, p. 168), he was a nephew of Matthew of Hathersage (see **161**, n. 1). He also inherited from Matthew half the manors of Barlborough, Clowne, and Whitwell in north-east Derbyshire (Turbutt, *Derbyshire*, II, p. 488).

163. Gift in free alms by Richard of Bernak to Beauchief abbey of common of pasture on his moor of Padley for all their animals at the grange of Strawberry Lee. Made in the year 1285.

Carta Ricardi Bernak de eodem[a]

Omnibus hoc scriptum visuris vel audituris Ricardus de Bernak' salutem in Domino sempiternam. Noverit universitas vestra me in anno Domini m° cc° octogesimo quinto, pro salute anime mee et omnium antecessorum et successorum meorum, dedisse, concessisse et hoc presenti scripto meo confirmasse abbati et conventui de Bello Capite comunam pasture ubique super moram meam de Paddeley ad omnia et omnimoda animalia sua morancia ad grangiam suam de Streberiley vel ibidem aliunde causa pascue quocumque anni tempore missas. Tenendam et habendam predictis abbati et conventui suisque successoribus in liberam, puram et perpetuam elemosinam, cum omnibus ac omnimodis aisiamentis et pertinenciis suis. Et ego predictus Ricardus et heredes mei totam predictam comunam pasture cum[b] omnibus ac omnimodis aisiamentis et pertinenciis suis, sicud predictum est, predictis abbati et conventui suis[que] successoribus in liberam, puram et perpetuam elemosinam contra omnes gentes inperpetuum warantizabimus, acquietabimus et defendemus. In cuius rei etc. Hiis testibus etc.

[a] *deodem.* [b] *cum (bis).*

[HAREWOOD]

164. Grant by Warin of Beeley,[1] with the consent of his wife and heirs, to Beauchief abbey of all Harewood[2] up to the

woods over which there is controversy between him and
Robert Brito[3] of Walton; of all pasture east of the great road
which leads to the Cross of Wadshelf[4] by Harewoodhead
Dereleyam;[5] and of common on Harland Edge[6] for 100 oxen
and cows and 20 mares with their young under 3 years
of age, and for 100 sheep. The canons, who gave Warin
5$\frac{1}{2}$ silver marks and his wife and Serlo his son 3 bezants[7]
each for this grant, shall render to him 10s annually and
confraternity. [1180–1210]

Carta Warini de Beghley[a] de Harewode[b]

Noverint universi tam presentes quam futuri tam clerici quam laici
tam Franci quam Anglici ad quos presentium pervenerit noticia[c] quod
ego Warnerius de Begalaia[d] de consensu et voluntate uxoris mee et
heredum meorum, concessi et dedi et hac carta mea[e] confirmavi Deo
et sancte Marie et sancto Thome martiri de Beauchef[f] et canonicis
ibidem Deo servientibus totam Harewdam[g] in dominico habendam
et possidendam usque ad nemus, de quo mota est controversia
inter me et Robertum Britonem[h] de Waletona, et totam pasturam
et que[i] ad me pertinet versus orientem a magna via que vadit de
cruce de Wadescelff[j] per Harewdeheved Dereleiam.[k] Concessi eciam
prefatis canonicis talem communiam qualem ego habeo de super
Harelundhegge, tam versus nort' quam versus orientem, numeratis
tamen eorum animalibus. Habebunt enim ibidem centum boves et
vaccas, cum toto exitu earum, et viginti equas cum toto exitu earum
usque in tres annos et anno tercio removebitur exitus remanente
predicto numero bovum vaccarum et equarum, que eque habebunt
pasturam per totam comunam meam extra haiam meam. Habebunt
eciam predicti canonici de Beauchef ibidem centum oves. Qui quidem
canonici tenebunt omnia prenominata de me et heredibus meis
libere et quiete, honorifice et pacifice inperpetuum, reddendo mihi et
heredibus meis singulis annis decem solidos argenti pro omni seculari
servicio, consuetudine et exactione duobus terminis, scilicet infra
octabas sancti Martini quinque solidos et ad Pentecosten quinque
solidos. Omnia vero que in hac carta continentur ego Warnerius[l] et
heredes mei sepedictis canonicis de Beauchef. contra omnes homines[m]
inperpetuum warantizabimus. Pro hac concessione et donacione
dederunt michi abbas et canonici quinque marcas argenti et dimidiam
et uxori mee tres bisancios et Serloni filio meo tres bisancios. Preterea
concesserunt mihi et uxori mee et heredibus meis fraternitatem domus
sue et tocius ordinis Premonstratensis in spiritualibus beneficiis, sicut
uni concanonicorum suorum. Hiis testibus Radulpho Basset canonico

de Rouecestre,[8] Hugone de Dronefeld, Roberto persona de Dereleia,[n] magistro Hugone de Cestrefeld, Galfrido clerico de Bramtona, Alano de Edelwasdeleia,[o] Nicholao de Bircheved,[p] Rogero[q] clerico de Schefeld, Rad[ulpho] de Nidhing,[r] Willelmo[s] dispensatore et aliis multis.[t]

W = British Library, Wolley charter, I, 13, with a very worn, round seal of green wax. Of the circumscription only ... + SIGIL... is legible. The figure is a galloping horse with a rider wearing a shield on his left arm (Jeayes, *Derbyshire Charters*, no. 244). Early thirteenth century.
B = Sheffield Archives, MD 3414 (Beauchief Cartulary), fo. 86r–v.
L = Derbyshire Record Office, D 1005 Z/E1 (Leake Cartulary, no. 1), p. 39.
R = Cambridge University Library, Add. MS 3897, pp. 1–3, transcript no. 1 by John Reynolds, junior, made in 1777. Reynolds, who copied the seal, found on the circumscription: + SIGILL(UM) ... (W)ARNER (II DE BEGALAI)A.

[a] note deleted.   [b] rubric *om.* LR   [c] *tam ... noticia:* etc. B   [d] *Warnerius de Beghleya* B
[e] *hac carta mea: hac presenti mea* B   [f] *Beuchef* B   [g] *Harewode* B *Harewodam* L
[h] *Britone* WL   [i] *quod* B   [j] *Wadeschelf* B   [k] *Dereleyam* B *derleiam* R
[l] *Warinus* B   [m] *gentes* B   [n] *derleia* R   [o] *Edelwaldeleia* R   [p] *burcheved* R
[q] *Roberto* R   [r] *cridling* R   [s] *Willelmo* W *Waltero* BL   [t] *Radulpho Basset ... multis:* etc. B

[1] Warin of Beeley and Liscelicia (Uscelin in the short version), his wife, were commemorated in the Obituary (14 August).
[2] Harewood is nine miles south of Beauchief as the crow flies. It occupied the easternmost extension of the manor and parish of Beeley. See the Introduction, pp. 15–16, for Harewood Grange (OS ref. SK 312680).
[3] i.e. the Breton, from Brittany; see **18**, n. 1. The National Archives CP 25/1/36/2/10 records a recognisance of grand assize that Serlo of Beeley (Warin's son) and Robert Brito had given 60 acres of land in Walton to Beauchief abbey in free alms. Serlo of Beeley and Robert Brito also granted 60 acres of land in Walton to Beauchief abbey on 19 November 1208 (Jeayes, *Derbyshire Charters*, no. 2745; J. Hunter (ed.), *Fines sive pedes finium; sive finales concordiae in Curia domini regis ... AD 1195–AD 1214*, II (London: Record Commission, 1844), p. 32). Serlo was commemorated as 'our canon and assistant brother' in the Obituary (4 November).
[4] The cross has gone; Wadshelf is in Brampton parish, OS ref. SK 315710.
[5] The parish of Darley extended to the top of the moor, within about a mile of Harewood Grange.
[6] OS ref. SK 290687. Both Harland Edge and Harewood derive their names from their position on a boundary (Cameron, *Place-names of Derbyshire*, I, pp. 44–45).
[7] A gold bezant was worth between a half-sovereign and a sovereign and was replaced by the noble during the reign of Edward III. A silver bezant was worth between a shilling and a florin.
[8] Rocester (Staffs).

165. Quitclaim by the same Warin of Beeley to Beauchief abbey of all his farm of Harewood, together with the body of Robert his son, to be taken within 2 years from the first Whitsun after Robert's death, during which 2 years the canons shall render to his heirs 80d annually, saving 40d from the 10s which they pay to him annually for the same grange, together with Warin's body. [1180–1210]

Relaxacio predicti Warini de eadem terra[a]

Sciant presentes et[b] futuri quod ego Warinus de Beghley[c] quietam clamavi totam firmam meam de Harewode[d] domui abbacie de Beauchef cum corpore filii mei Roberti a primo Pentecoste[e] post obitum ipsius Roberti in duos annos percipiendam, peractis vero duobus annis abbas et canonici predicte abbacie de Beuchef[f] heredibus meis pro ipsius loci grangia de Harewode[g] et omnibus pertinenciis suis dimidiam marcam duobus terminis, videlicet ad Pentecosten xl d[h] et infra octabas sancti Martini alios xl d[i] annuatim persolvent, salva xl d[j] de x s[k] quos michi[l] annuatim pro ipsius grangia solvere solebant cum corpore meo predictis abbati et canonicis de B.[m] pro salute anime mee[n] et omnium antecessorum et heredum meorum quietos inperpetuum clamavi. Hiis testibus etc.[o]

B = Sheffield Archives, MD 3414 (Beauchief Cartulary), fo. 86v.
L = Derbyshire Record Office, D 1005 Z/E1 (Leake Cartulary, no. 2), p. 39.

[a] rubric *om*. L   [b] *quam* L   [c] *Warnerius de Begleya* L   [d] *Harewt* L
[e] *Penthecosten* L   [f] *Beaucheft'* L   [g] *Harewt* L
[h] *quadraginta denarios* L   [i] *quadraginta denarios* L   [j] *quadraginta denarios* L
[k] *decem solidos* L   [l] *mihi* L   [m] *Beauchef* L   [n] *mee anime* L
[o] *etc.* omitted in L, instead: *Matheo sacerdote de Bachwelle, Richardo capellano de Nortona, Roberto de Hop, Petro de Hartill, Willelmo de Chateswre', Galfrido filio Warneri de Begley, Willelmo de Lidtun, et multis aliis.*

166. Release by the final testament of the same Warin of Beeley to Beauchief abbey of 40d of the farm of 10s of Harewood, together with his body, and of 1 palfrey and 2 oxen. The Leake copy of this charter includes other releases: to the mother church of Bakewell the land which William held and 3 oxen; to Beauchief abbey 1 ox; to the sick poor of Nottingham 12d; to the sick poor of Chesterfield 12d; to the 7 chapels [of ease] of Bakewell 12d each; to Tideswell church 2s; to Peak [Forest] church 12d and to their sick 12d, to Hope church 12d; to Edensor church 12d;

to Darley church 12d, and to the nuns of Derby 2s. [1180–1210]

Alia relaxacio eiusdem Warini per testamentum suum de eadem terra[a]

Hoc est testamentum extremum domini Warini de Beghley.[b] In primis cum corpore suo ad abbaciam de B. xl[c] denarios de firma de x[d] solidis de Harewode[e] relaxavit inperpetuum et palefridum cum strat' suo et lectum suum, scut' et ij boves[f] etc.[g] Hiis testibus etc.[h]

B = Sheffield Archives, MD 3414 (Beauchief Cartulary), fo. 86v.
L = Derbyshire Record Office, D 1005 Z/E1 (Leake Cartulary, no. 3), p. 39.

[a] rubric om. L   [b] *Warneri de Begley* L   [c] *Beauchef quadraginta* L
[d] *decem* L   [e] *Harewt* L   [f] *palefridum . . . boves* reads *palefridum suum cum toto staratio suo et lectum suum cum omnibus pertinentiis suis et scutum dedit et duos boves* in L.
[g] *etc.* omitted in L, instead: *Ad matricem ecclesiam de Bayckewelle terram quam aliquam eidem ecclesie dedit, quam Willelmus tenuit, quietam clamavit et tres boves, abbacie de Beuch' unum bovem, pauperibus lazaris de notincham duodecim denarios, pauperibus lazaris de Sesterfeult duodecim denarios, septem capellis de Bahekewelle uni cuius xii d, ecclesie de Tiddeswell duos solidos, ecclesie de Pec xii d, et infirmis eiusdem ville xii d, ecclesie de Hop' xii d, ecclesie de Eidenesower xii d, ecclesie de Dereleia xii d, sanctimonialibus de Derebi duos solidos.*
[h] *etc.* omitted in L, instead: *Matheo sacerdote de Bahikewell, Roberto de Hop, Petro de Hertill, Willemo de Schaterswrt, Galfrido filio Warneri de Begley, Willelmo de Lidtun, et multis aliis.*

167. Gift in free alms by Serlo son of Warin of Beeley[1] to Beauchief abbey of all his land called Harewood as is contained in the charter which they have from his father; and of common of pasture for 20 cows and a bull with their young under the age of 3 years (and, according to the Leake transcript, for 5 mares with their young under the age of 3 years), a plough-team, and 300 sheep in all the places mentioned in the same charter. [1200–1230]

[fo. 87r]

Carta Serlonis filii Warini de Beghley' de eadem terra[a]

Omnibus etc.[b] Serlo filius Warini de Beghley[c] salutem in Domino. Noverit universitas vestra me divine pietatis intuitu dedisse,[d] concessisse et hac mea presenti carta confirmasse Deo et sancte Marie et sancto Thome martiri de Beauchef et[e] canonicis ibidem Deo servientibus totam terram meam, que vocatur Harewode,[f] in dominico habendam per omnia, sicud[g] metas que continentur in carta, quam habent de patre meo. Et communem pasturam ad xx[ti][h] vaccas et taurum cum exitu earum trium annorum et ad[i] boves caruce sue et ad iij^{cj} oves in omnibus locis, que continentur in carta quam habent de patre meo, in liberam, puram et perpetuam elemosinam, pro salute anime mee et patris mei^k et omnium antecessorum et heredum meorum. Ego vero et heredes mei predictam terram cum pertinenciis et prenominatam^l pasturam dictis^m canonicis contra omnes homines acquietabimus et warantizabimus inperpetuum.^{n} Hiis testibus etc.^{o}

B = Sheffield Archives, MD 3414 (Beauchief Cartulary), fo. 87r.
L = Derbyshire Record Office, D 1005 Z/E1 (Leake Cartulary, no. 4), p. 40.

^{a}rubric *om.* L. ^{b}*etc.* omitted in L, instead: *sancte matris ecclesie filiis tam presentibus quam futuris.*
^{c}*Warin de Begleya* L ^{d}*dedisse et* L ^{e}*et* interlined in B ^{f}*Harewud* L
^{g}*secundum* L ^{h}*viginti* L ^{i}*quinque equas cum exitu earum trium annorum et ad* L
^{j}*trescentas* L ^{k}*et matris mee* L ^{l}*nominatam* L ^{m}*supradictis* L
^{n}*inperpetuum* omitted in L ^{o}*etc.* omitted in L, instead: *domino Roberto filio Willelmi de Alf', Matheo de Haderseg', Adam de Herthall, Ricardo de Edonesohona, Roberto de Stanton, et aliis.*

[1] Serlo of Beeley was one of the knights who perambulated the royal forest in East Derbyshire in 1225, as was Adam of Harthill, one of the witnesses here (Turbutt, *Derbyshire*, II, p. 584). Another witness, Matthew of Hathersage, appears with Serlo of Beeley as a witness to a Rufford abbey charter dated *c*.1166–1218 (Holdsworth, *Rufford Charters*, no. 98); see also **161** above.

168. Gift in free alms by Serlo son of Warin of Beeley to Beauchief abbey of an annual rent of $^1/_2$ silver mark from his mill in Beeley, together with his body. [1200–1230][1]

Carta Serlonis filii Warini de Beghley de dimidia marca redditus

Omnibus etc. Serlo filius Warini de Beghley salutem in Domino. Noverit universitas vestra me divine caritatis intuitu dedisse et concessisse et hac presenti carta mea confirmasse Deo et ecclesie sancti Thome martiris de Beuchef et canonicis ibidem Deo servientibus cum corpore meo, in liberam, puram et perpetuam elemosinam, dimidiam marcam argenti in molendino meo de Beghley, de me et heredibus meis annuatim ad festum sancti Martini inperpetuum percipiendam. Hiis testibus etc.

[1] Confirmed in 1316 (Appendix II, no. 50).

169. Grant by Warin son of Robert of Beeley, with the consent of his wife and heirs, to Robert son of Godric of Darley, for his homage and service, of all the land of Beeley

which Godric of Darley held; and of the land of Fallinge.[1] **Robert son of Godric shall render to Warin ¹/₂ silver mark annually. [1180–1210]**

[fo. 87r]

Item alia carta Warini de Beghley

[fo. 87v]

Sciant presentes et futuri quod ego Warinus filius Roberti, consensu uxoris mee et heredum meorum, dedi, concessi et hac presenti carta confirmavi Roberto filio Godrici de Derley, pro homagio[a] suo et servicio, totam terram de Beghley, quam pater suus tenuit, et terram de Fallinge. Tenendam de me et heredibus meis hereditarie et libere et quiete in pascuis et in cunctis[b] aysiamentis extra haiam meam. Annuatim inde reddendo dimidiam marcam argenti, medietatem ad Pentecosten et medietatem in festo beati Martini pro omni servicio michi et heredibus meis pertinente, excepta terra predicta[c] que ad molendinum meum pertinet et salvo servicio forensi. Hiis testibus etc.

[a] *humagio.*   [b] *cuntis.*   [c] *terre predicte.*

[1] OS ref. SK 270665.

170. Quitclaim in free alms by Susanna and Margery of Beeley daughters of Robert former dean of Beeley to Beauchief abbey of the territory of Beeley and Fallinge. [1200–1230][1]

Quieta clamacio Susanne et Margerie filiarum[a] Roberti quondam decani de terra de B.

Omnibus ad quos presens scriptum pervenerit Susanna et Margeria de Beghley filie Roberti quondam decani salutem in Domino. Noverit universitas vestra nos resignasse et quietum clamasse de nobis et heredibus nostris abbati et conventui de Beuchef et successoribus suis totum jus et clamium quod habuimus, vel habere poterimus, in territorio de Beghley et de Fallinge, cum omnibus pertinenciis, libertatibus, comunis et aysiamentis dicte terre de Beghley et de Fallinge pertinentibus. Tenendum et habendum in liberam, puram et perpetuam elemosinam. Ita quod nec nos nec heredes nostri, nec aliquis ex parte nostra, aliquod jus vel clamium in dicta terra de [fo. 88r] Beghley et Falling', cum pertinenciis et nativis et eorum sequela et catallis, decetero vendicare poterimus. In cuius rei testimonium etc. Hiis testibus etc.

[a] *filie.*

[1] See **171**, n. 1, for the date of this charter.

171. Gift in free alms by Luke of Beeley[1] to Beauchief abbey of the homage and service which Susanna and Margery daughters of Robert the former dean pay for the land which they hold of him in Beeley, together with his body. [1200–1230]

Carta Luce de Beghley' de terra in eadem terra de Beghley'

Omnibus ad quos presens scriptum pervenerit Lucas de Beghley salutem in Domino. Noveritis me[a] concessisse, dedisse et hac presenti carta mea confirmasse Deo et ecclesie beati Thome martiris de Beuchef in liberam, puram et [perpetuam] elemosinam cum corpore meo homagium et servicium cum redditibus, releviis et gardis, et aliis escaetis undecumque provenientibus, que michi facere solebant Susanna et Margeria filie Roberti quondam decani de terra quam tenent de me in villa de Beghley'. Ita quod nec ego nec heredes mei decetero in dicta terra cum homagiis, serviciis et aliis proventibus, sicud predictum est, aliquod jus vel clamium nobis vendicare poterimus, sed dicta Susanna et Margeria et heredes sui de dicta terra cum homagiis, redditibus et aliis proventibus, sicud de libera elemosina, abbatis et conventus dicte ecclesie de Beuchef decetero respondeant. Et ego Lucas et heredes mei omnia predicta dicte ecclesie de B. pro salute anime mee et omnium antecessorum et heredum meorum warantizabimus, acquietabimus et defendemus, sicud liberam, puram et perpetuam elemosinam. In cuius rei etc. Hiis testibus etc.

[a] *nos* deleted and *me* inserted above.

[1] In **172** Luke is identified as the son of Warin of Beeley, thus providing a date of about 1200–1230.

172. Gift in free alms by the same Luke son of Warin of Beeley to Beauchief abbey of all the land called Harewood; of pasture for 40 cows and 2 bulls with their young under the age of 2 years, 10 mares with their young under the

age of 3 years, the oxen of their plough-teams, 80 sheep, 30 pigs, and 40 goats on all the common of Beeley, *viz.* from the east part of the road which leads from the boundary of Darley called Galeghtres[1] to Harlandford and then up to Wodewardeston[2] and then through Tres Lauhes to Umberley Brook;[3] and of the freedom from fines for escaped animals for all animals beyond the aforesaid boundaries. [1200–1230][4]

Item alia carta Luce de Beghley'

Omnibus ad quos presens scriptum pervenerit Lucas filius Warini de Beghley salutem. Noveritis me divine pietatis intuitu et pro salute anime mee et omnium antecessorum et heredum meorum dedisse, concessisse [fo. 88v] et hac presenti carta mea confirmasse Deo et ecclesie sancti[a] Thome martiris de Beuchef et canonicis ibidem Deo servientibus totam terram que vocatur Harewode, cum pertinenciis in dominico habendam, scilicet metas quibus nunc clausa habetur et pasturam ad xl vaccas et duos tauros cum exitu duorum annorum et ad decem equas cum exitu trium annorum, et ad boves carucarum suarum, et ad octoginta[b] oves, et ad xxx porcos, et ad xl capras per omnem comunam de Beghley undique et ubique ab orientali parte vie que vadit a divisa de Derley que vocatur Galeghtres usque ad Harelundeford et inde usque ad Wodewardeston et sic per tres Lauhes usque in Humburley quantum dominium meum durat, cum libero introitu et exitu et aliis aysiamentis in omnibus rebus, in liberam, puram et perpetuam elemosinam, liberam et quietam ab omni exaccione seculari, sequela et demanda. Concessi eciam dictis canonicis liberum eschapium ultra predictos terminos de averiis omnibus capris et ceteris animalibus suis, sicud aliquod eschapium liberius haberi poterit. Et ego Lucas et heredes mei warantizabimus, acquietabimus et defendemus predictis canonicis, secundum formam prescriptam, totam prenominatam terram cum pertinenciis et cum pastura predictarum omnium caprarum, porcorum, equorum et ceterorum animalium ubicumque cubancia et levancia fuerint ab omni demanda et sequela, sicud puram elemosinam, contra omnes homines inperpetuum. Hiis testibus etc.

[a] *sancte* with *e* deleted and *i* inserted. [b] *octingenta*.

[1] Cameron, *Place-names of Derbyshire*, I, p. 84, interprets this lost name as Gallow Tree. Such gallows were normally sited at manorial boundaries.
[2] 'Forester's stone' – or derived from a personal name (*ibid.*, II, p. 227). A number of medieval boundary stones survive in the area.
[3] Tres Lauhes is a lost place-name. A medieval boundary stone survives by the Umberley Brook at SK 289696.
[4] Confirmed in 1316 (Appendix II, no. 29).

173. Gift in free alms by the same Luke of Beeley to Beauchief abbey of an annual rent of ¹/₂ mark in his mill of Beeley, together with his body. [1200–1230][1]

Item alia carta eiusdem Luce

[fo. 89r]

Omnibus etc. Lucas de Beghley salutem in Domino. Noverit universitas vestra me divine pietatis intuitu dedisse et hac presenti carta mea confirmasse Deo et ecclesie beati Thome martiris de Beuchef et canonicis ibidem Deo servientibus cum corpore meo, in liberam, puram et perpetuam elemosinam, redditum dimidie marce in molendino meo de Beghley de me et heredibus meis annuatim percipiendum et imperpetuum ad festum sancti Martini. Quod si ego vel heredes mei dictam dimidiam marcam cum alia dimidia marca quam habent in dicto molendino cum corpore Serlonis, fratris mei, sicud in[a] carta eius quam habent testatur,[1] predicto termino non solverimus, liceat abbati et conventui de Beuchef in curia ecclesiastica omni prohibicione regia postposita, sicud de pura elemosina sua, me et heredes meos ad solucionem plenam utriusque dimidie marce compellere. In cuius rei testimonium etc. Hiis testibus etc.

[a] *sicudi.*

[1] Confirmed in 1316 (Appendix II, no. 49).
[2] For Serlo's charter, see **168**.

[THE GREAVES]

174. Gift in free alms by Osbert son of Richard of Hore to Beauchief abbey of ¹/₂ bovate with a toft, croft, and meadow in the Greaves[1] in Beeley which John son of Luke of Beeley formerly held, together with his body. [1220–1250]

Carta Osberti filii Ricardi de Hore de terra in Beghley'

Universis Cristi etc. Osbertus filius Ricardi de Hore salutem in Domino. Noverit vestra me dedisse, concessisse et hac presenti carta mea confirmasse cum corpore meo pro salute anime mee Deo et ecclesie sancti[a] T. martiris de Bello Capite et canonicis ibidem Deo servientibus unam dimidiam bovatam terre cum tofto, crofto et prato in[b] le Grevis in territorio de Beghley' cum omnibus pertinenciis, libertatibus, comunis et aysiamentis, [fo. 89v] illam videlicet quam Johannes filius Luce de Beghley quondam tenuit. Tenendam et habendam sibi et succcssoribus suis de me et heredibus meis in liberam, puram et perpetuam elemosinam. Et ego prefatus Osbertus et heredes mei totam prefatam terram cum tofto, crofto et prato et omnibus libertatibus, comunis et aysiamentis et omnibus aliis pertinenciis dictis canonicis et successoribus suis in liberam, puram et perpetuam elemosinam contra omnes homines et feminas warantizabimus, acquietabimus et defendemus.[c] In cuius rei testimonium etc. Hiis testibus etc.

[a] *sancte.* [b] *en.* [c] *defendeus.*

[1] The Greaves was renamed Beeley Hilltop after William Saville purchased the estate in 1687, although the older name remained in use until the nineteenth century (Cameron, *Place-names of Derbyshire*, I, p. 44).

175. Confirmation by Margery daughter and heir of Luke of Beeley to Beauchief abbey of ½ bovate with a toft, croft, and meadow in the Greaves in Beeley which Osbert son of Richard of Hore, her late husband, gave to them together with his body. [1220–1250][1]

Confirmacio Margerie filie Luce de eadem terra

Omnibus etc. Margeria filia et heres Luce de Beghley' salutem in Domino. Noverit universitas vestra me, in libera potestate et legitima viduitate mea, concessisse et hoc presenti scripto confirmasse, pro salute anime mee et antecessorum meorum, abbati et conventui de Bello Capite et eorum successoribus, in liberam, puram et perpetuam elemosinam, illam dimidiam bovatam terre cum tofto, crofto et prato in le Grevis et territorio[a] de Beghley' cum pertinenciis, comunis et aysiamentis, quam Hosbertus filius Ricardi de Hore, quondam maritus meus, eis dedit cum corpore suo. Tenendam et habendam sibi et successoribus suis libere, quiete et integre. Ita quod nec ego nec aliquis pro me vel per me possit inposterum inde aliquod jus vel clamium exigere vel vendicare. In cuius rei etc. Hiis testibus etc.

[a] *territotorio.*

[1] Beauchief abbey gave this land to William de le Grevis for an annual rent of 30d in the reign of Henry III or Edward I (British Library, Wolley Charters, II, 45; Jeayes, *Derbyshire Charters*, no. 248). The witnesses are Peter de Baumford, Adam de Ronnesley, William de Chatteswrth (Chatsworth), and Peter le Rolund. The seal has gone. On 1 May 1398 Robert, abbot of Beauchief, gave licence to Thomas Gylesonne of le Greves to alienate a messuage and half a bovate of land which he held of the abbot in the Greaves (British Library, Wolley Charters, II, 51; Jeayes, *Derbyshire Charters*, no. 257).

[FALLINGE]

176. Grant by Robert the dean of Darley,[1] with the consent of his assigns, to Ralph of Fallinge of a certain toft and croft in Fallinge[2] which lie between the toft of Uchtred and the toft of William de Myrie with 4 acres in Fallinge thereunto belonging. Ralph shall render to Robert 12d annually. [1180–1210]

Carta Roberti decani de Derley

[fo. 90r]

Sciant presentes et futuri quod ego Robertus decanus de Derley, consensu et voluntate assignatorum meorum, dedi, concessi et hac presenti carta mea confirmavi Rad[ulpho] de Faling' et heredibus suis quoddam toftum et croftum in Fallinng', quod iacet inter toftum Huchcredi et toftum Willelmi de Myrie, cum quatuor acris terre in territorio de Falling' dicto tofto spectantibus. Tenendum et habendum sibi et heredibus suis in feodo[a] et hereditate, libere, quiete, pacifice et integre, cum omnibus comunis, libertatibus et aysiamentis ad predictum tenementum pertinentibus. Reddendo inde annuatim michi vel assignatis meis xij denarios, scilicet sex denarios ad festum Pent[ecostes] et sex denarios ad festum sancti Martini pro omni servicio seculari et exaccione vel demanda michi vel alicui assignatorum meorum pertinente, salvo forinseco servicio predicto tenemento pertinente et molitura bladi super predictum tenementum crescentis. Et ego dictus[b] Robertus et assignati mei warantizabimus predictum tenementum cum pertinenciis suis predicto Rad[ulpho] et heredibus suis contra omnes homines. Et ut hec mea donacio, concessio, confirmacio et warrantizacio rata sit, etc.[c]

[a] *et heredibus suis in feodo* (*bis*).   [b] *dictus predictus*.   [c] In Holles's *Excerpta* (British Library, Lansdowne MS 207B, fo. 357), the names of witnesses are given: *Dominus Willelmus de Vernun, Dominus Willelmus Basset testes cartae Roberti decani de Dereleye*. William de Vernun and William Basset together witnessed **191**; the latter also witnessed a grant by Ralph Musard to Beauchief abbey (see **222**, n. 4).

[1] See **104**.
[2] Fallinge is in the parish of Darley, about three miles across Beeley Moor from Harewood Grange.

177. Quitclaim by Simon son of Ralph of Fallinge to Hugh son of John of Duffield of 1 toft with a croft in the vill and territory of Fallinge with 4 acres thereunto belonging,

viz. **that toft which lies between the toft of Uchtred and the toft of William of Mirie. Hugh, who gave Simon a certain sum of money for this quitclaim, shall render to the chief lord of the fee 12½d annually. [1200–1230]**

Quieta clamacio de predicta terra Symonis filii Rad[ulphi] de Fall'

Sciant presentes etc. quod ego Symon filius Rad[ulphi] de Fallyng dedi, concessi, vendidi et presenti carta mea quietum clamavi omnino de me et heredibus meis et successoribus Hugoni filio Johannis de Duffeld, pro quadam summa pecunie quam michi premanibus donavit, illud toftum cum crofto in villa et in territorio de Falling, cum quatuor acris terre ad dictum toftum spectantibus, videlicet illud toftum cum crofto adiacente [fo. 90v] inter toftum Otheredi et toftum Willelmi de Mirie, absque[a] ullo retenemento. Habendum et tenendum ipsi Hugoni et heredibus suis vel cui et quando et ubi assignare voluerit quietam de me et heredibus et successoribus meis. Ita quidem quod nec ego Symon nec aliquis alius per me nec ex parte mea aliquod jus vel clamium in predicto tofto cum crofto et cum quatuor acris terre cum omnibus pertinenciis et libertatibus exigere vel vendicare poterimus inperpetuum. Faciendo inde servicium domino capitali illius feodi quod ad eum pertinet pro illo tenemento, scilicet xij denarios et obolum ad duos anni terminos, scilicet sex denarios ad Pent[ecosten] et sex denarios et obolum in festo sancti Martini pro omnibus rebus et demandis, excepto forinseco servicio, sicud carta feofeamenti testatur, quam habui de domino Roberto decano de Derley. Et ut hec mea donacio, concessio quietum etc. Hiis testibus etc.

[a] *asbsque.*

178. Gift in free alms by Hugh of Duffeld in Fallinge to Beauchief abbey of 4 acres with a toft and croft which he bought from Simon son of Ralph in Fallinge. [1200–1230]

Carta Hugonis Duffeld de eadem terra

Omnibus etc. Hugo de Duffeld in Falling salutem in Domino. Noverit universitas vestra me concessisse, dimisisse et omnino quietum clamasse pro me et heredibus meis imperpetuum domino abbati et conventui de Bello Capite et eorum successoribus, in liberam, puram et perpetuam elemosinam, quatuor acras terre cum tofto et crofto et omnibus aliis pertinenciis suis, quas emi de Symone filio Rad[ulphi] in Fallyng. Ita si quidem quod nec ego nec heredes mei nec aliquis alius per me vel pro me aliquod jus vel clamium in predictis quatuor acris terre, cum tofto et crofto et omnibus suis pertinenciis, decetero exigere vel vendicare poterimus inposterum. In cuius rei etc. Hiis testibus etc.

[ASHOVER]

179. Gift in free alms by Robert son of Ralph of Reresby[1] to Beauchief abbey of an annual rent of 4s 4d from the land which Roger of Marcham[2] formerly held in the soke of Ashover. [1260–1300][3]

[fo. 91r]

Esshover

Carta Roberti filii Rad[ulphi] de Deresby de quatuor[a] solidis et quatuor denariis in soca de Esshover

Omnibus Cristi fidelibus hoc scriptum visuris vel audituris Robertus filius Rad[ulphi] de Deresby salutem in Domino sempiternam. Noverit universitas vestra me dedisse, concessisse et hoc presenti scripto confirmasse abbati et conventui et eorum successoribus de Bello Capite, pro salute anime mee et antecessorum meorum, in liberam, puram et perpetuam elemosinam, quatuor solidos et quatuor denarios anni redditus percipiendos de terra quam Rogerus de Macham quondam tenuit de me in soca de Esshover ad duos anni terminos, videlicet ad festum sancti Martini in yeme duos solidos et duos denarios et ad festum Pent[ecostes] duos solidos et duos denarios. Tenendum et habendum predictis abbati et conventui et eorum successoribus totum predictum redditum cum wardis, releviis, escaetis, sectis ac omnibus aliis serviciis predictis redditui et terre aliquomodo spectantibus, libere, quiete et integre imperpetuum. Ego vero dictus Robertus et heredes mei vel assignati predictis abbatis et conventui et eorum successoribus totum predictum redditum cum pertinenciis, ut predictum est, contra omnes homines et feminas warantizabimus, acquietabimus et ubique[b] defendemus.[c] In cuius rei etc. Hiis testibus etc.

[a]*quatur.* [b]*uibique* with the first *i* deleted. [c]*defendeus.*

[1] In 1285 Robert de Reresby held the manor of Ashover (Turbutt, *Derbyshire*, II, p. 439); he was recorded at the 1281 Derbyshire eyre (Hopkinson, *Derbyshire Eyre*, pp. 26–27).
[2] Roger of Marcham and Albreda his wife are commemorated in the Obituary (14 September). Marcham is an early spelling of [East] Markham (Notts) (Watts, *English Placenames*, p. 399).
[3] Confirmed in 1316 (Appendix II, no. 47).

180. Gift in free alms by Richard Bernes to Beauchief abbey of 2 messuages with 2 tofts in the vill of Ashover which Sybil the weaver and Iseult former wife of Robert the smith held of him and which he had by the gift of Robert of Reresby.[1] **[1260–1300]**[2]

[fo. 91v]

Carta Ricardi Bernes de terre in Asshover

Pateat universis me Ricardum Bernes dedisse, concessisse et hoc presenti scripto confirmasse abbati et conventui de Bello Capite, in liberam, puram et perpetuam elemosinam, duo messuagia cum duobus toftis in villa de Asshover, que Sibilla textrix et Isolda, uxor quondam Roberti fabri, de me tenuerunt, que quidem habui de dono et concessione Roberti de Rerisby. Tenenda et habenda dictis abbati et conventui in liberam, puram et perpetuam elemosinam cum omnibus pertinenciis suis, libere, quiete, pacifice et integre. Et ego dictus Ricardus et heredes mei predicta duo messuagia cum toftis et aliis pertinenciis suis predictis abbati et conventui eorum[que] successoribus imperpetuum contra omnes homines warantizabimus, acquietabimus et ubique defendemus. In cuius rei testimonium presenti scripto sigillum meum apposui. Hiis testibus etc.

[1] Either Rearsby (Leics) or Reresby (Lincs).
[2] Confirmed in 1316 (Appendix II, no. 38).

181. Quitclaim in free alms by Robert of Reresby to Beauchief abbey of an annual rent of 1d from Richard of Bernes[1] **for 2 messuages and 2 tofts in the vill of Ashover which Sybil the weaver and Iseult former wife of Robert the smith held of him and for which 2 messuages and tofts he enfeoffed Richard. [1260–1300]**

Quieta clamacio Roberti de Rerysby

Universis ad quos presens carta pervenerit Robertus de Rerysby salutem in Domino sempiternam. Noverit universitas vestra me dedisse, concessisse et omnino quietum clamasse pro me et heredibus meis abbati et conventui de Bello Capite, in liberam, puram et perpetuam elemosinam, unum denarium annui[a] redditus, percipiendum de Ricardo de Bernes ad festum Pent[ecostes] pro duobus messuagiis et duobus toftis in villa de Asshover, que

Sibilla textrix [fo. 92r] et Ysolda, uxor quondam Roberti fabri, de me tenuerunt, de quibus duobus messuagiis et toftis cum eorum pertinenciis dictum Ricardum feoffavi. Ita quod nec ego dictus Robertus nec heredes mei nec assignati in dictis messuagiis cum toftis et pertinenciis suis aliquod jus vel clamium juris decetero exigere, capere vel aliquomodo reclamare poterimus. Et ego dictus Robertus et heredes mei vel assignati dictum denarium annui redditus cum suis pertinenciis predictis abbati et conventui et eorum successoribus, ut predictum est, contra omnes gentes warantizabimus ad sustentacionem luminis beate Marie Virginis in Bello Capite, acquietabimus et imperpetuum defendemus. In cuius rei testimonium etc. Hiis testibus etc.

[a] *anni.*

[1] Barnes Farm, Dronfield; OS ref. SK 337793.

182. Gift in free alms by Serlo of Pleasley[1] to Beauchief abbey of 1 bovate with a toft and croft in Upstall Field in the parish of Ashover which John son of Madoch quit to him. [1176–1195]

Carta Serlonis de Pleseleya de terra in Asshover

Omnibus sancte matris ecclesie filiis ad quos presens carta pervenerit Serlo de Pleseleia salutem in Domino. Sciatis me dedisse et hac presenti carta mea confirmasse Deo et sancte Marie et sancto Thome martiri de Beuchef et fratribus ibidem Deo servientibus unam bovatam terre cum tofto et crofto et cum omnibus pertinenciis suis in parochia de Essovr', scilicet in Ubbestoft. Quam videlicet bovatam Johannes filius Madoch posterius tenuit et michi [fo. 92v] quietam reddidit in puram et perpetuam elemosinam, libere et quiete ab omni exactione seculari[a] imperpetuum possidendam, pro salute anime mee et uxoris mee Mattildis et omnium heredum meorum et patris mei et omnium antecessorum meorum. Concessi eciam iamdictis fratribus vel ei qui[b] dictam bovatam de eis tenuerit comunionem uni bovate pertinentem liberam et quietam in bosco et plano, in viis et semitis et pascuis, et in omnibus locis. Hiis testibus: Rogero capellano, Serlo capellano, et multis aliis etc.

[a] *l* of *seculari* interlined.   [b] *qui* interlined.

[1] A Serlo de Pleasley held the manors of Ashover and Glapwell in 1086. His great-grandson, another Serlo de Pleasley, died *c.*1195 (Turbutt, *Derbyshire*, II, p. 481). This is therefore one of the earliest grants to the abbey.

183. Gift in free alms by Adam son of Ralph of Reresby to Beauchief abbey of common of pasture in the moor of Ashover for all their animals at their grange of Harewood, *viz*. the land contained in the area from Serleforkes[1] by Hereward's Street[2] south to the road which leads from Ashover to the bridge at Matlock, and then down by the same road to the Wringandstones, and then up to Eddlestow[3] through Wetemore to Shooterslea,[4] and then to Peasunhurst Roach,[5] and then down through the Moresyde to Stamfordsik and beyond the moor through Alwaldsetes to the boundaries of Wingerworth, and then to the boundaries of Walton and then up to Eastwood near Harewood; of license and free power to reap and carry to their grange at Harewood as much late hay and bracken in the aforesaid moor as they wish, but not turf or peat without his consent; and of the freedom from fines for escaped animals for the whole moor of Ashover beyond the aforesaid boundaries. Chirograph. [1290–1330]

Carta Ade filii Rad[ulphi] de Rerisby de pastura more de Essover[a]

Omnibus Cristi fidelibus hoc presens scriptum visuris vel audituris Adam filius Radulphi[b] salutem in Domino sempiternam. Noveritis me[c] concessisse, confirmasse religiosis viris abbati et conventui de Bello Capite et eorum[d] successoribus in liberam, puram et perpetuam elemosinam comunam pasture in mora de Essover infra divisas subscriptas ad omnia et omnimoda animalia sua ad grangiam suam de Harewode[e] qualitercumque pertinencia[f] seu ibidem sub nomine predictorum abbatis et conventus pro voluntate eorumdem quoquomodo commorancia, videlicet a Serleforkes per Herewardstrete[g] versus austrum usque viam que ducit de Essover versus pontem de Matlock[h] et sic descendendo per eandem viam usque le Wringandstones[i] et sic ascendendo usque Athelstowe[j] per Wetemore[k] usque Schiterley[l] et de Shyterley[m] [fo. 93r] usque Paystonhirstroche[n] et sic descendendo per le Moresyde usque Stamfordsik[o] et sic ultra moram per Alwaldsetes usque metas et divisas de Wyngurworth[p] et de metis et divisis de Wyngurworth[q] usque metas et divisas de Waleton'[r] et sic ascendendo usque Astwode iuxta Harewode,[s] cum libero introitu et exitu et omnibus aliis pertinenciis et aysiamentis que ad comunam predictam quocumquemodo spectant vel spectare poterunt vel pertinere, salvo michi et heredibus meis approvamento vasti mei extra predictas metas et divisas sine impedimento vel calumpnia predictorum abbatis et conventus et successorum suorum, non obstante facto Margerie matris mee. Concessi eciam et presenti scripto confirmavi predictis religiosis et eorum successoribus licentiam et liberam potestatem in mora predicta quibuscumque locis infra omnes divisas predictas licite et absque calumpnia seu inpedimento mei et heredum seu assignatorum meorum junctos sogg[agium] et feugerium[t] quantum voluerint singulis anni temporibus pro voluntate sua metere, falcare, levare, cariare,[u] asportare seu duci facere possint ad grangiam suam de Harewode[v] imperpetuum, sed non licebit predictis religiosis turbas vel petas fodere sine voluntate mei vel heredum meorum infra comunam predictam. Concessi insuper predictis abbati et conventui et eorum successoribus liberum eschapium per totam moram meam de Essover ultra divisas predictas, nisi fuerit per wardum factum. Concessi eciam quod [fo. 93v] quociens aliqua animalia sua aliquam seu aliquas predictarum divisarum metam vel metas transgredi seu aliqua loca per me vel heredes meos approbata[w] in predicto wasto intrare contigerit, eadem animalia per me vel per servientes meos nullatenus imparcentur, sed libere et quiete rehaiciantur,[x] sine aliquibus emendis inde michi vel heredibus meis faciendis seu petendis, nisi fuerit per wardum factum. Preterea ego predictus Adam omnia prenotata, cum omnibus suis pertinenciis qualitercumque contingentibus, concedo pro me et heredibus meis et assignatis meis prefatis abbati et conventui et eorum successoribus in liberam, puram et perpetuam elemosinam possidenda. Et ego vero Adam et heredes mei ea omnia et singula predicta eisdem abbati et conventui et eorum successoribus warantizabimus et defendemus[y] contra omnes gentes inperpetuum, quantum ad dominium meum pertinet. In cuius rei testimonium etc.[z] Hiis testibus etc.[aa]

B = Sheffield Archives, MD 3414 (Beauchief Cartulary), fos 92v–93v.
L = Derbyshire Record Office, D 1005 Z/E1 (Leake Cartulary, no. 10), p. 42.
R = Cambridge University Library, Add. MS 3897, pp. 13–16, transcript no. 5 made in 1777 by John Reynolds, junior, who describes a 'seal of common Bees-wax, on which is impressed an Escutcheon' but there was no circumscription.

[a] rubric om. LR   [b] *Radulphi de Rerisby* L   [c] *me dedisse* L   [d] *eorum: omnibus* L
[e] *Harwod* L   [f] *pertinentes* L   [g] *Herwardstrete* R
[h] *Mattlock* L; *Maatlock* R   [i] *Wringandestones* R   [j] *Ethalstowe* L; *Ethelstowe* R
[k] *Wetamore* L   [l] *Scheterley* L   [m] *Scheterley* L; *Schiterley* R
[n] *Paistonhirst roche* LR   [o] *Staniford* R   [p] *Wingarwaith* L; *Wingerworth* R
[q] *Wingarwaith* L   [r] *Walton* LR   [s] *Astwod iuxta Harwod* LR   [t] *feugeriam* R
[u] *carare* B   [v] *Harwod* LR   [w] *approbiata* B   [x] *rechaciantur* L   [y] *defendeus* B
[z] *etc.* B; *tam ego predictus Adam quam predicti abbas et conventus hiis scriptis alternatim divisis sigilla nostra apposuimus* L   [aa] *etc.* B; *Domino Henrico de Brailisford, domino Roberto de Dencokes* [*Deueck* R] *militibus, Roger le Breton, Stephano le Eir, Hugone de Linakre, Willelmo de Wynfeld* [*Winfeld* R], *Johanne Bate, et aliis* LR. Roger le Breton, Stephen le Eyr, and Hugh of Linacre appear

together in **37**, **46**, **81**, and **184**. John Bate, who also appears in **184** and **187**, witnessed two grants of land in Dore on 21 December 1341 (Jeayes, *Derbyshire Charters*, nos 1021, 1022).

[1] Cameron, *Place-names of Derbyshire*, II, p. 197: 'Serlo's fork-shaped land', a lost place-name.
[2] *Ibid.*, I, pp. 21–22; see A. Henstock, 'The course of Hereward Street: a reappraisal', *Derbyshire Archaeological Journal*, 100 (1980), pp. 35–42.
[3] OS ref. SK 328631; Cameron, *Place-names of Derbyshire*, II, p. 191: 'splendid place', or perhaps from a personal name.
[4] OS ref. SK 315647; *ibid.*: the 'well-manured clearing'.
[5] Roche Farm, OS ref. SK 312662; *ibid.*: 'stone'. Peasunhurst, OS ref. SK 318662; *ibid.*, II, pp. 191–192: a personal name and 'stone', to which 'hurst' (wooded hill) was added later.

184. Gift in free alms by Henry of Mousters[1] of Ashover to Beauchief abbey of common of pasture in the moor of Ashover for all their animals at their grange of Harewood, *viz.* **the land contained in the area from Serleforkes by Hereward's Street south to the road which leads from Ashover to the bridge at Matlock, and then down by the same road to the Wringandstones, and then up to Eddlestow through Wetemore to Shooterslea, and then to Peasunhurst Roach, and then down through the Moresyde to Stamfordsik and beyond the moor through Alwaldesetes to the boundaries of Wingerworth, and then to the boundaries of Walton and then up to Eastwood near Harewood; of license and free power to reap and carry to their grange at Harewood as much late hay and bracken in the aforesaid moor as they wish, but not turf or peat without his consent; and of the freedom from fines for escaped animals for the whole moor of Ashover beyond the aforesaid boundaries. Chirograph. [1290–1330]**

Carta Henrici Mousters de Essover de predicta pastura[a]

Omnibus Christi fidelibus hoc presens scriptum visuris vel audituris Henricus de Mousters de Essover salutem in Domino sempiternam. Noveritis me pro salute anime mee et antecessorum meorum dedisse, concessisse et hac presenti carta mea confirmasse religiosis viris abbati et conventui de Bello Capite et eorum successoribus, in liberam, puram et perpetuam elemosinam, communam pasture in mora de Essover infra divisas subscriptas ad omnia et omnimoda animalia sua ad grangiam suam de Harewode qualitercumque pertinencia seu ibidem sub nomine predictorum abbatis et conventus pro voluntate eorumdem quoquomodo commorancia, videlicet a Serleforkes per Herewardstrete versus austrum usque viam que ducit de Essover versus pontem de Mattelock et sic descendendo per eandem viam usque le Wringandstones et sic ascendendo usque Ethelstowe per Wetemore usque Shiterley et de Shiterley usque Paistonhirst Roche et sic descendendo per le Moreside usque Stamfordsik et sic ultra moram per Alwaldsetes usque metas et divisas de Wyngerwurth et de metis et divisis de Wyngerworth' usque metas et divisas de Walton' et sic ascendendo usque Astwode iuxta Harewod, cum libero introitu et exitu et omnibus aliis pertinenciis et aysiamentis que ad comunam predictam quocumque modo spectant vel spectare poterint vel pertinere, salvo michi et heredibus meis approvamento wasti mei extra predictas metas et divisas, sine impedimento vel calumpnia predictorum abbatis et conventus et successorum suorum. Dedi eciam et concessi et presenti carta mea confirmavi predictis religiosis et eorum successoribus licentiam et liberam potestatem in mora predicta quibuscumque locis infra omnes divisas predictas, licite et absque calumpnia seu impedimento mei et heredum seu assignatorum meorum, junctos sogg[agium] et feugerium quantum voluerint singulis anni temporibus pro voluntate sua metere, falcare, levare, cariare, asportare seu duci facere possint ad grangiam suam de Harwode inperpetuum, sed non licebit predictis religiosis turbas vel petas fodere, sine voluntate mei vel heredum meorum infra comunam predictam. Concessi insuper predictis abbati et conventui et eorum successoribus liberum eschapium per totam moram meam de Essover ultra divisas prescriptas, nisi fuerit per wardum factum. Concessi eciam quod quocienscumque aliqua animalia sua aliquam seu aliquas predictarum divisarum metam vel metas transgredi seu aliqua loca per me vel heredes meos in predicto wasto approvata intrare contigerit, eadem animalia per me vel per servientes meos nullatenus imparcentur, sed libere et quiete rethaciantur, sine aliquibus emendis inde michi vel heredibus meis faciendis seu petendis, nisi fuerit per wardum factum. Preterea ego predictus Henricus omnia prenotata, cum omnibus suis pertinenciis qualitercumque contingentibus, concedo pro me et heredibus meis et assignatis meis prefatis abbati et conventui et eorum successoribus in liberam, puram et perpetuam elemosinam possidenda. Ego vero Henricus et heredes mei ea omnia et singula predicta eisdem abbati et conventui et eorum successoribus warantizabimus et defendemus contra omnes gentes inperpetuum, quantum ad dominium meum pertinet. In cuius rei testimonium tam ego predictus Henricus quam predicti abbas et conventus his scriptis alternatim divisis sigilla nostra apposuimus.[b] Hiis testibus Domino Henrico de Braylisford, Domino Roberto de

Deverk, militibus, Rogero le Breton',[2] Stephano le Eyr, Hugone de Linakre, Willelmo de Winfeld, Johanne Bate et aliis.[c]

W = British Library, Wolley Charter III, 92 (Jeayes, *Derbyshire Charters*, no. 113). The seal has gone.
B = Sheffield Archives, MD 3414 (Beauchief Cartulary), fos 93v–94v.

[a] The heading is added by B   [b] *tam ... apposuimus*: etc. B   [c] *Domino Henrico ... aliis*: etc. B

[1] The Mousters family owned half the manors of Ashover and Pleasley (Turbutt, *Derbyshire*, II, p. 488); see also **209**.
[2] Roger le Breton also witnessed **71** (1301). See also **183**, note aa.

185. Quitclaim by Robert of Reresby son and heir of Ralph of Reresby to Beauchief abbey of an annual rent of 1d from Henry of Egmanton.[1] [1260–1300][2]

Carta Roberti de Rerisby de uno denario redditus

Omnibus ad quos presens scriptum pervenerit Robertus de Rerisby, filius et heres Rad[ulphi] de Rerisby, salutem in Domino sempiternam. Noveritis me dedisse, concessisse et omnino quietum clamasse pro me et heredibus meis [fo. 95r] et assignatis abbati et conventui de Bello Capite pro salute anime mee et omnium antecessorum meorum, in puram et perpetuam elemosinam, unum denarium annui redditus percipiendum de Henrico de Sgmanton'[a] coquo in festo sancti Johannis Baptiste ad sustentacionem luminis beate Marie in Bello Capite pro annuo redditu quatuor solidorum et quatuor denariorum, quem percipere solebam de Rogero de Marcham pro tenemento quod de me tenuit in feodo de Esshover, de quo redditu predictum Henricum feoffavi. Ita quod nec ego Robertus nec heredes mei vel assignati in predicto denario annui redditus cum suis pertinenciis, ut predictum est, aliquod[b] jus vel clamium juris decetero exigere, capere vel reclamare aliquomodo poterimus. Et ego predictus Robertus et heredes mei vel assignati predictum denarium annui redditus cum pertinenciis predictis abbati et conventui et eorum successoribus warantizabimus, acquietabimus et inperpetuum ubique defendemus. In cuius rei testimonium etc. Hiis testibus.

[a] *sic* for *Egmanton*.   [b] *aliqd*.

[1] Egmanton lies west of Marnham.
[2] For the earlier history of the rent of 4s 4d, see **179**.

186. Quitclaim in free alms by Ralph son of Robert of Reresby to Beauchief abbey of the tenements and buildings which Roger of Marcham and Sybil the weaver and Iseult the former wife of Robert the smith held in the vill and territory of Ashover. [1290–1330][1]

Quieta clamacio Rad[ulphi] filii Roberti de Rerisby de t[enementis] in Essover

Omnibus Cristi fidelibus hoc presens scriptum visuris vel audituris Rad[ulfus] filius Roberti de Rerisby salutem in Domino sempiternam. Noveritis me concessisse, relaxasse et omnino quietum clamasse religiosis viris abbati et conventui de B[ello] C[apite] [fo. 95v] [et] eorum successoribus, in liberam, puram et perpetuam elemosinam, totum jus et clamium quod habui vel habere potui vel habere potero in illis tenementis et edificiis et omnibus pertinenciis suis que Rogerus de Marcham et Sibilla textrix et Ysolda, quondam uxor Roberti fabri, tenuerunt in villa et territorio de Essover. Ita quod nec ego Radulphus nec heredes mei nec aliquis alius per nos vel nomine nostro aliquod jus vel clamium in predictis tenementis et edificiis vel eorum pertinenciis decetero exigere vel vendicare poterimus inperpetuum. In cuius rei testimonium etc. Hiis testibus etc.

[1] For earlier charters relating to these premises, see **179–181** and **185**.

187. Gift in free alms by the same Ralph son of Robert of Reresby to Beauchief abbey of common of pasture in the moor of Ashover for all their animals at their grange of Harewood, *viz.* the land contained in the area from Serleforkes by Hereward's Street south to the road which leads from Ashover to the bridge at Matlock, and then down by the same road to the Wringandstones, and then up to Eddlestow through Wetemore to Shooterslea, and then to Peasunhurst Roach, and then down through the Moresyde to Stamfordsik and beyond the moor through Alwoldsetes to the boundaries of Wingerworth, and then to the boundaries of Walton, and then up to Eastwood near Harewood; of license and free power to reap and carry to their grange at Harewood as much late hay and bracken in the aforesaid moor as they wish, but not turf or peat without his consent; of the freedom from fines for escaped animals for the whole moor of Ashover beyond the aforesaid boundaries; and of the tenements with buildings

which Roger of Marcham and Sybil the weaver and Iseult the former wife of Robert held in the vill and territory of Ashover. Chirograph. [1290–1330]

Carta Radulphi filii Roberti de Rerisby[a]

Omnibus Cristi fidelibus hoc presens scriptum visuris vel audituris Rad[ulphus], filius Roberti de Rerisby, salutem in Domino sempiternam. Noveritis me concessisse et confirmasse religiosis viris abbati et conventui de Bello Capite et eorum successoribus, in liberam [et] puram[b] elemosinam, comunam pasture in mora de Essover infra divisas subscriptas ad omnia et omnimoda animalia sua ad grangiam suam de Harewode[c] qualitercumque pertinencia[d] seu ibidem [fo. 96r] nomine predictorum abbatis et conventus pro voluntate eorumdem quoquomodo commorancia, videlicet a Serleforkes per Herewardestrete[e] versus austrum usque viam que ducit de Essover versus pontem de Matelock, et sic descendendo per eandem viam usque le Wryngandstones,[f] et sic ascendendo usque Ethelstowe per Wetemore usque Schiterley, et de Shiterley usque Paistonhurstroche[g] et sic descendendo per le Moresyde usque Stamfordsik'[h] et sic ultra moram per Alwoldsetes[i] usque metas et divisas de Wyngerworth et de metis et divisis de Wyngerwurth[j] usque metas et divisas de Walton' et sic ascendendo usque Astwode[k] iuxta Harewode,[l] cum libero introitu et exitu et omnibus aliis pertinenciis et aysiamentis que ad comunam predictam quocumquemodo spectant vel spectare poterunt vel pertinere, salvo michi et heredibus meis approvamento wasti mei extra predictas divisas et metas, sine impedimento vel calumpnia predictorum abbatis et conventus et successorum suorum, non obstante facto Roberti patris mei. Concessi eciam et presenti scripto confirmavi predictis religiosis et eorum successoribus licenciam et liberam potestatem in mora predicta quibuscumque locis infra omnes divisas predictas licite et absque calumpnia seu impedimento mei et heredum seu assignatorum meorum junctos[m] sogg[agium] et feugerium quantum voluerint singulis anni temporibus pro voluntate sua metere, falcare, levare, cariare, asportare seu duci facere possint ad grangiam suam de Harewode[n] inperpetuum, sed [fo. 96v] non licebit predictis religiosis turbas vel petas fodere sine voluntate mei vel heredum meorum infra comunam predictam. Concessi insuper predictis abbati et conventui et eorum successoribus liberum eschapium per totam moram meam de Essover ultra divisas prescriptas, nisi fuerit per wardum factum. Concessi eciam quod quociens aliqua animalia sua aliquam seu aliquas predictarum divisarum metam vel metas transgredi seu aliqua loca per me vel heredes meos in predicto wasto approvata intrare contigerit, eadem animalia per me vel per servientes meos nullatenus imparcentur, sed libere et quiete rethaciantur, sine aliquibus emendis inde michi vel heredibus meis faciendis seu petendis, nisi fuerit per wardum factum. Preterea concessi, relaxavi et omnino quietum clamavi predictis religiosis abbati et conventui et eorum successoribus totum jus et clamium quod habui vel habere potui vel habere potero in illis tenementis, cum edificiis et omnibus pertinenciis suis, queo[o] Rogerus de Marcham et Sibilla textrix[p] et Ysolda, quondam uxor Roberti,[q] tenuerunt in villa et territorio de Essover. Ita quod nec ego Rad[ulphus] nec heredes mei nec aliquis alius nomine nostro aliquod jus vel clamium in predictis tenementis vel eorum pertinenciis decetero exigere vel vendicare poterimus inperpetuum. Ego vero Rad[ulphus] predictus et heredes mei omnia et singula prenominata predictis abbati et conventui et eorum successoribus [fo. 97r] in liberam, puram et perpetuam elemosinam contra omnes gentes warantizabimus, acquietabimus et inperpetuum defendemus. In cuius rei etc.[r] Hiis testibus etc.[s]

B = Sheffield Archives, MD 3414 (Beauchief Cartulary), fos 95v–97r.
L = Derbyshire Record Office, D 1005 Z/E1 (Leake Cartulary, no. 11), p. 42.
R = Cambridge University Library, Add. MS 3897, pp. 6–10, transcript no. 3 by John Reynolds, junior, including a description of 'a small seal of white wax the impression whereon is a bird (perhaps a hawk) close with circumscription round it, but too dim to be read at this day (scil, 11° Februarii, 1777°)'.

[a] rubric *om.* LR   [b] *puram* B; *puram et perpetuam* LR   [c] *Harewod* LR
[d] *pertinentes* L   [e] *Herwardstrete* L   [f] *Wringandestones* R
[g] *Parstonhyrstroche* L; *Peystonhirstroche* R   [h] *Staniford Syk* R
[i] *Alwaldsetete* L; *Alwaldsetes* R   [j] *Wyngerworth* R   [k] *Astwod* LR
[l] *Harewod* L   [m] *juncos* BL   [n] *Harewod* L   [o] *quod* B   [p] *taty* R
[q] *Roberti fabri* L   [r] *etc.* B; *testimonium tam ego predictus Rad(ulf)us quam predicti abbas et conventus hiis scriptis divisis alternatim sigilla nostra apposuimus* LR   [s] *etc.* B; *domino Henrico de Breylesford* [*Braylesford* R], *domino Roberto de Denecke'* [*Deveck* R] *militibus, Rogero de* [*le* R] *Breton, Stephano le Eyr, Hugone de Linakre* [*Linacre* R], *Willelmo de Winfeld* [*Winefeld* R], *Johanne Bate, e aliis* L. Roger le Breton, Stephen le Eyr, and Hugh of Linacre appear together in **37** and **38** (1312). For John Bate, see **183**.

188. Gift in free alms by Robert of Reresby son and heir of Ralph of Reresby to Beauchief abbey of common of pasture in the moor of Ashover for all animals at their grange of Harewood, *viz.* the land contained in the area from Serleforkes by Hereward's Street south to the road which leads from Darley to Shooterslea, and then up through Peasunhurst to Dewyfyswode, and then up from the south part of Aylewaldsetes to the boundaries of Walton, and then

down by the same to Eastwood; and of the freedom from fines for escaped animals over all the moor of Ashover. [c.1269–1289]

Carta Roberti de Rerysby filii et heres Rad[ulphi] de Rerysby[a]

Omnibus Cristi fidelibus hoc scriptum visuris vel audituris Robertus de Rerysby, filius et heres Rad[ulphi] de Rerysby, salutem in Domino sempiternam. Noverit universitas vestra me divine caritatis intuitu concessisse et hoc presenti scripto[b] confirmasse abbati et conventui de Bello Capite et eorum successoribus comunam pasture in mora de Assover infra subscriptas divisas contentam omnibus animalibus suis pascualibus et aliis apud grangiam suam de Harewode cubantibus et levantibus, videlicet a Serleforkes[c] per Herewardstrete[d] versus austrum usque viam que ducit de Derley ad Shiterley,[e] et inde ascendendo per Paistonhirst[f] usque Dewyfyswode,[g] et inde ascendendo ex parte australi de Aylewaldsetes[h] usque divisas de Walton', descendendo per easdem usque ad Astwode.[i] Tenendam et habendam dictis abbati et conventui et eorum successoribus[j] in liberam, puram et perpetuam elemosinam, absque omni seculari servicio, secta et demanda. Concessi eciam et confirmavi dictis abbati et conventui et eorum successoribus in liberam, puram et perpetuam elemosinam, pro me et heredibus meis inperpetuum, liberum eschapium omnium predictorum animalium suorum ubique super moram de Assover.[k] Et ego, dictus Robertus, et heredes[l] mei [fo. 97v] dictam comunam pasture cum suis aysiamentis infra dictas divisas et predictum liberum eschapium omnium animalium suorum per omnem moram de Assover[m] dictis abbati et conventui et eorum successoribus in liberam, puram et perpetuam elemosinam contra omnes warantizabimus, acquietabimus et inperpetuum defendemus. In cuius rei testimonium etc.[n] Hiis t[estibus].[o]

B = Sheffield Archives, MD 3414 (Beauchief Cartulary), fo. 97r–v.
L = Derbyshire Record Office, D 1005 Z/E1 (Leake Cartulary), p. 43.
R = Cambridge University Library, Add. MS 3897, pp. 4–6, transcript by John Reynolds, junior, made in 1777, including a description of a seal of green wax embossed with a star of 6 points issuant from a crescent and circumscribed: +.S[IGILLUM]. ROBERTI : DE : RERISBI:.

[a] rubric om. LR [b] Scripto: scripto meo L, with meo struck through. [c] Serleforkys L
[d] Herewardestrete LR [e] Schiterley L; Schyterley R [f] Paystonhirst L
[g] Wyliswode L [h] Aylewaldsets R [i] Astewode LR
[j] in liberam puram et perpetuam elemosinam absque struck through L [k] Assovere L
[l] herede B [m] Assovere L [n] etc. B; presenti scripto sigillum meum apposui L
[o] t[estibus] B; testibus domino Willelmo de Steynsby [Steynisby R] milite, Roberto le Graunte [Graunt R], Johanne de Brimington, Ada de Taptover [Tapton R], Roberto Fraunk, Johanne de Peito [Pecco R]

in *Cesterfeld, Hugone de Takysford* [*Tokysford* R] *clerico de eadem, et aliis* LR. William of Stainsby succeeded his father *c.*1269 and died in 1289; see **26**, n. 4.

[WALTON]

189. Gift in free alms by Robert Brito of Walton,[1] **with the assent of Robert his son and heir, to Beauchief abbey of a certain part of his demense,** *viz.* **the land called Litestwood with all the wood from the place where Rutendecloch**[2] **goes down into the river Hipper, and then up through the same brook of Rutendecloch to Holinforde, and then up to the boundaries of Ashover, and then whatever is of his fee of Walton. [1200–1220]**

Carta Roberti Brito de Waltona de terra de Litestwd

Omnibus sancte matris ecclesie filiis tam presentibus quam futuris Robertus Brito de Walton' salutem in Domino. Noverit universitas vestra me, voluntate et assensu Roberti filii mei et heredis, dedisse et concessisse et hac mea presenti carta confirmasse Deo et sancte Marie et sancto Thome martiri de Beuchef et canonicis ibidem Deo servientibus quandam partem terre mee habendam in dominicum, illam scilicet que vocatur Litestwd, cum toto bosco ibidem existente, ab eo loco ubi Rutendecloch' cadit in aquam que vocatur Hyper et inde ascendendo per eundem rivulum de Rutendecloch' usque Holineforde et a Holyneford ascendendo[a] usque ad metas de Assovere et a metis de Assover, quicquid de feodo meo est, tam versus occidentem quam versus aquilonem, in bosco, in plano, in mora et in bruerio et quicquid infra easdem metas continetur. Tenendam in liberam, quietam, puram et perpetuam elemosinam pro salute [anime] mee et uxoris mee et omnium antecessorum et successorum meorum. Hiis testibus etc.

[a] *assendendo.*

[1] See **164**. Serlo of Beeley and Robert Brito of Walton jointly gave 60 acres of land in Walton to Beauchief (The National Archives, CP 25/1/36/2/10; made at Derby, 19 November 1208) and it is possible that this gift was granted about the same time. The 1208 charter is printed in W.H. Hart, 'A calendar of the fines for the county of Derby from their commencement in the reign of Richard I: 1196–1225', *Journal of the Derbyshire Archaeological and Natural History Society*, 7 (1885), no. 38; *Derbyshire Charters*, no. 2745; J. Hunter (ed.), *Fines sive pedes finium; sive finales concordiae in Curia domini regis . . . AD 1195–AD 1214*, II (London, 1844), p. 32.
[2] Cameron, *Place-names of Derbyshire*, II, p. 322: 'roaring clough'. All the minor place-names mentioned here are lost, but the only stream that flows into the Hipper in Walton that also

crosses the Ashover boundary is the one that runs south past Stonehay Farm, down a steep-sided valley that is presumably the 'roaring clough'. The woodland given to the canons is thus the small portion of Walton to the north and west of this stream around Hunger Hill. The younger Robert and his son Hugh (the grantor in **190**) were commemorated in the Obituary (29 December) for their gift of 'one part of Walton Hay in demesne which is called Hastewode', possibly Eastwood.

190. Confirmation in free alms by Hugh son of Robert of Walton[1] to Beauchief abbey of the wood called Litestwood[2] from the place where Rutendecloch goes down to the river Hipper, and then up through the same brook of Rutendecloch to Holinforde, and then up to the boundaries of Ashover, and then whatever is of his fee of Walton. [1210–1240]

[fo. 98r]

Confirmacio Hugonis filius Roberti de Walton'

Omnibus sancte matris ecclesie filiis tam presentibus quam futuris Hugo filius Roberti de Waleton' salutem in Domino. Noverit universitas vestra me pro amore dei et pro salute anime mee et patris mei et matris mee et omnium antecessorum et heredum meorum dedisse et concessisse et hac presenti carta mea confirmasse Deo et sancte Marie et sancto Thome martiri de Beuchef et canonicis ibidem Deo servientibus quicquid juris habui in bosco qui dicitur Litestwde ab eo loco ubi Rutendecloch' cadit in aquam que vocatur Hiper, et inde ascendendo per eundem rivulum de Rutendecloch usque ad Holineford et a Holineforde ascendendo usque ad metas de Assover et a metis de Assover, quicquid de feodo de Waleton' est, tam versus occidentem quam versus aquilonem, in bosco, in plano, in mora et in bruerio, et quicquid infra easdem metas continetur. Tenendum in liberam, puram et perpetuam elemosinam. Et ut hec mea donacio atque concessio robur optineat inperpetuum, presentem cartam sigilli mei apposicione roboravi. Hiis testibus etc.

[1] Robert Breton, lord of Walton, and Hugh his son were remembered in the Obituary (28 November) for the grant of **189** and **190**.
[2] Liteswood was said to be within a part of Walton Hay in demesne.

[BAKEWELL]

191. Sale by William the clerk of Saint John to Beauchief abbey for 4 silver marks of 1 burgage[1] in the vill of Bakewell

which he bought from Roger Cade. The canons shall render to the lord of the vill 4d annually. The canons also promised that they would say a special annual mass for Orayn, William's mother. [1180–1216]

Carta Willelmi clerici de terra in Bauquell'[a]

Sciant presentes et futuri quod ego Willelmus clericus de Sancto Johanne vendidi abbati et conventui de Bello Capite unum burgagium in villa de Bauquell' pro quatuor marcis argenti, quas michi [fo. 98v] premanibus solverunt, illud scilicet burgagium quod emi de Rogero Cade, cum omnibus suis pertinenciis et libertatibus ad predictam villam pertinentibus, absque aliquo retenemento, ad opus meum. Reddendo inde annuatim domino ville quatuor denarios pro omni servicio. Promiserunt eciam michi iidem abbas et conventus caritative semel in anno scilicet in crastino sancti Andree unam specialem missam pro fidelibus causa corporis Orayn, matris mee, ibidem requiescentis, que in martyrologio suo est memorata. Et ut hec mea vendicio inposterum stabilis et rata perseveret, huic scripto sigillum meum in testimonium apposui. Hiis testibus: Willelmo de Vernun', Willelmo Basset, etc.

[a] *Baghwel* in rubrics in the right margin.

[1] This is not certain evidence of burgage plots in Bakewell, but it is suggestive; see D. Hey, *Derbyshire: a history* (Lancaster, 2008), pp. 129–130.

[CHESTERFIELD]

192. Gift in free alms by William of Briges, burgess of Chesterfield, to Beauchief abbey of ½ toft in the south part of the new market[1] of Chesterfield, lying between the toft of Richard of Tapton and the toft of William of Normanton. The canons shall render to Matilda daughter of Gilbert of Hasland 3s in silver annually. Memorandum that William and Alice his wife wish to be buried at Beauchief. [1200–1240][2]

Carta Willelmi de Briges de terra in Chestrefeld

Omnibus sancte[a] matris ecclesie filiis ad quos presens carta pervenerit Willelmus de Brige burgensis de Chestrefeld salutem in Domino.

Noveritis me caritatis intuitu et pro salute anime mee et Alicie uxoris mee, in ligia potestate mea et plena corporis sanitate, concessisse, dedisse et hac mea presenti carta confirmasse Deo et ecclesie sancti Thome martiris de Beuchef et canonicis Premonstratensis ordinis ibidem Deo servientibus unum dimidium toftum in novo foro de Chestrefeld in australi parte, iacens inter toftum Ricardi de Tapton' et toftum Willelmi de Normanton', cum omnibus edificiis, utensilibus[b] et rebus aliis infra predictum toftum contentis. [fo. 99r] Tenendum et habendum et pacifice possidendum in liberam et perpetuam elemosinam cum omnibus pertinenciis et libertatibus et liberis consuetudinibus dicte ville burgagio pertinentibus, solutum et quietum de me et heredibus meis imperpetuum. Reddendo inde annuatim apud Chestrefeld Matilde filie Gilberti de Heselunt vel assignatis suis tres solidos argenti ad duos terminos, scilicet decem et viij denarios ad Pascha et decem et octo denarios ad festum sancti Michaelis pro omni servicio et exactione. Preterea memorandum quod ego Willelmus et dicta Alicia uxor mea apud prefatam ecclesiam beati Thome martiris de Beuchief nos sepeliendos fore connovimus cum ex vita hac Domino vocante subtracti fuerimus. Hiis testibus etc.

[a] *scancte* (with cross over the first *c*)   [b] *utensibibus*.

[1] i.e. on Low Pavement, the road flanking the southern side of the present market place.
[2] William of Brigge and Gilbert of Hasland both witnessed early thirteenth-century grants to Rufford Abbey (Holdsworth, *Rufford Charters*, I, nos 52 and 94) and William of Normanton witnessed a charter of William Brewer the elder as lord of Chesterfield between 1204 and 1226 (P. Riden and J. Blair (eds), *History of Chesterfield, V: records of the Borough of Chesterfield and related documents, 1204–1835* (Chesterfield, 1980), pp. 259–260). See also **160**.

193. Quitclaim by Matilda daughter of Gilbert of Hasland to Beauchief abbey of the toft which William of Briges once held in the vill of Chesterfield; and of an annual rent of 2s from the same toft. The canons, who gave Matilda 4 silver marks for this quitclaim, shall render to the exchequer of Chesterfield 12d annually.[1] **[1200–1240]**

Quieta clamacio Matildis filie Gilberti de Heselunt

Omnibus ad quos presens scriptum pervenerit Matilda filia Gilberti de Heselunt salutem. Noveritis me resignasse et quietum clamasse de me et de heredibus meis inperpetuum Deo et ecclesie beati Thome martiris de Beuchef quicquid juris vendicavi michi in tofto quod fuit aliquando Willelmi de Briges in villa de Chestrefeld cum omnibus edificiis et aliis pertinenciis. Remisi etiam predicte domui de Beuchef redditum duorum solidorum, qui michi contingebat de dicto tofto. Ita quod nec ego nec heredes mei decetero aliquod jus vel calumpniam in predicto tofto et redditu cum pertinenciis nobis vendicare[a] [fo. 99v] poterimus nec dictam domum in aliquo super hiis molestari, predicta vero domus de Beuchef satisfaciet scacario de Chesturfeld singulis annis de duodecim denariis, scilicet de sex denariis ad Pascha et de sex denariis ad festum sancti Michaelis dicto tofto pertinentibus. Pro hac autem resignacione et quieta clamacione dedit michi prefata domus de Beuchef quatuor marcas argenti. In huius rei testimonium feci dicte domui[b] de Beuchef hanc cartam sigillo meo munitam etc.

[a] *vendicare* repeated erroneously at beginning of folio verso.   [b] *domu.*

[1] The 'exchequer of Chesterfield' refers to a chief rent due to the lord of the manor.

194. Quitclaim by Peter of the hurst and Matilda his wife to Beauchief abbey of the toft and rent which William of Briges once held in Chesterfield, which toft and rent they held of the canons for their lives by a certain charter made between them. Made on Sunday 22 April 1263.

Quieta clamacio Petri del Hirst et Matilde uxoris eius de eadem terra

Omnibus ad quos presens scriptum pervenerit Petrus del Hirst et Matilda uxor eius salutem in Domino. Noverit universitas vestra nos anno regni regis Henrici filii Johannis xlvij° die Dominica proxima ante festum sancti Georgii martiris resignasse et omnino quietum clamasse de nobis pro salute animarum nostrarum toftum et redditum cum edificiis quod fuit Willelmi de Briges quondam in Chestrefeld abbati et conventui de Bello Capite et eorum successoribus. Que quidem toftum et redditum cum edificiis tenebamus de abbate et conventu in vita nostra per quamdam cartam inter nos confectam. Ita quod nec ego Petrus nec Matilda uxor mea nec aliquis ex parte nostra in predictis tofto, redditu et edificiis aliquod jus vel clamium decetero vendicare poterimus. In cuius rei testimonium presenti scripto sigilla nostra apposuimus. Hiis testibus: Roberto de Abeney, etc.

195. Gift in free alms by Hugh Wake[1] to Beauchief abbey of free rights of purchase and sale in his vill of Chesterfield and in the whole Wapentake of Scarsdale. [1233–1241]

[fo. 100r]

Carta Hugonis Wake duplicata de libertate empcionis et vendicionis in villa de Chestrefeld

Omnibus sancte Matris ecclesie filiis ad quos presens scriptum pervenerit Hugo Wake salutem in Domino. Noverit universitas vestra me caritatis intuitu et pro salute anime mee et pro animabus patris et matris mee et omnium antecessorum et successorum meorum concessisse et hac presenti carta mea confirmasse Deo et ecclesie beati Thome martiris de Beuchef et fratribus ibidem Deo servientibus liberam empcionem et vendicionem in villa mea de Chestrefeld, tam in domo quam in foro et per totum wapintake de Scaresdale, cum libero introitu et exitu et cariagio, absque omni tolneto et consuetudine *et omni seculari exaccione*.[2] Hanc vero concessionem et confirmacionem feci eidem in liberam, puram et perpetuam elemosinam. Et ego et heredes mei warantizabimus, defendemus et acquietabimus predictis fratribus de Beuchef totam prescriptam concessionem et confirmacionem contra omnes homines inperpetuum. Hiis testibus etc.

[1] Lord of Chesterfield 1233–1241; see **160**, n. 1.
[2] Apart from the inclusion of the phrase italicized here, this charter is identical to **160**.

196. Gift in free alms by John son of Isaac of Chesterfield[1] to Beauchief abbey of 1 toft in Chesterfield called Collesalfacra next to Robert the clerk of Walton. [1230–1260]

Carta Johannis filii Ysaac de terra in Chestrefeld

Omnibus sancte matris ecclesie filiis ad quos presens carta pervenerit Johannes filius Ysaac de Chestrefeld salutem. Sciatis me dedisse et hac mea carta confirmasse Deo et sancte Marie et sancto Thome martiri de Beuchef unum toftum in Chestrefeld de terra mea que vocatur Collesalfacra iuxta Robertum clericum de Waltona, habens sexaginta pedes in longitudine [fo. 100v] secus viam et latitudinem quantum terra illa extendit, in liberam et quietam, in puram et perpetuam elemosinam, pro salute anime mee et heredum meorum et omnium antecessorum meorum. Hiis testibus etc.

[1] John son of Isaac occurs as an abutting owner in a gift of land in Brampton by William son of Gilbert of Catcliffe to the guild of the Blessed Mary of Chesterfield of *c.*1240–1256. Riden and Blair, *History of Chesterfield*, V, pp. 135–136.

197. Grant by Alan son of Gunnild of Chesterfield to Beauchief abbey of an annual rent of 3d to be paid by him. [Undated]

Carta Alani filii Gunildi de Chestrefeld

Omnibus hoc scriptum visuris vel audituris Alanus filius Gunildi de Chestrefeld salutem. Noveritis me dedisse et hac presenti carta mea confirmasse Deo et ecclesie beati Thome martiris de Bello Capite pro salute anime mee et omnium antecessorum et heredum meorum tres denarios annuatim in die beati Thome martiris persolvendos apud Beuchef. Et cum de me Deus suam voluntatem fecerit, adhuc vivens constituo et promitto predictos tres denarios heredes meos ad predictum terminum predicte ecclesie reddituros. Hiis testibus etc.

198. Gift in free alms by Stephen son of Stephen the parson of Chesterfield[1] to Beauchief abbey of 1 furlong in the territory of Chesterfield which lies between the syke and the cross of Newbold and which Gervase son of Richard the good smith held. [1216–1272]

Carta Stephani filii Stephani persona de Chestrefeld

Omnibus sancte matris ecclesie filiis tam presentibus quam futuris Stephanus filius Stephani persona de Chestrefeld salutem. Noverit universitas vestra me divini amoris intuitu dedisse et hac presenti carta mea confirmasse Deo et sancte Marie et sancto Thome martiri de Beuchief et canonicis ibidem Deo servientibus unam culturam terre in territorio de Chestrefeld que iacet inter sicam et crucem de Newbold, quam scilicet culturam Gervasius filius Ricardi boni fabri tenuit de me. Tenendam et habendam, [fo. 101r] libere et quiete, in puram et perpetuam elemosinam, pro salute anime mee, patris mei et matris mee et omnium antecessorum meorum. Hiis testibus etc.

[1] Stephen the parson of Chesterfield witnessed a Brampton charter in Henry III's reign (Jeayes, *Derbyshire Charters*, no. 412).

199. Quitclaim in free alms by Henry the clerk of Chesterfield to Beauchief abbey of 1 burgage in the vill of Chesterfield lying between ½ toft which Robert son of Edwin held on the east and ½ toft which Thomas Hilde held on the west, bordering on the new market at one end and on the river Hipper at the other.[1] The canons shall render to the chief lord of the fee 12d annually. [Undated]

Carta Henrici clerici de Chestrefeld

Sciant presentes et futuri quod ego Henricus clericus de Chestrefeld concessi et dedi et hac presenti carta mea confirmavi et omnino quietum clamavi, pro salute anime mee et animarum antecessorum meorum, Deo et ecclesie beati Thome martiris de Bello Capite et canonicis ibidem Deo servientibus, in puram et perpetuam et liberam elemosinam, totum jus meum et clamium quod habui vel quod habere potero in uno burgagio in villa de Chestrefeld cum omnibus edificiis ibidem edificatis et cum omnibus aliis pertinenciis suis et libertatibus sibi pertinentibus, iacente inter dimidium toftum quod quondam Roberti filii Eedwyn ex parte orientali et inter dimidium toftum quod quondam fuit Thome Hilde ex parte occidentali, abuttante super novum mercatum ad unum et super aquam de Hypir ad aliud capud. Ita videlicet quod nec ego predictus Henricus nec heredes mei nec aliquis per nos neque pro nobis aliquod jus vel clamium in predicto burgagio nec in suis pertinenciis clamare, vendicare vel exigere decetero aliquomodo poterimus. Faciendo inde servicium capitali domino feodi, videlicet duodecim denarios ad duos anni terminos, ad Annunciacionem Marie sex denarios et ad festum sancti Michaelis sex denarios, pro omni seculari servicio, consuetudine, exactione vel demanda. Et quia volo quod hec mea concessio, [fo. 101v] donacio et presentis carte mee confirmacio et omnino quieta clamacio rata sit et inperpetuum duratura, huic presenti scripto sigillum meum apposui. Hiis testibus etc.

[1] i.e. on Low Pavement on the south side of the market place. Burgage plots typically stretched back from narrow frontages on the market place.

200. Notification by William son of Norman of Taddington that in full session of the port-moot[1] of Chesterfield he has constituted John of Taddington his brother to be his heir to ½ toft in the vill of Chesterfield which Norman their father bought from Thomas of Romerthwert in the new market of Chesterfield, and to 2 acres and 1 rod in the fields of

Chesterfield which he held of Robert and Thomas sons of Richard the good smith. John shall render to William's lord William Brier[2] 12d annually and to Beauchief abbey 12d annually. [1204–1234]

Carta Willelmi filii Normanni de Tadinton'[1]

Omnibus hoc scriptum visuris vel audituris Willelmus filius Normanni de Tadinton' salutem in Domino. Noverit universitas vestra me in pleno portumoto de Chestrefeld constituisse Johannem de Tadinton', fratrem meum, vel quem voluerit assignare heredum meum post decessum meum de uno dimidio tofto in villa de Chestrefeld cum pertinenciis, illud scilicet quod Normannus, pater meus, emit de Thoma de Romerthwert in novo mercato de Chestrefeld, salvo servicio domini mei Willelmi Brier, scilicet duodecim denariis, salvis eciam aliis duodecim denariis ecclesie sancti Thome martiris de Beuchief annuatim inperpetuum solvendis et de duabus acris terre et una roda in campis eiusdem ville de Chestrefeld, illas scilicet quas tenui de Roberto et Thoma, filiis Ricardi boni fabri. Et ne hoc factum meum futuris temporibus inirritum ducatur, presens scriptum tam sigilli mei apposicione quam testium subscriptione roboravi. Hiis testibus etc.

[1] The market court.
[2] William Brewer, the elder and younger, were lords of Chesterfield from 1204 to 1233–1234 (Riden and Blair, *History of Chesterfield*, V, p. 1). William Brewer son of William Brewer was recorded in the Obituary (17 March).

201. Grant by Richard the good smith of Chesterfield to Beauchief abbey of all that land with buildings in the new market of Chesterfield which Roger Ruffus and Gilbert the smith held. The canons shall render to him 2s in silver annually. [Undated]

Carta Ricardi boni fabri de Chestrefeld

Omnibus sancte matris ecclesie filiis ad quos presens [fo. 102r] carta pervenerit Ricardus bonus faber de Chestrefeld salutem in Domino. Sciatis me dedisse et hac mea presenti carta confirmasse Deo et sancte Marie et sancto Thome martiri de Beuchef et canonicis ibidem Deo servientibus totam illam terram cum edificiis in novo foro de Chestrefeld, quam Rogerus Ruffus et Gilbertus faber tenuerunt de me. Reddendo inde michi et heredibus meis annuatim duos solidos argenti pro omni seculari servicio michi et heredibus meis pertinenti, scilicet duodecim denarios ad Pascha et duodecim denarios ad festum sancti Michaelis. Hiis testibus etc.

202. Quitclaim by Margery the former wife of Richard the nailer of Chesterfield to Beauchief abbey of that moeity of 1 toft in the vill of Chesterfield which Richard her late husband held from them. [Undated]

Quieta clamacio Margerie uxoris[a] Ricardi Nayler de terra in C.

Omnibus ad quos presens scriptum pervenerit Margeria quondam uxor Ricardi le Nayler de Chestrefeld salutem in Domino. Noverit universitas vestra me concessisse de me et heredibus et quietum clamasse abbati et conventui de Bello Capite et successoribus suis totum jus et clamium quod habui vel habere potui nomine dotis in medietate unius tofti cum pertinenciis in villa de Chesterfeld, quam Ricardus quondam vir meus tenuit de eisdem abbate et conventu. Ita quod nec ego nec aliquis per me decetero aliquod jus vel clamium in dicta medietate cum pertinenciis aliquomodo nobis vendicare poterimus. In cuius rei etc. Hiis testibus etc.

[a] *uxori.*

[GLAPWELL]

203. Grant by Richard son of William of Glapwell to Beauchief abbey of 1 bovate in Glapwell which Weremund once held and 1 acre on Dunsill[1] in place of the messuage pertaining to that bovate; of pasture for 1 plough-team and 60 ewes with their lambs until Whitsun; and of common pertaining to 1 bovate. The canons, who gave Richard 20s for this grant, shall render to him 3s annually in silver. [1200–1220][2]

[fo. 102v]

Glapwell'

Carta Ricardi filii Willelmi de Glapwel de una bovata terre

Omnibus sancte matris ecclesie filiis ad quos presens carta pervenerit Ricardus filius Willelmi de Glapwella salutem in Domino. Sciatis me concessisse et presenti carta confirmasse abbati et conventui de Beuchef unam bovatam terre cum pertinenciis suis in Glapwella quam Weremundus aliquando tenuit et pro mesagio illi bovate pertinente unam acram terre de duabus super Dunshil, illam scilicet que est vicinior meridiei,[a] et pasturam averiis[b] uni caruce pertinentibus et sexaginta matricibus ovibus cum exitu earum donec a matribus separetur et tunc removebitur exitus semper singulis annis ad Pentecosten remanente numero predictarum ovium, et comunam per omnia uni bovate pertinentem in bosco, in plano, in viis et semitis, in aquis et in omnibus locis ad feudum de Glapwella pertinentibus, in quibus ego comunico. Tenendam de me et heredibus meis libere et quiete, honorifice et pacifice, in feudam firmam inperpetuum. Reddendo michi et heredibus meis singulis annis tres solidos argenti ad duos terminos, scilicet decem et octo denarios ad Pentecosten et decem et octo denarios infra octabas sancti Martini, pro omni seculari servicio, consuetudine et exactione, salvo domini regis servicio uni bovate pertinente. Hec vero prelibata predictis abbati et conventui de Beuchef ego et heredes mei warantizabimus. Pro hac concessione et confirmacione dederunt michi abbas et conventus xx solidos. Hiis testibus etc.

[a] *ri* of *meridiei* interlined.   [b] *averriis*.

[1] In Teversal (Notts).
[2] Another copy was printed in R.R. Darlington (ed.), *The Glapwell Charters, Derbyshire Archaelogical Journal*, 86–87 (1957–1959), no. 15. Witnesses are listed as 'Willelmo persona de Pleseleia, Willelmo filio Roberti de Alfertona, Radulfo Barri, Radulfo filio Hugonis, Roberto Britone de Waletona, Matheo de Hulma, Rogero de Heinecurt, Radulfo Silvano de Thorp, Simone filio Hugonis de Glapwella, Petro de Hertil, Roberto fratre suo, Roberto clerico de Waletona, Rogero filio Willelmi et multis aliis'. The date is given as early thirteenth century. Ralph Barri may be the Ralph Barre of Teversal who occurs in a transaction made in 1201–1202 and recorded in R. Thoroton, *Antiquities of Nottinghamshire* (London, 1677), p. 268; J. Throsby (ed.), *Thoroton's History of Nottinghamshire: republished with large additions*, 3 vols (Nottingham, 1790), II, p. 303. A later Ralph Barre son of Geoffrey Barre appears as the defendant in a plea made by the abbot of Beauchief in 1268–1269 to have restored to him the common pasture in Teversal of which his predecessor, abbot Roger, had been unjustly disseised by Geoffrey (Thoroton, *Antiquities of Nottinghamshire, loc. cit.*). For abbots Roger and Ivo, his successor (resigned 1278), see Smith and London, *Heads of Religious Houses*, II, p. 494. For two similar cases in 1269 and 1272 concerning unjust disseisin of lands belonging to the abbot of Beauchief, see **35**, n. 2. See **164** and **189** for Robert Brito of Walton.

204. Grant by Richard of Glapwell to Beauchief abbey of 6 acres of his demesne in the field of Glapwell, *viz.* in the field at Rowthorne[1] from his furlong called Schortbuttes 1 acre which lies between Hugh son of Sweyn and Eudes son of John and 1 acre between Simon son of Hugh and Roger

son of Arnold, in the field at Palterton from his furlong of Falwang 3 acres between him and Simon son of Hugh, and in the field at (Stony) Houghton 1 acre in Losk Corner next to the demesne of Lord Simon. The canons, who gave Richard 20s in silver for this grant, shall render to him 4d annually. [1200–1220][2]

[fo. 103r]

Carta Ricardi de Glapwella

Sciant omnes tam presentes quam futuri quod ego Ricardus de Glapwella dedi et concessi et hac mea carta confirmavi canonicis de Beuchef sex acras terre de dominico meo in campo de Glapwell', tenendas de me et heredibus meis in feodam firmam, libere et quiete. Reddendo michi et heredibus meis annuatim quatuor denarios pro omni servicio quod ad illam terram pertinet, scilicet duos denarios ad Pentecosten et duos denarios ad festum sancti Martini. Et sciendum quod sic iacent prefate sex acre terre in campo apud Ructhorne de cultura mea, que vocatur Schortbuttes, una acra terre que iacet inter Hugonem filium Suani et Eudonem filium Johannis, et altera acra terre inter Symonem filium Hugonis et Rogerum filium Arnaldi in campo apud Palterton' de cultura mea de Falwang', tres acre[a] terre inter me et Symonem filium Hugonis in campo apud Octonam, una acra terre in Loskecroftes iuxta dominicam domini Symonis. Quicquid vero in predictis locis de sex acris terre defuerit de cultura mea predicta de Falwang' eisdem canonicis implere concessi. Ego vero et heredes mei predictam terram iamdictis canonicis de Beuchef pro predicta firma de omni exactione et consuetudine adquietabimus et warantizabimus. Pro hac vero concessione dederunt michi pretaxati canonici xx solidos argenti. Hiis testibus etc.

[a] *acras.*

[1] In Ault Hucknall, OS ref. SK 478649; Cameron, *Place-names of Derbyshire*, II, p. 269: 'rough thorn-bush'.
[2] Another copy printed in Darlington, *Glapwell Charters*, no. 11. Witnesses are listed as 'Willelmo de Mainhil, Roberto le Bretun de Waletun, Ingeram de Bramtonna, Hugone persona de Dranefeld, Thoma et Michaele filiis suis, Simone de Glapwella, Rogero et Roberto fratribus suis, Roberto clerico de Waletona, Nicholao de Langeleya et Rogero filio eius, Waltero Dun de Dranefeld'. The date is given as early thirteenth century. See **164** and **189** for Robert Brito of Walton. Simon of Glapwell served on the jury for the wapentake of Scarsdale at the 1281 Derbyshire eyre (Hopkinson, *Derbyshire Eyre*, p. 193). Walter Dun was descended from a family who took their name from Bourg-Dun in Normandy (Turbutt, *Derbyshire*, II, pp. 475–476).

205. Grant by Richard son of William of Glapwell to Beauchief abbey of 2 bovates in Glapwell, 1 of which Weremund once held with 1 acre on Dunsill in place of the messuage pertaining to that bovate and the other which Roger held with a toft and croft; and of pasture for one plough-team and 100 sheep and rights of common. The canons, who gave Richard 60s in silver for this grant, shall render to him 2s in silver annually. [1200–1220][1]

[fo. 103v]

Alia carta Ricardi filii Willelmi de Glapwell

Omnibus sancte matris ecclesie filiis ad quos presens carta pervenerit Ricardus filius Willelmi de Glapwel salutem in Domino. Sciatis me dedisse et concessisse et hac mea presenti carta confirmasse abbati et conventui de Beuchef duas bovatas terre cum omnibus pertinenciis et libertatibus suis in Glapwella, quarum unam Weremundus aliquando tenuit et pro mesagio illi bovate pertinenti, unam acram terre de duabus super Dunneshil, illam scilicet que est vicinior meridiei, et alteram bovatam quam Rogerus aliquando tenuit cum tofto et crofto et pasturam averiis uni caruce pertinentibus et pasturam centum ovibus et comunam in bosco, in plano, in viis in semitis, in aquis et in omnibus locis ad feudum de Glapwel pertinentibus, in quibus ego et heredes mei comunicamus,[a] tenendas de me et heredibus meis libere et quiete, honorifice et pacifice, ad perpetuam firmam. Reddendo michi et heredibus meis singulis annis duos solidos argenti duobus terminis, scilicet duodecim denarios ad Pentecosten et duodecim denarios infra octabas sancti Martini pro omni seculari servicio et consuetudine et exactione, salvo domini regis servicio. Ego vero Ricardus et heredes mei predictas duas bovatas terre cum omnibus pertinenciis suis prenominatis abbati et conventui de Beuch' pro dicta firma adquietabimus[b] et warantizabimus[c] Pro hac autem concessione et confirmacione dederunt michi dicti abbas et conventus lx solidos argenti de gersuma. Hiis t[estibus] etc.

[a] *cominicamus.* [b] *adquietabius.* [c] *warrantizabius.*

[1] Another copy printed in Darlington, *Glapwell Charters*, no. 14. Witnesses are listed as 'Roberto filio Willelmi de Alfertone, Willelmo Barre, Roberto Britone de Waleton, Matheo de Hulmo, Radulfo Silvano de Torph, Symone filio Hugonis de Glapwella, Rogero clerico suo fratre et multis aliis'. The date is given as early thirteenth century. See **164** and **189** for Robert Brito of Walton.

206. Grant by Robert son of Hugh of Glapwell, with the consent of Roger the clerk his brother, to Beauchief abbey of 5 acres in the fields of Glapwell, *viz.* **2 selions below Morelestorth hill**[1] **and Stefnestubing**[2] **in another part of the field towards Scarcliffe and (Stony) Houghton next to the road from Bolsover, 2 selions at Wudemangatha;**[3] **3 selions between the Nottingham high road and the furlong of the lords of the vill called Five Acres, 2 selions in a third part of the field in Dunsill dale, and 2 selions to the east of Rowthorn road. The canons, who gave Robert 16s in silver for this grant, shall render to him 4d annually. [1200–1240]**[4]

[fo. 104r]

Carta Roberti filii Hugonis de Glapwel

Noverint omnes tam presentes quam futuri quod ego Robertus filius Hugonis de Glapwell', consensu et consilio Rogeri clerici fratris mei, dedi et concessi et hac mea presenti carta confirmavi Deo et sancte Marie et sancto Thome martiri de Beuchef et canonicis ibidem Deo servientibus quinque acras terre in campis de Glapwell', scilicet sub colle Morelestorth' et Stefnestubing' in alia parte campi versus Scarcheclif et Hocton' iuxta viam de Bolleshover duas selliones, apud Wudemangatha[a] duas selliones inter altam viam de Notingham et culturam dominorum ville que vocatur Quinque Acras tres selliones, in tercia parte campi in Dunneshil dale duas selliones, iuxta viam de Ruthorn ex parte orientali duas selliones. Habendas et tenendas ad perpetuam firmam de me et heredibus meis libere et quiete et pacifice ab omni servicio mundano forinseco et omnibus aliis demandis. Reddendo michi annuatim vel heredibus meis quatuor denarios ad Pascha. Ego vero Robertus et heredes mei predictis canonicis de Beuchef prenominatas quinque acras terre, cum libertate predicta, pro prefata firma acquietabimus[b] et warantizabimus. Pro hac donacione et concessione et confirmacione dederunt michi prenominati canonici sexdecim solidos argenti. Hiis testibus etc.

[a] *dale* deleted. [b] *a* of *acquietabimus* interlined.

[1] Cameron, *Place-names of Derbyshire*, II, p. 259: a family name and 'storth' ('brushwood'); a lost place-name.
[2] *Ibid.*: 'Stephen's clearing'; a lost place-name.
[3] *Ibid.*, p. 260: 'woodman's road'; a lost place-name.
[4] Robert son of Hugh of Glapwell appears as a witness in **204** and **208** and in Holdsworth, *Rufford Charters*, I, no. 134 (dated *c.*1210–1223). A Hugh of Glapwell witnessed *Rufford Charters*, I, nos 132 and 216 (dated 1170–1216). Another copy printed in Darlington, *Glapwell Charters*, no. 35. Witnesses are listed as 'Johanne Daincurth, Petro capellano de Glapwella, Rogero

de Sidenhale, Simone filio Hugonis de Glapwella, Ricardo filio Willelmi de eadem villa, Alano filio Ricardi, Johanne et Andrea fratribus, Willelmo filio Godriz, et multis aliis'. The date is given as early thirteenth century and probably before 1217-1218.

207. Grant by Richard son of William of Glapwell to Beauchief abbey of 1 furlong called Claiwang, 1 furlong called Falwang, 2 large selions bordering on the Nottingham road and everything contained in the furlong of Derebistret. The canons, who gave Richard 24s in silver for this grant, shall render to him 4d annually in silver. [1200-1220][1]

[fo. 104v]

Carta Ricardi filii Willelmi de Glapwella

Noverint omnes tam presentes quam futuri quod ego Ricardus filius Willelmi de Glapwella dedi et concessi et hac mea carta confirmavi Deo et sancte Marie et sancto Thome martiri de Beuchef et canonicis ibidem Deo servientibus totam culturam que vocatur Claiwang' et totam culturam que dicitur Fullwang', sine aliquo retenemento, et duas magnas selliones que pulsant super viam de Notingham et quicquid continetur in cultura de Derebistret'. Tenendas de me et heredibus meis in territorio de Glapwella ad perpetuam firmam, libere et quiete et pacifice. Reddendo michi et heredibus meis annuatim iiij denarios argenti duobus terminis, scilicet ij denarios ad Pentecosten et ij denarios ad festum sancti Martini, pro omnibus demandis et pro omni forinseco servicio. Ego vero Ricardus et heredes mei predictis canonicis de Beuchef prenominatas terras cum omni libertate prefata, pro predicta firma, adquietabimus et warantizabimus. Pro hac autem donacione et concessione et confirmacione dederunt michi predicti canonici xxiiij solidos argenti de gersuma. Hiis testibus etc.

[1] Another copy printed in Darlington, *Glapwell Charters*, no. 16. Witnesses are listed as 'Johanne Daincurth, Petro capellano de Glapwella, Rogero de Sidenhale, Simone filio Hugonis de Glapwell, Alano filio Ricardi, Johanne et Andrea fratribus, et multis aliis'. The date is given as early thirteenth century.

208. Gift in free alms by Richard son of William of Glapwell to Beauchief abbey of 1 toft with its croft in Glapwell which lies between the toft of Weremund which he gave to the

canons previously and the toft which Robert the cook once held. [1200–1240][1]

Alia carta eiusdem Ricardi

Omnibus sancte matris ecclesie filiis ad quos presens carta pervenerit Ricardus filius Willelmi de [fo. 105r] Glapwell' salutem in Domino. Sciatis me dedisse et presenti carta mea confirmasse Deo et sancte Marie et sancto Thome martiri de Beuchef et fratribus ibidem Deo servientibus unum toftum, cum crofto suo, in villa de Glapwell', quod iacet inter toftum Weremundi, quod predictis fratribus prius in elemosinam dedi, et toftum quod Robertus cocus aliquando tenuit, in puram et perpetuam elemosinam, ab omni seculari exactione et consuetudine liberam et quietam, pro salute anime mee et uxoris mee et heredum meorum et omnium antecessorum meorum. Hiis t[estibus] etc.

[1] Another copy printed in Darlington, *Glapwell Charters*, no. 12. Witnesses are listed as 'Willelmo persona de Pleseleya, Hugone persona de Dranefeld, Waltero de Heincurt persona de Mortun, Willelmo filio Roberti de Alfert, Johanne de Heincurt, Radulfo filio Hugonis, Roberto Britone de Waletun, Petro de Herthil, Roberto fratre suo, Roberto clerico de Waletun, Symone filio Hugonis de Glapwella et Roberto et Rogero fratribus suis, et multis aliis'. The date is given as early thirteenth century.

209. Grant by Simon son of Hugh of Glapwell to Beauchief abbey of 1 bovate in Glapwell which Roger son of William quitclaimed to him and 1 acre called Prestacra in place of the messuage pertaining to that bovate; of pasture for one plough-team and 60 ewes with their lambs until Whitsun; and of common pertaining to 1 free bovate. The canons, who gave Simon 20s for this grant, shall render to him 12d in silver annually. [1200–1240][1]

Carta Symonis filius Hugonis de Glapwella

Omnibus sancte matris ecclesie filiis ad quos presens carta pervenerit Symon filius Hugonis de Glapwella salutem in Domino. Sciatis[a] me concessisse et dedisse et hac mea presenti carta confirmasse abbati et conventui de Beuchef unam bovatam terre cum omnibus pertinenciis suis in territorio de Glapwella, quam Rogerus filius Willelmi michi post mortem patris mei quietam clamavit, et pro mesuagio illi bovate pertinente, unam acram terre que vocatur Presthacra et pasturam averiis[b] uni caruce pertinentibus, et pasturam sexaginta matricibus ovibus cum toto exitu earum donec a matribus separetur et tunc removebitur exitus semper singulis annis ad Pentecost[en] remanente numero supradictarum omnium et communam [fo. 105v] per omnia uni libere bovate terre pertinentem in bosco, in plano, in viis et semitis, in aquis et omnibus aysiamentis ad feudum de Glapwell' pertinentibus, in quibus ego comunico. Tenendam et habendam de me et heredibus meis, libere et quiete, honorifice et pacifice, ad perpetuam firmam. Reddendo michi et heredibus meis per annum duodecim denarios argenti duobus terminis, scilicet vj denarios ad Pentecosten et vj denarios infra octabas sancti Martini pro omni seculari servicio uni bovate pertinente. Hec vero prelibata predictis abbati et conventui de Beuchef ego et heredes mei pro predicta firma contra omnes homines acquietabimus et warantizabimus. Pro hac autem donacione et concessione et confirmacione dederunt michi abbas et conventus xx solidos de gersuma. Hiis testibus etc.

[a] *scyatis.*   [b] *averriis.*

[1] Another copy printed in Darlington, *Glapwell Charters*, no. 37. Witnesses are listed as 'Roberto Britone de Waletun, Ingelrammo de Bramtun, Galfrido de Musters, Rogero de Eynecurt, Rogero le Poer, Ricardo de Glapwella, Willelmo filio Thome de Sutton, Roberto clerico de Waletun, et Hugone filio eius, et pluribus aliis'. The date is given as early thirteenth century and probably earlier than 1217–1218. Galfrido (Geoffrey) of Mousters held half the manors of Pleasley and Ashover (Turbutt, *Derbyshire*, II, p. 488); see also **184**. Later in the reign of Henry III, Simon of Glapwell's grandson granted to Darley abbey the rent of 12d he received from Beauchief abbey for the bovate in Glapwell (**214**; also Darlington, *Cartulary of Darley Abbey*, II, H 61). Stephen abbot of Beauchief granted to Darley abbey, perhaps in 1217–1218, all the lands in Glapwell given to Beauchief by Simon son of Hugh of Glapwell and others; in return Darley abbey was to pay Beauchief abbey 12s 6d annually (*ibid.*, H 47). For some of this land in Glapwell held from Beauchief abbey an annual rent of 6d was payable by Darley abbey to Roger son of Adam of Glapwell who quitclaimed this rent in the later part of the reign of Henry III (Darlington, *Cartulary of Darley Abbey*, II, H 79).

210. Grant by Roger son of Hugh of Glapwell, with the consent of Robert his brother, to Beauchief abbey of 3 acres in the fields of Glapwell, *viz*. 2 selions below the hill at Calldwell and 1 selion called Longeroda, 1 selion towards Scarcliffe at Wudemangat and 1 selion towards (Stony) Houghton between the Nottingham high road and the furlong of the lords of the vill called Five Acres, 1 selion beyond the Pleasley road next to the furlong of lord Simon and 1 selion on Dunsill which borders on the furlong of Derebistret and 1 selion which borders on Ridding. The

canons, who gave Roger 8s in silver for this grant, shall render to him 2d annually. [1200–1230]¹

Carta Rogeri filii Hugonis de Glapwella

Noverint omnes[a] tam presentes quam futuri quod ego Rogerus filius Hugonis de Glapwella dedi et concessi et hac mea presenti carta confirmavi, consensu[b] et consilio Roberti fratris mei, Deo et sancte Marie et sancto Thome martiri de Beuchef et canonicis ibidem Deo servientibus tres acras terre in campis de Glapwell' sub colle, scilicet ad Calldwell' duas selliones et unam sellionem que vocatur Longeroda in alia parte campi versus Scarcheclyf', ad Wudemangat' unam sellionem versus [fo. 106r] Hocton' inter altam viam Notinghamie et culturam dominorum ville que vocatur Quinque Acras unam sellionem in tertia parte campi ultra viam de Pleseleya iuxta culturam domini Symonis unam sellionem et super Dunneshil, unam sellionem que pulsat super culturam de Derebistret, et unam sellionem que pulsat super Ridding'. Habendas et tenendas ad perpetuam firmam de me et heredibus meis, libere et quiete et pacifice ab omni servicio mundano forinseco et omnibus aliis demandis. Reddendo annuatim [michi] vel heredibus meis duos denarios ad Pascha. Ego vero Rogerus et heredes mei predictis canonicis de Beuchef prenominatas tres acras terre cum libertate predicta pro predicta firma acquietabimus et warantizabimus.[c] Pro hac donacione et concessione et confirmacione dederunt michi prenominati canonici octo solidos argenti. Hiis testibus etc.

[a] *universi* deleted and *omnes* interlined.   [b] *consesu*.   [c] *warantizabius*.

¹Another copy printed in Darlington, *Glapwell Charters*, no. 36. Witnesses are listed as 'Johanne Daincurth, Petro capellano de Glapwell, Rogero de Sidenhale, Simone filio Hugonis de Glapwell, Ricardo filio Willelmi de eadem villa, Alano filio Ricardi, Johanne et Andrea fratribus, et aliis'. The date is given as early thirteenth century.

211. Gift in free alms by Richard of Glapwell to Beauchief abbey of 1½ acres of his demesne in the field of Glapwell, viz. 1 acre in the field at (Stony) Houghton which lies between Ralph Hospitalis and Alan son of Richard on the Bolsover road and ½ acre at Rowthorne in Dunusilldale next to Ulf. [1200–1230]¹

Carta Ricardi de Glapwella

Omnibus sancte matris ecclesie filiis ad quos presens carta pervenerit Ricardus de Glapwella salutem in Domino. Sciatis me dedisse et hac mea carta confirmasse Deo et sancte Marie et sancto Thome martiri de Beauchef et canonicis ibidem Deo servientibus unam acram[a] terre et dimidiam de dominico meo in campo de Glapwella, libere et quiete in puram et perpetuam elemosinam inperpetuum possidendam, scilicet unam acram[b] [fo. 106v] terre in campo apud Hoctonam, que iacet inter Rad[ulphum] Hospitalem et Alanum filium Ricardi ad viam de Bolleshover, et unam dimidiam acram terre apud Ructhorne in Dunusilldale iuxta Ulf, pro salute anime mee et uxoris mee et patris mei et omnium antecessorum meorum. Hiis testibus etc.

[a] *de* deleted.   [b] *unam acram* erroneously repeated at beginning of folio verso.

[1] Another copy printed in Darlington, *Glapwell Charters*, no. 13. Witnesses are listed as 'Willelmo de Mainil, Roberto le Bretun de Waletun, Ingeram de Bramton, Hugone persona de Dranefeld, Thoma et Michaele filiis suis, Simone de Glapwella, Rogero et Roberto fratribus suis, Roberto clerico de Walton, Nicholao de Langeleya, Rogero filio eius, Waltero Dun de Dranefeld'. The date is given as early thirteenth century.

212. Grant by Simon son of Hugh of Glapwell to Robert and Roger his brothers of 2 bovates which Itho and Avice held in the vill of Glapwell. Robert and Roger shall render to him 6d annually. [1200–1240]

Carta Symonis filius Hugonis de Glapwell'

Sciant omnes tam presentes quam futuri quod ego Symon filius Hugonis de Glapwell' concessi et hac mea carta confirmavi Roberto et Rogero, fratribus meis, duas bovatas terre, sicut carta patris mei testatur, illas scilicet quas Itho et Avice[a] tenuerunt in villa de Glapwell' cum omnibus pertinenciis pro homagiis et serviciis suis inperpetuum. Tenendas de me et heredibus meis illi et heredes sui, libere et quiete, pro omni servicio quod ad me vel heredes meos pertinet, salvo forinseco. Reddendo inde michi annuatim vj denarios ad Pascha. Hiis testibus etc.

[a] Or *Anice*?

213. Notification by Roger son and heir of Adam of Glapwell that he has quitclaimed to the canons of Darley an annual rent of 6d which Beauchief abbey owe him for certain lands which the canons of Darley hold of them. Roger

acknowledges to Beauchief abbey that he has no claim to this rent in the future. [1260–1290][1]

Quieta clamacio Rogeri filii et heredis Ade de Glapwell'

Noverint universi hoc scriptum visuri vel audituri[a] quod cum ego Rogerus filius et heres Ade de Glapwell' dederim et omnino quietum clamaverim de me et heredibus meis abbati et conventui de Derley' et eorum successoribus, in puram et perpetuam elemosinam, [fo. 107r] sex denarios annui redditus, quos abbas et conventus de Bello Capite michi solvere tenebantur annuatim pro terris et tenementis cum pertinenciis, quas habuerunt ex dono et concessione antecessorum meorum in Glapwell', et quas terras cum pertinenciis abbas et conventus de Derley tenent de abbate et conventu de Bello Capite simul cum aliis terris in Glapwell, concedo pro me et heredibus meis dictis abbati et conventui de Bello Capite, quod imposterum nichil juris vel clamii in predictis sex denariis annui redditus vel in eorum proventibus seu recognicionibus exigemus vel vendicabimus inperpetuum. Set nichilominus ego dictus Rogerus et heredes mei seu assignati dictas terras et tenementa cum pertinenciis dictis abbati et conventui de Bello Capite in puram et perpetuam elemosinam contra omnes gentes warantizabimus et defendemus. In cuius rei testimonium etc. Hiis testibus etc.

[a] *visuris vel audituris.*

[1] Another copy printed in Darlington, *Glapwell Charters*, no. 128. Witnesses are listed as 'Roberto le Graunt de Languat, Thoma filio Willelmi de Glapwell, Symone filio Hugonis de eadem, Willelmo de Hokenal, Roberto Harang, Ricardo de Aula et aliis'. The date is given as late Henry III or early Edward I. A similar charter, without a witness list and for which the date is given as late Henry III, is printed in Darlington, *Cartulary of Darley Abbey*, II, H 79.

214. Notification by Simon son of Hugh of Glapwell and grandson of Simon of Glapwell that he has quitclaimed to the canons of Darley an annual rent of 12d which Beauchief abbey paid him for 1 bovate in Glapwell which they had by the gift of Simon of Glapwell his grandfather and which the canons of Darley hold of Beauchief abbey. Simon acknowledges to Beauchief abbey that he has no claim to this rent in the future. [1282][1]

Quieta clamacio Symonis filii et heredis Hugonis de Glapwell'

Notum sit universis hoc scriptum visuris vel audituris quod cum ego Symon filius et heres Hugonis de Glapwell' dederim et omnino quietum clamaverim de me et heredibus meis abbati et conventui de Derley et eorum successoribus in liberam, puram et perpetuam elemosinam duodecim denarios annui redditus, quos abbas et conventus de Bello Capite michi solvere tenebantur annuatim ad duos terminos pro una bovata terre cum pertinenciis, quam habuerunt ex dono Symonis [fo. 107v] de Glapwell', avi mei, et quam terram abbas et conventus de Derley tenent de abbate et conventu de Bello Capite in Glapwell', concedo pro me et heredibus meis dictis abbati et conventui de Bello Capite, quod inposterum nichil juris vel clamii in predictis duodecim denariis annui redditus vel in eorum proventibus seu recognicionibus exigemus vel vendicabimus inperpetuum. Set nichilominus ego dictus Symon et heredes mei seu assignati dictam bovatam terre cum pertinenciis dictis abbati et conventui de Bello Capite vel tenentibus eandem terram de eisdem in liberam et perpetuam elemosinam, quietam et solutam ab omnibus secularibus serviciis, sectis curie, releviis et omnimodis aliis escaetis et demandis ad me seu ad heredes meos pertinentibus, preter orationes in Domino, salvo tamen forinseco servicio domini regis, contra omnes gentes warantizabimus et defendemus. In cuius rei testimonium etc. Hiis testibus etc.

[1] Another copy printed in Darlington, *Glapwell Charters*, no. 54. Witnesses are listed as 'Roberto le Graunt, Thoma filio Willelmi de Glapwell, Rogero Bate, Willelmo de Hokenale, Roberto Harang, Ricardo de Aula et aliis'. The date is given as 24 February 1282 (*Datum in festo sancti Mathie apostoli anno gratie M° CC° LXXX° primo*). A similar charter, without a witness list and for which the date is given as late Henry III, is printed in Darlington, *Cartulary of Darley Abbey*, II, H 61.

215. Confirmation in free alms of Thomas of Glapwell son and heir of William of Glapwell[1] to Beauchief abbey of all lands, tenements, rents, and possessions which they have in fee of his ancestors by the gifts or sales of those ancestors. [1200–1240]

Confirmacio Thome de Glapwel' de omnibus terris nostris in G.

Noverint universi hoc presens scriptum visuri vel audituri[a] quod ego Thomas de Glapwell, filius et heres Willelmi de Glapwell', concessi et hoc presenti scripto pro me et heredibus meis seu assignatis confirmavi abbati et conventui monasterii sancti Thome martiris de Bello Capite eorumque successoribus, in liberam, puram et perpetuam elemosinam, omnes terras et tenementa, redditus et [fo. 108r] possessiones que habent et habuerunt in feodis antecessorum meorum, de donis vel vendicionibus eorumdem vel mei ipsius, cum wardis, releviis, sectis curiarum et omnimodis escaetis et demandis que poterunt ad me vel heredes meos seu assignatos aliquomodo vel eventu pertinere vel inperpetuum escadere de predictis terris et tenementis cum redditibus dictorum feodorum. Ita quod nec ego dictus Thomas nec heredes mei seu assignati nec aliquis alius nomine nostro in predictis terris, tenementis et redditibus cum hiis que dicta sunt serviciis, sectis vel escaetis aliquod jus vel clamium consuetudinem vel demandam exigere vel vendicare poterimus inperpetuum. Sed et ego dictus Thomas et heredes mei seu assignati dictas terras et tenementa cum redditibus, escaetis et omnibus appendiciis suis, nominatis et non nominatis, dictis abbati et conventui eorumque successoribus in liberam, puram et perpetuam elemosinam contra omnes gentes warantizabimus, acquietabimus et inperpetuum defendemus. In cuius rei testimonium etc. Hiis t[estibus] etc.

[a] *visuris vel audituris.*

[1] Thomas son of William of Glapwell was a witness to **214**.

216. Quitclaim by William son of Richard of Glapwell to Beauchief abbey of an annual rent of 32d which they pay to him in the vill of Glapwell. The canons gave William 2 silver marks for this quitclaim. [1220–1270]

Carta Willelmi filii Ricardi de Glapwell'

Omnibus ad quos presens scriptum pervenerit Willelmus filius Ricardi de Glapwell' salutem in Domino. Noveritis me resignasse et quietum clamasse de me et heredibus meis inperpetuum Deo et ecclesie beati Thome martiris de Beuchief et canonicis [fo. 108v] ibidem Deo servientibus redditum triginta duorum denariorum, quem michi solvere tenebantur annuatim in villa de Glapwell'. Ita quod nec ego nec heredes mei aliquod jus vel clamium in predicto redditu triginta duorum denariorum decetero nobis vendicare poterimus. Pro hac autem quieta clamacione et confirmacione dederunt michi abbas et conventus de Beuch' duas marcas argenti in gersuma. In huius rei testimonium feci eis hanc cartam sigillo meo signatam. Hiis testibus etc.

[WIGLEY AND BRAMPTON]

217. Grant by Robert of Wigley senior to John of Ridgeway, chaplain,[1] and William his brother of all lands and tenements which he had by the gift and feoffment of John

THE BEAUCHIEF ABBEY CARTULARY 249

of Wigley his late father, and of all the lands and tenements which he had by the gift and feoffment of Roger of Wigley, his brother, in the vills and fields of Wigley[2] and Brampton.[3] [1370–1400]

Carta Roberti de Wyggeley de terra in eadem[a]

Sciant presentes et futuri quod ego Robertus de Wyggeley senior dedi, concessi et hac presenti carta mea confirmavi domino Johanni de Ryggeway capellano et Willelmo fratri suo omnia terras et tenementa cum edificiis, pratis, boscis cum omnibus pertinenciis suis, que et quas habui de dono et feoffamento Johannis de Wyggeley, quondam patris mei, et omnia terras et tenementa, pratos, boscos cum pertinenciis suis, que et quas habui de dono et feoffamento Rogeri de Wyggeley, fratris mei, in villis et in campis de Wyggeley et Brampton'. Habenda et tenenda omnia predicta terras et tenementa cum edificiis, pratis et boscis[b] cum omnibus pertinenciis suis predictis Johanni et Willelmo heredibus et assignatis [fo. 109r] de capitalibus dominis feodorum illorum per servicia inde debita et de iure consueta imperpetuum. Ego vero predictus Robertus et heredes mei omnia predicta terras et tenementa cum edificiis, pratis et boscis cum omnibus pertinenciis suis prefatis Johanni et Willelmo heredibus et assignatis suis contra omnes gentes warantizabimus inperpetuum. In cuius rei testimonium huic presenti carte sigillum meum apposui. Hiis testibus etc.

[a] *Wygley* marginated.   [b] *boscos*.

[1] A chaplain named John of Ridgeway occurs in a Chesterfield deed of 1383 (Riden and Blair, *History of Chesterfield*, V, p. 261).
[2] In Brampton parish, about 1 mile west of the church, OS ref. SK 316719.
[3] According to an agreement made between the dean, William de Thornaco (Thorney), and chapter of Lincoln and the abbot, Gilbert, and convent of Beauchief on 22 April 1237, the abbey held tithes of the lands in the parish of Brampton to which the church belonged as a chapel to Chesterfield (Foster and Major (eds), *'Registrum Antiquissimum'*, III, pp. 62–63).

218. Grant by John of Ridgeway of Chesterfield, chaplain, to Ralph Barker of Dore and William of the Barkhouse of Norton[1] of all lands and tenements which he had by the gift and feoffment of Robert son of John of Wigley in Wigley and Brampton. [1370–1400]

Carta Johannis de Ryggeway

Sciant presentes et futuri quod ego Johannes de Ryggeway de Chestrefeld capellanus dedi, concessi et hac presenti carta mea confirmavi Rad[ulph]o Barker de Dore et Willelmo del Barkhowse de Norton' omnia terras et tenementa cum omnibus pertinenciis suis que et quas habui ex dono et feoffamento Roberti filii Johannis de Wygley in Wyggeley et Brampton'. Habenda et tenenda omnia predicta terras et tenementa cum omnibus pertinenciis suis predictis Rad[ulph]o et Willelmo heredibus et assignatis suis de capitali domino feodi illius per servicia inde debita et de jure consueta. Et ego vero predictus Johannes et heredes mei omnia predicta terras et tenementa cum omnibus pertinenciis suis prefatis Rad[ulph]o et Willelmo heredibus et assignatis suis contra omnes gentes warantizabimus et inperpetuum defendemus. In cuius rei etc. Hiis testibus etc. Dat' etc.

[1] Ralph Barker and William of the Barkhouse are well attested in the Dronfield district between c.1384 and 1416 (Jeayes, *Derbyshire Charters*, nos 231, 1053, 1055, 1778, 1398, 2442) and appear to have been in partnership at a tannery at Beauchief from c.1383 (*ibid.*, no. 241; Sheffield Archives, Bagshawe Collection, no. 3184, dated 1383/1384). The surname Barker was an occupational name for a tanner. Ralph Barker lived in Dore and was instrumental in founding the guild of St Mary chantry chapel in 1392. He transferred his right of the advowson of Dronfield to the abbey in 1399 (Nottinghamshire Archives, DD/CW/Ib/4 and 8). This process took several years to reach fulfilment, for a licence was granted on 1 December 1389 to the abbey to acquire and appropriate in mortmain for £20 the advowson of Dronfield from John de Wodehouse, dean of the collegiate church of St John, Chester, Robert de Barley, and Ralph Berker (*Calendar of Patent Rolls, Richard II, 4: 1388–1392*, p. 164). Robert de Berley occurs as a witness in a grant of property in the new market of Chesterfield made by Sir Thomas Chaworth IV on 26 March 1412 (Hall and Thomas, *Jackson Collection*, p. 122). Garratt, *Derbyshire Feet of Fines*, p. 69, records that in 1398 Ralph Barker of Dore bought the advowson of Dronfield church from John Bassett, knight, and his wife, Joan (see also **50**). Turbutt, *Derbyshire*, II, p. 720, says that the benefice of Dronfield was appropriated to Beauchief in 1399.

219. Grant by Ralph Barker and William of Barkhouse to Beauchief abbey of 1 messuage and 20 acres in Wigley. Made at Brampton. [c.1393][1]

[fo. 109v]

Carta Radulphi le Barker et Willelmi de Barkhous

Sciant presentes et futuri quod nos Rad[ulph]us Barker et Willelmus de Barkehouse dedimus, concessimus et hac presenti carta nostra confirmavimus abbati et conventui de Bello Capite unum messuagium et viginti acras terre cum pertinenciis in Wyggelay. Habenda et tenenda predictum messuagium et predictas viginti acras terre cum pertinenciis prefatis abbati et conventui et eorum successoribus inperpetuum de capitalibus dominis feodi illius per servicia inde debita et consueta. Et nos vero predicti Rad[ulph]us et Willelmus et heredes nostri predictum messuagium et predictas viginti acras terre cum pertinenciis prefatis abbati et conventui et eorum successoribus contra omnes gentes warantizabimus et inperpetuum defendemus. In cuius rei testimonium etc. Hiis testibus etc. Dat' apud Brampton' etc.

[1] On 17 September 1392 licence was given for 2 marks paid to the king by the abbey for the alienation in mortmain by Ralph Barker and William del Barkehous of 3 messuages, 2 bovates of land, and 2 acres of meadow in Wigley and Chesterfield in aid of the maintenance of the abbey (*Calendar of Patent Rolls, Richard II, 4: 1391–1396*, p. 159). In July 1393 an inquest jury found that it would not be to the damage of the king if Ralph Barker and William Barkhouse gave 5 messuages, 3 or 4 bovates of land, and 3 acres of meadow in Wigley, Beeley, and Chesterfield to Beauchief abbey. 2 messuages, 2 bovates, and 2 acres in Wigley were held of the abbot as tenant of Ralph Frescheville, who held of the king in chief; a messuage in Chesterfield was held of the dean of Lincoln, who held of the Crown in pure alms; and 2 messuages, 2 bovates, and an 1 acre of meadow in Beeley were held of undertenants of the Duchy of Lancaster (The National Archives, C 143/417/23; the writ specifies 3 bovates but the jury mention 4). Some evidence of the abbey's role in supplicating for the souls of deceased commoners in this part of Derbyshire is found in the grant of a licence on 8 May 1409 to Henry Coke chaplain, Thomas Rodes chaplain, and John de Normanton of Chesterfield to grant in mortmain to the abbey 3 messuages, 6 cottages, 60 acres of land, 12 acres of meadow, and 46s of rent in Chesterfield, Brampton, Newbold, Boythorpe, Hasland, and Heath, all worth 41s 8d yearly, for the maintenance of a chaplain to celebrate divine service daily for the souls of Hugh Draper of Chesterfield and Cecily de Thomworth, sometime his wife, and Cecily Leche, late his wife, in the church of All Saints, Chesterfield (*Calendar of Patent Rolls, Henry IV, 4: 1408–1413*, pp. 89–90); Hugh le Drapier, formerly an owner of tenements in the new market of Chesterfield, also appears in a charter of Sir Thomas Chaworth IV dated 26 March 1412 (Hall and Thomas, *Jackson Collection*, p. 122). On 23 November 1406 the abbey had paid £10 for a licence to acquire lands and rents in mortmain to the value of £10 yearly (*Calendar of Patent Rolls, Henry IV, 3: 1405–1408*, p. 278).

220. Final concord made in the court of the Lord King at York in the third week after Easter 1328[1] between John of Wigley, plaintiff, and John son of Walter of Buildwas[2] and Alice his wife, deforciants, concerning 1 messuage, 1 bovate, and 2 acres in Wigley and Brampton. John son of Walter and Alice acknowledged that the aforesaid tenements were John of Wigley's by right by their gift. John of Wigley gave John son of Walter and Alice 100s in silver for this acknowledgement. [1328]

Finalis concordia de Wyggeley

Hec finalis concordia facta in curia domini regis apud Ebor' a die Pasche in tres septimanas anno regni regis Edwardi[a] tercii a conquestu secundo, coram Willelmo de Herle, Henrico le Scrop, Johanne de Mutford de Stonore et Johanne de Bousser, justiciis et aliis domini regis fidelibus tunc ibi presentibus, inter Johannem de Wyggeley querentem et [fo. 110r] Johannem filium Walteri de Byldeswath'ᵃ et Aliciam uxorem eius deforcientes, de uno messuagio una bovata et duobus acris terre cum pertinenciis in Wyggeley et Brampton'. Unde placitum convencionis summonitum fuit inter eos in eadem curia, scilicetᵇ quod predicti Johannes filius Walteri et Alicia recognoverunt predicta tenementa cum pertinenciis esse jus ipsius Johannis de Wyggeley, ut illa que idem Johannes habet ex dono predictorum Johannis filii Walteri et Alicie. Habendos et tenendos eidem Johanni de Wiggeley et heredibus suis de capitalibus dominis feodi illius per servicia que ad predicta tenementa pertinent inperpetuum. Et preterea idem Johannes filius Walteri et Alicia concesserunt pro se et heredibus ipsius Alicie quod ipsi warantizabunt predicto Johanni de Wyggeley et heredibus suis predicta tenementa cum pertinenciis contra omnes homines inperpetuum. Et pro hac recognicione, warancia, fine et concordia, idem Johannes de Wyggeley dedit predictis Johanni filio Walteri et Alicie centum solidos argenti.

ᵃ *Ewardi.* ᵇ *sicilicet.*

[1] i.e. between 18 April and 24 April.
[2] Buildwas (Shrops).

[NOTTINGHAM]

221. Indenture made between Beauchief abbey and Adam Barry of Nottingham. Since Adam holds 1 messuage of the canons in the vill of Nottingham in the Littlemarsh for 2s 8d in silver, they have given Adam their part in the said messuage. Adam shall render to the canons 18d in silver annually, with power of distraint for the canons. [1347–1389]

Indentura inter abbatem et conventum de Beuchef et Adam
Barry etc.
[fo. 110v]

Notyngham

Hec indentura facta inter Robertum de Radclyf, abbatem de Bello Capite,[1] et eiusdem loci conventum ex parte una, et Adam Barry de Notyngham ex altera testatur, que cum dictus Adam tenet unum messuagium cum pertinenciis in villa de Notyng' in le Litelmersh', quod quidem messuagium cum pertinenciis tenebatur nobis in duobus solidis et octo denariis argenti. Noveritis nos dictum Robertum abbatem et eiusdem loci conventum dedisse et hiis scriptis indentatis confirmasse pro nobis et successoribus nostris predicto Ade heredibus et assignatis eius propartem nostram in predicto messuagio cum pertinenciis inperpetuum pro octodecim denariis argenti per annum percipiendis ad duos anni terminos, scilicet ad festa sancti Martini in hyeme et Invencionis sancte Crucis per equales porciones. Et si predictus redditus in parte vel in toto ad aliquem terminum supradictum aretro fuerit, bene liceat abbati et conventui seu suis successoribus predictum messuagium cum pertinenciis intrare et eodem distringere, districciones capere, asportare et penes se retinere, quousque de predicto redditu plenarie eis fuerit satisfactum. In huius rei testimonium etc. Hiis testibus etc.

[1] Robert was abbot between 1347 and 1389 (Smith, *Heads of Religious Houses*, III, p. 563). This stray Nottingham deed is probably placed here because one of the parties was a member of the Barry family of Teversal (Notts), whose gifts to the abbey in Stanley in Teversal follow.

[STANLEY]

222. Gift in free alms by William Barry of Teversal to Beauchief abbey of 1 bovate in his demesne with 2 tofts and crofts in Stanley,[1] ***viz.*** **the moiety of that land west of the road which leads from Frankbridge to Stanley, and then up westward by the mansion of William son of Geoffrey, and then by the house of the canons to the land ditch, and then to the river which runs through the boundaries between the counties of Nottingham and Derby at Biggin (Farm), and then down by the same river to Frankbridge;**[2] **of all the moeity of the woods and plains contained with the aforesaid boundaries; and of pasture for 300 sheep, of which 200 shall be ewes with their lambs until separated each year on St Botulf's day,**[3] **20 cows and a bull and 8 mares with their young under the age of 3 years, and 16 oxen in the soke of Teversal. [1190–1225]**[4]

[fo. 111r]

Stanleya

Carta Willelmi Barre de Stanley

Omnibus sancte matris ecclesie filiis ad quos presens carta pervenerit Willelmus Barre de Tiveresholt salutem in Domino. Sciatis me dedisse, concessisse et hac mea presenti carta confirmasse Deo et sancte Marie et sancto Thome martiri de Beuchef et canonicis ibidem Deo servientibus unam bovatam terre in dominicam, semper habendam et possidendam cum duobus toftis et croftis et cum omnibus pertinenciis suis in Stanleya, scilicet: totam medietatem illius terre que est ex parte occidentali vie que tendit a Frankebrigga usque ad ipsam villam de Stanleya, et sic ascendendo apud occidentem iuxta mansionem Willelmi filii Galfridi, et per mansionem ipsorum canonicorum usque ad terram fossatam et per ipsam terram fossatam usque ad rivulum que currit per metas inter comitatum de Notingham et de Derby apud Neubiggine et sic descendendo per ipsum rivulum usque ad predictum Francbrigga; et totam medietatem de bosco et plano que continetur infra metas predictorum terminorum, sine aliquo retenemento michi inde vel heredibus meis habendo; et pasturam trescentis ovibus quarum ducente erunt matrices cum exitu suo quolibet anno usque ad festum sancti Botulphi, et tunc [fo. 111v] amovebitur exitus remanente numero predictarum trescentarum ovium, et pasturam viginti vaccis et tauro suo et octo equabus cum toto exitu suo tam vaccarum quam equarum donec sint[a] trium annorum, et pasturam sexdecim bobus, et comunam ad sua necessaria habenda et facienda in bosco, in plano, in exitu, in redditu, in viis, in semitis, in quarrariis, in pascuis, in terris cultis et non cultis, in aquis et pontibus, in pratis et pasturis, et in omnibus locis ubicumque ego et heredes mei et homines de soka de Tiveresholt habemus aysiamenta et communam extra pratum meum, in liberam et puram et perpetuam elemosinam, libere et quiete ab omni seculari exactione inperpetuum possidendam, pro salute anime mee et patris mei et omnium antecessorum et heredum meorum. Hiis testibus etc.

[a] *sit.*

[1] Stanley Grange Farm, OS ref. SK 459623.
[2] The reference to the stream forming the county boundary running to Frankbridge locates the bridge as that on Stanley Lane near the Hardwick Inn (Ault Hucknall). From there the bounds follow Stanley Lane to the hamlet of Stanley (in Teversal, about 1 mile west of the church) before striking westward, past the canons' own house (Stanley Grange), to the county boundary near Biggin Farm (in Tibshelf) and then following the stream northward back to the bridge.
[3] 17 June.
[4] Confirmed in 1316 (Appendix II, no. 43). Thoroton, *Antiquities of Nottinghamshire*, p. 270 (Throsby, *Thoroton's History of Nottinghamshire*, II, p. 305), printed, from an original then in the possession of John Molyneux of Teversal, an abstract of **222** with its witness list: Richard abbot of Welbeck, Robert son of William de Alfreton, Ranulph his brother, John de Eincuria, Robert Briton of Waleton, Roger de Sidenhale, William de Meinil, Roger de Eincurth, Ralph son of Richard de Bramton, Simon son of Hugh, Richard son of William of Glapwell, Robert de Briminton, Hugh de Linacre, and others. Richard was recorded as

abbot of Welbeck between 1196 and 1215 (Colvin, *White Canons*, p. 418; see also **137** and **138**). William of Menil, Roger of Eyncurt, and Hugh of Linacre witnessed the donation by Ralph Musard to Beauchief abbey of the village of Hanley (now Handley, north of Staveley in Derbyshire), together with his body, in the reign of Henry III; it was copied from an original in the possession of John Freschevile by the antiquary Gervase Holles (1607–1675) in his *Memorials* (G. Holles, *Memorials of the Holles Family, 1493–1656*, ed. A.C. Wood, Camden 3rd series (London, 1937), p. 137); for Holles, see also the *Oxford Dictionary of National Biography*). Two other witnesses to this gift appear in the Cartulary (William Basset, Geoffrey of Musters) and two do not (William of Heriz, Hasculphus Musard). The Obituary (June) commemorates Ralph Musard as 'our canon and brother' who gave Hanley and also Wadshelf (west of Chesterfield in Derbyshire) and a golden chalice. Three of Ralph's charters and one of his son's were confirmed in 1316 (Appendix II, nos 30–33); none survives in the Cartulary. The income received by the abbey from temporalities in Handley and Wadshelf was valued in the *Taxatio* in 1291 at 40s (http://www.hrionline.ac.uk/taxatio).

223. Quitclaim in free alms by the same William Barry of Teversal to Beauchief abbey of all lands, rents, and tenements with pasture for 400 sheep, of which 200 shall be ewes with their lambs until separated each year on St Botulf's day, 20 cows and a bull and 8 mares with their young under the age of 3 years, and 16 oxen in the soke of Teversal; of common beyond his park; and of all charters, feoffments, gifts, grants, quitclaims, and muniments which the canons have from him or his ancestors. [1190–1225]

Alia carta eiusdem Willelmi

Omnibus sancte matris ecclesie filiis hoc presens scriptum visuris vel audituris Willelmus Barry de Tiveresholt salutem in Domino sempiternam. [fo. 112r] Noverit universitas vestra me pro salute anime mee et omnium antecessorum et successorum meorum concessisse et confirmasse et omnino quietum clamasse de me et heredibus meis et assignatis Deo et ecclesie beati Thome martiris de Bello Capite et abbati et conventui illius loci eorumque successoribus, in liberam, puram et perpetuam elemosinam, omnes terras, redditus, sectas, sequelas, servicia, possessiones, jura, consuetudines et libertates ac omnia tenementa, cum pastura quatuor centum ovibus quarum ducente erunt matrices cum exitu suo quolibet anno usque ad festum sancti Botulphi et tunc removebitur exitus remanente numero predictarum quatuor centum ovium, et cum pastura viginti vaccis et tauro suo et octo equabus cum toto exitu suo, tam vaccarum quam equarum, donec sint trium annorum, et cum pastura sexdecim bobus et comunam ad sua necessaria habenda et facienda in bosco, in plano, in exitu et redditu, in viis et semitis, in quarrariis et pascuis, in terris cultis et non cultis, in aquis et pontibus, in pratis et pasturis, et in omnibus locis ubicumque[a] ego et heredes mei et homines de soka de[b] [fo. 112v] Tyveresholt habemus aysiamenta et comunam extra parcum meum cum omnibus eorum proventibus et pertinenciis, quibus terris, redditibus et tenementis, cum aliis rebus et pertinenciis, pretitulatis abbas et conventus monasterii predicti de Bello Capite vestiti sunt et seysiti infra feodum meum de Tyveresholt. Concedo eciam ac confirmo ac quietum clamo pro me et heredibus meis seu assignatis dictis abbati et conventui [et] eorum successoribus, in liberam, puram et perpetuam elemosinam, omnes cartas, feofamenta, donaciones, quietum clamaciones, concessiones et omnia munimenta que dicti abbas et conventus habent de antecessoribus meis vel de me ipso. Ut hoc scriptum solum cum necesse fuerit pro omnibus aliis munimentis suis sufficiat dictis abbati et conventui et eorum successoribus inperpetuum ad eorum tranquillum statum in omnibus rebus pretitulatis cum suis pertinenciis conservandis. Et ego predictus Willelmus et heredes mei ac assignati et heredes assignatorum meorum omnes terras, redditus ac tenementa, cum pastura superius nominata, sectas, sequelas, servicia, possessiones, donaciones, consuetudines et libertates, cum [fo. 113r] omnimodis aysiamentis proventibus ac pertinenciis suis, ut dicitur,[c] quibus sepedicti abbas et conventus vestiti sunt vel seysiti infra feodum meum de Tyveresholt, eisdem abbati et conventui eorumque successoribus in liberam, puram et perpetuam elemosinam, sicudi per me vel meos liberius potest vel poterit fieri, contra omnes homines et feminas et omnes gentes warantizabimus, acquietabimus et ubique inperpetuum defendemus. In cuius rei testimonium etc. Hiis testibus etc.[1]

[a]*uibicumque.*   [b]*de* repeated erroneously on folio verso.   [c]*dicitur est.*

[1] As with **222**, Thoroton (*Antiquities of Nottinghamshire*, p. 270; Throsby, *Thoroton's History of Nottinghamshire*, II, p. 305) gives the list of witnesses from an original in the possession of Molyneux: John de Heriz, Roger le Bret, William his brothers [*sic*], John Deynkurt, Roger le Breton, etc.

224. Grant by the same William Barry of Teversal to Beauchief abbey of ½ bovate which Thomas son of Nigel the smith held in Stanley with a toft and croft and pasture for 300 sheep, 200 of which should be ewes with their lambs until separated, 15 cows and 5 mares with their young, and 8 oxen in the soke of Teversal; and of common beyond his park. The canons, who gave William 5½ [marks] of silver

for this grant, shall render to him 40d annually. [1190–1227]

Alia carta eiusdem Willelmi

Omnibus sancte matris ecclesie filiis ad quos presens carta pervenerit Willelmus Barre de Tiveresholt salutem in Domino. Sciatis me dedisse et concessisse et hac mea carta confirmasse Deo et sancte Marie et sancto Thome martiri de Beuchef et canonicis ibidem Deo servientibus unam dimidiam bovatam terre, videlicet totam terram quam Thomas filius Nigelli fabri de me aliquando tenuit in Stanleya cum tofto et crofto et omnibus pertinenciis suis, et pasturam trescentis ovibus quarum ovium[a] ducente debent esse oves matrices cum exito suo,[b] donec a matribus suis quolibet anno separetur, pasturam eciam quindecim vaccis et quinque equabus cum exitibus suis semper tamen aliorum [fo. 113v] et octo bobus in bosco, in plano, in exitu, in redditu, et in omnibus locis ubicumque ego et heredes mei et homines de soka de Tiveresholt habemus aysiamenta et communam extra parcum meum. Tenendam de me et heredibus meis in feodofirmam libere et quiete. Reddendo michi et heredibus meis annuatim quadraginta denarios, scilicet viginti denarios ad Invencionem sancte Crucis et viginti denarios ad festum sancti Martini pro omni servicio et exactione et consuetudine michi vel heredibus meis, pro predicta terra et pastura, pertinenti, salvo domini regis forensi servicio predicte dimidie bovate terre pertinenti. Habebunt eciam predicti canonici de Beuchef de bosco de Tiveresholt ad edificandum et ad cetera necessaria sua in prefata terra utenda per visum forestarii mei et heredum meorum. Hec omnia prelibata iamdictis canonicis de Beuchef ego et heredes mei pro predicta firma inperpetuum per omnia et in omnibus acquietabimus [et] warantizabimus, salvo domini regis, sicud predictum est, forensi servicio. Pro hac vero donacione et concessione dederunt michi predicti canonici quinque et dimidiam [marcas] argenti. Hiis testibus etc.

[a] *oviu.*   [b] *cum sua.*

225. Gift in free alms by William of Stanley son and heir of Geoffrey of Stanley to Beauchief abbey of 4 pieces of land separately lying in the territory of Stanley, *viz.* 2 called Hirnynghuldoles bordering at one end on Somersall to the south, 1 called Birkinshache lying similarly, and 1 called

**Frankbridgedole bordering at one end on Frankbridge.
[1190–1225]**

[fo. 114r]

Carta Willelmi de Stanleya etc.

Omnibus Cristi fidelibus ad quorum noticiam vel audienciam presens scriptum pervenerit Willelmus de Stanley, filius et heres Galfridi de Stanley, salutem in Domino sempiternam. Noverit universitas vestra me dedisse, concessisse et hac presenti carta mea confirmasse in liberam, puram et perpetuam elemosinam abbati et conventui de Bello Capite quatuor placeas terre divisim iacentes in territorio de Stanley, quarum due vocantur Hirnynghuldoles buttantes ad unum capud super Somerlesole versus austrum, tercia vocatur Birkinshache similiter sicud iacet in longitudine et latitudine, quarta vocatur Frauncbrigdole buttans ad unum capud super Fraunkebrigge. Tenendas et habendas dictis abbati et conventui et suis successoribus inperpetuum in liberam, puram et perpetuam elemosinam de me et heredibus meis cum omnimodis pertinenciis et aysiamentis suis, libere, quiete, bene et in pace. Et ego dictus Willelmus et heredes mei vel assignati predictas quatuor placeas terre cum suis pertinenciis et aysiamentis in puram et perpetuam elemosinam predictis abbati et conventui vel suis successoribus imperpetuum contra omnes gentes warantizabimus, acquietabimus et ubique defendemus. In cuius rei etc. Hiis t[estibus] etc.

226. Quitclaim by the same William son of Geoffrey of Stanley to Beauchief abbey of 8 pieces of land lying separately in the territory of Stanley, *viz.* 1 called Arnedwodedole, 1 called Conslopdole, 1 called Worhuldole bordering on the great road which goes between Nottingham and Chesterfield,[1] 1 in Hirnynghulhal bordering on Somersall, 1 called Birkinschache, 2 called Hirnynghuldoles bordering similarly at one end at Somersall (Hall) to the south, and 1 called Frankbridgedole bordering at one end on Frankbridge.[2] [1190–1225]

[fo. 114v]

Alia carta eiusdem Willelmi

Sciant presentes et futuri quod ego Willelmus filius Galfridi de Stanleia dedi, concessi et omnino quietum clamavi de me et heredibus meis abbati et conventui de Bello Capite capitalibus dominis meis octo placeas terre divisim iacentes in territorio de Stanley, quarum una vocatur Arnedwodedole, alia Conslopdole, tercia Worhuldole buttantes super magnam viam que ducit inter Notyngham et Chestrefeld, et quarta iacet in Hirnynghulhal buttantes super Somerlesow, quinta vocatur Birkinshache, sexta et septima vocantur Hirnynghuldoles buttantes similiter ad unum capud super Somerlesow versus austrum, octava vocatur Frauncbrigdole buttans ad unum capud super Fraunkebrig. Tenendas et habendas dictis abbati et conventui et suis successoribus libere, quiete et integre, cum omnibus pertinenciis et aysiamentis suis, sine impedimento vel calumpnia mei vel heredum vel assignatorum meorum et sine omni demanda, servicio et consuetudine. Ita quod nec ego Willelmus nec heredes mei nec assignati mei nec aliquis alius nomine nostro quoquomodo aliquod jus vel clamium amodo in dictis octo placeis terre cum suis pertinenciis, nec in aliqua parte eorumdem, exigere vel vendicare poterimus. In cuius rei testimonium.[a]

[a]Charter left unfinished; confirmed in 1316 (Appendix II, no. 4).

[1]i.e. Stanley Lane and Silverhill Lane.
[2]See **222**, n. 2.

APPENDIX I: LEAKE CARTULARY DOCUMENTS RELATING TO BEAUCHIEF ABBEY

The Leake Cartulary is held at Derbyshire Record Office (D 1005 Z/E1). It was compiled *c.*1574 for Sir Francis Leake of Sutton, near Chesterfield (d. 1588), and contains extracts from several monastic cartularies relating to estates acquired by his family after the Dissolution. Twelve charters relating to Beauchief abbey's Harewood Grange estate in Beeley are transcribed on pages 39–43. Seven of these documents appear in the abbey's cartulary (**164–167, 183, 187–188**). The Leake copies were most probably transcribed from originals, rather than from this cartulary, and contain lists of witnesses and other details omitted there. These omissions have been given in the textual apparatus of the relevant documents printed above.

The documents printed below are those concerning the abbey but which do not appear in its cartulary. They have been given in full. The manuscript references (L) refer to the Leake Cartulary.

1. See **164**.

2. See **165**.

3. See **166**.

4. See **167**.

5. Gift in free alms by Walter Chauz,[1] son and heir of Thomas Chauz of Brampton, to Beauchief abbey of common of pasture at Harewood Grange and in the soke of Brampton. [1260–1289]

Omnibus Cristi fidelibus ad quorum noticiam presens scriptum pervenerit Walterus Chauz, filius et heres Thome Chauz de Bramton, salutem in Domino sempiternam. Noveritis me pro salute anime mee et omnium antecessorum[a] et successorum meorum dedisse, concessisse et hac presenti carta mea confirmasse abbati et conventui de Bello Capite et eorum successoribus, in liberam, puram et perpetuam elemosinam, communem pasture ad omnia animalia sua levancia vel cubancia ad grangiam suam de Harwod, vel ibidem causa pascue aliquo tempore[b] morancia, ubicumque voluerint in soka de Brampton, tam super moram quam super alias terras cultas et non cultas, ubi ego predictus Walterus vel alii liberi homines de soka de Bramton' communem antea habuimur. Tenendum et habendum dictis abbati et conventui et eorum successoribus in liberam, puram et perpetuam elemosinam, sine aliquo contradictione mei vel heredum meorum, sicut aliqua elemosina liberius haberi potuerit vel teneri. Ego vero dictus Walterus et heredes mei vel assignati predictum communem pasture predictis abbati et conventui et eorum successoribus in liberam, puram et perpetuam elemosinam, ut predictus est, cum libero introitu et exitu et omnibus aliis aisiamentis et pertinentiis suis contra omnes gentes warantizabimus, acquietabimus et ubique imperpetuum defendemus. In cuius rei testimonium presenti scripto sigillum meum apposui. Hiis testibus: domino Thome de Chaworth, domino Willelmo de Steynsbye et Johanne de Bramton,[1] cum aliis.[c2]

L p. 40.

W = British Library, Wolley Charters, III, 35 (I.H. Jeayes, *A Descriptive Catalogue of Derbyshire Charters in Public and Private Libraries and Muniment Rooms*, no. 426). The seal is missing.

R = Cambridge University Library, Add. MS 3897, pp. 18–19, transcript no. 6 by John Reynolds, junior, made in 1777; Reynolds notes that the seal is gone.

[a] *ancessorum* L   [b] *tempore* interlined.
[c] *Willelmo de Steynsbye et Johanne de Bramton, cum aliis*: Willielmo de Staynesby, Roberto le Graunt, Johanne de Bramton, Roberto de Reresby, Hugone de Linhaker, Nicholao de Holm, Thoma de Wodhuse, Petro de Le Bernes, et aliis R.

[1] His family came from Pays de Caux in Normandy. From the late twelfth century until the fifteenth century their Derbyshire seat was Caux Hall, Brampton, now Caushouse Farm (G. Turbutt, *A History of Derbyshire*, 4 vols (Cardiff, 1999), II, pp. 484–485, 491).
[2] Robert le Graunt witnessed **60** (1279); Sir William of Stainsby and Robert of Reresby together witnessed **90**.

6. Gift in free alms by Thomas of Beeley[1] to Beauchief abbey, for the sake of his soul and of that of his wife Cecily, of common of pasture for 80 she goats and their young under one year, of heather, turf, bracken, and quarry stone for all their needs, at Harewood grange below the common pasture at Beeley. Confirmation by Thomas of grants of

land, tenements, dues, and services made in Beeley by his ancestors. 24 December 1335.

Omnibus Cristi fidelibus hoc scriptum visuris vel audituris Thomas de Belegh' salutem in Domino. Noveritis me divine pietatis intuitu et pro salute anime mee et Cecelie uxoris mee et omnium antecessorum meorum et heredum meorum dedisse et concessisse Deo et ecclesie beati Thome martiri de Bello Capite et abbati et conventui ibidem Deo servientibus et eorum successoribus imperpetuum communem pasture ad octoginta capras cum eorum exitu unius anni, brueram, turbas, feugerium, cirpos et quarreram pro lapidibus fodiendis et cariandis ad necessaria sua apud grangiam suam de Harewod infra communem pasturam de Belegh=. Concessi enim et confirmavi eisdem abbati et conventui et eorum successoribus imperpetuum omnes terras et tenementa, redditus et servicia quorumque tenementorum et tenencium in Belegh = in liberam, puram et perpetuam elemosinam, que habuerunt ex dono et concessione quorumdam antecessorum meorum. Habenda et tenenda omnia hec predicta sibi et successoribus suis in liberam, puram et perpetuam elemosinam cum omnibus pertinentiis suis. Et ego predictus Thomas et heredes mei predictam communam pasture, brueram, turbas, feugerium, cirpos[a] et quarreram, terras et tenementa, redditus et servicia cum omnibus pertinentiis suis in Belegh', sine aliquo retenemento seu impedimento, contra omnes gentes warantizabimus, acquietabimus et ubique[b] defendemus. In cuius rei testimonium huic[c] presenti scripto sigillum meum apposui. Hiis testibus: Johanne Bard', Roberto de Muffeld de Bramton, Roberto de Gratton, Roberto de Knyveton, et aliis.[d] Dat' apud Belegh' die Dominica proxime[e] ante festum Natalis Domini anno Domini millesimo ccc^{mo} xxx^{mo} v^{to}.

L p. 40.

[a] possibly *cropas*, that is cropping (of trees).   [b] *uibique* L   [c] *hui* L
[d] *alii* L   [e] *post* struck through.

[1] Thomas de Belay, who confirmed the charters and grants of his ancestors, is commemorated in the Obituary (26 October).

7. Gift by Ralph of Freshmall, keeper of the property of Robert of Reresby,[1] to Beauchief abbey of common of pasture on the moor of Ashover and of dues and services from the tenement of Roger of Marcham and from two

cottages given by Robert of Reresby. Chirograph. [1260-1290]

Omnibus ad quos presens scriptum pervenerit Rad[ulph]us de Freshemall, custos terre et Seŕ Roberti de Reresby, salutem in Domino. Noveritis me concessisse religiosis viris abbati et conventui de Bello Capite quod ipsi habeant[a] pacificam possessionem communis pasture in mora de Esschoure, et quod habeant[b] possessionem redditus et servic[iorum] pertinentium de ten[emento] quod fuit Rogeri de Marcham et de duobus cotagiis que habuerunt ex donacione Roberti de Reresbye, prout in scriptis sibi factis per Robertum de Reresby et Margeriam, que fuit uxorem Rad[ulph]i de Reresby, continetur. Ita quod predicti religiosi viri per me vel aliquem meorum, ratione custodie Rad[ulph]i, filii et heredis Roberti de Reresby, vel ratione custodie heredis Galfridi, de monasteriis nullatenus de predictis redditibus vel serviciis, pastura vel cotagiis inquietent quoquomodo seu graventur. In cuius rei testimonium presenti scripto cirographato sigilla nostra alternatim apposuimus.

L p. 40.

[a] *heant* L   [b] *habeat* L

[1] Robert of Reresby witnessed **26** (*c*.1269–1289).

8. Gift in free alms – following a dispute in the wapentake of Scarsdale between abbot William of Folkingham[1] and the convent of Beauchief on the one hand and Margery, widow of Ralph of Reresby, on the other over pasture on the moor of Ashover – by Margery to Beauchief abbey of common of pasture on the moor of Ashover for all animals kept at their grange at Harewood within the following boundaries, *viz.* the land contained in the area from Serleforkes by Hereward's Street south to the road which leads from Darley to Shooterslea and then up past Peasunhirst to Wiliswodd and then to Alwaldsetes and Walton, then down to Eastwood; and of freedom from fines for escaped animals for the whole moor of Ashover beyond the aforesaid boundaries. Chirograph. [1290–1320]

Omnibus Cristi fidelibus hoc presens scriptum visuris vel audituris Margeria, quondam uxor Rad[ulph]i de Rerisby, salutem in Domino sempiternam. Noverit universitas vestra quod cum contencio mota fuit[a] in wapintak' de Scarnesdale[b] inter fratrem Willelmum de Folkingham[c] abbatem de Bello Capite et eiusdem loci conventum ex parte una et meipsam ex altera, super certis divisis in pastura more de Essover in qua predicti abbas et conventus et eorum predecessores communicaverunt[d] a tempore cuius non exstat[e] memoria cum omnimodis animalibus suis ad grangiam suam de Harewod quocumque modo pertinentibus, tandem communibus amicis intervenientibus quievit predicta contencio in hac forma: videlicet quod ego predicta Margeria concessi, in legittima viduitate mea, et de me et heredibus meis et quibuscumque assignatis meis omnino quietum clamavi,[f] in liberam, puram et perpetuam elemosinam, predictis abbati et conventui et eorum successoribus predictam communam[g] pasture in mora de Essover infra subscriptas divisas contentam ad omnimoda animalia sua ad grangiam suam de Harewod'[h] qualitercumque pertinencia et nomine dictorum abbatis et conventus de predicta grangia ad pascua exeuncia et per voluntatem[i] eorundem quoquomodo ad dictam grangiam commorancia, videlicet a Serlforkes per Herewardstrete versus austrum usque viam que ducit de Derley ad Scheterley,[j] et inde ascendendo per Paystonhirst usque de Wiliswodd,[k] et de Wiliswod[l] ascendendo usque in Alewoldsettes,[m] et inde usque divisas de Walton descendendo per easdem divisas usque Astwode, cum libere introitu et exitu et aliis quibuscumque aysiamentis suis. Concessi etiam et omnino quietum clamavi de me et heredibus meis et quibuscumque assignatis meis eisdem abbati et conventui et eorum successoribus, in liberam, puram et perpetuam elemosinam, liberum et quietum eschapium omnimodorum animalium suorum ad predictam grangiam de Harewode eorundem[n] quoquomodo ad predictam grangiam commorancium per totam moram de Essover ultra predictas divisas, sine omni calumpnia et perturbacione mei et heredum meorum et quorumcumque assignatorum meorum. Et ego predicta Margeria et heredes mei et assignati mei dictam communam[o] pasture et predictum eschapium ad omnimoda animalia sua, prout superius dictum est, cum libero introitu et exitu et aliis aysiamentis suis predictis abbati et conventui et eorum successoribus, in liberam, puram et perpetuam elemosinam, contra omnes gentes warantizabimus, adquietabimus et inperpetuum defendemus. In cuius rei testimonium tam ego predicta Margeria pro me et heredibus meis et assignatis quam predicti abbas et conventus hiis scriptis cirographatis alternatim sigilla nostra apposuimus. Hiis testibus: domino Willelmo de[p] Reyrisby,[q] Waltero de Mighale,[r] Willelmo de

Foliambe,[s] Roberto le Graunt, Johanne le Brimington,[t] Rogero le Bret, Hugone de Taxforth,[u] Hugone de Linakre,[2] Petro de Bernis.[v]

L p. 41.

R = Cambridge University Library, Add. MS 3897, pp. 4–6, transcript no. 4 by John Reynolds, junior, dated 11 February 1777. Reynolds describes an oval seal of green wax, almost all broken off; of the circumscription nothing remains except ...IS + SIG...

[a] *fuerit* R   [b] *Scaruesdale* R   [c] *Folkigham* R   [d] *communucaverunt* L
[e] *extat* L   [f] *quieteclamaui* R   [g] *communiam* R   [h] *Harewode* R
[i] *pro uoluntate* R   [j] *Scheterleye* R   [k] *Deruiliswode* R   [l] *Deruiliswode* R
[m] *Alewoldsetes* R   [n] *Harewode eorundem: Harewod qualitercunque pertinencium et nomine dictorum abbatis et conventus de dicta grangia ad Pascua exeuncium et pro uoluntate eorundem* R
[o] *communiam* R   [p] *le* R   [q] *Steynesby* R   [r] *repinghale* R   [s] *Folejambe* R
[t] *Brummington* R   [u] *Tuxforth* R   [v] *Bernis: Bernis, Johanne de bircheved* R

[1] Abbot William of Folkingham occurs 1296 (see above no. **99**), died 1324 (D.M. Smith and V.C.M. London (eds), *Heads of Religious Houses: England and Wales, II: 1216–1377* (Cambridge, 2001), p. 494; H.M. Colvin, *The White Canons in England* (Oxford, 1951); see also Leake **9** (below).

[2] John of Brimington, Roger le Bret, and Hugh of Linacre appear together as witnesses in **18**, **33**, **39**, **40**, **51**, and Leake **9**.

9. Gift in free alms – following a dispute in the wapentake of Scarsdale between abbot William of Folkingham and the convent of Beauchief on the one hand and Robert of Reresby, son and heir of Ralph of Reresby, on the other over the boundaries of the pasture on the moor of Ashover – by Robert to Beauchief abbey of common of pasture on the moor of Ashover for all their animals kept at Harewood grange within the following boundaries, *viz.* the land contained in the area from Serleforkes by Hereward's Street south to the road which leads from Darley to Shooterslea, and then up past Peasunhirst to Develiswode and up further to Alwaldesetes, then from Walton down to Eastwood; and of freedom from fines for escaped animals for the whole moor of Ashover beyond the aforesaid boundaries. Chirograph. [1290–1320]

Omnibus Cristi fidelibus hoc scriptum visuris vel audituris Robertus de Rerysby filius et heres Rad[ulph]i de Rerysby salutem in Domino sempiternam. Noverit universitas vestra quod cum contencio mota fuerit in wapentak de Skerinsdale inter fratrem Willelmum de Folkyngham abbatem de Bello Capite et eiusdem loci conventum ex una parte et meipsum ex altera, super certis divisis in pastura[a] more de Essover in qua predicti abbas et conventus et eorum predecessores communicaverunt a tempore cuius[b] non existat[c] memoria cum omnimodis animalibus suis ad grangiam suam de Harewod quocumque modo pertinent[ibus], tandem communibus amicis intervenientibus quievit predicta contencio in hac forma, videlicet quod ego predictus Robertus concessi et de me et heredibus meis et quibuscumque assignatis meis omnino quietum clamavi, in liberam, puram et perpetuam elemosinam, predictis abbati et conventui et eorum successoribus predictam communam pasture[d] in mora de Essover infra supradictas divisas contentam, ad omnimoda animalia sue ad grangiam suam de Harewod qualitercumque pertinentes, et nomine dictorum abbatis et conventus de predicta grangia ad pascua exeuncia et per voluntatem eorumdem quoquomodo ad predictam grangiam commorancia, videlicet a Serleforkes per Herwardstrete versus austrum usque viam que ducit de Derley ad Scheterlei, et inde ascendendo per Paystonhyrst usque Develiswode, et de Develiswode ascendendo usque in[e] Alewoldsetes' et inde usque divisas de Walton[f] descendendo per easdem divisas usque Astwode, cum libero introitu et exito et aliis quibuscumque aysiamentis suis. Concessi enim et omnino quietum clamavi de me et heredibus meis et quibuscumque assignatis meis eisdem abbati et conventui et eorum successoribus in liberam, puram et perpetuam elemosinam liberum et quietum eschapium omnimodorum animalium suorum ad predictam grangiam[g] de Harewod qualitercumque pertinentium, et nomine dictorum abbatis et conventus de dicta grangia ad pascua exeuncium et per voluntatem eorumdem quoquomodo ad predictam grangiam commorancium, per totam moram de Essover ultra predictas divisas, sine omni calumpnia et perturbacione mei et heredum meorum et quorumcumque assignatorum meorum. Et ego predictus Robertus et heredes mei et assignati mei dictam communam pasture et predictum eschapium ad omnimoda animalia sua, prout superius dictus est, cum libero introitu et exitu et aliis aysiamentis suis predictis abbati et conventui et eorum successoribus, in liberam, puram et perpetuam elemosinam, contra omnes gentes warantizabimus, acquietabimus et inperpetuum defendemus. In cuius rei testimonium tam ego predictus Robertus pro me et heredibus meis et assignatis meis quam predicti abbas et conventus hiis scriptis cyrographatis alternatim sigilla nostra apposuimus. Hiis testibus: domino Willelmo de Staynesbye, Waltero de Bringhale, Willelmo Foleiaumbe, Roberto le Graunte, Johanne de

APPENDIX I

Brimyngton, Roger le Bret, Hugone de Tuxforth, Hugone de Lynacre, Petro de Herris, Johanne de Byrgeved, et aliis.[1]

L p. 41.

[a] *de* struck through. [b] *not* struck through. [c] *extat* L
[d] *pasture* interlined. [e] *Alewoldstettes* struck through. [f] *decess* struck through.
[g] *comorancium per totam moram de Essover ultra d predictas divisas sine* struck through.

[1] See also Leake **8**. John of Brimington, Roger le Bret, and Hugh of Linacre appear together as witnesses in **18**, **33**, **39**, **40**, **51**, and Leake **8**. Petro de Herris may be a misreading by the Elizabethan scribe of Petro de Bernis, a frequent witness of contemporary charters.

10. See **183**.

11. See **187**.

12. See **188**.

APPENDIX II: THE ROYAL CONFIRMATION OF 1316

Willliam Dugdale (see W. Dugdale *Monasticon Anglicanum*, ed. J. Caley, Sir H. Ellis, and B. Bandinel, 6 vols (1817–1830), VI.2, pp. 884–886) printed the royal confirmation, made at Lincoln on 20 February 1316, of fifty-five charters relating to Beauchief abbey, of which summaries were entered on the Patent Roll, 9 Edward II, p. 1 m. 3. Each item in this confirmation, reproduced here from Dugdale, is given a number so that, with the aid of the Concordance in Appendix III, corresponding items in the Cartulary and in the Confirmation of 1312 (**38**) can be found. Eighteen of the charters confirmed in 1316 are not recorded in the extant part of the Cartulary; of these an English summary is given.

Carta Regis Edwardi Secundi, Concessiones Donatorum recitans et confirmans.

REX omnibus ad quos, etc. salutem.

1. Donationem quam Robertus filius Ranulphi fecit Deo et sanctae Mariae, et sancto Thomae martyri, et fratribus in ordine Praemonstratensi professis, de loco, qui dicitur Beauchef, cum pertinentiis, qui in Dorhesele situs est, ad abbaciam construendam; et de ecclesiis de Norton, Alferton, Wymandeswald, et Edwaldeston; et de molendinis de Norton, cum omni multura et operibus suis; et de sarto Hugonis, juxta Meresbrok; et uno tofto in Leys; et uno tofto juxta domum Alani; et de tota decima pannagii totius terrrae suae; et de duabus bovatis terrae in Wymundwald de dominio suo; et de uno tofto continente tres acras terrre cum pertinentiis.
2. Donationem etiam et confirmationem, quas dictus Robertus fecit praefatis fratribus de una bovata terrae in Wymundwold quae fuit Alexandri, cum tofto suo, et de una bovata terrae quae fuit Lunechild viduae, cum pertinentiis.
3. Donationem etiam, et confirmationem, quas idem Robertus fecit eisdem fratribus, de loco qui dicitur Brokhirst cum pertinentiis.

4. Donationem etiam et confirmationem quas Willielmus filius Roberti fecit eisdem fratribus de molendino de Aston, cum omni multura.
5. Donationem, concessionem, et confirmationem, quas Robertus filius Willielmi de Alfertona fecit eisdem fratribus de illa terra cum pertinentiis, quas Helias de Touey de eo tenuit.
6. Donationem etiam, concessionem, et confirmationem quas idem Robertus fecit canonicis loci praedicti, de sexaginta acris terrae, per perticam viginti quatuor pedum in Alferton, cum bosco supercrescente.
7. Donationem etiam concessionem, et confirmationem, quas idem Robertus fecit eisdem canonicis de tribus acris terrae, per perticam vigniti quatuor pedum, juxta rivulum qui descendit ab abbatial ad majorem rivum de Shewe, ex parte aquilonis; et de una libra cimini de terra de Sireokkes.
8. Donationem, etc. quas idem Robertus fecit eisdem canonicis, de xxiv acris terrae per perticam xxiiii pedum, in Nortone, cum bosco supercrescente.
9. Donationem, etc. quas Thomas filius Willielmi de Chaworth fecit dictis canonicis de una bovata terrae cum pertinentiis, quam Adam filius Johannis del Cliff aliquando tenuit de ipso in Nortona, et de quinque acris assarti cum uno parcello in bosco de Nortone, quas idem Adam de ipso tenuit; et de ipso Adam cum tota sequela sua, et eorum catallis; et de una bovata terrae in Bradewaye; et de octo acris assarti in eodem bosco de Nortona cum pertinentiis quas Thomas filius Hugonis de Bosco de ipso tenuit; et de ipso Thoma cum tota sequela sua, et eorum catallis; et dimidia bovata terrae, cum pertinentiis in Cokshet, quam Winora de ipso tenuit, et de ipsa Wynora, cum tota sequela sua, et eorum catallis; et de uno assarto cum uno tofto, cum pertinentiis, in eadem villa, quae Henricus le Bercher de ipso tenuit; et de vi acris terrae, cum pertinentiis, jacentibus juxta aquam de Sewe, quas Ricardus de Mora de ipso tenuit; et de quater viginti acris terrae cum pertinentiis in bosco de Nortone, jacentibus ex parte aquilonari parci abbatis et conventus de Beauchef.
10. Donationem etiam, etc, quas praedictus Thomas fecit abbati et conventui loci praedicti, de xviii s redditus, quos Robertus le Redsmith sibi reddere consuevit, pro tenemento quod de ipso tenuit in Swanwyk, juxta Alfertone, cum pertinentiis; et de toto illo assarto cum tofto et crofto et pertinentiis, quod Rogerus Faber de ipso tenuit in Birchewode in soca de Alfertone; et de una bovata terrae, cum pertinentiis, quam Adam de Birchewode, de ipso tenuit in eadem villa; et de tota illa terra, cum pertinentiis, quam Rogerus le Bercher de ipso tenuit in praedicta soca de

Alfertone; et de toto illo assarto, quod vocatur Robert...Rideings, cum pertinentiis; et de duabus solidatis redditus et tenemento quod Rogerus Mous tenuit in Alfarton; et de duodecim denariatis redditus de tenemento quod Nicholaus Thorald de ipso tenuit in Alfertone; et de illa bovata terrae cum pertinentiis, quam Ricardus Horeghe de ipso tenuit in Bradeweye; et de Roberto del Grene nativo suo, cum tota sequela sua, et omnibus catallis suis; et de toto tenemento quod de ipso tenuit in bondagio in soca de Norton cum pertinentiis.

11. Donationem, etc, quas idem Thomas fecit etc. de tota illa terra, cum pertinentiis, quam Ricardus de Mora de ipso tenuit in Cokshet.

12. Concessionem, etc. quas idem Thomas fecit, etc. de toto illa assarto integre cum pertinentiis in bosco de Norton, jacente ex parte aquilonari parci dictorum abbatis et conventus, cum tota longitudine et latitudine usque ad filum aquae de Sheue. [Grant by Thomas son of William Chaworth of all the assart in Norton wood to the north of the abbey's park and along its whole length and width as far as the middle of the river Sheaf.] [1247–1316]

13. Donationem, etc. quas idem Thomas fecit, etc. dictis canonicis, de uno tofto et crofto, cum aedificiis et pertinentiis suis in Cokshete, quod Johannes Faber de ipso tenuit, et de uno cartilagio in Aufertone, juxta orreum praedictorum canonicorum.

14. Donationem, etc. quas idem Thomas fecit praedictis abbati [et conventui] de tota illa placea terrae, quae vocatur Eycliffe, cum bosco supercrescente.

15. Donationem, etc. quas idem Thomas fecit, etc. de tota illa terra, quae vocatur le Whittek et de xii acris terrae in loco qui vocatur Barsfeld; et de illa placea terrae, quam Petrus Textor de ipso tenuit in Alferton.

16. Donationem, etc. quas idem Thomas fecit, etc. de quodam assarto, quod Robertus Forestarius de ipso tenuit juxta bercariam dictorum canonicorum; et de tribus acris terrae. quas Robertus del Childre de ipso tenuit infra clausum dictorum canonicorum ; et de octo acris terrae, et dimidia, quas Ranulphus de Storches de ipso tenuit, et de quinque acris terrae et dimidia quas Ricardus Everard de ipso tenuit in Alferton, cum pertinentiis.

17. Donationem, etc. quas idem Thomas fecit etc. de tota illa terra, cum pertinentiis, quam Thomas de Bosco et Willielmus Tynet de ipso tenuerunt in le Wodesetes.

18. Donationem, etc. quas idem Thomas fecit, etc. de tota illa bovata terrae, cum toftis, croftis, aedificiis, et omnibus aliis pertinentiis suis, quam Richardus Hore de ipso tenuit in le Bradeway.

19. Donationem, etc. quas idem Thomas fecit, etc. de illo annuo redditu quinque solidorum, quem sibi solvere consueverunt pro illa terra, quam dicti abbas et conventus de eo tenuerunt in soca de Nortone.
20. Donationem, etc. quas idem Thomas fecit, etc. de libero et quieto passagio habendo ad feriam suam de Marnham, tam terris quam familiae suae, de abbacia praedicta: et de omnibus aliis locis suis, cum omnibus animalibus, rebus, ac cariagiis suis quibuscunque et quandocunque opus habuerint in meliori navigio feriae suae praedictae.
21. Donationem, etc. quas idem Thomas fecit, etc. de una placea terrae, jacente ex parte occidentali aulae suae, in Alferton.
22. Donationem, etc. quas Thomas de Chaworth miles, dominus de Norton, fecit dictis abbati et conventui, de toto illo hameleto in soca de Nortone quod vocatur Grenehill, simul cum mora de Grenehil, et cum homagiis, wardis, releviis, etc. Et de omnibus terris et tenementis, quae Hugo de Parva Norton de ipso tenuit in villenagio, in Parva Norton et Wodesetes; et de ipso Hugone cum tota sequel sua, et omnibus catallis suis.
23. Remissionem, etc. quas idemThomas fecit, etc. de xii s et viii d redditus, quas praefati abbas et conventus sibi reddere solebant pro diversis tenementis, quae de ipso tenuerunt in Alfertone et Nortone.
24. Donationem, etc. quas idem Thomas fecit, etc. de omnibus terris, etc. quae de ipso tenentur in villenagio in Wodesetes, juxta Norton; et de omnibus villanis suis ibidem cum totis sequelis suis, et omnibus catallis suis. [Gift by Thomas Chaworth of all lands held of him in villeinage in Woodseats by Norton, and of all their villeins with all their households and chattels.] [1247–1316]
25. Donationem, etc. quas idem Thomas fecit, etc. de Rogero de Bradewaye, Gileberto de Bradewaye, et Emma, ad novum molendinum, nativis suis, cum omnibus catallis, sequelis, sectis, et serviciis suis et cum omnibus terris, toftis, croftis, et aedificiis, quae de ipso tenuerunt in Nortone.
26. Nortone, cum pertinentiis; et de terra ubicunque eisdem necesse fuerit, per totum wastum suum, ad fossas suas ampliandas, et levandas, capiendum. Et de terra et turbis ad domus suas emendandas, et cooperiendas.
27. Donationem, etc. quas idem Thomas fecit, etc. de licentia et libera potestate ad carbones fodendos, levandos, asportandos, et cariandos, ad utilitatem et profectum suum, et eorum tenentium, tam liberorum quam nativorum, quocienscunque sibi necessse fuerit, tam in terris tenentium, dictorum abbatis et conventus,

quam in terris suis propriis, et wastis inter terras suas, infra socas de Alfertone et Nortone.

28. Concessionem etiam, quam idem Thomas fecit, etc. de terris suis et terris tenentium suorum, tam liberorum quam nativorum, a goldis mundandis per se et suos, secundum consuetudinem in socis de Alferton et Norton usitatam. [Leave granted by Thomas Chaworth to clear corn marigolds from his lands and those of his tenants, both free and villein, as is the custom of the sokes of Alfreton and Norton.] [1247–1316]

29. Donationem, etc. quas Lucas filius Warneri de Beygle fecit dictis canonicis, de tota terra, quae vocatur Harewode, cum pertinentiis; et de pastura ad xl vaccas, et duos tauros cum exitu duorum annorum, ad decem equas cum exitu trium annorum: et ad boves carucarum suarum; et ad octingentas oves et xxx porcos, et ad xl capras per omnem communiam de Beygle, undique et ubique, et de concessione liberi eschap, de omnibus animalibus praedictis.

30. Donationem, etc. quas Radulfus Musard fecit dictis canonicis de villula de Hauley [*sic*] cum hominibus, absque ullo retenemento. [Gift by Ralph Musard of the vill of Handley with men and with no restrictions.] [1200–1229][1]

31. Donationem, etc. quas idem Radulfus fecit, etc. de tota terra, quam habuit in villa de Wadeself, cum pertinentiis; et cum hominibus et eorum serviciis. [Gift by Ralph Musard of land in the vill of Wadshelf with men and their services.] [1200–1229][2]

32. Donationem, etc. quas idem Radulfus fecit dictis canonicis de tota terra, cum bosco super existente in Hauley [*sic*], cum multurae libertate. [Gift by Ralph Musard of all the land and wood on it in Handley with free multure.] [1200–1229][3]

33. Donationem, etc. quas Radulfus Musard filius Radulfi Musard fecit, etc. de tota terra, et toto prato in Hinkershull, de feodo suo de Staveleye. [Grant by Ralph Musard son of Ralph Musard of all the land and meadow in Inkersall of his fee of Staveley.] [1219–1250]

34. Donationem, etc. quas Walterus de Furneus filius Roberti de Furneus fecit, etc. de tribus bovatis, et una acra terrae, et duobus

---

[1] See **222**, n. 4. Both Ralph I and Ralph II appear in C.J. Holdsworth (ed.), *Rufford Charters*, 4 vols (Nottingham, 1972–1981), nos 62, 65, 69, 79, and 83; dates given for Ralph I are before 1230 and for Ralph II before 1270.

[2] On 1 July 1230 the sheriff of Nottingham was instructed that, notwithstanding the king's retention of the lands of Ralph Musard, land given by Ralph to the abbey in Handley and Wadshelf should be held by the abbey in peace (*Calendar of Patent Rolls, Henry III: 1227–1231*, p. 357).

[3] See the previous note.

toftis in Birlay; et de una placea prati in Bettona, quae vocatur Ormesmedwe; et de duabus acris terrae et dimidia, quae vocantur Ormesland. [Grant by Walter of Fourness son of Robert of Fourness of 3 bovates, 1 acre of land and 2 tofts in Birley, a parcel of meadow in Beighton called Ormesmeadow, and $2\frac{1}{2}$ acres called Ormesland.] [1230–1260]

35. Donationem, etc. quas Willielmus filius Andreae de Hetone fecit dictis canonicis de xxs. redditus, percipiendis de tenentibus suis in Golthorp.
36. Donationem, etc. quas Johannes filius Ricardi Daniel fecit dictis canonicis, de xi s redditus cum pertinentiis, in Swyntone et Billingley.
37. Donationem, etc. quas Gerardus de Furnival fecit dictis canonicis de pastura herbagii in foresta sua de Folwode, sufficiente ad xxx vaccas, et ad earum exitum trium annorum: et de una acra terrae in eadem foresta, ad logias faciendas ad praedictas vaccas. [Gift by Gerard of Furnival of pasture for thirty cows and their calves under three years in Fulwood and of an acre of land to provide lodges for them there.] [1195–1219]
38. Donationem, etc. quas idem Gerardus fecit dictis canonicis de xxs. redditus, percipiendis de molendino suo de Sheffeld. [Gift by Gerard of Furnival of rent of 20s from his mill in Sheffield.] [1195–1219]
39. Donationem etiam, etc. quas Matildis de Lovetot fecit dictis canonicis, de una marcata redditus, percipienda de molendino suo de Sheffeild. [Gift by Matilda of Lovetot of rent of 1 mark from her mill in Sheffield.] [1219–1250]
40. Concessionem etiam, etc. quas eadem Matildis fecit dictis canonicis de tota elemosina, quam Gerardus de Furnival, vir suus, eis dedit. [Grant by Matilda of Lovetot of all the free alms granted by her husband, Gerard of Furnival.] [1219–1250]
41. Concessionem etiam et confirmationem, quam Thomas de Furnival dominus de Halumshire, fecit dictis abbati et conventui, de grangia sua de Folewode, et de tota terra ad praedictam grangiam pertinente, cum pertinentiis, et de communia pasturae sufficiente, in liberis chaceis et pasturis suis de Folewode, et Rynelingdene, ubique ad omnia animalia sua, exceptis capris; et de omnimodo aisiamento bruerii, quarrerii, turbarii, junctii, et feugerii ad domos suos cooperiendos; et alia necessaria sua facienda; et de terra de wasta suo sufficienter capienda, ad fossas suas emendandas et relevandas. [Grant by Thomas of Furnival, lord of Hallamshire, of his grange and all its land in Fulwood; of common of pasture in Fulwood and Rynelingdene for all the animals except she-goats; of every right to take heather, stone,

peat, rushes, and bracken to roof their houses and to meet other needs; and to take from the waste sufficient earth to keep their ditches in repair.] [1225–1260]

42. Donationem, etc. quas Thomas de Furnival, filius et haeres Thomae de Furnival, filii Gerardi de Furnival, fecit dictis abbati et conventui, de quatuor acris prati cum pertinentiis in Sheffelde, in le Brodenge, ex parte occidentali de Halleker. [Gift by Thomas of Furnival son and heir of Thomas of Furnival son of Gerard of Furnival of four acres of meadow in Sheffield in le Brodenge (Broad Inge?) on the west side of Halleker.] [1225–1260]

43. Donationem, etc. quas Willielmus Barre de Tiversholte fecit dictis canonicis, de una bovata terrae, cum duobus toftis et croftis cum pertinentiis, in Stanelcia; et de pastura trescentis ovibus, xx vaccis, uni tauro, et octo equabus, cum toto exitu suo, tam vaccarum, quam equarum, donec sit trium annorum, et xvi bobus; et de communia ad necessaria sua facienda in bosco et plano.

44. Donationem, etc. quas Willielmus filius Galfridi de Stanleia fecit, etc. de octo placeis terrae, divisim jacentibus, cum pertinentiis, in Stanley.

45. Donationem,etc, quas Willielmus filius Radulfi Barry, de Tiversand, fecit, etc. de dimidia marcata redditus, cum pertinentiis, quam Willielmus filius Galfridi de Stanley ei reddere solebat. [Grant by William son of Ralph Barry of Teversal of rent of half a mark which William son of Geoffrey of Stanley used to pay to him.]

46. Donationem, etc. quas Gervasius de Bernak fecit, etc. de toto redditu, cum pertinentiis, in Brom, quem emit de Jordano Heryng de Heringthorp. [Gift by Gervase of Bernak of all the rent in Broom which he bought from Jordan Herring of Herringthorpe.] [1240–1280]

47. Donationem, etc. quas Robertus filius Radulfi de Reresby fecit, etc. de quatuor solidatis et quatuor denariatis redditus, percipiendis de terra, quam Rogerus de Markham quondam tenuit de eo in soca de Essover.

48. Donationem, etc. quas Ricardus del Bernes fecit, etc. de duobus messuagiis et duobus toftis, cum pertinentiis, in Ashover.

49. Donationem, etc. quas Lucas de Beygle fecit, etc. de redditu dimidiae marcae in molendino suo de Beygle. [1200–1230]

50. Donationem, etc. quas Sarlo, filius Waneri de Begley, fecit dictis canonicis de dimidia marca in molendino suo de Begley annuatim percipienda. [1200–1230]

51. Relaxationem, etc. quas Tho. de Chaworth fecit, etc. de toto illo servicio calcarium deauratorum, quae sibi annuatim solvere tenebantur ad Pascha, pro tota illa terra et tenemento, cum

pertinentiis, quae de ipso tenuerunt in Wymondwold, et quae habuerunt de dono Rogeri de Allirtone.

52. Concessionem, etc, quas Tho. de Chaworth filius Willielmi de Chaworth, fecit, etc. de omnibus terris, etc. quas iidem abbas et conventus habent de dono et concessione Tho. de Chaworth, avi sui, caeterorumque antecessorum suorum in Wymundwold et Marnham, et in socis de Norton et Alferton.

53. Remissionem, etc. quas Willielmus filius Ricardi filii Alani de la Bradwaye, fecit, etc. de toto jure et clamio quod habuit in tota illa terra, cum pertinentiis, quam Petrus de Bircheheved dedit praedicto Ricardo patri suo in liberum maritagium, cum Margeria filia sua. [Release by William son of Richard son of Alan of Bradway from all his right and claim over all the land which Peter of Birchitt gave to the said Richard, his father, on his marriage to his daughter Margery.] [1270–1300]

54. Remissionem, etc. quas Tho. filius Rogeri, filii Adae del Clyf, fecit, etc. de toto jure suo et clamio quod habuit in tota illa placea prati, quod vocatur Moseker, et de duabus acris terrae in le Wodesetes. [Release by Thomas son of Roger son of Adam of the Cliff from all his right and claim over all the parcel of meadow called Moseker and two acres of land in Woodseats.]

55. Remissionem, etc. quas Rogerus filius Willielmus [*sic*] de Holyns fecit, etc. de toto jure et clamio quod habuit in toto illo tenemento, cum pertinentiis, quod habent de dono et concessione Willielmi del Holyns, patris sui, in le Holyns; habendas et tenendas in puram et perpetuam elemosinam praefatis abbati, fratribus, et canonicis, et successoribus suis, ratas habentes et gratas, eas pro nobis et haeredibus nostris, etc. confirmamus, etc. T. rege apud Lincoln. xx die Februarii.

APPENDIX III: CONCORDANCE

Concordance A

Entries in the Cartulary that are recorded in the General Confirmation in 1312 by Thomas Chaworth of grants made by him and his ancestors or in the Royal Confirmation in 1316 by King Edward II or in both; entries in the General Confirmation in 1312 and the Royal Confirmation in 1316 which are not found in the Cartulary.

Cartulary	Confirmation in 1312	Confirmation in 1316
4	1	1
5	2	2
6	3	3
7	4	4
8	5	5
–	7	6
9	6	7
10	8	8
21	9	9
22	10	10
23	11	11
–	–	12
24	13	13
25	12	14
26	14	15
27	15	16
28	16	17
29	17	18
30	18	19
31	19	20
32	20	21
33	22	22
33	22	23
–	–	24
35	–	25
36	–	26

APPENDIX III

Cartulary	Confirmation in 1312	Confirmation in 1316
37[1]	–	27
–	–	28
–	–	30
–	–	31
–	–	32
–	–	33
–	–	34
60	21	51
62	–	52
106	–	35
109	–	36
–	–	37
–	–	38
–	–	39
–	–	40
–	–	41
–	–	42
154	–	55
168	–	50
172	–	29
173	–	49
179	–	47
180	–	48
222	–	43
226	–	44
–	–	45
–	–	46
–	–	53
–	–	54

[1] Copied in **81**.

Concordance B

Entries in the Cartulary which are not found in the General Confirmation in 1312 or in the Royal Confirmation in 1316.

Cartulary	Confirmation in 1312	Confirmation in 1316
1–3	–	–
11–20	–	–
34	–	–
38–59	–	–
61	–	–
63–105	–	–
107–108	–	–
110–127	–	–
129–153	–	–
155–167	–	–
169–171	–	–
173–178	–	–
180–221	–	–
223–225	–	–

BIBLIOGRAPHY

Addy, S.O., 'A contribution to the history of Norton in Derbyshire', *Journal of the Derbyshire Archaeological and Natural History Society*, 2 (1880), pp. 2–27

────── 'The discoveries at Beauchief', *Transactions of the Hunter Archaeological Society*, 4 (1935), pp. 249–252

────── *Historical Memorials of Beauchief Abbey* (Oxford, London, and Sheffield, 1878)

────── 'Some ancient documents relating to Totley, Dore, and Holmesfield, near Dronfield', *Journal of the Derbyshire Archaeological and Natural History Society*, 3 (1881), pp. 95–107

Alexander, J. and P. Binski (eds), *Age of Chivalry: art in Plantagenet England, 1200–1400* (London, 1987)

Andrewes, C.B. (ed.), *The Torrington Diaries*, II (London, 1935)

Armitage, H., *Chantrey Land* (London, 1910)

Astle, T., S. Ayscough, and J. Caley (eds), *Taxatio ecclesiastica Angliae et Walliae auctoritate P. Nicolai IV, circa A. D. 1291* (London, 1802)

Backmund, N., *Monasticon Praemonstratense, id est historia circariarum et canoniarum candidi ordinis praemonstratensis*, 3 vols (Straubing, 1949–1956)

Ball, C., D. Crossley, and N. Flavell (eds), *Water Power on the Sheffield Rivers*, 2nd edn (Sheffield, 2006)

Battye, K., *Unstone: the history of a village* (privately published, 1981)

Bestall, J.M., *Early and Medieval Chesterfield* (Chesterfield, 1974)

Black, W.H., *A Descriptive, Analytical and Critical Catalogue of the Manuscripts Bequeathed unto the University of Oxford by Elias Ashmole* (Oxford, 1845)

Brown, W. (ed.), *Yorkshire Lay Subsidy*, Yorkshire Archaeological Society Record Series 16 (1894)

Burton, J., *Monastic and Religious Orders in Britain, 1000–1300* (Cambridge, 1994)

Calendar of Charter Rolls, Henry III, I, 1226–1257

Calendar of Close Rolls, Henry III, I, 1227–1231

Calendar of Patent Rolls, Edward I, III, 1292–1301

Calendar of Patent Rolls, Henry IV, III, 1405–1408

Calendar of Patent Rolls, Henry IV, IV, 1408–1413

Calendar of Patent Rolls, Richard II, IV, 1388–1392

Calendar of Patent Rolls, Richard II, V, 1391–1396

Caley, J. and J. Hunter (eds), *Valor Ecclesiasticus Temp. Henr. VIII. auctoritate regia institutus*, 6 vols (London, 1810–1834)

Cameron, K., *The Place-names of Derbyshire*, 3 vols (Cambridge, 1959)

Chatfield, M., *Churches the Victorians Forgot* (Ashbourne, 1979)

Colvin, H.M., *The White Canons in England* (Oxford, 1951)

Cox, J.C., 'The abbey of Beauchief', *Victoria County History: Derbyshire*, II (1907), pp. 63–69

Crook, D., 'Hardwick before Bess: the origins and early history of the family of Hardwick, of Hardwick, co. Derby', *Derbyshire Archaeological Journal*, 107 (1987), pp. 41–54

Cross, C. and N. Vickers, *Monks, Friars and Nuns in Sixteenth Century Yorkshire*, Yorkshire Archaeological Society Record Series 150 (1995)

Darlington, R.R., *The Cartulary of Darley Abbey*, 2 vols (Kendal, 1945)

──── *The Glapwell Charters, Derbyshire Archaeological Journal*, 86–87 (1956–1957)

Dugdale, W., *Monasticon Anglicanum*, ed. J. Caley, H. Ellis, and B. Bandinel, 6 vols (1817–1830)

Elgar, W.H., 'Beauchief abbey', *Transactions of the Hunter Archaeological Society*, 3 (1926), pp. 162–164

Emden, A.B., *Biographical Register of the University of Oxford to A.D. 1500*, 3 vols (Oxford, 1957–1959)

Farrer, W. (ed.), *Early Yorkshire Charters*, III, Yorkshire Archaeological Society Record Series, extra series (Edinburgh, 1916)

──── *Honours and Knights' Fees*, I (London and Manchester, 1923)

Foster, C.W. and K. Major (eds), *The 'Registrum Antiquissimum' of the Cathedral Church of Lincoln*, 10 vols, Lincoln Record Society 27–29, 32, 34, 41, 46, 51, 62, 67 (1931–1973)

Fowkes, D.V. and G.R. Potter (eds), *William Senior's Survey of the Estates of the First and Second Earls of Devonshire, c.1600–1628*, Derbyshire Record Society 13 (1988)

Garratt, H.J.H. (ed.), *Derbyshire Feet of Fines, 1323–1546*, Derbyshire Record Society 11 (Chesterfield, 1985)

Gibbs, V. and H.A. Doubleday (eds), *The Complete Peerage of England, Scotland, Ireland, Great Britain and the United Kingdom*, VI (London, 1926)

Gover, J.E.B., A. Mawer, and F.M. Stenton, *The Place-names of Nottinghamshire* (Cambridge, 1940)

Hall, T.W., *A Descriptive Catalogue of . . . Ancient Charters and Instruments of Ughill, Waldershelf and Norton Lees* (Sheffield, 1930)

―――― *A Descriptive Catalogue of Charters, Copy Court Rolls and Deeds Forming Part of the Wheat Collection* (Sheffield, 1920)

―――― *A Descriptive Catalogue of Early Charters Relating to Lands In and Near Sheffield* (Sheffield, 1938)

―――― *A Descriptive Catalogue of Miscellaneous Charters and Other Documents Relating to the Districts of Sheffield and Rotherham* (Sheffield, 1916)

―――― *A Descriptive Catalogue of Sheffield Manorial Records*, III (Sheffield, 1934)

―――― and A.H. Thomas, *A Descriptive Catalogue of the Charters . . . Forming the Jackson Collection at the Sheffield Public Reference Library* (Sheffield, 1914)

Hart, W.H., 'A calendar of the fines for the county of Derby from their commencement in the reign of Richard I: 1196–1225', *Journal of the Derbyshire Archaeological and Natural History Society*, 7 (1885), no. 38

Harte, R. and C. Merrony, 'Two way traffic: the importance of Beauchief Abbey as a case study for the Premonstratensian Order in England', in *A Review of Archaeology in South Yorkshire, 1994–1995*, compiled by the South Yorkshire Archaeology Service (Sheffield, 1995), pp. 81–88

Hearnius, T. (ed.), *Johannis . . . Glastoniensis sive historia de rebus Glastonieansibus*, 2 vols (Oxford, 1726)

Henstock, A., 'The course of Hereward Street: a reappraisal', *Derbyshire Archaeological Journal*, 100 (1980), pp. 35–42

Hey, D., *Derbyshire: a history* (Lancaster, 2008)

―――― *Historic Hallamshire* (Ashbourne, 2002)

Holdsworth, C.J. (ed.), *Rufford Charters*, Thoroton Society Record Series 29, 30, 32, 34 (Nottingham, 1972–1981)

Holles, Gervase, *Memorials of the Holles Family, 1493–1656*, ed. A.C. Wood, Camden 3rd series 55 (London, 1937)

Hopkinson, A. (ed.), *The Rolls of the 1281 Derbyshire Eyre*, Derbyshire Record Society 27 (2000)

Hunter, J. (ed.), *Fines sive pedes finium; sive finales concordiae in Curia domini regis . . . AD 1195–AD 1214*, II (London, 1844)

―――― *Hallamshire: the history and topography of the parish of Sheffield*, ed. A.S. Gatty (London, 1875)

——— *South Yorkshire: the history of the deanery of Doncaster*, 2 vols (London, 1828–1831)

Jeayes, I.H., *A Descriptive Catalogue of Derbyshire Charters in Public and Private Libraries and Muniment Rooms* (London and Derby, 1906)

Johnson, R., *A History of Alfreton* (Ripley, no date)

Kiernan, D., *The Derbyshire Lead Industry in the Sixteenth Century*, Derbyshire Record Society 14 (1989)

Kirke, H., 'The Praemonstratensian abbey of Beauchief', *The Reliquary*, 7 (1866–1867)

Knowles, D., *The Religious Orders in England, III: the Tudor age* (Cambridge, 1959)

———, C.N.L. Brooke, and V. London (eds), *The Heads of Religious Houses: England and Wales, I: 940–1216*, 2nd edn (Cambridge, 1972)

Leach, P. and N. Pevsner, *The Buildings of England: Yorkshire: the West Riding*, 2nd edn (London, 2009)

Lloyd, S., *English Society and the Crusade, 1216–1307* (Oxford, 1980)

Logan, F.D., *Runaway Religious in Medieval England, c.1240–1540* (Cambridge, 1996)

Lugard, C.E. (ed.), *Calendar of the Cases for Derbyshire from the Eyre and Assize Rolls (Henry III, 1256–1272)* (Barnston, Cumbria, 1938)

McKinley, R., *The Surnames of Lancashire* (London, 1981)

Matthew, H.C.G. and B. Harrison (eds), *Oxford Dictionary of National Biography*, 60 vols (Oxford, 2004)

Meredith, R. 'Beauchief abbey and the Pegges', *Derbyshire Archaeological Journal*, 87 (1967), pp. 86–126

Merrony, C.J.N., 'More than meets the eye? A preliminary discussion of the archaeological remains of Beauchief abbey and park', in *A Review of Archaeology in South Yorkshire, 1993–1994*, compiled by the South Yorkshire Archaeology Service (Sheffield, 1994), pp. 60–67

Migne, J.P., *Patrologia latina, 201* (Paris, 1903), *Lucius III Pontifex Romanus, epistolae et privilegia*, cols 1069–1380

Morgan, P., *Domesday Book: Derbyshire* (Chichester, 1978)

Mott, R.A., 'The water mills of Beauchief abbey', *Transactions of the Hunter Archaeological Society*, 9 (1969), pp. 203–220

Page, W. (ed.), *Victoria County History of Leicestershire*, I (London, 1907)

——— *Victoria County History of Nottinghamshire*, I (London, 1906)

——— *Victoria County History of Suffolk*, II (London, 1907)

Pegge, S., *An Historical Account of Beauchief Abbey* (London, 1801)

Pevsner, N., *The Buildings of England: Derbyshire*, 2nd edn, revised by Elizabeth Williamson (Harmondsworth, 1979)

——— *The Buildings of England: Leicestershire and Rutland* (Harmondsworth, 1960)

——— *The Buildings of England: Nottinghamshire*, 2nd edn, revised by Elizabeth Williamson (Harmondsworth, 1979)

Platt, C., *The Monastic Grange in Medieval England: a reassessment* (London, 1969)

Potter, G.R., summary of a lecture he gave on the Cartulary of Beauchief Abbey in *Derbyshire Archaeological Journal*, n.s. 12 (1938), pp. 160–162

Poynton, E.M., 'A rental of Beauchief abbey', *The Genealogist*, n.s. 27 (1910), pp. 15–21

Postles, D., *The Surnames of Leicestershire and Rutland* (Oxford, 1998)

Proceedings of the Society of Antiquaries of London, 17 November 1870 to 3 April 1873, second series, vol. 5

Riden, P. and J. Blair (eds), *History of Chesterfield, V: records of the borough of Chesterfield and related documents, 1204–1835* (Chesterfield, 1980)

Saltman, A., *The Cartulary of Dale Abbey*, Derbyshire Archaeological Society Record Series 2 (1967)

Scott-Gatty, A.S. 'Records of the Court Baron of the manor of Sheffield', *Transactions of the Hunter Archaeological Society*, 1:3 (1914), pp. 257–329.

Smith, A.H., *The Place-names of the West Riding of Yorkshire* (Cambridge, 1961)

Smith, A.V., *Beauchief Abbey: notes on the layout and remains – the abbey and surrounding area* (Sheffield, 1993)

Smith, D.M. (ed.), *Heads of Religious Houses: England and Wales, III: 1377–1540* (Cambridge, 2008)

——— and V.C.M. London (eds), *Heads of Religious Houses: England and Wales, II: 1216–1377* (Cambridge, 2001)

Southern, R.W., 'Master Vacarius and the beginning of an English academic tradition', in J.J.G. Alexander and M.T. Gibson (eds), *Medieval Learning and Literature: essays presented to Richard William Hunt* (Oxford, 1976), pp. 257–286

Tanner, T., *Notitia Monastica* (London, 1744; reprinted with addition, Cambridge, 1787)

Thoroton, R., *Antiquities of Nottinghamshire* (London, 1677)

Throsby, J. (ed.), *Thoroton's History of Nottinghamshire: republished with large additions*, 3 vols (Nottingham, 1790)

Turbutt, G., *A History of Derbyshire*, 4 vols (Cardiff, 1999)

Walker, J.W. (ed.), *Abstracts of the Cartularies of the Priory of Monkbretton*, Yorkshire Archaeological Society Record Series 66 (1926)

Walton, M. and R. Meredith, *Beauchief Abbey Past and Present*, 2nd edn (Sheffield, 1975)

Watson, A.G. (ed.), *Supplement to the Second Edition of Medieval Libraries of Great Britain: a list of surviving books*, ed. N.R. Ker, Royal Historical Society Guides and Handbooks 15 (London, 1987)

Watts, V. (ed.), *The Cambridge Dictionary of English Place-names* (Cambridge, 2004)

Wheeler, P., *Beauchief Abbey: its buildings and lands, with special reference to the granges* (dissertation for the Certificate in Archaeology of the University of Sheffield, 1996)

INDEXES

Numbers in Roman type provide references for persons and places mentioned in the documents, including the Leake copies (Appendix I) and the summaries in the royal confirmation (Royal Conf.) in 1316 (Appendix II). Italics are used when personal or place-names are otherwise mentioned. Persons and places in the Introduction are noted with the relevant page number (e.g. 'Intro. *6*').

All persons are listed by first name. Some entries may conceal separate identities; likewise some entries may refer to the same person or place. 'De' (as in 'Nigel de Stokes', for example) has always been replaced in the Indexes by 'of'. Place-names are given in their modern form wherever possible.

D = historic county of Derbyshire; L = Leicestershire; N = Nottinghamshire; SH = ancient parish of Sheffield; SY = South Yorkshire; fd. = found.

INDEX OF PERSONS

i) Persons other than witnesses

Adam Barry of Nottingham 221
Adam of Birchwood, D 22, 38
Adam le Blunt Intro. *29*
Adam the carter of Brincliffe, SH 126–128, 139–141, 149
Adam the cook of Sheffield 129, 150–151
Adam of Glapwell, D 213
Adam of Greenhill, D 52, 55
Adam Hutun son of Eudes (Odo) Leneire 88
Adam Lawnder Intro. *19*
Adam of Milum (Cumberland?) 66
Adam of Saint Mary (of Rawmarsh, SY) Intro. *6*, 137–138

Adam son of John of the Cliffe, D 21, 38, 49
Adam son of Ralph of Reresby, L and of Margery 183
Adam son of Richard the ditcher 155
Agnes of Birchwood, D 68
Agnes daughter of Robert of England 151
Agnes of Orby (Lincs) *4 n. 3*
Agnes wife of William of Dronfield, D 159
Alan 4, 38
Alan son of Gunnild of Chesterfield, D Intro. *11*, 197
Alan son of Richard 211
Albert of Bradway, D 38
Alexander 5, 38

Alexander son of Alexander of Birchwood, D 89
Alice of Alfreton Intro. 7
Alice daughter of William son of Robert of Alfreton, D Intro. *10*, 64, 76
Alice Loole 43
Alice wife of Walter of Buildwas (Shrops) 220
Alice wife of William of Briges 192–194
Amice (Amitia), wife of Nigel of Stokes Intro. *30*
Andrew of Hooton, SY 106
Avice 212

Beatrice wife of Robert Hauselin (of Little Sheffield, SH) 129
Boniface IX, pope 13
Brun Gerard 134

Cecily aunt of Hugh of Scholes, SY 97
Cecily Leche *219 n. 1*
Cecily of Tamworth (Staffs) *219 n. 1*
Cecily wife of Ralph of Ecclesall, SH 111
Cecily wife of Thomas of Beeley, D Leake 6
Christopher Blackwall Intro. *15*
Christopher Haslam Intro. *20*
Clebern 3

Daniel the butler, brother of Walter 104

Edmund Deincourt Intro. *10*
Edward Pegge Intro. *14*, Intro. *23*
Edward of Scholes, SY 100
Edwin 199
Ellen wife of Adam the cook of Sheffield 129
Ellis the carpenter Intro. *11*, 98
Ellis the steward 125
Ellis of Troway, D 8, 38
Emma at the new mill, SH 35
Emma wife of Richard the redsmith 69
Emma wife of William of Lovetot Intro. *6*, *129 n. 2*

Francis Leake, knight, of Sutton, D Intro. *16*, Intro. *17*, Intro. *23*
Francis Talbot, 5th earl of Shrewsbury Intro. *15*, Intro. *23*

Gamel Intro. *11*, 3
Gamel of Ecclesall, SH 117
Gamel son of Solon 135

Geoffrey (Galfrid) Leake 7
Geoffrey Barre, knight, of Teversal, N 66, 203
Geoffrey Blythe, bishop of Conventry and Lichfield Intro. *12*, Intro. *29*
Geoffrey of Stanley, N 222, 225–226, Royal Conf. 45
George son of Sir Thomas Chaworth Intro. *7n*
Gerard Intro. *11*, 3, 136
Gerard of Furnival, knight Intro. *6*, Intro. *8*, Intro. *15*, Royal Conf. 37–40, Royal Conf. 42
Gerard of Greenhill, D 6, 38
Gertrude Strelley Intro. *23*
Gervase Intro. *11*, 3
Gervase son of Richard the good smith 198
Gilbert, abbot of Beauchief Intro. *28*, *217 n. 3*
Gilbert of Bradway, D 35
Gilbert of Hasland, D 192–193
Gilbert of Perlethorpe, N 95–96
Gilbert the smith 201
Godric of Darley, D 169
Gunnild of Chesterfield, D 197
Gunnild of Sheffield 148

Hacon Intro. *11*, 3
Henry the bercher 21
Henry, clerk of Chesterfield, D 199
Henry Coke, chaplain *219 n. 1*
Henry of Egmanton, N 185
Henry Fraunc 109
Henry of Herries *26 n. 4*
Henry the mason of Ecclesall, SH Intro. *20*
Henry of Mousters of Ashover, D 184
Henry of Scholes, SY 94
Henry son of Gunnild of Sheffield 148
Henry son of Laurence 101
Henry son of Thomas of Bradwell, D 105
Henry son of William the tanner 134
Henry Stafforth, knight Intro. *21*
Herbert of Orby (Lincs) *4 n. 3*
Hugh Intro. *11*, 4, 38
Hugh II, abbot of Prémontré Intro. *26*, 1, 2
Hugh of Avallon (St Hugh), bishop of Lincoln *59 n. 1*
Hugh of the Barkhouse Intro. *19*
Hugh Bauzan 109
Hugh Bridde 101
Hugh the cook 137–138
Hugh Draper of Chesterfield, D *219 n. 1*
Hugh of Duffield, D 178

Hugh of Glapwell, D 206, 209–210, 212, 214
Hugh Hauselin of Little Sheffield, SH 118, 126–127, 130–133, 149, 156, 158
Hugh, knight and rector of Handsworth, SY Intro. *21*
Hugh of Linacre, D *18 nn. 1 and 2*
Hugh of Little Norton, D 33, 38, 40
Hugh of Scholes, SY 98, 103
Hugh the smith 136
Hugh son of Adam at the spring in Greenhill, D Intro. *10*, 55
Hugh son of Albert of Bradway, D 6, 38
Hugh son of John of Duffield, D 177–178
Hugh son of Ralph of Scholes, SY 105
Hugh son of Robert of Scholes, SY 93–94, 97
Hugh son of Robert of Walton, D 190
Hugh son of Sweyn 204
Hugh son of William 94
Hugh Wake (of Chesterfield) 160, 195
Hugh of Wells, bishop of Lincoln 59 *n. 1*

Idonea of Leyburn (N. Yorks) 99
Ingram Intro. *5*
Isaac of Chesterfield, D 196
Iseult former wife of Robert the smith 180–181, 186–187
Itho 212
Ivo, abbot of Beauchief *203 n. 2*

James Oates Intro. *19*
Joan Bassett, lady *218 n. 1*
Joan daughter of Sir Robert of Lathom (Lancs) 66
Joanna of Alfreton, D Intro. *7*
Joanna wife of John Ormond Intro. *8n*
Jocelin of Stainsby, D *26 n. 4, 56 n. 1, 90 n. 1*
John of Abbernun *35 n. 2*
John, abbot of Beauchief Intro. *29*
John of Annesley, N, knight Intro. *29*
John Austin Intro. *16*
John Basset, knight *50 n. 1, 218 n. 1*
John Blackiswalle, knight Intro. *15*
John Blythe of Norton, D Intro. *19*
John Calton of Totley, D Intro. *18*
John of the Cliffe, D 38
John Croke Intro. *12*
John Downham, abbot Intro. *22*
John of Duffield, D 177
John Fanshawe (Faunchall) Intro. *14–15*
John Greenwood, alias Sheffield, abbot Intro. *12*, Intro. *23*

John Moor of Greenhill, D Intro. *20*
John at the new mill, SH 19
John of Normanton, D *219 n. 1*
John of Ridgeway, D, chaplain 217–218
John Rocester of Dore, D Intro. *6*
John of Rotherham, SY 102–103
John Sargant of Alfreton, D 75
John the smith 24, 38
John son of Adam at the spring in Greenhill, D 55
John son of Isaac of Chesterfield, D 196
John son of Luke of Beeley, D 174
John son of Madoch Intro. *11*, 182
John son of Walter of Buildwas (Shrops) 220
John the swane son of Adam of Greenhill, D Intro. *10*, 52
John Swift, canon Intro. *22*
John of Taddington, D 200
John Tonk 47
John of Wigley, D 217–220
John Wolaton 82
John of the wood 25
John Woodhouse, dean of St John, Chester *218 n. 1*
John Wykwall, vicar of Dronfield Intro. *13*
Jordan of Attercliffe, SH 113
Jordan Herring of Herringthorpe, D Royal Conf. 46
Juliana daughter of Adam the carter (of Brincliffe, SH) 129, 139, 141

Laurence the smith 101
Lettice wife of Andrew of Hooton, SY 106–107
Lovechild, widow 5, 38
Lucius III, pope 1
Lucy daughter of Robert of Alfreton, D 57
Luke son of Warin of Beeley, D 171–175, Royal Conf. 49

Madoch 182
Margaret of the Brom Intro. *21*
Margaret daughter of Walter the shepherd 147
Margery of Beeley, D, daughter of Robert, former dean of Beeley 170–171
Margery daughter of Luke of Beeley, D 175
Margery the former wife of Richard the nailer of Chesterfield, D 202
Margery widow of Ralph of Reresby, L Leake 8
Matilda of Ashover, D Intro. *21*

Matilda daughter of Gilbert of Hasland, D 192–193
Matilda (Maud) of Louvetot, SH Intro. *15*, Royal Conf. 39–40
Matilda mother of Simon 162
Matilda wife of Peter of the hurst 194
Matthew of Hathersage, D Intro. *14*, 161–162
Michael of Hathersage, D Intro. *20*

Nicholas of Lathom (Lancs) 66
Nicholas of Longford Intro. *18–19*
Nicholas son of John of Rotherham, SY 102
Nicholas Strelley, knight Intro. *15*, Intro. *18*, Intro. *23*
Nicholas Torald 22
Nigel of Lisurs Intro. *30*
Nigel the smith 224
Nigel of Stokes Intro. *30*
Norman father of William and John of Taddington, D 200

Odo (Eudes) Leneire 88
Odo (Eudes) son of John 204
Orayn mother of William the clerk of Saint John 191
Osbert son of Richard of Hore 174, 175
Osbert of Wadsley, SY 145

Peter Intro. *11*, 4, 38
Peter of Bradfield, SY 139–141
Peter of Goxhill (Lincs) *18 n. 2*
Peter of the hurst 194
Peter at the mill of Bradway, D 35
Peter the weaver Intro. *11*, 26, 38, 90

Ralph, abbot of Beauchief *30 n. 3*
Ralph Barker of Dore, D Intro. *9*, Intro. *13*, Intro. *19*, 82, 218–219
Ralph Barre I of Teversal, N 203, Royal Conf. 45
Ralph Barre II son of Geoffrey Barre of Teversal, N 203
Ralph, clerk of Sheffield 143
Ralph the cobbler 181
Ralph of Ecclesall, SH 120, 124–125
Ralph of Fallinge, D 176–178
Ralph Frescheville *219 n. 1*
Ralph of Freshmall Leake 7
Ralph of the Hospital 211
Ralph Musard Intro. *8*, Intro. *30*, *222 n. 4*, Royal Conf. 30–32

Ralph Musard son of Ralph Musard Royal Conf. 33
Ralph, reeve of Wymeswold, L 16
Ralph of Reresby, L, husband of Margery 179, 183, 185, 188, Leake 8–9
Ralph of Scholes, SY 105
Ralph son of Geoffrey Barre *203 n. 2*
Ralph son of Robert of Ecclesall, SH Intro. *8–9*, Intro. *18*, 111, *111 n. 5*, 112–116, 122–123
Ralph son of Robert of Reresby, L 183, 186–187
Ranulf 3–6, 11, 38, 59, Royal Conf. 1
Ranulf of Alfreton, D Intro. *5*, Intro. *31*
Ranulf brother of Robert of Alfreton, D 12–15, 57
Ranulf son of William son of Robert of Alfreton, D 64, 76
Ranulf of Storthes, D 27, 38
Reyner of Bullon (Boulogne?) 136
Richard Bars 82
Richard of Bernak (Cambs?), lord of Beighton, SY 163
Richard of Bernes, D 181
Richard, bishop of Coventry Intro. *3*, 3
Richard Costenoth 142–144, 146
Richard Daniel 109
Richard the ditcher Intro. *11*, 155
Richard Edward 38
Richard Everard 27
Richard of Glapwell, D Intro. *6*, 204, 211, 216
Richard the good smith 198, 200–201
Richard of Hore (or Horegh) 22, 29, 38, 174–175
Richard of the moor 21, 23, 38
Richard Musard Intro. *8n*
Richard the nailer of Chesterfield, D 202
Richard Oxley, knight Intro. *21*
Richard the redsmith of Swanwick, D 69
Richard of Scholes, SY 99, 100–102
Richard Scyvel 134
Richard the serjeant 133
Richard son of Adam 25
Richard son of Adam the cook of Sheffield Intro. *11*, 150
Richard son of Edward of Scholes, SY 100
Richard son of Gerard 136
Richard son of Hugh of Scholes, SY 95, 98, 103
Richard son of Jordan of Attercliffe, SH 113
Richard son of Richard Costenoth 142–144
Richard son of Thoke Intro. *11*, 131

Richard son of William Daniel of Tideswell, D 107, 109
Richard son of William of Glapwell, D 203, 205, 207–208, 214
Richard son of William of Thorpe, SY 103
Richard the squire 56
Richard Swappocke 34
Richard of Tapton, D 192
Robert Intro. *11*, 4, 38
Robert, abbot of Beauchief *175 n. 1*
Robert of Alfreton son of William of Alfreton, D 8–10, 12–17, 38, 57, 64, 76, 89, Royal Conf. 5–8
Robert of Barley (Barlow, D) *218 n. 1*
Robert of Beeley, D 169–171
Robert Bele, miller Intro. *19*
Robert of Bella Aqua Intro. *30*
Robert Brito of Walton, D Intro. *6*, 164, 189
Robert Chaworth Intro. *7*
Robert of Childre 27, 38
Robert, clerk of Hooton, SY 114
Robert, clerk of Masbrough, SY 98
Robert, clerk of Walton, D 190, 196
Robert the cook 208
Robert, dean of Beeley and father of Susanna and Margery of Beeley 171
Robert, dean of Darley, D 176–177
Robert of England 129, 139–141, 151
Robert Ferrers, 2nd earl of Derby Intro. *6*
Robert the fletcher 30, 38, 49
Robert the forester 3, 27, 38
Robert of Furness, knight Intro. *6*, Intro. *16*, Royal Conf. 34
Robert of the Greaves, D 20, 22, 38, 48
Robert of Grendun Intro. *30*
Robert Hauselin (of Brincliffe, SH) 128
Robert of Hooton son of William of Hooton Roberts, SY 110
Robert Ladde, clerk of Burton 65
Robert of Lathom (Lancs), lord 24, 38, 66
Robert the mason 144
Robert of the mill of [Coal] Aston, D 38
Robert nephew of Robert of Scholes, SY 93–94
Robert Putrell (of Cotes, L) 59
Robert Pykard 42
Robert of Radclyffe, abbot of Beauchief 83–84
Robert the redsmith of Swanwick, D 22, 38, 71–73, 78
Robert of Reresby, L 181, Leake 7, Leake 9
Robert Rivers, knight and rector of Eckington Intro. *21*

Robert Scarlet 27, 38
Robert the smith 180–181, 186–187
Robert son of Alice and nephew of Robert 97
Robert son of Edwin of Chesterfield, D Intro. *11*, 199
Robert son of Gilbert of Perlethorpe, N 95–96
Robert son of Godric of Darley, D Intro. *11*, 169
Robert son of Hugh of Glapwell, D 206, 210, 212
Robert son of Hugh of Little Sheffield, SH 126
Robert son of John of Wigley, D 218
Robert son of John (of Wymeswold, L) 65
Robert son of Osbert of Wadsley, SY 145
Robert son of Ralph of Ecclesall, SH 121
Robert, knight, son of Sir Ralph of Ecclesall, SH Intro. *18–19*, 119
Robert son of Ralph of Reresby, L 179, 185–188
Robert son of Ranulf Intro. *2*, Intro. *4–5*, Intro. *10–12*, Intro. *24*, Intro. *31*, 3–6, 11, 38, 59, 64, 76, Royal Conf. 1–3
Robert son of Richard of Lathom (Lancs) Intro. *7*
Robert son of Richard the good smith 200
Robert son of Robert Brito of Walton, D 189
Robert son of Robert of Masbrough, SY 96
Robert son of Robert Wyden of Wadsley, SY 144
Robert son of Roger of Dronfield, D 115
Robert son of Walter of Brampton, D Intro. *28n*
Robert son of Warin of Beeley, D 165
Robert son of Wido (of Wadsley, SY) 145–146
Robert son of William of Alfreton, D 8–10, 12–17, 34, 38, 64, 76, 89
Robert son of William of Hooton, SY 110
Robert son of William of Wymeswold, L 62
Robert Swift Intro. *19*
Robert of Wigley, D, senior 217
Robert Wyden 144
Roger 3, 205
Roger, abbot of Beauchief *35 n. 3, 203 n. 2*
Roger of the alder-grove 147
Roger of Alfreton, D 12, 13, 15, 57–58, 60, 64, 76
Roger Barker Intro. *18*
Roger the bercher 22, 38, 80
Roger of Birley Intro. *29*

292   INDEXES

Roger of Bradway, D 35
Roger Cade 191
Roger of Chesterfield, D, knight Intro. *20*
Roger the clerk, son of Hugh of Glapwell, D (*see* Roger son of Hugh)
Roger of Dronfield, D 115
Roger Eyre Intro. *19*
Roger of Marcham, N 179, 186–187, Leake 7
Roger Mons 22, 38
Roger of Poitou (France) Intro. *5n*
Roger Pycard 42
Roger of Ridding, D 9, 38
Roger Ruffus 201
Roger the smith of Birchwood, D 38, 68
Roger son of Adam of Glapwell, D *209 n. 1*, 213
Roger son of Arnold 204
Roger son of Hugh of Glapwell, D, and clerk 206, 210, 212
Roger son of Hugh Hauselin (of Little Sheffield, SH) 158
Roger son of Juliana the carter 129
Roger son of Peter of Bradfield, SY 139–141
Roger son of Richard the squire of Norton, D 53
Roger son of William 209
Roger son of William of Hollins, SH 152–154, 158, 209
Roger of Wadsley, SY 145
Roger of Wigley, D 217
Roscelin of Bromp (Broom Hall, SH) 67, 130

Salinwell 38
Samson 27, 38
Serlo of Pleasley, D Intro. *6*, 182
Serlo son of Warin of Beeley, D Intro. *6*, 164, 167–168, Royal Conf. 50
Siggrit daughter of Henry of Scholes, SY 94
Simon, lord 204
Simon of Cromwell, N Intro. *30*, 214
Simon of Goxhill (Lincs) 162
Simon son of Henry son of Gunnild of Sheffield Intro. *11*, 148
Simon son of Hugh of Glapwell, D *16 n. 1*, 204, 209, 212, 214
Simon son of Matthew 162
Simon son of Ralph of Fallinge, D 177–178
Simon son of Rocelin of Bromp (Broom Hall, SH) 130
Simon of the Storthes, D 26, 38, 82
Solon 135
Stephen Nevil 62

Stephen son of Stephen the parson of Chesterfield, D 198
Suard 38
Susanna of Beeley, D, daughter of Robert, former dean of Beeley 170–171, 175
Sweyn 204
Sweyn of Boulogne 114
Sybil the weaver 180, 181, 186–187

Theobald of Valoines *12 n. 1*
Thoke 131
Thomas of Alfreton Intro. *7*, Intro. *12*
Thomas of Beeley, D Leake 6
Thomas of Bella Aqua (SY) 109
Thomas of Bradwell, D 105
Thomas of the Chamber (de Camera) Intro. *29*
Thomas Chauz of Brampton, D Leake 5
Thomas Chaworth I, lord Intro. *7*, Intro. *17*, Intro. *29*, 17–43, 45, 47–49, 52–53, 56, 58, 60, 66–68, 70–71, 87
Thomas Chaworth II, lord Intro. *7*, Intro. *28*, 44, 46, 61
Thomas Chaworth III, lord Intro. *7*, 50, 83–86
Thomas Chaworth IV, lord 218, 219
Thomas Chaworth I or II, lord Intro. *17*, Intro. *29*, 51, 54, 72–73, 77–81
Thomas Chaworth I, II, or III, lord Intro. *32*, 55, 88
Thomas of Dronfield Intro. *12n*
Thomas the forester of Alfreton, D 74
Thomas of Furnival I, lord Intro. *8*, Intro. *15*, Royal Conf. 41–42
Thomas of Furnival II, lord Royal Conf. 42
Thomas Gilbert, canon Intro. *29*
Thomas Gory 54
Thomas Greenwood Intro. *19*
Thomas Gyleson of the Greaves, D *175 n. 1*
Thomas Hilde 199
Thomas North Intro. *15–16*
Thomas Rodes, chaplain *219 n. 1*
Thomas of Romerthwert 200
Thomas son of Adam at the spring in Greenhill, D 55
Thomas son of Hugh of the wood 21, 38
Thomas son of John of the wood 25, 38
Thomas son of Nigel the smith 224
Thomas son of Richard the good smith 200
Thomas son of Richard the redsmith 69
Thomas son of Robert of Masbrough, SY 96
Thomas son of Roger of Gotham, N 18

INDEXES

Thomas son of William of Glapwell, D 215
Thomas of the Wood 18, 28, 33

Uchtred Intro. *11*, 176–177

Walter the baker 134–136
Walter Barry of Teversal, N Intro. *6*
Walter brother of Daniel the butler 104
Walter of Buildwas (Shrops) 220
Walter Chauz, son of Thomas Chauz of Brampton, D Intro. *9*, Leake 5
Walter of Furness Royal Conf. 34
Walter the shepherd 147
Walter son of Robert of Furness Intro. *16n*
Walter of Ufton, D 71–73
Warin of Beeley, D Intro. *6*, Intro. *15*, 164–168, 171–172
Warin son of Robert of Beeley, D 169
Weremund Intro. *11*, 203, 205, 208
Wido son of Roger of Wadsley, SY 145
William 166, 209
William, abbot of Beauchief 65
William, abbot of Welbeck, N *137 n. 3*
William of the Barkhouse of Norton, D Intro. *19*, 218–219
William Barry of Teversal, N Intro. *16*, 203, 222–224, Royal Conf. 43
William Barry son of Ralph Barry of Teversal, N Royal Conf. 45
William Blackwall Intro. *15–16*
William Bolles Intro. *17*, Intro. *23*
William Brewer 200
William of Briges 192–194
William of Brincliffe, SH 128
William Chaworth, knight, son of Sir Thomas Chaworth Intro. *7*, 44, 61, 90–91
William the clerk of Saint John 191
William the cook 56
William of Cressy (France) Intro. *30*, 120, 124
William Dolphin of Eckington parish, D Intro. *20*
William of Dronfield, D Intro. *9*, 159
William of Folkingham, abbot of Beauchief *30 n. 3*, 99, Leake 8–9
William of Glapwell, D 203, 205, 207–208
William of the Greaves *175 n. 1*
William of Gringley, N, knight Intro. *21*
William Holland Intro. *15*
William of Hollins, SH 150, 152–155, 157
William of Hooton Roberts 110
William Jorrs 63
William Kitchen (Kychyne) Intro. *12*
William of Little Sheffield, SH 129
William of Lovetot (France) Intro. *6*, *129 n. 2*
William of Meynell [Langley], D 159
William the merchant of Sheffield 147, 157
William of Myrie 177
William of Normanton, D 192
William Picard 51
William of Retford (Radeford), tanner Intro. *19–20*
William son of Andrew of Hooton, SY 106
William son of Daniel the butler 104
William son of Gamel of Ecclesall, SH Intro. *11*, 117
William son of Geoffrey of Stanley, N 222, 225–226, Royal Conf. 45
William son of Gilbert of Catcliff, SY, *196 n. 1*
William son of Hugh Hauselin of Little Sheffield, SH 126–127, 149
William son of Norman of Taddington, D 200
William son of Ralph Barry of Teversal, N Royal Conf. 45
William son of Richard of Dore, D 102
William son of Richard of Glapwell, D 216
William son of Richard the squire 56
William son of Robert of Alfreton, D 7, 11, 38, 64, 76, Royal Conf. 4
William son of Sunun 49
William of Stainsby, D, knight Intro. *29*
William of Stone of Harewood Intro. *15*
William Swift Intro. *19*
William the tanner of Sheffield Intro. *11*, 134–135, 148
William of Thorney, dean of Lincoln cathedral Intro. *28n*, *217 n. 3*
William of Thorpe (Hesley), SY 103
William Tinett of [Norton] Woodseats, D 18, 28, 33, 38, 50
William West, knight Intro. *24*
William Widdowson Intro. *22*
Winnora of Cockshutt 21, 23, 38

ii) Witnesses

Note: the witnesses were always male.

A., abbot of Welbeck, N 59, 63
A., prior of Worksop, N 59
Adam, abbot of Welbeck, N 5–6, 11
Adam of Berne, SY 103
Adam of Birchett, D 143
Adam le Blunt Intro. *29*
Adam, chaplain of Normanton, D 10
Adam, chaplain of Rotherham, SY 105
Adam, chaplain of Wentworth, SY 97
Adam, clerk of Sheffield 157
Adam the cook of Sheffield 150–151, 154–155
Adam of Everingham (East Riding), knight and lord of Stainborough and Rockley, SY 18, 33, 39–41, 44, 61
Adam of Gotham, N 50
Adam of Harthill, D 104, 167
Adam of Kucton 5
Adam of Normanville (France) 106
Adam of Reresby, L 37, 41, 46, 81
Adam of Ronnesley 175
Adam son of Phillip of Huston 4, 11
Adam of Stretton, D 3, 11, 63
Adam of Taptover 188
Adam of Wadsley, SY 149
Adam of Wandell 127
Adam of the wood (*de bosco*) in Sheffield Intro. *29*, 134–136, 139–141, 143, 147–148, 154
Alan of Edelwasdeleia 164
Alan son of Richard of Glapwell, D 206–207, 210
Albinus, abbot of Derby Intro. *3*, 3–4
Alexander of Birchwood, D 75
Andrew of Hooton, SY 108
Andrew son of Richard of Glapwell, D 206–207, 210
Arnold of Wymeswold, L 62

Daniel, chaplain of Sheffield 139, 151

Edmund of Ainecourt (or Deincourt), knight and lord of several local manors 38
Edmund of Wasteneys (France), knight and lord of Todwick, SY 110
Egidio (*see* Giles)
Ellis of Ecclesall, SH 121–123
Ermemot of Wenham (Suffolk) 104
Eudes (*see* Odo)

Eustace clerk of the lord of Sheffield 108, 130, 149
Eustace of Lilleshall (Shrops), Brother 3–4
Eustace parson of Handsworth, SY 132–133
Eustace son of Hugh 4

Galfrid (*see* Geoffrey)
Gamel son of Serlo 134–136, 147–148
Geoffrey Barry, lord of Teversal, N 66
Geoffrey brother of Henry of Shelton, N 6
Geoffrey, clerk of Beighton, D 23, 60
Geoffrey, clerk of Brampton, D 164
Geoffrey, clerk of Osberton, N 7
Geoffrey, clerk of Sulcholm 59
Geoffrey of Hodsock, N 120, 124
Geoffrey of Musters 209, 222 n. 4
Geoffrey son of Stephen of Westwold (i.e. Wymeswold, L?) 62, 65
Geoffrey son of T. of Lond' 59
Geoffrey son of Warin of Beeley, D 165–166
German of Mortomley, SY 149
Gervase of Bernaby 111
Gervase of Bernak (Barnack, Cambs?), lord of Beighton, D 24, 34–35, 43, 106, 109
Gervase of Kenilworth (Warwicks), magister 59
Gilbert of Bernston 4
Gilbert, prior of Blyth, N 124
Gilbert of Sucton 4
Giles of Meynell (lord of Meynell Langley, D) Intro. *29*, 38, 90
Giles of Rossale (Shrops) 67, 72–74, 78

Hacon the reeve 5
Hasculphus Musard 222 n. 4
Henry of Berengerville (or Bergerville) 7, 63, 92
Henry of Birchwood, D 57, 66
Henry of Brailsford, D, knight Intro. *12*, 36, 38, 46, 183–184, 187
Henry, clerk of Horchent 63
Henry Daate 50
Henry of Edwalton, N 12–13
Henry Lecard 102
Henry of Longcroft 69, 71, 73, 79–80, 87
Henry of Masbrough, SY 95–96
Henry of Newbold, D 28
Henry of Pierrepoint, lord of Holme Pierrepont, N, and Langwith, D 26, 90
Henry of Shelton, N 6

INDEXES

Henry son of Godolf 131
Henry son of Roger of Wadsley, SY 120, 124, 145
Henry son of Stephen of Harley, SY 103
Henry of Spina (i.e. thorn) 144
Henry of Stead, SY 103
Henry of Tankersley, SY 121–123, 156
Henry of Tinsley, SY 101, 109
Henry Wylte Intro. *29*
Herard of Bernest 63
Hugh of Birchett, D 42
Hugh of Brom (Broom Hall, SH) 117, 130, 133
Hugh of the Canons Intro. *29*, 27, 38, 67–68, 70, 72
Hugh of Chesterfield, D, magister 164
Hugh of Dronfield, D 164
Hugh Hauselin (of Little Sheffield, SH) Intro. *19*, 117, 130, 142, 146
Hugh of Huletotes 92
Hugh Kent 148
Hugh of Linacre, D Intro. *29*, 18–19, 22, 32–33, 36–41, 44, 46, 51, 54–55, 61, 81, 183–184, 187, 222, Leake 5, Leake 8–9
Hugh Lunt 135
Hugh, parson of Dronfield, D 204, 208, 211
Hugh of Sandiacre, D 7
Hugh son of Godolf 131
Hugh son of Henry 92
Hugh son of Peter of the Woodhouse, D 17, 21
Hugh, son of Robert, clerk of Walton, D 209
Hugh of Southwell, N 5, 7
Hugh of Tankersley, SY 98
Hugh of Tuxford, N, clerk 53, 188, Leake 8–9
Hugh of Ulgerthorp (Oakerthorpe), D 68, 72, 74, 77–80
Hugh of Wadsley, SY 32, 105, 114, 130, 132, 145, 149, 156
Hugh of Windhill, SY 103
Hugh of Woodhouse 23–24, 43, 58, 98, 116

Ingelram or Ingram of Brampton, D 204 n. 2, 209 n. 1, 211 n. 1
Ivan of Prestwold, L 63

Jeremy of Leysers 94
John of Ancourt (France; otherwise Ayencourt, Deyncourt, Deynecourt, Eyncourt, Eynecourt, or Eynecourt),
knight 18–19, 22, 28, 33, 37–41, 44, 51, 54, 61, 71, 81
John of Annesley, N, lord Intro. *29*, 26–27, 38, 90
John Bard Leake 2
John Basset, lord 50
John Bate 183–184, 187
John of the Beyle 159
John of Birchitt, D Intro. *11*, 20, 24–25, 29, 31–32, 35, 42–43, 45, 48–49, 52–53, 56, Leake 8–9
John of Brampton, D Leake 5
John of Brimington, D Intro. *29*, 18, 22, 26, 30, 33, 38–39, 40, 51, 53, 55, 90, 188, Leake 8–9
John Broune of [Coal] Aston, D 54
John Buk, lord 31
John, chaplain of Campsey Ash (Suffolk) 16, 64, 76
John, chaplain of Ecclesfield, SY 121–123
John, chaplain of Wymeswold, L 63
John the clerk 13, 16, 64, 76
John, clerk of Stubley, D Intro. *11*, 19, 20, 22, 25, 28, 51, 53, 55
John, clerk of Wentworth, SY 100
John, clerk of Wymeswold, L 12
John of the Cliff, D 129
John, constable of Sheffield 156
John Daincurth (otherwise de Heincurt, Deynkurt, or de Eincuria) 206–208, 210, 222–223
John of Darley, D 104
John Dorli, lord 95–96, 98
John Friend 140–141, 157
John of the hall of Alfreton, D 74, 87
John of Heriz, knight and lord of Tibshelf and South Wingfield, D Intro. *29*, 26, 38, 78, 80, 90, 223
John of Huntingfield (Suffolk) 15
John Ingram 65
John of Langley, D 118
John of Midhope, SY 149, 156
John of Orby (Lincs) 4
John of Peito in Chesterfield, D 188
John the Poher, brother of Ralph 9–10, 12–16, 64, 76
John Putrell of Wymeswold, L 62
John of Rossington, SY Intro. *29*
John the servant of Kimberworth, SY 93
John of Siwoldby, L 62
John son of Adam the spenser 65
John son of Giles, parson of Foxton, L 16
John son of Peter of Birchett, D 116

John son of Richard of Glapwell, D 206–207, 210
John son of Sweyn 137–138
John of the Stead, SY 102
John of Vilers in Marnham, N 31, 34, 62
John of Wigley, D 46, 54
John of Wiresdale (Lancs) 102
Jordan of Apetoft 115
Jordan, chaplain of Norton, D 92
Jordan, chaplain of Sheffield 117–118, 126
Jordan Foliot 120, 124

Lambekyn Gamel son of Serlo 134
Lambert the dyer of Sheffield 150–153
Laurence of Chaworth (France), knight 38
Lisiard, magister 59

Matthew, abbot of Rufford, N 59
Matthew of Bakewell, D, priest 165–166
Matthew, canon of Welbeck, N 137–138
Matthew of Eston 3
Matthew of Hathersage, D 167
Matthew of Holme, D 203, 205
Matthew son of Hugh and brother of Ralph 3–4, 11
Matthew of Welbeck, N, Brother 5
Michael(?) of Holme, D Leake 5
Michael son of Hugh, parson of Dronfield, D 204, 211

Nicholas of Bakewell, D 82
Nicholas of Birchitt, D 164
Nicholas of Boby, knight 62
Nicholas of Holm, D Leake 5
Nicholas, lord of [Meynell] Langley, D 89, 204, 211
Nicholas son of Nicholas of Wortley, SY 94
Nicholas Wake, knight Intro. *29*, 38
Nicholas of Woodhouse 92, 101
Nicholas of Wortley, SY 94, 121–123, 156
Nigel of Lisurs Intro. *30*

Odo 3
Odo son of Ralph 63
Osbert Thakall 93
Osbert of Wachesh 16

Peter of Alfreton, D 74
Peter of Bamford, D 175
Peter of Barnes, D Intro. *11*, 20, 23, 25, 29, 32, 42, 45, 48–49, 52–53, 55–56, 60, 70, Leake 5, Leake 8
Peter of Birchitt, D Intro. *11*, 17, 21, 34, 58, 88, 112–113, 115, 126–127, 142, 144, 146

Peter of Brimington, D 41
Peter, chaplain of Glapwell, D 206–207, 210
Peter of Doncaster, SY, magister 59
Peter of Harthill, D 165–166
Peter of Harthill, D or SY, brother of Robert 5–7, 92, 203, 208
Peter Herries Leake 9
Peter of Kilnhurst, SY 137–138
Peter of Leys (Norton Lees), D 30
Peter Payne of Norton, D 20
Peter of the Peak 135, 148
Peter of Roydes 110
Peter of the Woodhouse 17, 126
Phillip of Huletotes 7
Phillip son of Gerard of Styrrup, N 11

Radolf (*see* Ralph)
Ralph of Avers (France) 120, 124
Ralph Barri (of Teversal, N) 203
Ralph Basset, canon of Rocester (Staffs) 164
Ralph Bercher 82
Ralph of Bredon, L 89
Ralph of the Cemetery 117–118, 131
Ralph the clerk 98, 105, 128
Ralph, clerk of Sheffield 106, 111–113, 116, 126–128, 142, 146
Ralph, clerk of Wentworth, SY 93
Ralph of Ecclesall, SH, lord 34–35, 93, 97, 101, 105, 109, 145
Ralph Hauselyn (of Little Sheffield, SH) 116
Ralph of Nidhing 164
Ralph of Normanvile (France), lord 107, 121–123
Ralph the Poer 8–10, 12–13
Ralph, rector of the church of Heckington (Lincs) 10
Ralph of Reresby, L 23, 37, 81
Ralph the seneschal 5–6
Ralph Silvanus of Thorpe, SY 203, 205
Ralph son of Ralph 63
Ralph son of Richard of Brampton, D 222
Ralph son of Robert of Ecclesall, SH 94
Ralph son of Hugh 3–4, 11, 63, 203, 208
Ralph of Tideswell, D, magister 104
Ralph of Wingfield, D 75
Ralph of Wortley, SY 111–113
Ranulph of Acton 113
Ranulph of Jorr 64, 76
Ranulph the seneschal of Sheffield 116
Ranulph son of William of Alfreton, D 222
Ranulph of Swanwick, D 73
Ranulph, vicar of Norton, D 49, 126–127
Ranulph of Wadsley, SY, lord 66, 90

INDEXES

Reginald, abbot of Roche, SY 120, 124
Reginald of Bullon (Boulogne?) 136, 148
Reginald of Colwick, N 124
Reginald of Glewit 120
Reginald of the Hollins, SH 77
Reginald of the island 63
Remigius, prior of Shelford, N 59
Reyner Bullon (Boulogne?) 134, 147
Reyner, clerk of Sheffield 128, 143
Reyner, parson of Treeton, SY 95–96
Richard, abbot of Welbeck, N 137–138, 222
Richard the chaplain 7
Richard, chaplain of Ecclesfield, SY 121–123
Richard, chaplain of Norton, D 92, 165
Richard, chaplain of Rawmarsh, SY 137–138
Richard, chaplain of Sheffield 108
Richard, clerk of Marnham, N 31
Richard of [Coal] Aston, D 142, 146
Richard the cook 136
Richard Corbard of Sheffield 129
Richard the dean 5–6
Richard, despenser of Alfreton, D 9–10, 12–13, 15–16, 64, 76
Richard of Edensor, D 104, 108, 167
Richard of Finningley, N 11
Richard of Flintham, N 107, 158
Richard of Furness, knight and lord of Beighton, D 18, 33, 39–41
Richard of Gotham, N 106
Richard of the Hall 213–214
Richard of Handley, D 142, 146
Richard of Harthill, SY 8
Richard of Heeley, SH 129
Richard of Lavender (Lavendon, Bucks?) 136, 147
Richard of Leake, N 62
Richard of Loversall, SY 110
Richard, marshal of Norton, D 42, 49, 56
Richard Peche 104
Richard, smith of Thorpe, SY 100
Richard son of Adam 125
Richard son of Arthur 114
Richard son of Henry of Thorpe, SY 100
Richard son of William of Glapwell, D 206, 209–210, 222
Richard Torkard of Sheffield 151
Richard Walteroc' 135, 148
Robert of Abney, D 194
Robert of Aldwark, SY 116, 126–127, 158
Robert of Anjou 63
Robert the archer 104
Robert of Belgrave, L 62

Robert Blanckaim the clerk 65
Robert the Blount 88
Robert of Blyth the parson of Misterton (Lincs) 108, 132
Robert the Breton, seneschal of Hallamshire 133
Robert Brien 76
Robert of Briminton 222
Robert Brito (otherwise le Breton or le Bretun) of Walton, D 203–205, 208–209, 211, 222
Robert of Brom (Broom Hall, SH) Intro. *29*, 128, 143, 157
Robert brother of Peter of Harthill, D or SY 6, 7, 203, 208
Robert brother of Roger, clerk of Glapwell, D 209
Robert brother of Simon of Glapwell, D 211
Robert Bulmer 36
Robert, chaplain of Alfreton, D 8, 10, 89
Robert, chaplain of Campsey Ash (Suffolk) 16, 64, 76
Robert, clerk of Totley, D 108
Robert, clerk of Walton, D 203–204, 208–209, 211
Robert of the Cliff, D 152–153
Robert, dean of Darley, D 104, 164, 176
Robert of Dethick (Dencokes, Deverk), D, knight 183–184, 187
Robert of Ecclesall, SH, knight Intro. *10*, 18, 33, 37–38, 40, 110, 133, 149, 154
Robert Frank 188
Robert the forester 58
Robert of Gratton, D Leake 6
Robert the Graunt (of Langwith, D) Intro. *29*, 23, 26, 30, 32, 38, 42, 56, 60, 188, 213–214, Leake 5, Leake 8–9
Robert of Greenhill, D 87
Robert of Grendun Intro. *30*
Robert Harang 213–214
Robert Hasard 139–141
Robert Hauselin (of Little Sheffield, SH) 113, 116, 128, 139–141, 157–158
Robert of Hope, D 165–166
Robert of Jorr 63
Robert of Kelesehold 89
Robert of Knyveton, D Leake 6
Robert of Mattersey, N 12
Robert of Muffield of Brampton, D Leake 6
Robert of Munteney (France), lord of Cowley and Shirecliffe, SY 113
Robert, nephew of Peter and Robert of Harthill, D or SY 7

Robert the official of Westhind, magister 95–96
Robert of Ogston, D 17
Robert Picot 16
Robert, prior of Worksop, N 120, 124
Robert Putrell of Wymeswold, L 12–13, 16, 57, 64, 76
Robert of Pyrhohe (Pirehill, Staffs?) 15
Robert of Rearsby or Reresby, L 90, Leake 5
Robert Ro 5
Robert Sautcheverel, knight Intro. 29, 38
Robert Scarlet 27, 32, 67–68, 70, 72–73, 78, 90
Robert Seller of Rotherham, SY 102
Robert, seneschal of Sheffield 114, 120, 124
Robert son of Brian 15, 64, 76
Robert son of Henry 92
Robert son of Hugh of Glapwell, D 204, 208, 211
Robert son of Ranulph and father of William 11
Robert son of Roger of Aldwark, SY 107
Robert son of Roger of Ridding, D 75
Robert son of Wido of Wadsley, SY 114, 131
Robert son of William 97
Robert son of William of Alfreton, D 64, 76, 167, 205, 222
Robert of Stanton, D 167
Robert of Swanwick, D 69
Robert of Thorpe, SY 63
Robert of Wadsley, SY, knight 44, 61
Robert of Warnwike 65
Robert of Watnall, N, lord 66
Robert of Wentworth, SY 94, 105
Robert of Willoughby, L 5
Robert of Wombwell, SY 109
Robert of Woodhouse 98, 103, 105
Roger, abbot of Beauchief 66
Roger of Aldwark, SY 133
Roger of Alfreton, D 7, 9–10, 14–16, 108, 130
Roger (1) of Ayncourt (France; or Heinecurt, Eynecurt, Eincurth) 203, 209, 222
Roger (2) of Ayncourt (France; or Eynecourt) 66
Roger Bate 214
Roger of Berche 106
Roger of Birchwood 7
Roger of Brailsford, knight and rector of the church of Dronfield, D 18, 33, 38–41, 44, 61
Roger of Brecton 38

Roger (1) Breton or le Breton or le Bret 18, 22, 28, 33, 37–41, 46, 51, 54, 71, 81, 183–184, 187, Leake 8, Leake 9
Roger (2) le Bret 223
Roger (3) le Breton 223
Roger (4) le Brett, knight 46
Roger brother of Simon of Glapwell, D 204 n. 2, 211
Roger, carpenter of Norton, D 30, 48, 53
Roger chaplain 182
Roger, clerk of Glapwell, D *see* Roger son of Hugh
Roger, clerk of Sheffield 164
Roger, clerk of Wymeswold, L 62
Roger of the Cliff, D 25
Roger of Cuckney, N 137–138
Roger of Duckmanton, D 38
Roger of Fimeleya of Scholes, SY 92
Roger of Fletburgh in Norton, D 31, 52
Roger of Fungl' 6
Roger of the Green in Norton, D 55
Roger Hauselin (of Little Sheffield, SH) Intro. 29, 128–129, 139–141, 150, 154–155, 157
Roger of Hollins, SH 113, 128
Roger of Mattersey, N 12–13, 120, 124
Roger of Newhouse, Brother 5
Roger of Ollerton, N 75
Roger of Osbaston, L 57
Roger of Padley, D 50
Roger the Poer 209
Roger, rector of half of the church of Rotherham, SY 110
Roger of Ridding, D 75
Roger of Sidenhale 206–207, 210, 222
Roger of Somervill 27, 56, 60, 66
Roger son of Hugh of Glapwell, D, and clerk 204–205, 208, 211
Roger son of Nicholas of Langley, D 204, 211
Roger son of Ralph 4
Roger son of Reyner (or Reynes) of Aldwark, SY 95, 121–123
Roger son of William 203
Roger of Swanwick, D 74, 80
Roger of Ufton, D 69
Roger of Wadsley, SY 145

Serlo of Beeley, D 7–8
Serlo the chaplain 182
Serlo of Pleasley, D 3
Simon brother of Robert of Brimintun, D 209

INDEXES

Simon, chaplain of Wortley, SY 94
Simon, clerk of Greenhill, D 78
Simon of Cromwell, N Intro. *30*
Simon Friend 134, 135, 148
Simon of Greenhill, D 36, 77
Simon of Reresby (L or Lincs) 18, 22, 33, 39, 40
Simon son of Hugh of Glapwell, D 203–208, 210–211, 213, 222
Stephen, abbot of Beauchief 16
Stephen of Bella Aqua, lord of Rawmarsh, SY 100
Stephen of Birchwood, D 8
Stephen of Birley, SY 98
Stephen brother of Eustace and son of Hugh 4
Stephen the Eyr 19, 37, 38, 46, 54, 81, 183–184, 187
Stephen of Harley, SY 94, 103
Stephen the Joesu 154
Stephen Manluel (Meynell Langley, D?) 57
Swaro(?) the Buliona 114
Sweyn of Heriz 8

T. of Lond' 59
Thomas, lord 91
Thomas Barbot (Brabot Hall, Greasbrough, SY) 93, 97–98, 102, 121–123
Thomas of Bella Aqua (*de Beleuu*), lord of Rawmarsh, SY 106
Thomas of Bradfield, SY 9, 10, 12–13, 15, 57, 64, 76
Thomas of Brampton, D 21, 88
Thomas the Breton 110
Thomas Brom (Broom Hall, SH) 144
Thomas Chaworth, knight 62, 115, Leake 5
Thomas, clerk of [Dronfield] Woodhouse, D Intro. *11*, 20, 24–25, 29–31, 35, 42, 45, 48–49, 52, 53, 88, 111–112, 115, Leake 5
Thomas, clerk of Morton, D 24, 27, 42
Thomas, clerk of Wadswick (Wilts) 49
Thomas Doylly 109
Thomas Foljambe of Tideswell, D, lord 24, 35, 45, 70, 109
Thomas of Furnival (France), knight and lord of Hallamshire 18, 33, 38, 40, 44, 61, 111–113
Thomas of Gotham, N 152–153
Thomas of Gunton (Suffolk) 15, 64, 76
Thomas Gylesonne of the Greaves in Beeley, D 175
Thomas of Hazelhurst, D 35
Thomas of Heton 25

Thomas of Huntingfield (Suffolk) 15
Thomas of Leys (Norton Lees, D) Intro. *11*, 17, 21–22, 28–31, 43, 51, 52, 57, 88, 111, 115–116, 126–127
Thomas of Masbrough, SY 93
Thomas of Mounteney (France), lord of Cowley, SY and Shirecliffe, SH 109
Thomas of the Peak 64, 76
Thomas of Saint Quentin (France) 120, 124
Thomas Selwyn 9–10
Thomas serjeant 151
Thomas of Sheffield 155
Thomas son of Hugh the parson of Dronfield, D 204, 211
Thomas son of William of Glapwell, D 213–214
Thomas of Stannington, SY 144–145
Thomas of Wadshelf, D 88
Thomas of Wheatcroft 137–138
Thomas of the wood of Sheffield 118, 129, 131, 150–151, 154–155
Thurstan, abbot of Garendon, L 59

Vicarius, magister 59

Walter of Ancourt, parson of Morton, D 208
Walter the baker 148
Walter of Bringhale (*see also* Walter of Mighale) Leake 9
Walter of Campo Remigii 149
Walter, clerk of Osbaston, L 4
Walter, dean of Stretton, D 4
Walter the despenser 164
Walter Dun of Dronfield, D 204, 211
Walter of Easthwaite (lord) 12–13
Walter of Elmton, D 50
Walter of Goxhill (Lincs), knight 18, 31, 33, 36, 39–41
Walter of Kanrenn 130
Walter of Kibuf (lord) 60
Walter of Lindsey (Lincs) 159
Walter of Mighale (*see also* Walter of Bringhale) Leake 8
Walter the physician (medicus), magister 4
Walter of Southwell, N 5
Walter of Ufton, D 32, 36, 46, 66, 68, 79–80, 90
Warin of Beeley, D 165–166
William, abbot of Welbeck, N 120, 124
William of Adderley (Shrops or Staffs) 82
William of Alfreton, D 131
William of Arnehall (Darnall?, SH) 143

William of Aubeny, lord 34
William Basset 104, 176, 191, 222
William le Bret (1) 223
William le Bret (2) (or le Brett, de Brett, le Brect, le Breton) 18–19, 22, 28, 33, 36–41, 44, 46, 51, 61, 71, 81, 107
William Brom (Broom Hall, SH) 158
William Bulmer 71, 87
William of Burton 6
William of the Chamber, lord 144–145
William, chaplain of Sheffield 118
William of Chatsworth, D 165, 175
William Chaworth, lord 27, 34, 58
William Clarell (of Aldwark, SY), knight 110
William, clerk of Scholes, SY 93
William Colt 70, 72–73
William the cook 5
William of Cressy Intro. *30*
William the dagge 104
William of Darley, D 104
William Foljambe 45, 109, Leake 8–9
William the forester 27
William Fraunceys 28, 77, 79
William of Gotham, N 35, 43, 88, 106, 111–113, 116
William Hauselin (of Little Sheffield, SH) 129, 150, 154
William of Hazlebarrow, D 54
William of Heriz 222
William of Hollins, SH 141
William of Hucknall, D 213–214
William of Huntingfield (Suffolk) 15–16
William the Latemer 107
William of Little Sheffield, SH 129
William of Litton, D 165–166
William Matiney of Gravesend (Kent) 23, 25, 29, 48–49, 70
William of Matynesby (lord) 60
William of Meadow Hall, SY 93, 98
William of Meynell, lord of Meynell Langley, D Intro. *29*, 38, 204, 211, 222
William of the moor 129
William of Mundisder 101, 102
William Norm' (Normannicus?), magister 59
William, parson of Pleasley, D 203, 208
William Peck (or Pice, Pid', Pitt, Pyce) 26–27, 56, 135, 148

William, prior of Blyth, N 120
William Putrell of Wymeswold, L 58
William of Pyrhohe (Pirehill, Staffs?) 15
William of Rennes (France) 98, 137–138
William of Reresby (L or Lincs) Leake 8
William of Saint John 104
William of Sapperton (Lincs) 110
William Scarlet 67–68, 70
William of Schaterswrt (Chatsworth), D 166
William of Somerville (Norfolk?) 67, 77, 80
William son of Andrew of Hooton, SY 109
William son of Dolphin 145
William son of Godric 206
William son of Hugh of Wentworth, SY 93–97, 105
William son of Matyne 56
William son of Ranulf 3–4, 63
William son of Robert 3–4, 63, 92
William son of Robert of Alfreton, D 203, 208
William son of Robert of Ogston, D 17
William son of Robert of Wentworth, SY 98, 103
William son of Robert son of Ranulph 6
William son of T. of Lond' 59
William son of Thomas of Sutton, D 209
William son of William of Wentworth, SY 103
William Spynke of Little Sheffield, SH 152–153
William of Stainsby, D, lord Intro. *29*, 26, 38, 56, 90, 188, Leake 5, Leake 9
William the tailor 69
William of Tocham (Tockenham, Wilts?) 34
William of Ufton, D 27
William of Ughill, SY 117
William Underway of Wentworth, SY 100
William the Vavassur, lord of Denaby, SY 110
William of Vernon (France) 176, 191
William of Welbeck, N, Brother 3
William of Wentworth, SY 101, 106
William of Westhall 15, 64, 76
William of Wingfield, D 22, 183–184, 187
William the Waleys 69
William the Wyte 79–80, 87

INDEX OF PLACES

These places do not include those used in personal names; modern place-names are given where possible.

Abbey Brook, D 4, 38
Abbey Lane, SH Intro. 25
Abbeydale, SH Intro. 25
Aldefelde (fd. in Norton), D 4, 38
Aldwark, SY *110 n. 2*
Alfreton, D Intro. *2*, Intro. *4–7*, Intro. *10–12*, Intro. *17–18*, Intro. *20*, Intro. *23*, Intro. *28*, Intro. *31n*, 3–4, 17, 22, 24, 26–27, 32–33, *35 n. 2*, 36–38, 40, 44, 46–47, 61, 65–67, 69–81, 83–85, 87, 89–91, Royal Conf. 6
Alwaldsetes, D 183–184, 187–188, Leake 8–9
Annesley, N Intro. *8n*
Apperknowle, D Intro. *23*
Arnedwodedole (fd. in Stanley), N 226
Ashbourne, D Intro. *9*
Ashover, D Intro. *6*, Intro. *9*, Intro. *11*, Intro. *15*, 179–184, 186–190
Ashover Moor, D 183–184, 187–188, Leake 7–9
Aston (*see* Coal Aston, D)
Attercliffe, Intro. *9*, SH 112–113
Auvers (France) *120n*

Bakewell, D 166, 191
Barlborough, D *18 n. 2*, *162 n. 1*
Barlow, D Intro. *9*
Barsfelde (fd. in Alfreton), D 26, 38, 90
Beauchief, D Intro. *passim*, 3–4, 27, 38, 69, 71, 111, 119, 192
Beeley, D Intro. *15*, Intro. *19*, 168–175, Leake 6, Royal Conf. 49–50
Beighton, D Intro. *5–6*, Intro. *16*, *24 n. 3*, Royal Conf. 34
Bentt, the (fd. in Alfreton), D 74
Biggin Farm, D Intro. *16*, 222
Bilby, N Intro. *5*
Billingley, SY Intro. *5*, Intro. *9*, 109
Birchitt, D Intro. *4*, *6*, *36 n. 2*, 38, *50 n. 2*
Birchwood, Lower (fd. in Alfreton), D 22, 27, 38, 67–68, 89
Birkinschache (fd. in Stanley), N, 225–226
Birley, D Intro. *6*, Intro. *16*, *24 n. 3*, Royal Conf. 34
Blackwell, D Intro. *5n*
Blankney (Lincs) Intro. *10*

Blyth, N Intro. *5*, *108 n. 2*
Bolsover, D 205, 211
Bolton-on-Dearne, SY *109 n. 2*
Botheclyfesyke, the, SH 150
Boythorpe, D *219 n. 1*
Bradfield, SY *144 n. 1*, *149 n. 2*
Bradway, D Intro. *13*, Intro. *16*, Intro. *18*, Intro. *25*, 6, 21–22, 29, 35, 38
Bramcote, N Intro. *5n*
Brampton, D Intro. *9*, Intro. *24*, *46 n. 2*, *196 n. 1*, *198 n. 1*, 217–220, Leake 5
Brincliffe, SH 126–129, 139–141, 151
Brodenge, SH, Royal Conf. 42
Brockford (fd. in Norton), D 4, 38
Brockholeclive, SH 135, 147
Brockhurst (fd. in Norton), D 6, 38
Broom, SY, *24 n. 3*, Royal Conf. 46
Burbage Brook, D 161

Calldwell (fd. in Glapwell), D 210
Calver, D Intro. *5n*
Campsey Ash (Suffolk) 12–13, 15–16, 64, 76
Caushouse Farm (fd. in Brampton, D) Leake *5 n. 1*
Chancet Wood, D 3
Chaurces (France) Intro. *7*
Chesterfield, D Intro. *6–10*, Intro. *21*, Intro. *24*, *38 n. 2*, 160, 166, 192–196, 198–202, *217 n. 1*, *219 n. 1*, 226
Claiwang (fd. in Glapwell), D 207
Cliffe, the (fd. in Norton), D 30, 38
Clowne, D *162 n. 1*
Coal Aston, D Intro. *19*, Intro. *23*, 7, 38, 42, 45, 91
Cockshutt (fd. in Norton), D 21, 23–24, 38
Collesalfacra (fd. in Chesterfield), D 196
Comberdale (Kumbardall) (fd. in Wymeswold), L 38
Conslopdole (fd. in Stanley), N 226
Cotespark Farm, D 77
Coumbeclyffe (fd. in Norton), D 34
Cousewellende (fd. in Wymeswold), L 4
Cowley, Intro. *23*, *109 n. 4*
Crokesbero (fd. in Alfreton), D 75

Dale abbey, D Intro. *2*
Darley, D 166, 172, 188, Leake 8–9

Darley abbey, D Intro. *2*, Intro. *13*, Intro. *30*, 213–214
Denaby, SY *110 n. 2*
Derby 166, Intro. *2*
Der(e)bistret (fd. in Glapwell), D 207, 210
Dewyfyswode/Devellswode/Willswodd (fd. in Ashover), D 188, Leake 8–9
Doncaster, Intro. *2*
Dore, D Intro. *4–6*, Intro. *13*, Intro. *18–19*, *161 n. 7*, *218 n. 1*
Doreheg, D 3
Doreheseles, D 3–4, 43
Dronfield, D Intro. *4*, Intro. *5n*, Intro. *9*, Intro. *12–13*, Intro. *15*, Intro. *19–20*, Intro. *23–24*, 18 n. 2, 115, *218 n. 1*
Dronfield Woodhouse, D Intro. *13*
Dunsill, N 203, 205, 210–211
Dunstorthes Intro. *29*, *141 n. 2*

Eastwood Hall (fd. in Ashover), D 183–184, 187–188, Leake 8–9
Ecclesall, SH Intro. *4n*, Intro. *9*, Intro. *18–19*, Intro. *23*, Intro. *25*, 111–112, 119, 133, 153–154, 158
Ecclesfield, SY *100 n. 1*, *109 n. 4*, *149 n. 2*
Eckington Intro. *19–21*, Intro. *24*
Edensor, D 166
Eddlestow (fd. in Ashover), D 183–184, 187
Edwalton, N Intro. *2*, Intro. *5*, Intro. *11–12*, Intro. *20*, Intro. *23–24*, 3–4, 38, 66
Egmanton, N Intro. *5*
Eycliff (fd. in Norton), D 25

Fallinge (fd. in Beeley), D 169–170, 176–178
Falwang (fd. in Palterton), D 204, 207
Five Acres (fd. in Ault Hucknall), D 206, 210
Forest of the Peak (*see* Peak (Forest), D)
Frankbridge (fd. in Stanley), D 222, 225–226
Frankbridgedole (fd. in Stanley), D 225, 227
Fulsyke (fd. in Norton), D 49
Fulwood, SH Intro. *6*, Intro. *9*, Intro. *14–15*, Intro. *18*, Intro. *23*, 161, Royal Conf. 37, Royal Conf. 41

Galeghtres (fd. in Darley), D 172
Glapwell, D Intro. *6*, Intro. *13*, Intro. *30*, 16 n. 1, *182 n. 1*, 203–216
Goldthorpe, SY Intro. *5*, Intro. *9*, 106–108, 110
Gosedyrtker, SH 136
Greaves, the (fd. in Beeley), D 174–175
Greenhill, D Intro. *4*, Intro. *20*, Intro. *24–25*, 3–4, 6, 18, 33, 38–41, 43, 55

Greenhill Moor, D 33, 38, 41
Grenoside, SY *135 n. 2*

Hackenthorpe, SY Intro. *16*
Hagnaby (Lincs) *4 n. 3*
Halches (Upper Haugh, Rawmarsh, SY), 137–138
Hallamshire, SH Intro. *6*, Intro. *8–10*, Intro. *15*, *18 n. 2*, 153–154, 161, Royal Conf. 41
Halleker, SH Royal Conf. 42
Handley, D Intro. *8*, Royal Conf. 30, Royal Conf. 32
Handsworth, SY Intro. *16*, Intro. *21*, *101 n. 1*, *108 n. 3*, *133 n. 1*
Harewood Grange, D Intro. *6*, Intro. *9*, Intro. *15*, Intro. *23*, 164–167, 172, 183, 187–188, Leake 5–6, Leake 9
Harewoodhead Dereleyam (fd. in Darley), D 164
Harland Edge (fd. in Beeley), D 164
Harlandford (fd. in Beeley), D 172
Harthill, SY Intro. *7*
Hasland, D *219 n. 1*
Hassop, D Intro. *5n*
Hathersage, D Intro. *9*, Intro. *14*, Intro. *19*, 161–162
Hazelhurst (fd. in Coal Aston), D Intro. *19*, 42, 91
Heath, D *219 n. 1*
Hereward's Street (fd. in Ashover), D 183–184, 187–188, Leake 8–9
Herewise (fd. in Alfreton), D 74
Herringthorpe, D Royal Conf. 46
High Melton, SY *120 n. 1*
Hipper river, D 189–190, 199
Hirninghuldoles (fd. in Stanley), N 225–226
Holineforde (fd. in Walton), D 189–190
Holleford, SH 156
Hollins, the (Holt House, SH) 152–154
Holmesfield, D Intro. *10*
Hope, D 166
Horepittes, SH 135
Houghton, Stony, D 204, 206, 210–211
Hungerhill (fd. in Wymeswold), L 4, 38
Hurkelwell (*see* Ulkelwell)
Hutcliffe Wood, D Intro. *4*, Intro. *16*, Intro. *18–19*, Intro. *25*
Hyggehou (Higger Tor) (fd. in Hathersage) D 161

Inkersall, D Royal Conf. 33

Killamarsh, D Intro. *16*
Kilnhurst, SY *101 n. 1*, *106 n. 4*, *133 n. 1*

INDEXES 303

Kimberworth, SY Intro. 5, 93 n. 1, 99
Kumbardall (fd. in Wymeswold) L (see also Comberdale) 4

Lady's Cross, (fd. in Hathersage), D Intro. 14, 161
Lady's Spring Wood, D Intro. 18
Langar, N Intro. 8n
Langwith, D 26 n. 4
Leicester, 61
Lenton priory, N Intro. 9
Lightokford (fd. in Hathersage), D 161
Lincoln Intro. 9
Littlemarsh (in vill of Nottingham), N 221
Litestwood (fd. in Walton), D 189–190
Little Norton (see Norton, Little, D)
Little Sheffield Intro. 19
Longbenelondichend (fd. in Wymeswold), L 4, 38
Longeroda (fd. in Glapwell), D 210
Losk Corner (fd. in Stony Houghton), D 204
Louth Park abbey (Lincs), Intro. 9
Lower Birchwood (see Birchwood, Lower)

Markham, N Intro. 5n
Marnham, N Intro. 5, Intro. 7, Intro. 31n, 31, 38, 44, 61
Marthegravegate (fd. in Wymeswold), L 4, 38
Martynhaw (fd. in Wymeswold), L 4, 38
Marwaterlandes (fd. in Wymeswold), L 4, 38
Matlock Bridge, D 183–184, 187
Mattersey, N Intro. 9, 120–125
Meersbrook, D Intro. 4, 4, 38
Mikylwaterlandes (fd. in Wymeswold), L 4, 38
Millhouses, SH Intro. 18–19, 111 n. 2, 152 n. 1
Milnhill (fd. in Wymeswold), L 4, 38
Monk Bretton priory, SY 18 n. 2
Monyash, D Intro. 5n
Morelestorth hill (fd. in Glapwell), D 206
Morton, D Intro. 10
Moss Beck (fd. in Eckington) Intro. 19
Mousewelehende (fd. in Wymeswold), L 38
Mylneclyff, SH 157

Nether Padley (see Padley, Nether, D)
Netherbromebergh (fd. in Wymeswold), L 4, 38
New Mill, SH Intro. 19, 156
Newbold, D Intro. 24, 198, 219 n. 1
Newhouse abbey (Lincs), Intro. 3, 18 n. 2

Norton, D Intro. 2–7, Intro. 10–13, Intro. 17–20, Intro. 28, Intro. 31n, Intro. 32, 3, 4, 10, 17–22, 30, 33, 35–40, 43 n. 1, 44–45, 47–48, 50–51, 53–54, 56, 61, 66, 81, 86, 90–91, 106 n. 4, 152 n. 2, Royal Conf. 12
Norton Green Intro. 12
Norton Hammer, D Intro. 4
Norton Lees, D Intro. 4, Intro. 12, Intro. 24, Intro. 29
Norton, Little, D Intro. 24, 33, 38, 40
Norton Wood, D 34, 38
Norton Woodseats, D Intro. 4, Intro. 19, Intro. 24–25, 18, 28, 33, 38, 50, Royal Conf. 24
Nottingham 166, 206–207, 210, 221, 226
Nuthall, N Intro. 5n

Ollerton, N Intro. 5n
Ormesland/Ormesmedwe (fd. in Beighton), D Royal Conf. 34
Osberton Hall, N Intro. 5n, 66

Padley, Nether, D Intro. 9, Intro. 14, 23 n. 2, 161, 163
Palterton, D 204
Peak (Forest), D 24 n. 3, 104 n. 3, 107 n. 2, 166
Peasunhurst (fd. in Ashover), D 183, 187–188, Leake 8–9
Perlethorpe, N Intro. 5
Pleasley, D Intro. 5, 23 n. 2, 184 n. 1, 210
Povey, D Intro. 23
Prémontré abbey Intro. 3–4
Prestacra (fd. in Glapwell), D 209
Priestcliffe, D 106 n. 2

Qwythenegrenes (fd. in Alfreton), D 74
Qwytekere (fd. in Alfreton), D 26, 38, 90

Rawmarsh, SY Intro. 6, Intro. 7n, 100 n. 1, 106 n. 4, 109 n. 4, 110 n. 2, 137–138
Ridding (fd. in Westnall), N 82, 210
Riddings (fd. in Alfreton), D Intro. 12
Rikisike (fd. in Wymeswold), L 4, 38
Rivelin Valley, SH Royal Conf. 41
Roach House (fd. in Ashover), D 183–184, 187
Robbewong (fd. in Wymeswold), L 4, 38
Robert Rydding (fd. in Alfreton), D 22, 38
Rockley, SY 18 n. 2
Rotherham, SY Intro. 29, 44 n. 2
Rowsley, D Intro. 5n
Rowthorne, D Intro. 5, 204, 206, 211
Rufford abbey, N 7 n. 3, 167 n. 1, 192 n. 2
Rutendecloch (fd. in Walton), D 189–190

St Quentin abbey (France) Intro. *3*
St Wandrille abbey Intro. *6*
Scarcliffe, D 206, 210
Scarsdale, wapentake of, D Intro. *7*, Intro. *10*, *18 n. 2*, 160, 195, Leake 8–9
Scholes, SY Intro. *5*, Intro. *9*, 92–101, 103
Schortbuttes (fd. in Glapwell), D 204
Serleforkes (fd. in Ashover), D 183–184, 187–188, Leake 8–9
Sheaf river, D/SH Intro. *4*, Intro. *6*, Intro. *9*, Intro. *18–19*, 4, 9–10, 18, 21, 28, 33, 34, 38, 49, 50, 116, 156, Royal Conf. 12
Sheffield, Intro. *4*, Intro. *6*, Intro. *9*, Intro. *21*, 111–119, *113 n. 1*, 114, *118 n. 1*, *128 n. 2*, *129 n. 1*, 130–136, *139 n. 2*, *143 n. 1*, 147–150, *151 n. 2*, *155 n. 1*, 156–157, Royal Conf. 38, Royal Conf. 42
Sheffield, Little (*see* Little Sheffield)
Shirecliffe, SH *109 n. 4*
Shireoaks, D 9, 38
Shooterslea (fd. in Ashover), D 183, 184, 187–188, Leake 8–9
Smaligesikend (fd. in Wymeswold), L 4, 38
Smithy Wood, D Intro. *19*
Somercotes (fd. in Alfreton), D 74
Somersall Hall, D 225–226
Stainborough, SY *18 n. 2*
Stainsby, D *56 n. 1*
Stamfordsike (fd. in Ashover), D 183–184, 187
Stanley, N Intro. *6*, Intro. *16*, Intro. *23*, 222, 224–226
Staveley, D Intro. *5*, Intro. *24*, Royal Conf. 33
Stefnestubing (fd. in Glapwell), D 206
Stony Houghton (*see* Houghton, Stony, D)
Storthes, the (fd. in Alfreton), D 90
Strawberry Lee, D Intro. *9*, Intro. *14–16*, Intro. *18*, Intro. *23*, 159, 161, 163
Swanwick, D Intro. *18*, 22, 38, 69, 84
Swinton, SY Intro. *5*, Intro. *9*, 104, *106 n. 4*, 109

Tacheleforde (fd. in Norton), D 6
Taddington, D *106 n. 2*
Teversal, N Intro. *6*, Intro. *16*, *203 n. 2*, 222–224, Royal Conf. 45
Thorpe Hesley, SY Intro. *5*, Intro. *9*, 99–103
Thortley (fd. in Alfreton), D 79
Thurgaton priory, N Intro. *5n*, *18 n. 2*
Tibshelf, D *26 n. 4*
Tickhill, Honour of Intro. *5*, Intro. *7*, *92 n. 1*, *104 n. 1*, *106 n. 1*, *132 n. 1*
Tideswell, D *106 n. 2*, 166

Todwick, SY, *110 n. 2*
Tokeby (unidentified) 66
Tomelingreve (fd. in Alfreton), D 74
Totley, D Intro. *4*, Intro. *14*, Intro. *18*, *159 n. 1*, *161 n. 7*
Treeton, SY Intro. *21*, *24 n. 3*
Tres Lauhes, D 172
Troway, D Intro. *6*, 8, 38
Tugby, L *66 n. 2*
Twentywell Lane, D Intro. *3*
Twentywellsick (fd. in Beauchief), D 4, 38

Ulkelwell/Urkelwelsike, SH 134–136
Umberley Brook, D 172
Unstone, D Intro. *23*, *36 n. 2*
Upper Haugh, SY (*see also* Halches) Intro. *6*
Upstall Field (fd. in Ashover), D 182

Wadshelf, D Intro. *8*, 164, Royal Conf. 31
Wadsley, SY Intro. *9*, 142–146
Wadworth, SY Intro. *7*
Walton, D Intro. *6*, Intro. *15*, Intro. *24*, *164 n. 3*, 183–184, 187–190, Leake 8–9
Watnall, N Intro. *5n*, 82
Welbeck abbey, N Intro. *2–3*
Westerley (fd. in Norton), D 6, 38
Westwood (fd. in Beighton), D Intro. *16*
Wetemore (fd. in Ashover), D 183–184, 187
Whitwell, D *162 n. 1*
Wigley, D 217–220
Willswodd (*see* Dewyfyswode/Devellswode/Willswodd)
Wingerworth, D *36 n. 2*, 183–184, 187
Wiverton, N Intro. *8n*
Wodewardeston (fd. in Brampton), D 172
Woldhyll (fd. in Wymeswold), L 65
Wombwell, SY *109 n. 4*
Woodborough, N Intro. *5n*
Woodhouse, SY Intro. *16*
Woodseats (fd. in Thorpe), SY 101
Worhuldole (fd. in Stanley), N 226
Worksop priory, N Intro. *5*, Intro. *6*
Wormhill, D *106 n. 2*
Wringandstones (fd. in Ashover), D 183–184, 187
Wudemangatha (fd. in Glapwell), D 206, 210
Wymeswold, L Intro. *2*, Intro. *4–6*, Intro. *11–12*, Intro. *17*, Intro. *20*, Intro. *22*, Intro. *24*, Intro. *29*, 3–5, 12–16, 38, 44, 57–66, 76, 90–91
Wyntersedecrofte (fd. in Alfreton), D 74

York, 220